COUNCIL AND COURTS IN ANGLO-NORMAN ENGLAND

BY

GEORGE BURTON ADAMS, Litt.D., LL.D.

Emeritus Professor of History in Yale University

De curia loquor et nescio, Deus scit, quid sit curia.

Walter Map

THE LAWBOOK EXCHANGE, LTD.
Clark, New Jersey

ISBN 978-1-58477-449-5

Lawbook Exchange edition 2004, 2019

The quality of this reprint is equivalent to the quality of the original work.

THE LAWBOOK EXCHANGE, LTD.
33 Terminal Avenue
Clark, New Jersey 07066-1321

Please see our website for a selection of our other publications and fine facsimile reprints of classic works of legal history:
www.lawbookexchange.com

Library of Congress Cataloging-in-Publication Data

Adams, George Burton, 1851-1925.
Council and courts in Anglo-Norman England / by George Burton Adams.
p. cm.
Originally published: New Haven: Yale University Press, 1926. (Yale historical publications. Studies ; 5.)
Includes bibliographical references.
ISBN 1-58477-449-5 (cloth : alk. paper)
1. Law--Great Britain--History. 2. Courts--Great Britain. I. Title. II. Yale historical publications. Studies ; 5.

KD608.A32 2004
347.42'01'09--dc22 2004040733

Printed in the United States of America on acid-free paper

YALE
HISTORICAL PUBLICATIONS

STUDIES

V

THE ELEVENTH VOLUME
PUBLISHED UNDER THE DIRECTION OF
THE DEPARTMENT OF HISTORY ON THE
KINGSLEY TRUST ASSOCIATION PUBLICATION FUND
ESTABLISHED BY
THE SCROLL AND KEY SOCIETY
OF YALE COLLEGE

COUNCIL AND COURTS IN ANGLO-NORMAN ENGLAND

BY

GEORGE BURTON ADAMS, LITT.D., LL.D.

Emeritus Professor of History
in Yale University

De curia loquor et nescio, Deus scit, quid sit curia.

WALTER MAP

NEW HAVEN: YALE UNIVERSITY PRESS
LONDON: HUMPHREY MILFORD
OXFORD UNIVERSITY PRESS
MDCCCCXXVI

Printed in the United States of America

CONTENTS

PREFACE

Most of the chapters of this book have been published separately in the *Yale Law Journal* or in the *Columbia Law Review* and I am indebted to their editors, and as regards the Appendix to the officers of the Royal Historical Society, for permission to reprint them here. As originally published they had little relation to one another, apart from a common general subject, and no attempt has been made to work them into a continuous account. The gaps between them are to some extent filled by the chapters which are new, but they also are largely detached studies of periods or subjects which seemed to need further investigation. Some repetitions in the original articles have been left standing as not undesirable for the sake of emphasis or clearness. It is difficult to indicate the advantage I have gained from the opportunity to discuss many subjects treated in this book with Professor George E. Woodbine of the Yale Law School. His extensive and accurate knowledge of the substantive law of the period has been an invaluable safeguard to one whose interest in chiefly institutional. I am alone responsible, however, for the conclusions stated.

G. B. A.

Such is the preface to this book as my father left it. Proofs have been corrected and the index has been made since his death. There are various matters that he undoubtedly would have ordered otherwise had he been able to make the final revision himself; and doubtless errors will be found. That the latter are not more frequent is due to the advice and ever ready help of Professor George E. Woodbine and Professor Sydney K. Mitchell. The courtesy and patience of the Yale University Press and the encouragement of Professor Charles M. Andrews have also made this task much easier.

It is to be hoped that other students may take up the lines of investigation indicated in these papers, and carry on the work here left unfinished.

RUTH ADAMS

Yelping Hill, September, 1925.

ABBREVIATIONS

A.H.R.	American Historical Review.
C.R.R.	Curia Regis Rolls.
E.H.R.	English Historical Review.
Holdsworth.	Holdsworth's History of English Law.
Liebermann.	Liebermann's Gesetze der Angelsachsen.
Origin.	Adams's Origin of the English Constitution.
P. and M.	Pollock and Maitland's History of English Law.
R.C.R.	Rotuli Curiae Regis.
R.S.	Rolls Series.
Stubbs.	Stubbs's Constitutional History of England.
Stubbs S.C.	Stubbs's Select Charters.
V.C.H.	Victoria County History.

INTRODUCTION

THE governmental structure which the Normans erected in England after the Conquest of 1066 rested on a broad foundation of Anglo-Saxon institutions. The structure, the general constitution of the state, which they built upon that foundation was new to England and determined her future history in that particular. In that constitution, even at that early date, several groups of institutions can be distinguished from one another, or at least the institutions of that time can be classified in groups in view of the functions which they performed, though some institutions from their undifferentiated character may need to be placed in more than one class. These groups can be separately described and held more or less completely apart in the study of their history. For example, this has already been done with distinction for the group of institutions which are administrative in character.[1] Among these possible groups there is one which in two respects, in determining the character and direction of the first age of constitutional growth after the Conquest, and in constructive influence upon the present government of the Anglo-Saxon world, probably exceeds in importance any other of the groups of early institutions which we may form. It is the group of judicial institutions which the Normans introduced. There are then three constituent elements which go to make up any constitutional study of Anglo-Norman England: The Anglo-Saxon foundation, the general constitution of the central government, and

[1] Professor T. F. Tout, *Chapters in the Administrative History of England,* 2 vols., 1920, and cf. Vol. I, p. 10.

the separate groups, or a separate group, of particular institutions in their proper place in the whole.[2]

It is the purpose of this book to trace the history of English judicial institutions from the Norman Conquest through their first age of growth; to attempt to show what they were in themselves and how they were transformed; to indicate their setting in the general constitution of the state, and to trace the influence upon that constitution of the changes which they underwent; and thirdly in some cases at least to point out the Anglo-Saxon foundation upon which they rested, or the lack of that foundation, and to what extent in the former instance the character of the final building was affected by the character of the foundation. It hardly needs to be said that this is a programme of constitutional history, since the first age of English constitutional history was brought about and its results determined by changes in the judicial system. From this fact, however, it follows that the primary object of this book is special, not general, constitutional history and that the latter will be included only so far as it is involved in the history of the judicial system, its place in the state and its influence upon the central government.

By way also of introduction the reader may be advised

[2] It is almost impossible to write the institutional history of any community, even of an early community, without using such general words as "state" and "constitution." Their use in such connections has been strongly objected to because they seem to carry ideas which are politically advanced back into a primitive society which could not yet have formed them from its own experience. It should be noticed, however, that in such uses as the above no political idea is ascribed to the society concerned, but it is only said that it did possess some degree of general organization which may be called for our convenience a state, and that the machinery of that organization may be called a constitution. The fact that an early people does not consciously understand the institutions which it has, should not prevent us from recognizing them for what they are and calling them by their proper names.

in advance that the writer still holds to the explanation of the early English constitution and the character of the changes which took place in it which he proposed some years ago.[3] England in the two centuries to be studied was a feudal state. It was a state as nearly ideally feudalized as any that existed in western Europe. Feudal principles were carried into operation and applied to the public and private relations of life more thoroughly and logically than has yet been generally recognized. It is true that a good deal of progress has been made during the last dozen years in the understanding of English feudalism and of the place which should be allowed to feudal ideas and feudal law in shaping institutions and general constitution.[4] This may be seen in any recent book on law or institutions. But how much is still lacking in this direction may also be seen in the fact that this interpretation is not often carried out to logical conclusions in all particulars. The final work will not be done upon this period of history until the feudal influence is traced out in all details and given its proper place among the various factors which produced the complex result. This has hardly been done as yet.

If I may judge by some criticisms of the views which have been referred to above, it is necessary to explain that I do not hold to the existence anywhere of an ideally logical feudalism expressed in practical arrangements of government. England comes as near to such an ideal

[3] *The Origin of the English Constitution,* Yale University Press, New Haven, 1912; second edition, enlarged, 1920.

[4] See Dr. Ernest Barker, "The Origin and Future of Parliament," *Edinburgh Review,* July, 1921, Vol. 234, 58-73, especially p. 64: "We have beeu taught of late years that we cannot draw any contrast between English and Continental feudalism: there is a common European feudalism, and the English species only differs (perhaps owing to the peculiar conditions created by the fact of a conquest in 1066) in being more completely logical than any other variety."

feudalism as any contemporary state, but there are exceptions to a perfect feudalism in every country. There are institutions which do not belong to feudalism surviving from an earlier period. There are functions and powers vested in institutions and in officials which are not feudal and which are sometimes anti-feudal. These exceptions are pretty generally alike in all feudal states and what is especially important to be noticed is that when we are speaking of the feudalism of western Europe these features are included in it. The feudal system, the feudal society, is the total make-up of society as it existed in that age, the exceptions included. The king with his non-feudal rights surviving from an earlier age is as much a part of it as the baron with his independent jurisdiction who was one of the products of the age itself. To point out these exceptions is not to prove nor to admit that a given state was not feudal, or even logically feudal.[5] The actual feudalism of Europe's feudal age is the sum total of all that existed in the society of the period to which feudalism gave its prevailing character. The theoretical prerogatives which the kings of the twelfth century retained may be exceptions in an ideal feudalism, but they are not exceptions in the actual feudalism which prevailed throughout the Europe of that date. They are characteristics of it.

It is desirable here also to call attention to the distinction, made elsewhere,[6] between political and economic feudalism, their distinct origins, place in the community life, and historical outcome. It is with political, not economic, feudalism that we have to do in constitutional history. Though economic feudalism had quite as much to do with the life and welfare of the individual man, it is only in minor and local affairs that it touches the general in-

[5] Liebermann in the *Historische Zeitschrift,* 1914, CXII, 408-409.

[6] Hunt and Poole, *The Political History of England,* II, 14-18.

stitutional life of the state. What affects government and institutions, the law of the free man, his public duties and most of his private obligations, is the regime of contractual relationships into which free men generally enter with other free men who stand to them in consequence in a relation of lordship, theoretical or actual. So controlling is this regime that it draws under its own peculiar interpretations relationships which are not originally or in their nature feudal, like socage and fee-farm tenures. It is this regime of contract which creates, or gives their character to, institutions, which is the source of law, and which furnishes the starting point for the limited monarchy. The serf, wholly immersed in economic feudalism, the feudalism of the manorial cultivators, can neither make nor enforce a contract. He cannot appeal to the courts of the free man, and the customary manorial law which regulates his life has no influence outside the local sphere. By way of qualification of too absolute statement, it must be added that, while this was the strict law, exceptions sometimes occur to it, as to almost every feudal fact, in the practical operation of affairs. But the ease with which exception may be mistaken for law, the difficulty of distinguishing between the exception and the rule, this is what gives rise to the constantly besetting temptation to wrong conclusions which leads the student of feudal institutions astray.

Considered primarily with reference to permanent results, the Norman conquest of England was a conquest of institutions by institutions rather than of men by men. The human element added to the population of the country was comparatively small and its influence upon national characteristics is negligible. The new legal and constitutional elements on the contrary were from the moment of William's coronation in dominating control, and they were destined during the next two centuries to an increasing influence which has given them the largest place in the foundations of our constitution. To call the institutional result a conquest is, however, in one sense to convey a wrong impression. Few institutions were driven from the field. Many remained in form to all appearance unchanged for generations. But in these cases the old institutions were soon brought under a new controlling spirit and new conditions of growth, so that in the end they either dropped out of sight or were absorbed in a new institutional whole to which often their independent contribution can with difficulty be traced.

The new elements added by the Conquest may be grouped together under four heads:

1. A new kingship which supplanted the old and became for many generations the central feature of the constitution. This change might be considered a change of conception or emphasis merely, but, so far as we can now tell, it was a wholly practical one with no reasoning about it and no conscious change in ideals. There was, however, a real change in the emphasis placed upon the kingship in the practical operation of government, and it was not long before the new place given the king affected ideals which were consciously stated.[7] 2. A new interpretation of institutions and governmental processes. Interpretation may be too strong a word, since here again there was no conscious reasoning or attempt at explanation, but there was a new way of looking at these things. For example there was a new way of looking at the national assembly in the light of a prevailing feudalism which leads to such statements about it as those in the Constitutions of Clarendon c. XI and in Magna Carta c. 14. 3. There was an addition of a positive

[7] Note for example the theory of the duty of the king to make justice prevail, on which rested some of the reforms of Henry II. See *Origin*, pp. 82-83, and below Chapter VII at note 11.

kind in a new body of law, the feudal law, which was at the same time both public and private law, and which affected not merely future law in the technical sense but also constitution and constitutional law. 4. Certain specific institutions which were either new or were brought for the first time so prominently into use as to appear new and which became permanent in themselves or in their derivatives, for example, the small continual council and the king's local court. These new elements brought in by the Normans will be considered here not in all cases in their full influence upon the constitution but only with reference to the special topic of the book.

As a result of the Conquest, after the lapse of two hundred years, the whole body of English law had been made over, the judicial system had been entirely reconstructed, and a new legislative system, if there may be said to have been one before, had begun to be formed whose further formation and development was to constitute one great feature of the next age of constitutional growth. Constitutionally even more important than these changes was the fact that there had been discovered in the feudalism introduced from Normandy the foundation of the limited monarchy, and this foundation had been so securely laid that it was never afterwards to be removed and never afterwards changed to the present time.

In his account of the early Germans, Tacitus attributed to the general assembly of all the free men of the tribe the function of making judicial decisions in lawsuits as well as of deciding questions of policy.[8] In the small community of the primitive German tribe, such a mass-meeting court may have done its necessary work easily

[8] Tacitus, *Germania,* Chapters XI and XII; Adams, *Constitutional History of England,* p. 16.

and satisfactorily. It would be impossible to carry it on in the larger states which these tribes carved for themselves out of the Roman Empire. In political matters some faint traces of the national assembly of all the free men may have survived, but none can be found of its judicial function. The council of the tribal chiefs on the other hand, which Tacitus describes as a separately organized feature of the assembly, preparing questions to submit to the larger body and apparently arguing before it in favor of decisions which it had itself previously reached, may well have been the ancestor or prototype of the actual national assembly in these states. This latter assembly at any rate was made up of magnates only; it inherited the judicial as well as political powers of the earlier full assembly, but the decisions which it reached by itself were now final. It occupied in all the new German states, whose institutions we can study in detail, the position of the highest tribunal not merely as a court of appeals in occasional use but also in dignity and rank.[9]

If such an assembly of all the nobles and officials of the kingdom met occasionally, it could not meet frequently. The same difficulties of distance and of serious interruption of regular duties which prevented the meeting of all the free men would make it impossible to gather an as-

[9] On the national assembly and the king's court in the Frankish and other Teutonic states, see Brunner, *Deutsche Rechtsgeschichte,* II, 130-141; Waitz, *Deutsche Verfassungsgeschichte,* 1882, II, 2, 135 ff.; 1884, IV, 472 ff.; Dahn, *Koenige der Germanen,* VII, 3, 40 ff., 517 ff.; VIII, 4, 32 ff.; Glasson, *Histoire du Droit et des Institutions de la France,* III, 276-291; Fustel de Coulanges, *La Monarchie Franque,* 1888, Chaps. III, XIII; Beauchet, *Histoire de l'Organisation Judiciaire en France, Époque Franque,* pp. 47-73, 327-353; Liebermann, *The National Assembly in the Anglo-Saxon Period.* These authorities are not in entire agreement on all details. I have stated in the text the opinion which I believe to have the best evidence in its support.

sembly of all the magnates many times in the year. One meeting, or at most two, in spring and autumn, seems to have been all that was possible, unless a military campaign or some other unusual reason made something like an assembly necessary. Manifestly none of its functions as the supreme governing body of the kingdom, legislative or judicial, those of counsel upon policy or administrative supervision, could be efficiently exercised by an assembly meeting so infrequently. Its place was therefore generally taken for continuing business in the Germano-Roman states by a small assembly or council, which seems to have formed itself naturally, without special constitutional planning, from the officers of the king's household and the magnates who happened to be with the king at any given time, or who were specially summoned. So far as we can now tell from the evidence we have, it seems to have been assumed without theorizing but as a practical matter that this small council could legitimately exercise the functions and powers of the larger.

In the Frankish state we know much more of the smaller court than we do of the larger national assembly.[10] While the central formative body was always the household officials and a fluctuating number of magnates, bishops, dukes, counts, and other vassals, in early times there was also a larger body in or around the central one of men in various and uncertain capacities, minor and local officials, witnesses, *referendarii, domestici, fideles,* even *vulgi.* In Carolingian times this body became more feudal, practically limited to king's vassals, and there is less evidence of outside attendants. Their presence, however, continued to be represented by formal expressions, sometimes in words that startlingly suggest later phrases used in England for the same purpose, as when a judg-

[10] Cf. Fustel de Coulanges, *La Monarchie Franque,* p. 332, note 1.

ment is rendered by magnates and "ceteris quam plures fidelibus qui ibidem aderant."[11] Probably the words indicate no more real participation in the judgment than in the English cases, but they may imply a surviving feeling that the national assembly was the body which should be acting and that the smaller one should be made to seem as nearly like it as circumstances would permit. There is no doubt but that such words were used later to imply conformity to a tradition which was nothing more than a tradition.

This body was council; its action was *consilium* as well as *judicium;* its members were *consiliarii;* "cum consilio suo" was said when the king followed its advice. It possessed also the legislative function so far as there was any legislation; it advised, approved and consented to laws and regulations which the documents represent in form as coming from the king. In a sense it supervised the administration of the kingdom since by its advice the king exercised the administrative function, and before it were brought complaints and accusations against local officials of every grade. In judicial matters its competence seems at first to have been universal, but a growing tendency to ignore the local courts in order to get a decision of the king's court made limitation of the privilege necessary. It was a court of first instance and in some cases at least a court of appeals. It enforced local law as well as king's law and was also a court of equity. It was called during the Frankish period variously *curia, placitum, conventus, colloquium, synodum, concilium,* and it was sometimes described by the word *generalis* even when it seems clear that the smaller not the larger assembly was meant. Its members were *magnates, optimates, primates* or *primores, regni principes, proceres.* Most of these

[11] Waitz, *Deutsche Verf.*, IV, 493, note 4.

terms included ecclesiastics of high rank. Its procedure was the same as that of the popular courts, the same as that which is familiar to us in the later feudal courts which will be discussed hereafter. This central body without change of composition or function, still the undifferentiated organ of central government for the kingdom, was inherited by the Capetian dynasty from the Carolingian,[12] and it was the model upon which was formed, deliberately in some cases, without conscious thought because it was the natural thing to do in others, the central governing organ of the great baronies. This baronial court performed the same functions within its territory and used the same terms of itself and of its members as the curia regis.

So far as positive evidence shows, the Anglo-Saxon state seems to have been an exception among contemporary Teutonic states in this feature of its organization. It had a national assembly, the witenagemot, composed of the same class of persons, bishops, *principes, optimates, nobiles,* etc., as the Frankish national assembly, serving the same purposes in government, both legislative and judicial in character, and meeting two or three times a year. But there is no direct evidence to show that there was a smaller assembly, like the Frankish small council, which carried on the business of the larger during the intervals between its meetings. It is difficult to understand how the government could be conducted without such a body, and one is tempted to assume that it must have existed, and yet the mass of Anglo-Saxon material,

[12] In addition to the references in note 9, above, see: Flach, *Origines de l'Ancienne France*, III, 419-454; Luchaire, *Manuel des Institutions Françaises*, pp. 201, 250 f., 534, 556; *Institutions Monarchiques de la France*, I, 246-254; II, 45 f.; Viollet, *Institutions Politiques de la France*, I, 229, 235; II, 104 f. On continuity from Carolingian to Capetian see Viollet, *Institutions*, II, 214.

in which proof positive of its activity ought to be found but is not, is so large that there is equal difficulty in making such an assumption.[13] The question must be left for the present at least undecided, and we must regard the national assembly as the only central national court of which we have definite knowledge. There is no doubt, however, of the general governmental functions of this assembly including the judicial or of the position of authority which it occupied in the central government.[14]

The territory of the Anglo-Saxon state, to which corresponded on the institutional side the national assembly, was divided into shires, called also counties after the Conquest, irregular in size and diverse in origin, but notwithstanding all differences everywhere serving the same purposes. They divided the country into administrative units of a size that could be readily managed by a single agent and supervised by the crude central government of the time, and they served as the largest unit for the operation of local self-government to which fell originally large responsibilities. To the shire corresponded institutionally first the sheriff, or shire reeve, at once the head of the local government and the agent of royal authority; and second the shire court, of uncertain composition but acting in doing its business as an assembly court, at once legislative and judicial in function for the shire, and an

13 Professor Liebermann holds, *National Assembly*, pp. 17-18, 68-69, that such a small council and court did exist. The conclusion does not seem to be necessitated by the evidence, but it is a possible explanation of a limited number of facts which also may be otherwise explained. See Larson, *The King's Household in England before the Norman Conquest*, pp. 202 f., and below, Chapter IV, at note 25.

14 On all points regarding the witenagemot see Liebermann's *National Assembly*. On its judicial functions see pp. 68 ff., where the evidence is fully collected. H. Adams, *Essays in Anglo-Saxon Law*, pp. 309-383, prints, text and translation, a selection of cases illustrating judicial action in various courts. Cases 9 to 14 incl. are particularly interesting.

organ made use of by the sheriff in the conduct of his office. In jurisdiction the shire court was divided off by no sharp line from the witenagemot on one side or from the court of its own subdivision, the hundred, on the other. It was the same system of law which was administered in all three courts, and what decided in what court a case should be brought was rather the importance of the case, or the rank of the parties concerned, than any rules as to sphere of jurisdiction.

The shire in its turn was divided into hundreds which were also units of local self-government acting through a court probably of similar composition to the shire court, of especial importance in police jurisdiction and increasingly made use of by the sheriff in some of his functions. Lower still in range was the town and the town court, acting as an organ of self-government in small neighborhood affairs and as a police court for minor offences not important enough to attract the interest of the sheriff.[15] At the time of the Conquest the courts of these two lower territorial units had in many cases passed into private possession. The lowest, the town court, had become the private manorial, that is domanial, court by the natural operation of economic causes, there being no

15 Not all students of early English institutions hold to the existence of a town court. Notably Maitland, while allowing to the town its full importance in the territorial organization, argues strongly against the existence of any corresponding court. Pollock and Maitland, *History of English Law*, 1895, I, 514, 554, 599, cf. 596. The difficulty of accounting for the later development unless there was a court of the primitive town is almost a sufficient answer to Maitland's contention, but the arguments of Vinogradoff and Liebermann are still more convincing. Vinogradoff, *Growth of the Manor*, pp. 194, 273, 361; Liebermann, *Gesetze der Angelsachsen*, II, 2, 354, 451 c. 11b, 747, c. 23e: *Ueber die Leges Edwardi Confessoris*, p. 78. References throughout the book are to the first edition of Pollock and Maitland. They are so easily located in the second that it seemed best to make both editions available.

public interest to oppose. In the hundred court the government had a larger interest since it was the chief organ for the enforcement of criminal justice, even in the case of capital crimes, and since the income from the fines collected was large. The hundred court would therefore legally pass into private possession by a special grant only which should transfer the income to the lord and put him in the place of the king or the sheriff. It was probably often the case that the grant did not create a new relationship but recognized a fact already completed by gradual usurpation, and no doubt in many cases successful usurpation had established private possession without a grant. It was the natural tendency of private possession also to make the sheriff's employment of the hundred court as an agent of the central government more and more difficult.

So much may be said in brief of the general organization of the Anglo-Saxon judicial system. A mere outline is sufficient to indicate the foundation upon which the Normans began to build immediately after the Conquest. They had no disposition to change what they found in working order, and they were probably not aware of the changes which they did unintentionally make. Men who were not interested to analyze their government scientifically, who had no suspicion that they ought to inquire whether two institutions, superficially alike and performing the same functions in government, were institutionally identical, would naturally identify the witenagemot with their own curia ducis and, introducing in fact this latter, would seem to themselves to have made no change. So it was also with shire and sheriff, with the hundred whether still in the king's hands or in private possession, and with the domanial court of the great estate which they called the manor. The Normans had in their own organization at home things sufficiently like the Saxon institutions to make an identification natural, and it was easy for them to introduce such modifications as the real differences led them to make with a consciousness of what they were doing in a few cases only, and with no changes even then that were felt to be revolutionary.

CHAPTER I

THE AGE OF THE CONQUEST

THE central governing body of the Anglo-Norman state, national in character, was the *curia regis,* the *magnum concilium,* corresponding in position in the state and in function to the Saxon witenagemot and to the *generalis conventus,* the *placitum generale,* of the Frankish kingdom contemporary with the Saxon. It was itself also known by these names, witenagemot naturally to those who were writing in English and general *conventus* or *placitum* or *curia regis* to those writing in Latin. In its history during the first period we are to consider three things: the change in it which resulted from the Conquest; the evidence which we have bearing upon its membership; and what traces have survived to us of its legislative action.[1]

There is no evidence in any contemporary material that has come down to us that the men of the time noticed any change in the national assembly as a result of the Norman Conquest. Names, historical accounts and various allusions, though somewhat different in minor particulars, continue mainly the same. The fact, though indicating clearly enough that no revolutionary break was felt to

[1] I am considering in this chapter only a few points in regard to the councils of the eleventh century which seem to me to admit of further discussion. Most of the topics concerning them have been so fully and conclusively treated by Bishop Stubbs in sections 123, 125 and 127 of his *Constitutional History of England* and by Professor Liebermann in section IX of his *National Assembly in the Anglo-Saxon Period* that the repetition involved in a complete treatment would be out of place.

have occurred, must not be considered as proof that no change of the kind took place. Contemporaries rarely understand the nature of an institutional change, or are conscious that it is occurring, unless it is of deliberate intention as this was not. Accounts and records of the time usually enable us to discover what happened and to make out the character of the change, but they do not often show a knowledge of it themselves or spare us the necessity of getting at it by inference. The institutional change in the character of the national assembly at the end of the thirteenth century was as little understood by those who took part in it as that at the end of the eleventh.

The change which took place as a result of the Conquest was the feudalization of the national assembly.[2] These words are so easy to misunderstand, exactly what the change was is so easy to escape us, that pains even to weariness must be taken to make it clear. It is not meant that an assembly which was a product of feudalism, which had been given shape and purpose solely by feudalism, as was the ceremony of homage, was put in the place of the older Saxon assembly. It is not meant that the assembly was a necessary constituent element of feudalism without which that system could not exist, like the vassal relationship. What is meant is that an institution not produced by feudalism, much older than that system and continuing long after it disappeared, came during the feudal age under feudal control, was seized upon by feudal ideas, interpreted by them and temporarily made over by them in principle and structure. The same trans-

[2] See note A at the end of the chapter. Stubbs's statement (*S.C.*, ed. 8, p. 22) that under Henry II the composition of the national council was that of "a perfect feudal court," is retained by Davis in the ninth edition, p. 24.

formation in varying degrees befell other institutions: the monarchy, the manorial system of agriculture, the army which also contained non-feudal elements brought in by the king, the ecclesiastical organization, all of which were older than feudalism and long survived its fall.

The change which was made by the Conquest was a change in the principle of composition which affected both the institutional character of the assembly and its position in the state. The members of the assembly no longer came together because they were the chief men of church and state.[3] They were summoned and came because they had entered into a personal obligation to the king to perform this service when called upon to do so in return for the fiefs which he had given them. In briefest form, the public duty had become a private obligation. The change in the character of the assembly was only part of a larger change which affected in general the aspect and character of the state. Everything took on, not with absolute completeness but prevailingly, the form of private possession and personal agreement. Public law, community interest, a national sense and feeling, almost wholly disappeared. The kingdom became the king's private lordship;[4] portions of it were shared with his vassals, but the lands which they held had been loaned to them to secure personal services which were a part of what may be called the king's estate, and which assisted him in carrying on the whole, as the lord's domain lands in the manor were cultivated by the services of his manorial tenants. The revenue of the state was the king's private income. The institutions of the state were no

[3] See note B at the end of the chapter.

[4] See *The Song of Lewes*, ed. Kingsford, 11, 485 ff. and notes, for this idea as expressed by the feudal party in the thirteenth century; also Madox, *Exchequer*, I, 2, *b;* Vinogradoff, *Oxford Studies*, VI, 1, 39; Holdsworth, I, 19, 246 ff.

longer public institutions. They were the king's machinery for conducting his private business, as the institutional organization of the manor was the machinery for the private business of the lord. In this changed aspect and atmosphere, the assembly was involved as largely as any part of the state. It was no longer national or public. It was the king's private court for the business of his great manor of England. It was this fact which was institutionally expressed in the new principle of composition, in the assembly as an assembly of vassals.

There is to be noticed another aspect of the vassal relationship besides that of service to the king which affected the history if not the character of the assembly. It is one which has been somewhat obscured by the emphasis which it was necessary a generation ago to put upon the idea of required service, that is upon the fact that attendance at the assembly was not a privilege but a burden, in order to correct mistaken views of the early history of the institution. The feudal relationship was a mutual one. If it implied service on the part of the baron, it implied protection on the part of the king. It was founded on a contract, and that contract created rights for the vassal as truly as it did for the lord. In the case of the assembly, while unquestionably in practice emphasis was most often and most strongly laid on the idea of service, it must not be overlooked that there were corresponding rights of the baron on which he could insist. The curia was his in one sense as much as the king's. He would no doubt most frequently feel the service as a burden but, if ever occasion arose, he quickly perceived the other side of the relationship. It was a part of his duty of service that he was bound to bring his cases to the king's court and to submit to its judgments, but in return he could demand justice of the court, the judgment of his peers, for himself and his own cases.[5] The unwritten conventions and the written law of feudalism recognized his right to deny all service and to withdraw from his allegiance, if the justice he demanded was denied him. It was of course in the action of the curia as a court of law that the rights of the baron would be most often concerned, but his right to be a counsellor of the king, to be consulted and to offer his advice in the feudal council was unquestionably what gave rise to the later assertion of the right of every member of the house of lords to go to the king at any time and tender him counsel.[6] In the details of the period we shall find many evidences that the baron was not unmindful of the rights which he possessed in the various functions of the assembly.

The necessary formative and constructive membership of the great council was therefore the baronial body, the body of king's vassals. If they alone were present, the assembly was still a great council, competent for all the business of a national assembly. If they alone are specified in a formal charter or notification, it is sufficient to attest the action of the great council even if it be a legislative act of constitutional significance like the ordinance separating ecclesiastical from secular jurisdiction in the

[5] It will be noticed that the relation of the baron to the new judicial processes, writ, jury, special court of justices, when they came into use, was quite different, for these were prerogative processes, that is, they belonged to the king as king not as feudal lord and they formed no part of feudalism. Therefore the baron could claim no use of them as a part of what the king owed to him. He must obtain a special permission if he wished to use them and naturally he must pay for it.

[6] L. O. Pike, *Constitutional History of the House of Lords,* pp. 151-154; Blackstone, *Commentaries,* I, 228.

For convenience I am using the term ''member'' of those who made up the medieval council, great or small. It must not be understood to mean that at the time there was any theory of official membership. Those attended a given meeting who were summoned for that occasion or who had business there, without reference to whether they had attended before or would again.

courts.[7] Whatever members of other classes may seem to be associated with the royal tenants-in-chief in meetings of the assembly, whatever share may seem to be assigned to them in any particular meeting, it is made abundantly evident by the documents we possess that their presence was not necessary to validate assembly action or to the exercise of any assembly function.

During the present period at least, 1066-1100, there is no evidence that such outside elements had any part in assembly action. From the accounts of actual meetings and references to them, all that we can affirm with confidence is the attendance of tenants-in-chief, almost exclusively the great barons of the kingdom, lay and ecclesiastical, and of officials. It is clear from the evidence of later times that frequently, especially at the annual meetings on the three great feast days, Christmas, Easter, and Pentecost, the great council was surrounded, or it would be better to say that the king and the magnates who compose the council were attended, by a crowd of persons of lesser rank, clergy of minor dignities, monks and clerks, rear vassals, minor vassals, and officials of all grades. We cannot doubt that this would be true of eleventh century meetings also.[8] These persons attended upon their lords, added to their dignity and consideration and served as their personal council and advisers when their interests were involved. There is some evidence that attendance and counsel of this sort were occasionally provided for in the feudal arrangements, and that the kings desired such attendance to increase the pomp and display of the social court. Sometimes apparently persons of these minor

[7] The words of this document specifying those who were acting in the legislation are quoted below in note 34. Although there are mentioned great barons only, there can be, I think, no doubt but that the assembly was composed of all the elements usually going to make it up.

[8] See note C at the end of the chapter.

ranks were present in formal meetings of the great council, but there is no indication that they were regarded as members of it for the purpose of doing its business. Charters which record the decisions of the curia regis often distinguish between these attendants and regular members, sometimes by a descriptive term attached to the name of a witness, sometimes by grouping these nonmembers apart from the witnesses proper. The natural desire of a successful party in a lawsuit to secure as many witnesses as possible to the charter, which is the evidence of a judgment in his favor and becomes an especially valuable one of his title deeds, leads often to including many in the list who were only spectators and sometimes, it is probable, to omitting any marks which would indicate their exact capacity. This happens frequently enough to make it impossible to say that the presence of a name among the witnesses shows us a member of the court, unless there is something besides the mere name to serve as confirmation, like a statement of rank or office. This means no more than that the evidence must be examined with care and that ordinary lists of witnesses cannot be trusted to give us the membership of the court. There is no doubt but that good evidence proves the occasional presence apparently among the members of the court of minor barons, minor clergy and minor officials, especially after the eleventh century.[9]

[9] An interesting example, because illustrating more than one point, is the account of a lawsuit between the churches of York and Gloucester which came before a mixed ecclesiastical and baronial assembly in December, 1157, and was decided by compromise. The account is given in a notification by the archbishop of York which is printed in the Gloucester Cartulary, II, 105-107 (Bigelow, *Placita Anglo-Normannica,* pp. 189-191). The assembly is called curia regis in the account itself and manifestly is that, though of exceptional composition and though the case had evidently been appealed to the pope and by him referred to three English bishops for decision. It contained besides the king, five bishops, four abbots, two deans, two archdeacons, two priors, four canons, two earls, one constable, eleven ''barones

In nearly every case without doubt, the officials who were present, who were not great barons, were minor tenants-in-chief. Others of this class may have been present as well from the neighborhood, and there would be likely to be in the assembly also vassals of the king who were not yet tenants. The actual possession of a benefice was no more necessary to the vassal's obligation of court service, if called upon to serve, than it was to his military service. It is probable also that from the Conquest on in some though not in all cases, the minor tenants-in-chief of each county were summoned collectively through a writ directing the sheriff to make the summons.[10] It is not

regis,'' and three dapifers. These are mentioned in the notification undoubtedly by way of witnesses, but they are so given that it is impossible to distinguish between mere witnesses and members of the court. All seem to be members. Then the archbishop proceeds to name those who were acting with him for the church of York, eight names, among which it is especially interesting to find that of ''Thomas, provost of Beverley, chancellor of the king,'' who was acting in this case not as a member of the court but as one of the archbishop's advisers.

10 This fact is so firmly established for the later time that, when we add the slight evidence we have for the eleventh century, there seems no reason to doubt the statement in the text. William's writ to Abbot Æthelwig in 1072 indicates plainly a twofold military summons, one direct to the abbot for his own service, and one through the abbot to the knights of his liberty or of the shires which he administered—''qui sub ballia et justitia sunt.'' Stubbs, *S.C.*, p. 96; Round, *Feudal England*, p. 304. See *Origin*, p. 226, n. 21. Mr. Round objects (*Magna Carta Commemoration Essays*, 1917, p. 52) to the reference made to Domesday Book in this last note but, while his comment explains why the unit used was six instead of five and therefore that the particular reference does not extend to all England, I do not see that it affects the fact of the payment of small reliefs to the sheriff instead of to the king which is the point here. That in other cases there was a division of payments between the sheriff and the king, only makes it more likely that the same method would be used if there was to be a division in the payment of reliefs. For France in the eleventh century see Flach, *Origines*, III, 442. The line drawn in Magna Carta c. 14 could be left more vague than that in c. 2 (Round, *l.c.* p. 49) because of the king's prerogative right of summons. There was nothing to prevent him from issuing a personal summons to any minor tenant, if he pleased, and the line between major and

likely, however, that many of them responded, and the only occasions on which we can be sure that a considerable number of the small tenants-in-chief were present at the time of a meeting are those which coincide with a general summons of the *servitium debitum,* or a part of it, for military purposes. In connection with the three great feasts of the church, the chroniclers so frequently record that the king "tenuit curiam suam," that the phrase is almost technical. The reference is primarily no doubt to an unusual gathering at the social court of the king at which frequently there was great display. The great barons were expected to bring with them to these meetings some at least of their own vassals,[11] and minor tenants-in-chief and rear tenants as well should be expected to be present, among the spectators from the neighborhood at least. It is not likely that the numbers from these classes would be large. It is to be remembered that the whole number of minor tenants-in-chief was not large; in determining how large, we should be careful to cross out from the list which we can draw up for any county the names of those who were also great barons for other holdings or in other counties, and these are a considerable proportion of the whole.

There was always present in the assembly an official element which probably furnished the working core of the institution. There is, however, no evidence at hand to show that it was considered at the time to be an element

minor might be moved about without violating any principle or property right. This could not be done with the line between these classes in c. 2 because definite property rights were involved.

11 Whatever may have been expected, it is clear that the court service of rear vassals at great councils with their lords, whether for display or as counsel for the lord, was not supervised by the overlord, the king, as their military service was. If it had been we should have a far larger mass of evidence bearing upon it. Very likely it could more safely be left to the natural interests of the lords.

in the composition of the curia different in kind, or in the duty which determined its presence, from the ordinary baronial element. The chronicle sources in describing the composition of the assembly almost never use any term which distinguishes an official element from the baronial, nor do the charters more frequently in their narrative portion or in the enumeration of the classes present. It is from the signatures to the charters and from incidental references that we are able to prove its presence. In the lists of witnesses titles are naturally given and to some extent classified, but in only a few of the cases where we know that more than one title was possible are two used, and there is never anything to indicate that the title named was the only relationship to the king or the ground of membership. The share of royal officials in the assembly would be *a priori* practically certain from the fact that the important interests of the realm in the daily carrying on of government, financial, judicial, military and administrative were in the hands of the household officers of the king. Chancellor, constable, treasurer or chamberlain, marshal and steward, did not find the mere management of the king's household the limit of their duties, or perhaps, having regard to the feudal conception of the state described above, it would be better to say that, because they managed personally or through subordinates the king's household in certain particulars, they also managed the same things, or something like the same things, for the state. As executive and administrative heads of departments, if we may use a modern term, they would almost of necessity be members of the great council.

It does not follow that this was the ground of their membership, or at least it is certain that these officials make no exception to the general rule that the great council was composed of the king's vassals. We know that the great offices of the household were, almost without exception, filled by men who were before and during their official service great barons lay and ecclesiastic. That is to say that, even if in a given meeting of the assembly their presence may not have been desired because of the office which they held, they would nevertheless have been summoned to the meeting, as they would also have been if they had not been in office. The exceptional cases, with other exceptions to the rule of vassal membership, will be discussed under a later date because there is practically no evidence concerning them in this period. Here it may be said that it is unlikely that at the height of the feudal age these minor personages were not held to their duties by a feudal obligation.[12] The practice was apparently universal of providing pay, or partial pay, for all sorts of services about the court, by a grant of lands to be held by a serjeanty tenure, which would involve a special oath of fealty. The custom also still continued, which had been common in early feudalism, of attaching to the court men who were bound only by a personal tie to the king, who became his vassals but received no fief, or did not until after some time of service at least.[13] Evidence of the

[12] The fact of an oath of fealty from the household officer, as well as of the conflict of oaths sometimes growing out of double feudal relations, is illustrated by the story of Adam, vice-chancellor of the young King Henry, told by the writer of the *Gesta Regis Henrici*, under the year 1176 (I, 122-123). Reckoning his allegiance of more binding force to the father than to the son, he revealed to the former secrets of the latter, and was by him accused of treason, tried by his court, and condemned. An oath to the son is not specifically mentioned, but there could be a condemnation for treason on no other ground. He must have been the man of the young king. See also oaths taken from his household officers, *ibid.*, p. 43.

[13] Called in England most frequently *milites* (sometimes *barones*) *domestici, dominici*, or *de familia*. "Then Henry of Pomeroy and Alan of Dunstanville answered 'quod illi fuerunt de privata familia domini Regis jurati quod si illi aliquid audirent quod fuisset contra dominum Regem quod domino Regi illud intimarent.' Maitland, *Select Pleas of the Crown* (Selden Society), p. 70, no. 115. Maitland says, *ibid.*, n. 3, that this "looks like a very

presence of such men in occasional meetings of the assembly need cause no surprise nor difficulty.

During the eleventh century evidence that any persons who may be taken to stand for the mass of the people were present occurs only once;[14] even the formal words to denote their presence which are found in both Saxon and Frankish documents are lacking. These phrases come into more frequent use after the middle of the twelfth century, but it is improbable that any change in actual practice was denoted by the change in language. The words are always purely formal.

There are few recorded meetings of the great council in the first two Norman reigns, and the number about which any details are given is fewer still.[15] Once the *servitium debitum* was called out for a date when a meeting was probably held, and twice it was called out near, but not at, the time of a meeting.[16] In 1094 before beginning his campaign, William II went up from Hastings to attend the dedication of Battle Abbey church and we are told that *vulgi* in great numbers crowded around,[17] a phrase which doubtless indicates the only share which

early trace of the privy councillor's oath,'' but it is merely the feudal obligation long common throughout the feudal world. ''. . . et alius miles est de familia et non habet terram . . .'' *Bracton's Note Book,* pl. 1450. *Summa de Legibus Normannie,* ed. Tardif, c. XXVII, 4. Cf. Professor A. B. White, *A.H.R.,* XIX, 868.

14 See below, note 18.

15 See note D at the end of the chapter.

16 In 1072 the *servitium debitum* was called out for the octave of Pentecost. Stubbs, *S.C.,* p. 97, and in 1088 it was called out near the time of Easter. *Liber Eliensis* (Anglia Christiana Soc.), p. 276. Probably a meeting and a military levy came together early in 1094, but not certainly. Eadmer, *Historia Novorum,* p. 47; Freeman, *William Rufus,* I, 442. The summons to a meeting near the end of 1095 (Anglo-Saxon Chronicle) and that for the Salisbury meeting in 1086 (Florence of Worcester, Engl. Hist. Soc., II, 19) may imply the *servitium debitum.* If so it was summoned in these two cases for a great council and not for a military campaign.

17 *Chronicon Monasterii de Bello* (Anglia Christiana Soc.), pp. 40-41.

they could take in a general assembly. Once in a passage written probably a generation after the event, we have it said, in a "clerical phrase" more frequent in the twelfth century than in the eleventh, that Lanfranc was elected archbishop of Canterbury by the seniors of that church "cum episcopis et principibus, clero et populo Angliae."[18] Once the word "knights" is used where "barons" would be expected in a charter of doubtful authenticity.[19] Once again knights are mentioned[20] and twice the presence of sheriffs[21] and once that of minor officers is noted.[22]

The question of the composition of the great council during the feudal period is one that may seem difficult from the variety of the facts presented, but it is not difficult from the side of the principles involved. The essential point to be remembered is that we have in this case, as in other features of the feudal age, in all countries alike, what seem to be and in a sense are, two opposing principles. One is the feudal obligation to serve when summoned. The other is the king's prerogative right, over and above his right as the lord of vassals, to command service of any one for any purpose. The first of these is a fundamental principle of the political system which gives organization to the western world during these centuries and by which the business of the state is in the main carried on. The second is a survival from an older system, which once prevailed and was destined to prevail again but which was for the present, not indeed

18 *The Latin Acts of Lanfranc* in Earle and Plummer, *Two Saxon Chronicles*, I, 287. This phrase occurs again in the letter of Henry I to Anselm announcing his accession to the throne in 1100. Stubbs, *S.C.*, p. 120.

19 Davis, *Regesta*, no. 137, *c.* 31 March, 1081.

20 1086, Salisbury. Florence Worc., II, 19. In its general statement the Anglo-Saxon Chronicle includes knights. (R.S.), I, 355; II, 189.

21 1086, Salisbury. Florence Worc., II, 19. At the trial of Bishop William, 2 November, 1088. Simeon of Durham (R.S.), I, 183.

22 2 November, 1088, as in note 21.

in total, but in nearly total eclipse. In other words to understand the apparent anomaly presented by the non-feudally summoned members of the assembly, it is necessary to remember that they represent not a feature continued from the earlier assembly but a survival of the king's earlier position. What is anomalous from the feudal point of view is not the assembly but the king. The king's anomalous position affects the assembly as it does the army, but in both the real principle which determines the character of the institution is the feudal. The argument against the feudal character of the assembly based on the non-feudal elements in it proves too much. Prerogative action in equity does not prove that there is no common law, though it does away with its rules in the particular case. Prerogative wardship does not prove that wardship is not feudal and exercised by regular rule on feudal grounds, though in the particular case the rule is not followed. If the introduction of non-feudal elements into the assembly by the king's prerogative proves that the assembly is not feudal, then it can be proved that the feudal system itself did not exist, for the prerogative on occasion modified essentially almost every principle of the system.

The way of one who approaches the legislation of this period has been smoothed because Professor Liebermann has made a very complete list of the changes in the law, or of definitions of the law, which resulted from the Conquest and which may possibly have been made by legislation.[23] To enumerate these before comment upon them, and in the classes into which they naturally fall: In the first place we have three acts which have come down to us in a documentary form which must be very near to the originals, in content certainly. These are, first, William's

[23] Liebermann, II, 735, "Wilhelm I," cc. 4 and 5; III, 272. On legislation in the feudal period in general, see *Origin*, Chapter IV, note B.

writ regarding procedure in trials between Englishmen and Normans;[24] second, the ordinance, as it is often called, separating the ecclesiastical and secular courts;[25] and third, William's notification addressed to the bishop and portreeve of London assuring the citizens that no change in the law was intended.[26] This last is not legislative in character. It makes no new law, but it may be said to define the law; it continues the old law in its place as the rule of conduct and business enforceable in the courts.[27]

In another class we have a number of things of which there is no documentary record, but which we know to have been changes, or the results of changes, innovations, in the body of the law as a result of the Conquest. In this class there are:[28] the *murdrum* fine, forest and hunting regulations, the *misericordia regis, monetagium,* that is, a tax to take the place of the royal right to change the coinage, the truce of God, emasculation as a punishment for certain crimes according to the Saxon annalist, the prohibition of blood revenge in any case, this last being a larger modification than was made in the current law on that subject in Normandy, and the development of the frankpledge system. In a third class are to be put certain unofficial, private compilations of a later date of what the

24 Liebermann, I, 483 f.; III, 271 ff. Below, note 41.

25 *Ibid.,* I, 485 f.; III, 274 f.; Stubbs, *S.C.,* pp. 99 f.

26 Liebermann, I, 486; III, 276; Stubbs, *S.C.,* p. 97.

27 Hunt and Poole, *The Political History of England,* II, 11.

28 On these respectively see the articles "Murdrum," "Forst," "Jagd," "Misericordia regis," "Münzänderung," "Treuga Dei," "Entmannung," "Blutrache," "Zehnerschaft," in Liebermann, II, *Rechtsglossar.* On blood revenge see Liebermann, I, 499 n. *a;* III, 272 and the references there: *Annalis Historia Cadomensis,* in J. A. Giles, *Scriptores Willelmi,* 1074, and *Anglo-Saxon Chron.,* 1087 (1086), and add Robert of Torigni (R.S.), p. 41, and Orderic Vitalis, V, 158. If this innovation was made by William, it was not permanent. On the development of the frankpledge system, see also W. A. Morris, *The Frankpledge System.*

law was said to be in William's time in the form of codes and one general statement. Of the codes there are two, the *Hic intimatur*[29] and the *Leis Willelmi*,[30] and the general statement is the historian Eadmer's about William's canons for the government of the church.[31] To all these may be added inferences by way of confirmation from other sources like those which may be drawn from the coronation charter of Henry I.

Of these different matters some certainly represent legislation, as the ordinance regarding the church courts for example; some like the forest regulations probably had no formal authorization of any kind behind them but were brought in as incidental to the general change, as the rules of feudal landholding were, because it was the natural and the only natural thing for Normans to do; others were very likely administrative orders, or perhaps mandates of the monarch of his absolute prerogative. The later codes and writings give us more items of William's innovations than we can otherwise prove, but some of their statements are supplemented by indirect evidence and others are probable in themselves.[32] The sum total, even noting how much of it can be called no more

[29] Liebermann, I, 486-491; III, 277-283; Stubbs, *S.C.*, pp. 98 f.

[30] Liebermann, I, 492-520; III, 283-292; J. E. Matzke, *Lois de Guillaume le Conquérant*, Paris, 1899.

[31] Liebermann, I, 520; III, 292; Eadmer, *Hist. Nov.*, pp. 9-10. Liebermann notes that Eadmer in this passage refers to his knowledge of secular laws of William's which he intentionally omits.

[32] Cf. Liebermann, III, 285, c. 14. These include the protection of cultivators, the prohibition of the exportation of slaves, the improvement of trade and commerce, the protection of the highways, further substitution of mutilation for the death penalty, improvement of the judicial summons, severer punishment for offences against women and for poisoning, and the regulation of Peter's-pence. Perhaps besides the great addition of the feudal law noted below, there should be added for a complete sum total of what may be legislation the requirement of the Salisbury oath and the regulations for the Domesday survey.

than probable, is impressive. It indicates active interest in a wide range of problems and the careful consideration of such changes as a violent break in the continuity of government and the introduction of much that was new would make necessary.

Upon the method of legislation, the make up of the legislating body and its proportionate share in the making of new law, the material of this period gives us very little information. Negatively it may be said that the legal writers of the next age furnish no direct or indirect evidence of any change in the method of legislation or in the composition of the legislating body between the date of the Conquest and their own day. Considering their interest in constitutional and legal questions and the numerous passages in their writings which would have suggested a reference to the subject, and adding the interest which they plainly felt in whatever was done by the Conqueror, it is not likely that any really essential change in either of these matters would have failed in some way to be referred to. It is fair to conclude that the information that we shall gain from the later age also indicates with a high degree of probability the facts of the first period.

From the period of the first two reigns there is only one document or recorded statement of any kind which gives us a hint as to the process or organ of legislation. This is the so called ordinance of William I separating the spiritual and temporal courts.[33] It is in form a notification sent without doubt to each shire, or usual combination of shires, and to each bishopric. Of it we have two examples, later copies, one which was sent to the sheriffs of Essex, Hertfordshire and Middlesex and the other to the diocese of Lincoln, and some fragments which go back to other copies. The variations in readings with one ex-

[33] See above, note 25.

ception do not affect any point of importance.[34] In this notification, as commonly quoted, the king says that "episcopales leges . . . communi concilio et consilio archiepiscoporum et episcoporum et abbatum et omnium principum regni mei emendandas judicavi." These words indicate, so far as they go, and as we must suppose they were intended to be understood, both the process of legislation and the legislating institution. Upon the first point they imply in the form of words used that the final decision was with the king and that he made his decision after taking the counsel of the magnates, ecclesiastical and lay of the kingdom.[35] They have no bearing one way or the other on the question whether the king was obliged to take such counsel or whether he might have issued an edict as far reaching in its consequences as this without consulting any one. As to the legislating body and its composition, the words indicate that in a change so sweeping as this it was not thought necessary to declare that the step was taken with the counsel and consent of any except the magnates of the kingdom. In all these

[34] The expression which is used in this document for the legislating body and the legislative act, "communi concilio et consilio archiepiscoporum et episcoporum et abbatum et omnium principum regni mei," occurs no where else. Of the later copies, which Liebermann (III, 274; Davis, *Regesta*, nos. 93-94) supposes to go back to four originals, two agree in this reading but, so decidedly is it at variance with the usage common to any period before the reign of Edward I, that there is less difficulty in believing the text corrupt than in believing that these words were written as they stand in the reign of William I. In the "Gravamina cleri" of 1309, which goes back to an independent one of the four originals, the phrase reads "de communi consilio archiepiscoporum, etc." This is quite in accordance with usage and probably is what was originally written. For the first suggestion of this explanation, see Professor A. B. White, *A.H.R.*, XXV, 15-16. The text printed in the *Registrum Palatinum Dunelmensi* (R.S.), III, 82, reads "communi consilio et consilio archiepiscoporum . . ." It should be noted that the courts were bound by this ordinance.

[35] On anything that may seem to be implied by the word "judicavi," see below, Chapter III, note 3.

respects the indications are what we should be led to suppose they ought to be from the evidence of later times.

From a date—1100—which is technically still of the eleventh century, though not of the first two reigns, there comes another official document of the first importance, the coronation charter of Henry I.[36] As it was issued immediately after the close of the second Norman reign, it must be taken as indicating what the practice of these reigns would be. There are in it four references to action which, if not in every case precisely legislative—it is in one case—is the decision of important questions approaching the legislative in character. In c. 1 Henry, it is said, has been crowned "communi consilio baronum totius regni Angliae," though as a matter of fact only a few were present; in c. 3 Henry promises that he will give in marriage female heirs "consilio baronum meorum"; in c. 13, which does imply legislation, he says that his father amended the "lagam Edwardi consilio baronum suorum." These are all alike; they all use the same phrase, and they all agree with but add nothing to what we learned from the Conqueror's ordinance on

[36] Liebermann, I, 521-523; III, 293-299; Stubbs, *S.C.*, pp. 116-119. The coronation charter of Henry has been called an amplification, a more detailed phrasing, of the coronation oath (Stubbs, *S.C.*, p. 116) and with reference to logical content the statement is true. The coronation oath, however, is stated in such general terms that almost any promises of good government, specific in character, that could be framed would be an amplification of it. On the other hand the connection of the provisions of the charter with the institutional situation at the death of William Rufus and with the principles of feudal law is too clear and immediate to allow us to suppose that its authors had anything else in mind. That the charter may seem to be an expansion of the coronation oath is due, not to an intention to make it so, but to the fact that what it is trying to do, that is, to reëstablish law and justice and specific rights which have been violated, necessarily falls within the general promises of the coronation oath. See Henry L. Cannon, "The Character and Antecedents of the Charter of Liberties of Henry I," *A.H.R.*, XV, 37-46, and McKechnie, *Magna Carta*, pp. 95-101. The coronation oath may be found in Stubbs, I, 329, note 5.

ecclesiastical jurisdiction. The fourth instance is somewhat different. In c. 10 Henry says: "Forestas communi consensu baronum meorum in manu mea retinui sicut pater meus eas habuit." This clause seems clearly to imply that before the charter was issued, before it was drawn up undoubtedly, there had been discussion with the barons and agreement as to what should be surrendered by the king and what he should retain. In a document composed of renunciations the presence of a clause of the opposite tenor, which affirms the retention of what was universally regarded with dislike, and probably as an abuse, can mean only one thing. It implies that there had been a general demand and expectation that here also there would be a renunciation, and because there was not, the expectation was met with the statement that the king retains the forests as his father had them "communi consensu baronum." The sentence is more instructive of the range of the baronial consent and of the nature of the king's dependence upon it than any we have yet noticed. It implies, though these things are not explicitly affirmed either in words or in the facts made known to us, in the first place that the consent of the barons is sufficient answer to the general demand[37] and in the second that the king could not have retained the forests as his father had them if the barons had stubbornly refused their consent.[38] What would happen when consent was refused is more clearly shown in an incident of the reign of William II.[39] In a meeting of the great council at Rockingham in 1095 the king, if we may judge from the evidence which we

[37] It is likely that as affecting the king the demand would arise practically from the barons alone.

[38] Three times in the charter Henry speaks in the first person, commanding or forbidding, as if by his own authority, cc. 4, 5, 12, but he is speaking in these cases as executive, not as legislator.

[39] Eadmer, *Hist. Nov.*, pp. 53-67; *Political History of England,* II, pp. 101-103.

have, demanded of the council the forfeiture of Archbishop Anselm's spiritual office as a punishment for a secular offence, an offence against the sovereignty of the king as William asserted. Of the legality of this action he could not convince the barons and he was obliged to abandon his demand. What was going on in this case was a judicial trial and not legislative action, but there was in the thoughts of the men of the time so little distinction between these acts that we may be sure that what holds true in one set of facts will hold true also in the other.[40]

Of the other two official documents which make up the first class noted above, little is to be said. One is a writ upon procedure in the courts addressed generally in which the king says: "Mando et precipio per totam Anglie nationem custodiri . . ."[41] These words William might use if the act were one of his sole royal prerogative with no advice sought or taken. He might use the same words unchanged if he were carrying into effect an act adopted after full discussion and a decision in the great council. We are given no information beyond the mere fact that in such a proclamation the king could properly speak as if the command emanated from himself alone. The proclamation to the Londoners speaks in the same way: "Ego vobis notum facio quod volo . . .," "ego nolo pati . . .," and adds nothing further. The incidental

[40] A letter of Henry I's to Anselm of the same date as the coronation charter, though it emphasizes consultation very strongly, cannot be allowed the same weight because of the evident motives of policy which might influence the writer. Stubbs, *S.C.*, 119-120.

[41] Liebermann, I, 483 f. The fact should not be overlooked that this mandate grants to the Saxon plaintiff the right to appeal to the Norman law in certain cases if he wishes, and so makes a change in the Saxon law which the courts could not disregard, and on the other hand denies to the Norman plaintiff the right to insist upon his own law, and finally modifies both these provisions if the case involves outlawry. Whatever in the way of legislation may lie behind this mandate, it has upon existing common law the full modifying effect of a statute.

references to other innovations that were said to have been made give us no information as to a legislative body or legislative methods, and the codes of laws attributed to William add nothing, hardly even confirmation, to our information from other sources. The *Hic intimatur* says: "statuimus"—"volo"—"interdicimus"—"decretum est"—but without details, and the longer statement of the *Leis Willelmi*—"Ces sunt les leis e les custumes, que li reis Will. grantad al pople de Engleterre aprés le cunquest de la terre, iceles que le reis Edward sun cusin tint devant lui"—is also not instructive.[42]

In conclusion we can say that our information derived from the period itself though scanty covers the really fundamental matters. There was a central council composed of the magnates of the whole kingdom by whose advice and counsel the king acted in questions of legislation and policy. It was able to withhold its consent if it did not agree with the king, in which case, sometimes at least, what the king had intended was abandoned. In proclaiming the decisions which king and council had reached, the king made use of words which seem to imply that he was making laws or issuing executive orders by his sole prerogative power.[43]

[42] See note D at the end of the chapter.

[43] In such conception of government as prevailed in the feudal age, in the more or less unconscious theorizing which lay back of action and which became more conscious as time went on, the legislative function was regarded as vested in the king, as were most, probably all, government functions. Luchaire, *Institutions,* I, 243. As the king was theoretically the source of justice, so it was by action of the crown that law was made. This theory, that all government is the act of the king, has remained a permanent feature of the constitution to the present day, and its frequent expression in the field of executive action in the king's speech at the opening of parliament is a most interesting survival. In one respect, however, the theory in feudal days corresponded more exactly with the facts: the king possessed an absolute veto. It was by the formal act of the king in publishing the law, in what contemporaries and the documents themselves often called *decreta* or

In these paragraphs on the legal changes of the first period I have confined myself to those which are enumerated by Liebermann in the passages I have referred to, and they cover those commonly included in the legislation of the first two Norman kings. To them, however, should be added the bringing in of the whole body of feudal law, regulating landholding by feudal tenure and allied matters. This was in William's time a great and well developed body of law, having behind it a history of more than two hundred years. Its growth was not yet complete,[44] for the growth of no body of law is complete until it is dead, but its fundamental principles are all clearly to be recognized in English feudalism of the eleventh century and in their application in the most distinctive features of the system as we know it in western Europe.[45] It was probably only a half dozen years after the composition of the *Leis Willelmi* and a little before the middle of Henry I's reign that a statement of feudal law was made in England, the most advanced that had yet been made in the history of feudalism.[46] There is in fact nothing of the kind which can be compared with it at

constitutiones, that what had been determined on in the curia became actual law and, without such publication by the king, any determination of the curia remained without effect. To this same function or prerogative of the king, as exercised in the trial of cases in the curia, the German writers have given the name Rechtsgebot, and there has been more discussion of that aspect of this royal power by historians than of its exercise in legislation, perhaps because the whole subject of feudal legislation has been less minutely studied. It must, however, of necessity have been the same prerogative and it must in many cases have been exercised in the formal way of a legislative veto. It too has survived in theory to the present time.

44 Later developments in this body of law in England were not to change it in any important details of practice but were to be in some points away from its fundamental principles.

45 The debt which English history owes to Dr. J. Horace Round for establishing this fact in many particulars can hardly be overstated.

46 The *Leges Henrici*. On date and significance see Liebermann, III, 312-314, and *Ueber das Englische Rechtsbuch Leges Henrici*, Halle, 1901.

that date except the *Usatici Barchinone,* written down in the last half of the eleventh century but clearly representing institutions in a less developed stage.[47] The *Leges Henrici* portray the feudal law in one respect certainly as it was in William I's day—a definite body of law extending over the whole kingdom, but standing beside another definite body of law extending over the same territory but quite different in character, the local customary law of Saxon times. Perhaps to say that they are different in character is to convey a wrong impression. They regulated quite different things, quite different interests. There was in consequence no clash between them, nor did they come into collision with one another. Where collision would have been likely, or at least disagreement in forms and principles, if the Saxon had remained in force, the Saxon disappeared and the feudal took its place. Much Saxon land law, so far as it regulated the holdings of the actual cultivators and so far as it related to payments that were due, *consuetudines,* tolls, and the like, remained unchanged.[48] The law which regulated the rights in land of persons above the actual cultivators and the services due for their lands from their own class became feudal. So in respect to other matters. The spheres of the two bodies of law were distinct, and probably they no more had an effect to confuse one another in the carrying on of practical affairs in the time of William I than they have in the statements of the *Leges Henrici.*

One other characteristic of the feudal law as intro-

47 Printed in Ch. Giraud, *Histoire du Droit Français,* II, 465-509. For a critical study of the date and character of this code, see Ficker, *Mitth. d. Instituts f. Oesterreichische Geschichtsforschung,* 1888, *Ergänzungsband,* II, 236-275. The fragments from which the Lombard *Libri Feudorum* were to be formed in the course of the thirteenth century were beginning to appear at the end of the eleventh and the beginning of the twelfth centuries.

48 See below, Chapter III, n. 3.

duced by the Conquest is to be noticed. It was itself a body of customary law. It had not been created by legislation, nor was it ever put into statute or official code. This made its introduction beside another body of customary law a simple matter.[49] It need not be, and it was not, done by legislation. It was not consciously done at all. The feudal military system, the whole governmental organization, so far as that was different from the old, was of unavoidable necessity introduced. The feudal in these respects was the only system which the Normans could have operated. So far in the way of deliberate, probably conscious, change they must go, but all the rest followed as incidental, as unconsidered corollaries of the necessary change. And the practical operation at the same time of the two bodies of law was simple from another reason. Each had its own system of courts—the Saxon local courts on one side, the king's general and local courts, and the private courts of barons, on the other. To each of these two sets of courts belonged primarily its own law. When necessity arose each recognized and enforced the law of the other, but in the main the fields of the courts, like the fields of the law, were distinct. When the king made use of the Saxon local court for his own purposes, he plainly changed its character.

NOTE A

FEUDALIZATION

The feudalization of the assembly is not a change which took place in England. What happened there was that the Normans without thinking about it at all set up what seemed to them the

49 Round, *Studies in Peerage and Family History*, p. 186, calls attention to the fact that on the Welsh border with the consent of the king some lands were held of William Fitz Osbern according to Norman custom and some according to Welsh.

natural and normal national assembly. This inevitably was constructed according to the only model with which they were familiar, and the feudalized assembly was at a stroke put in place of the old witenagemot, with no evolution of form or principle intervening between them. The feudalizing process had really been completed in the Frankish kingdom a century or more before the Norman Conquest. There the transformation of an assembly of the great men of church and state into an assembly of king's vassals was also an unconscious change, and it had gone on through several generations. The history of the change is really the history of the growth of feudalism and its absorption of more and more of the public life of the time. As the great men of church and state were taken over into the vassalage of the king, it became more and more difficult to distinguish between a national assembly of the old type and an assembly of king's vassals. The purely official positions of the state were affected along with everything else. It became customary to attach fiefs to offices. Offices were themselves regarded as fiefs and granted and held as such. Fiefs were specially bestowed to reward efficient service or to secure it in the future. The transformation affected church as well as state. The endowment lands of the ecclesiastical office which had been given for its support by the faithful, of a bishopric for example, became a fief held of the king on the same terms of feudal service as lay fiefs, and was as naturally connected with an office of state or of the household. In the English transformation this change in ecclesiastical arrangements had to be carried through suddenly, as it had not been on the continent, and as it touched men closely in their money interests we find it noticed in the writers of the time. See Makower, *Const. Hist. of the Church of England,* 1895, pp. 245-247, and references, especially *Hist. Eliensis,* p. 274; *Chron. Abingdon,* pp. 3, 35; and M. Paris, II, 6. Thus gradually in the Frankish kingdom without the knowledge or intention of anyone, the national assembly, the *placitum generale,* the *concilium* in all its forms, was feudalized; it became a feudal assembly or assembly of king's vassals. And because court service became a more and more important dependence as the state became more feudal, it took its place as a coördinate duty, always to be expected of the vassal, beside military service which had been in the beginning more essential. See with the references they give Waitz, *Deutsche Verfassungsgeschichte,* 1896, VI, 31-33; Dahn, *Koenige der Germanen,* VIII, 4, 32; 6, 134, 145-147; Brunner, *Deutsche Rechtsgechichte,* II, 125-135. All this was a completed development more than a century before the Norman Conquest, and it is the result not the process that affected the witenagemot. In other words the necessary feudalizing of landholding which lay back of the change of the assembly was carried through in England for reasons of its own with no special thought of what would be its effect on the witenagemot, but having been carried through, that effect was not to be escaped.

No change of the sort which took place in the Frankish kingdom affected the assembly in contemporary Saxon England because there was no development of political feudalism there. Exactly what did take place in England, carried as far towards later feudalism as the facts will warrant, can best be studied in the writings on Saxon institutions of Professor Felix Liebermann, especially in the articles in his *Rechts und Sachglossar, Gesetze der Angelsachsen,* II, Abt. 2. Great care must be taken, however, not to misinterpret Dr. Liebermann's statements. He holds with Brunner (See *A.H.R.* VII, 30, note 2) that the institutional origin of vassalage is to be found in the *comitatus,* and he consequently sees in England a nearer approach to the continental vassalage of the eleventh century than would otherwise be recognized. Still it must be said that no objection can be made on the ground of accuracy to the use of the terms vassal and vassalage of Saxon personal relations, for the same terms were used in the course of the development of Frankish feudalism for very similar and contemporary arrangements, that is contemporary not in time, not in the eleventh century, because French feudalism had then passed far beyond these things, but contemporary in the stage of development which they represent. Nor, if exception be made of the identification of some Teutonic practices of the *mundium* type with vassalage, can Liebermann's conclusions be objected to, for he recognizes clearly enough the incompleteness of the Saxon results and shows plainly that it is only by a combination of vassalage and the fief that political feudalism is created, a combination which does not take place in Saxon times. See *Rechtsglossar,* Article, "Lehnwesen," and *Zeitschrift für Geschichtswissenschaft,* 1889, II, 463. Cf. *Origin,* pp. 44 ff.

To my mind what was produced in the Saxon state—a considerable development of the *comitatus* relationship but none of the benefice or fief to combine with it, even through a period of centuries in favoring conditions—proves that the institutional basis of the later vassalage was not the *comitatus* and indicates the contribution which the Teutonic institution did make to the feudal system, chiefly social, affecting the interpretation given to the relationship and its social consideration. There is also a contribution from it to the ceremonial side of feudalism which does not show itself in Saxon England. See *Encyclopaedia Britannica,* 11th ed., X, Article, "Feudalism." It would seem that the belief that vassalage is institutionally a development from the *comitatus,* rather than from the Roman *patrocinium,* arises from putting too great emphasis on the social influences which assisted in the formation of feudalism and too little upon the purely institutional, which are the elements in any development which determine form. It is the work of the social elements to give impulse not form.

It is easy to believe in the continuity of the national assembly from witenagemot to great council unless one makes clear to himself with precision what the problem really is. Beyond question the great council occupies the same place in the state, fulfils the same functions, and is composed of the same classes of men as the witenagemot. Certainly also contemporaries saw no noteworthy change in passing from one to the other. There is continuity in the sense of these particulars. But if evidence of this sort proves institutional continuity, there is almost never any institutional change in history. There would be when there occurs deliberate action, like the adoption of federal government in the constitution of the United States, but there would not be when the British cabinet system was formed nor when the representative system was introduced. A change of function or a change in the elements forming an institution may be a sign of institutional change, though this must be proved by other evidence, but a continuance without change of these things is never a sign of institutional continuity. Institutional differences are differences of structure, institutional changes are changes of structure; they are necessarily changes in principle, not necessarily changes in form or product. If this were not true, then it would be quite right to say that an institutional change, like basing the court service of the bishops on their feudal relationship, has no particular importance (Liebermann, *Assembly,* p. 79), and historians then would hardly be justified in giving the time and effort which it requires to establish institutional facts. To insist that there was continuity because of identity of function and of composition is not to notice that the same facts would prove continuity with the Norman curia ducis or even with the curia regis of the kings of France. See on the character of the Norman curia ducis, with the references given, Charles H. Haskins, *Norman Institutions,* pp. 54-58; Powicke, *The Loss of Normandy,* p. 59; Valin, *Le Duc de Normandie et sa Cour,* pp. 101-106; and on the French assembly, Luchaire, *Institutions Monarchiques,* I, 246-252, 254, 275-276. The assemblies of practically all contemporary states performed the same functions and were made up from the same aristocratic classes. "Hortatu itaque et consilio archiepiscoporum, episcoporum, ducum, marchionum, comitum, palatinorum, ceterorumque nobilium, simul etiam judicum hac edictale lege in omne evum Deo propicio valitura decernimus." (1136). *Monumenta Germania Historica,* Legum, Sectio IV, Tomus I, 176. "[Curia] in qua sunt principes, episcopi, abbates, comites et vicecomites, comitores et vasvassores, philosophi et sapientes atque judices." (*c.* 1076) *Usatici Barchinone Patrie,* c. 80, from Giraud, *Histoire du Droit Français au Moyen Age,* II, 481. It follows that these similarities have no value as evidence of historical connection. It follows also that practically the same history of function and composition lies back of the curia regis of William I whether we suppose the Saxon or the Norman assembly to be its immediate ancestor.

Some of the evidence which has been brought forward to show that the writers of Henry I's time believed the curia regis to be a continuation of the witenagemot cannot, I think, be accepted in the sense in which it is used. What these writers understood well, as a standard of comparison, was the institution as it existed in their own time. Their knowledge of the Saxon institution was antiquarian knowledge, not the intimate personal knowledge of men who saw it in operation or helped to operate it themselves, as they did the Anglo-Norman. It was natural that they should overlook the fundamental but subtle institutional difference and be deceived by the superficial but not organic resemblances. What they did, however, is what would be always natural to men in their situation, they projected their institutional ideas and understandings back into Saxon times. They did not identify their institution with the witenagemot, but the witenagemot with the curia regis. See *Leges Edwardi Confessoris,* 8.3, 15.4, 34.3. That the writer of these Leges was not familiar with the earlier history is well known. See Prolog 9 and 34 to 34 1b, and Liebermann, *Ueber die Leges Edwardi Confessoris.* They identified in the same way the Anglo-Saxon tithing system with the frankpledge, and Anglo-Saxon land relationships with the feudal. W. A. Morris, *Frankpledge System,* pp. 33-35; Liebermann, *Leges Edwardi Confessoris,* p. 81; *Gesetze,* II, 2,568, c. 4.

It is likely that I have labored this argument more than was necessary. It has seemed worth while because the doctrine of the continuity of the national assembly from Saxon to Norman times, held unconsciously perhaps as a feeling that the assembly as the ancestor of parliament escaped Norman remaking, has a further bearing. It appears to be one of the chief defences of the belief that there was something peculiarly English about the early constitution, something coming from Saxon times and different from anything possessed by any continental people, which explains the development of a free constitution in England alone. In my opinion this belief, often as I have implied unconsciously or only half consciously held, is the most serious obstacle which prevents a clear understanding of the Anglo-Norman constitution and of the way in which the limited monarchy arose. The beginning of such an understanding is to see that there is nothing of real significance which distinguishes the English national constitution from the French in the period, except such beginnings of growth as show themselves after 1066 of institutions which in France remained without power of growth. It is in these beginnings in

England after 1066 that the peculiarity of English constitutional history is to be found.

NOTE B

GROUND OF SERVICE IN THE ASSEMBLY

The institutional principle by virtue of which the bishops had their place in the great council is a sufficient test of this fact. Their ecclesiastical office remained unchanged from Saxon to Norman days and their importance as chief men of the community had if anything increased. If any persons whatever sat in the great council by virtue of the ancient principle, because they were the chief men of church and state, the bishops would certainly be among them. That they had their position in the great council because they were barons and not because they were bishops, and in modern times have continued to sit in the house of lords for a corresponding reason and not as representatives of the church, is generally though not universally admitted. See Pike, *Constitutional History of the House of Lords,* 1894, Chapter IX. For our purpose the early period only is important, and it is fortunate that the fact is firmly established by evidence from the first hundred years after the Conquest, and indeed from before the close of the eleventh century. Probably the most familiar bit of evidence comes from almost the very end of the first Anglo-Norman century, but it is worth quoting again because, apart from its bearing on this point, it is, as I have said before, one of the best statements of the fundamental principle of the feudal assembly which we have from any country. C. XI of the Constitutions of Clarendon of 1164 reads: "Archiepiscopi, episcopi, et universae personae regni qui de rege tenent in capite, et habent possessiones suas de domino rege sicut baroniam, et inde respondent Justitiis et ministris regis et sequuntur et faciunt omnes rectitudines regias et consuetudines, et sicut barones ceteri, debent interesse judiciis curiae domini regis cum baronibus, usque perveniatur in judicio ad diminutionem membrorum vel mortem." Stubbs, *S.C.,* p. 166. The Constitutions of Clarendon were drawn up as the result of a national inquiry undertaken by the great council to ascertain the ancient customs of the kingdom with special reference to the rights of the king concerning the church, particularly during the time of Henry I, roughly the first third of the twelfth century. That is, the assembly was stating in this formal declaration the principle of its own composition and the ground of the bishop's position in it as they judged it to be during the first part of the twelfth century. It was only a few months later in another meeting of the assembly that the bishops themselves repeated the same declaration in other words. An eye witness who had considerable knowledge of the law and was likely to represent the clerical point of view, William Fitz Stephen, a clerk and assistant of Becket's, tells us that, when the lay barons proposed that the bishops should pronounce the judgment of the curia upon Thomas Becket, the bishops in explaining their refusal replied: "Non sedemus hic episcopi, sed barones. Nos barones et vos barones pares hic sumus." Robertson, *Materials for the History of Thomas Becket,* III, 52.

This is exactly the position which had been taken by Lanfranc, archbishop of Canterbury, in 1082 in the trial of Odo, bishop of Bayeux, and in 1088 in the trial of William bishop of Durham. See below, Chapter II. The judgment in the case of Odo asserts that his consecration as bishop did not relieve him of the responsibility to the great council which rested on him as earl of Kent, but that he remained subject to trial and punishment by it like any lay baron. The case is a famous one, but it is well to notice how thoroughly established the essential matter is. Two of the best historians of the next generation, Orderic Vitalis, ed. Le Prevost, III, 191, and William of Malmesbury, *Gesta Regum* (R.S.), IV, 306, quite independent of one another, state the crucial point, and the latter attributes the suggestion to Lanfranc. Six years later than the trial of Odo, in the trial of William bishop of Durham for treason, Lanfranc himself, according to one who was probably an eye witness, makes exactly the same point and fortifies it by a reference to the case of Odo. The evidence here cited is so controlled that there can be no doubt as to the fact, nor as to the opinion of Lanfranc who had been trained in the law. But the trial of 1088 is still more explicit on the subject, for Bishop William made repeated and skillful attempts to evade the jurisdiction of the court on the ground of his ecclesiastical office and was met with equal skill by Lanfranc at every turn. The point is again involved in the trial of Archbishop Anselm for default of fealty to William II in 1095, but this time Bishop William of Durham was on the king's side and insisted on the baronial position of the bishop and his consequent responsibility to the court, which in 1088 he had refused to accept. The king's demand that Anselm's spiritual office should be involved in his secular fault shows how far he was willing to carry this principle, but the barons refused to take that view. See further on these cases below in Chapter II. The abbot's position, if he held a barony, was the same as that of the bishop. The declaration of Abbot Samson of St. Edmunds towards the end of the twelfth century—"se non posse demembrare baroniam"—in answer to a suggestion that he transfer a church to the convent, is interesting as stating a feudal principle not often referred to in England in that form, though it is that upon which primogeniture rests. *Chronica Jocelini de Brakelonda* (Camden Society), p. 46.

There is also an interesting document from the reign of William I which by inference gives us a glimpse into the institutional ideas of the time and has an indirect bearing upon this point. It is the record of a decision in 1072 of the question of the primacy between Canterbury and York, Davis, *Regesta Regum Anglo-Normannorum*, I, nos. 64 and 65. In the list of signatures to no. 64 occur these words: "Ego Odo Bayocensis episcopus et comes Cantiae consensi. Ego Godefridus Constantiensis et unus de primatibus Anglorum consensi." The second title of Geofrey is omitted by Davis, but it is found in all the copies of the document which give the signatures. See William of Malmesbury, *Gesta Regum*, III, 298; Eadmer, *Historia Novorum*, p. 252. The second designations in both these cases are clearly no accident and they should be significant to us. The pope had directed that the question should be decided "tocius regni episcoporum et abbatum testimonio et judicio." The document commonly called the "constitution of Windsor," no. 64, though it embodies in fact the decision of the great council, is put into form corresponding to the pope's reference of the case. It has the signatures of 15 bishops and 12 abbots, and no lay signatures except the king's and queen's, which would be quite in place even if witnessing the decision of an ecclesiastical synod. But the two bishops named above were not "episcopi regni," and the one who drew up the document plainly had in mind the fact that as bishops these two had no standing either as conforming to the pope's reference of the case or as members of the great council, and so he adds in each case the designation which explains their presence in the council which, as suggested below, probably made the legal decision.

This incident is so interesting and important institutionally that, though it bears only incidentally on our present subject, it may be well to notice some points of doubt concerning it. The best text of all the material, including Davis's no. 64 without the signatures, is to be found in Boehmer, *Die Fälschungen Erzbischof Lanfranks von Canterbury,* 1902, pp. 165-173, cf. pp. 141-143; not referred to by Davis, as also is not the facsimile of no. 65 in Series I, Vol. III, plate 170, of the Paleographical Society. The one link in Boehmer's chain of argument in regard to the Canterbury forgeries which seems too weak is that which makes the connection between the two meetings of the great council. He supposes that Lanfranc found at the Easter meeting at Winchester that he could not prove the Canterbury claim with the evidence which he then had, and that the case was therefore adjourned to the Pentecost meeting at Windsor for decision. In the meantime Lanfranc provided the necessary evidence—a *gesta* or chronicle account and six forged and four expanded papal privileges, necessitating the destruction of four genuine ones. This supposition as to when the evidence was produced does not seem to me necessary either to Boehmer's proof of the forgery and the forger, which I am obliged to accept, or to the explanation of the evidence as we have it. Boehmer also sets forth so clearly the difficulty which the forger would have had to complete his work between the time of his arrival at Canterbury from Winchester and the time when he must set out for Windsor as to convince one that it would be really impossible.

All the conditions I think are met, and more simply, by supposing that the evidence had been provided before the Easter meeting; that there was a decision then by the great council but that, in order to conform to the terms of the pope's reference of the case to England as above, the final notification of the decision was postponed to the Windsor meeting at which an especially large number of prelates was got together; that at Winchester a record was made of the decision which was witnessed and given to Lanfranc for the Canterbury archives, for which it would be especially important as the legal decision; while the other document with the added sentence about the two meetings, as it appears in no. 64 but not in 65, and witnessed by all the ecclesiastics present, was the record intended as a general notification and distributed generally to the churches and abbeys. It is asking a good deal to require us to suppose that Lanfranc thought he could suppress the evidence that there were two meetings about the case, in the first of which he failed, from the Canterbury archives and from the news that went to Rome (Boehmer, p. 26), when in the archives of the churches and monasteries generally, including Canterbury itself, there was plain evidence of the facts. If there was only one trial, confirmed perhaps at Windsor and certainly with the preparation of the record in final form reserved for the ecclesiastical signatures possible there, while the legal evidence was furnished to Canterbury at the Winchester meeting, all the facts seem to me to be explained and the apparent discrepancy between the Windsor document and Lanfranc's letter to the pope (Boehmer, p. 169), accounted for. He gives an account of only one trial because there was only one actual trial. The facsimile of the Winchester document, which is published as above, shows that the signatures are all autographs, a very important fact in the case, and that the document ended with the word "episcopi," having only the signatures of bishops, and does not add "et abbates," which are the last words of the Constitution of Windsor. In this latter document the archbishop of York adds to his signature "subscripsi," while in the other he says "concedo," an expression likely only at the time of the first decision. It has not been noticed I think that St. Albans had a copy of the Windsor document. Matthew Paris, ed. Luard, II, 10.

If this explanation is correct, it can be seen why it was desirable that the presence among the English witnesses of two who were not "episcopi regni" should be accounted for by indicating their baronial position which gave them a voice in the legal decision. Also if it is correct, the order given the documents in Davis's *Regesta* should be reversed since his no. 64 is the Windsor record made at Whitsuntide for the churches generally and no. 65 the Winchester record made at Easter for Canterbury.

Davis's no. 63, which as it reads calls for the assembly of the *servitium debitum* at Clarendon on the octave of Easter of this year for the Scottish expedition, Round, *Feudal England,* p. 304, would make the meeting of a great council at Pentecost difficult. The correct reading, however, is the octave of Pentecost, not Easter. See Davis's edition of the same year as the *Regesta,* of Stubbs, *S.C.*, p. 97, which gives correctly the reading of the manuscript.

Upon the main subject of this note, certain words of Lanfranc's in his letter to the pope are significant. After saying how there had come together "ad regalem curiam apud Uuentanam civitatem in Pascali solemnitate episcopi, abbates, ceterique ex sacro et laicali ordine" and a reference to the pope's authority, he goes on to say: "Deinde regia potestas per semet ipsam contestata est eos per fidem et sacramentum, quibus sibi colligati erant, quatinus hanc causam intentissime audirent, auditam ad certum rectumque finem sine partium favore perducerent." Boehmer, p. 169; Giles, *Opera Lanfranci,* I, 23. The "fides et sacramentum" by which they were bound to the king is the ground on which he bases their duty to act as members of the great council.

NOTE C

COMPOSITION OF THE CURIA REGIS

A cartulary has preserved an account, informal and narrative in character, of a trial held by King William and his curia, probably in 1086, which is interesting as bearing on the composition of the court. Davis, *Regesta,* no. 220, App. no. xxxii, text; Round, *Calendar,* no. 114. The plea occupied the whole of a Sunday at a manor of William of Eu's in Wiltshire, called in the text Ala

Chocha, probably Lackham, which at the time of the Domesday survey was held by a tenant of William's. Round suggests (*Calendar,* index) Laycock, but Lackham was in the parish of Laycock and no other part was held at that time by William of Eu. The assembly was hardly a great council, nor was it an ordinary small council. It was what I have called elsewhere (*Origin,* pp. 197 f.) a reinforced small council, but so largely reinforced as to be almost a great council. The names of those who were present—"viderunt hunc finem"—are enumerated in an informal list. They are given, not as signatures, but as they would be in a chronicle account, perhaps reclassified by the writer. They are called "hii barones" and include the king's two sons, William and Henry, two archbishops, eight bishops including Geoffrey of Coutances who was a baron in England, three earls and eighteen barons, two of whom in the middle of the list have official designations. Then are given the names of three monks and six *laici* who had attended evidently as representatives of the abbot of Féchamp, one of the parties to the suit. It clearly seemed to the writer a normal thing to include bishops and officials among the barons. It did also somewhat later to the writer of a similar record, in 1103. Round, *Calendar,* no. 118; Dugdale, *Monasticon,* 1846, VI, 1083. After the names of the king and queen, it continues: "Ad haec barones fuerunt Robertus episcopus Lincoln" and two others. Here also the chancellor, Waldric, is named in the midst of the barons. This record refers definitely to the preceding one: "De theoloneo quod injuste recipiebant homines Philippi . . . post illam narrationem quae de ipso theoloneo facta est alachoche in praesentia Willielmi regis antiquioris ac baronum ejus . . ."

Attendance of the rear vassal at the king's court in the train of his lord is implied in the statement of the services due from Nigel D'Oilly to the abbot of Abingdon early in the twelfth century: "In curia etiam regis si abbati placitum aliquod forte habendum contigerit, ipsius abbatis parti idem aderit, nisi contra regem placitandum forte fuerit." *Chronicon Monasterii de Abingdon,* II, 133. In 2 John the question was put to a grand assize jury whether Nigel de Broc owed to the bishop of Winchester for a fee the service of one knight or "debet ei assurgere in curia Domini Regis et facere ei locum ut possit loqui cum Domino Rege." *Placitorum Abbreviatio* (Record Commission), p. 34. On the right of a lord to the counsel of his men, which implies their attendance with him at the curia regis but not their membership of the court, see below, Chapter II, note 42. A notification of William II's speaks of the reduction of the service of the abbot of Ramsey "de servitio decem militum in festis" to three north of the Thames. *Ramsey Cartulary,* I, 235; Davis, *Regesta,* no. 462. William of Malmesbury states both fact and motive in speaking of the three annual courts: "omnes eo cujuscunque professionis magnates regium edictum accersiebat ut exterrarum legati speciem multitudinis apparatumque deliciarum mirarentur." *Gesta Regum,* II, 335; cf. Orderic Vitalis, II, 168, and Stubbs, I, 399 and n. 3. The attendance of rear vassals upon their lords at important meetings of the national assembly was common in other countries. Waitz, *Deutsche Verf.,* VI, 437; Luchaire, *Institutions,* I, 262. In Germany the attendance of the rear vassal with his lord at the Reichstag was so regular that it was reckoned a part of his court service to his immediate lord. So also the dignitaries of the church were accompanied by clergy of minor rank to such meetings from similar motives. That minor officials of the king's were present in formal meetings of the assembly is noted very infrequently, only once in the first two reigns in the trial of the bishop of Durham (Chap. II, at note 11) and then not in such a way as to imply that they were members of the court. These facts are well known but they are not always kept in view in considering the membership of the assembly. Descriptive terms attached to the names of witnesses are very numerous and most of them indicate a doubtful member of the court: vicecomes, sheriff, minister, forester, cook, scribe, chaplain, cleric, priest, monk, canon, the chancellors, dapifers, seneschals, etc., of others than the king, and women's names other than the queen, and even the queen if the king is present. See Haskins, *Institutions,* pp. 180-182. Instances of the distribution of witnesses into classes are: Round, *Calendar,* nos. 116, 1114, 1115, 1410; Davis, *Regesta,* no. 423 (text p. 137); Haskins, *Institutions,* p. 95, no. 5; *Gloucester Cartulary,* II, 106; Valin, *Le Duc de Normandie,* pp. 261, 266; a charter of confirmation by Henry Count of Eu, *The*

Genealogist, XIII, 12; Brunner, *Schwurgerichte,* pp. 196-199; Teulet, *Layettes du Trésor des Chartes,* I, no. 509. Cf. Davis, *Regesta,* nos. 2, 3, 48, 55, 56, 117, 118, 121, 270. Not all the above are charters recording the action of courts, though charters of grant and confirmation may do so, but all go to show that lists of witnesses cannot be used with certainty to prove the composition of a court, and incidentally I think they show that Luchaire, *Institutions,* I, 317, goes a little too far in supposing that the parties before the court could in this way modify its composition.

The chancellor, as the king's secretary and therefore very probably something like what we might call the secretary of the council, stood, it would seem, in a rather different relationship to it from the ordinary household officers. As sending out the summonses to others and as the council scribe, he may have had a right, or a duty, to attend its meetings without a formal summons made out to himself. We know that at meetings of the council acting as a court scribes were often present officially, but not necessarily as helping to form the court. See the claim advanced for Thomas Becket that the chancellor had a right to attend the meetings of the council without a summons. *Materials,* III, 18. This relationship of the chancellor to the council survived to modern times. Pike, *House of Lords,* pp. 352-354; Round, *E.H.R.,* XXXIII, 463; Pollard, *Evolution of Parliament,* pp. 21-24.

NOTE D

THE ASSEMBLY IN THE CHRONICLES

A few incidental references to the operations of the great council in this period, mostly in chronicle accounts, while they say little in themselves are not uninstructive in the light of our other information. In a notification of 1074 the archbishop of Rouen says that a "petitio Rogerii de Mortuomari et uxoris eius Advisae ad nos venit, ad dominum Guillelmum regem Anglorum et ad me, sedentes et tractantes de negotiis ecclesiasticis et secularibus cum episcopis in quodam concilio congregato in urbe Rotomagensi . . ." Davis, *Regesta,* no. 77; cf. Orderic Vitalis,

V, 158. This was an ecclesiastical council presided over by the king and the archbishop, but it evidently considered secular business. In 1085 "the king had a great council and very deep speech with his witan about this land," resulting in the Domesday survey. Anglo-Saxon Chronicles, II, 186. Orderic Vitalis, III, 316-317, puts into the mouth of William II a speech supposed to be addressed to the barons in the Easter assembly at Winchester, 1089, to persuade them to invade Normandy with him. It can mean to us no more than what Orderic, writing more than thirty years later, thought it natural and to be expected that William would say. But there is no reason to suppose that what Orderic would think at the end of the reign of Henry I to be a natural mode of address for the king to use in speaking to the great council would not also be natural in 1089. If the drift of events in the meantime had any influence at all, it would be to make such a speech seem less natural and so Orderic less likely to put it in that form. The speech is wholly one of persuasion and it closes: "Colligite, quaeso, concilium, prudenter inite consilium, sententiam proferte, quid in hoc agendum sit discrimine. Mittam, si laudatis, exercitum in Normanniam . . ." See Freeman, *William Rufus,* I, 222-224. Under date of 1098 (IV, 44) Orderic records a closely similar occurrence. With these passages agree the brief references to procedure and purpose in Eadmer's accounts of assemblies at some of which he was present as an attendant upon Archbishop Anselm. At Christmas, 1092, before Anselm became archbishop, when "omnes regni primores ad curiam regis pro more venissent, contigit ut eorum optimi quique uno sensu inter se de communi matre regni quererentur, quod viduata suo pastore tam diu . . . Hujusmodi ergo de hoc ab eis consilium sumptum est, ut supplici prece dominum suum regem convenirent" that he would allow public prayers for the appointment of an archbishop. The king though somewhat angry consented, adding that without doubt he should do whatever he pleased. Eadmer, *Hist. Nov.,* p. 29. The passage illustrates the position the king could sometimes take as well as the procedure of the assembly. William of Malmesbury, who in his *Gesta Pontificum* (R.S.), pp. 79-80, gives an independent account of the same incident, adds another at the same assembly illustrating procedure (p. 80). He says: "Item cum in consessu procerum de Anselmo haberetur verbum, unus intulit ipsum esse solum nostro tempore nullius honoris cupidum." To this the king made answer and finally declared that he would be archbishop himself. Eadmer's long account, *ibid.*, pp. 53-67, of the assembly at Rockingham in 1095, at which Anselm was tried, agrees in all particulars with the foregoing. The assembly, "ex regia sanctione ferme totius regni nobilitas," came together at Rockingham. He indicates the presence also of spectators—"assistentem monarchorum, clericorum, laicorum numerosam multitudinem"—and that the open discussion in the assembly was at times somewhat turbulent. He shows even more clearly than does the passage cited from Orderic Vitalis above the dependence of the king on the result of the discussion. He makes him exclaim: "Quid placet, si haec non placent? Dum vivo parem mihi in regno meo utique sustinere nolo. Et sic sciebatis eum tanto in causa sua robore fultum, quare permisistis me incipere placitum istud contra eum? Ite, consiliamini, quia, per Vultum Dei, si vos illum ad voluntatem meam non damnaveritis, ego damnabo vos." Of the final refusal of the barons he says: "Quod ille [rex] repressa sustinuit ira, ratione eorum palam ne nimis offenderentur contraire praecavens." Of the Whitsuntide assembly in 1097 he says (p. 79): "Peractis igitur festivioribus diebus, diversorum negotiorum causae in medium duci ex more coeperunt," and of that in the following August: "Cum de statu regni acturus rex episcopos, abbates et quosque regni proceres in unum praecepti sui sanctione egisset." It should be added that a writer, probably towards the end of the reign of Henry I, records the participation of the barons in taxation to raise the money that was loaned to Duke Robert for his crusade. He says: "Et hanc libertatem habuit sancta ecclesia usque ad tempus Willelmi iunioris, qui de baronibus totius patrie auxilium petiit ad Normanniam retinendam de fratre suo Rodberto eunte in Ierusalem. Ipsi autem concesserunt ei quatuor solidos de unaquaque hyda, sanctam ecclesiam non excipientes." *Leges Edw. Conf.*, 11, 2; Liebermann, I, 636. This statement is not confirmed elsewhere, though Eadmer says (p. 74) that the money was "partim data," and we have no record of an assembly in the year of the transaction,

1096, but the details mentioned are so completely in accord with what we know of later times that they may be taken as highly probable. See Freeman, *William Rufus,* I, 556. The participation of the barons, lay and ecclesiastic, in the granting of money, one of the most important acts of a legislative assembly, may be inferred, at least for an occasion so important as the one referred to. And these passages together imply that the writers of one or two generations later believed that the assembly of the first period was composed of the magnates of the realm, that they reached their conclusion by consultation together, that they discussed the general interests of the kingdom, and that in some cases the action which the king was about to take depended upon their decision.

CHAPTER II

PROCEDURE IN THE FEUDAL CURIA REGIS[1]

To us who must form our opinion of a past age by the evidence from it which has come down to us, it may naturally seem that in the eleventh and twelfth centuries judicial processes, litigation in the courts, exceeded greatly in importance and frequency any other governmental activity.[2] Certainly the evidence which we have of litigation greatly exceeds in amount that of any other function of the great council and is much more specific in character. A little reflection will convince us, however, that this appearance of greater activity is probably due to the conditions which determined first what evidence should be put into definite form, easily preserved, and afterwards its actual preservation. When we consider how many and what permanent interests of person and property depended upon the decisions of courts, it is not strange that these decisions were carefully formulated and not left to mere chance for their preservation.

It may perhaps be in place here also to say that to regard the greater frequency of judicial evidences as meaning that to the men of the time the judicial was made the standard of all other activities of the curia regis, is to take into the account only a part of the determining

1 This Chapter first appeared as an article with the same title in the *Columbia Law Review*, April, 1913, XIII, 277-293. It is here reprinted with slight additions and changes.

2 This is regarding the matter relatively of course. Regarded absolutely the amount of litigation during the first Anglo-Norman century, of which we have the evidence, was not great, is surprisingly small indeed.

conditions. They were in one way more interested in the judicial activity of the government than in any other of its activities, but this was in a practical way only, because of the immediate and tangible concerns which were involved, not from any reasoning about government nor on any theoretical ground. Even when they applied terms taken from the judicial side—*judicium, sententia, consideratum est*—to action which to us seems plainly legislative or administrative, they were not identifying one kind of action with the other as a species of government activity.[3] They were not thinking of the character of the action. They were not saying: "This is a judicial act; we are acting as a court of law." They were merely identifying procedure. They were saying: "We are acting as we always do."

Procedure was the one thing about government action

[3] Conversely in a French charter of 1016 the judgment of a court is called *haec constitutio*. Langlois, *Textes Relatifs a l'Histoire du Parlement*, in the *Collection de Textes pour Servir a l'Étude et l'Enseignement de l'Histoire*, p. 2. In the word *placitum* we have also a development in the reverse direction. From meaning "what was pleasing," "opinion," it came to mean the assembly in which the opinion was reached (Gregory of Tours, VII, 7), a use frequent in the Anglo-Norman sources, and then became a technical word for a suit at law—a plea. It is certainly not justifiable to use the fact that a legislative act was sometimes called *judicium* to show that the early "constitutional theory" was that the national assembly, or curia regis, or parliament was, or was thought to be, primarily a court of law and that its other powers grew out of its judicial function, which is what the theory means. Pollard, *The Evolution of Parliament*, p. 24. There was no theory behind the use. The various applications and sometimes seeming confusion in the use of the terms *judicium, sententia, placitum, constitutio, assisa, statutum,* carry in them no declaration as to the constitutional character of the act or of the body acting; they do declare that the men so using them did not yet make careful constitutional distinctions. As will be seen below in this chapter, the judicial procedure followed so closely in its general features, and even in details, that of a legislative assembly that it is not to be wondered at that the actors, not yet aware of the importance of minuter technical distinctions, should interchange the technical terms. They would no doubt have been able to pass an excellent examination on the distinction if they had been obliged to do so.

in which distinctions and differences concerned them. The importance of forms to their minds, of following the established models correctly, of using the regular procedure, is well known. In an endeavor to understand the legal and institutional history of the Anglo-Norman period, it is indispensably necessary as the condition of all else that the law of procedure and the changes in procedure be understood. In such an important matter as the origin of the common law, for example, the changes which brought it about were changes in procedure rather than changes in substantive law. Some part of the misunderstanding of c. 39 of Magna Carta is due to a neglect of the principles of procedure which are involved. It is true also that the introduction of the new prerogative forms of procedure in the twelfth century marks in itself a great constitutional as well as legal epoch, and the fact that these forms were never adopted by the great curia regis is of importance in understanding peculiarities of the present day constitution. A recent writer on the history of the law has also called attention to the importance of the early procedural rules of Parliament, and through them to the large debt which Parliament owed to its close alliance with the law.[4] It is therefore of great importance that we should obtain as full and accurate a knowledge of early procedure as the material at our command will allow.

At first glance it would seem as if the exact information to be found in the sources is too slight to justify any detailed account of procedure in the feudal curia regis, and that is probably why none has yet been attempted. It is possible, however, that a comparison of sources may enable us to reach some conclusions which will have at least the value of a working hypothesis.

[4] Dr. W. S. Holdsworth in the *Columbia Law Review,* XII, 15-16. See below, the last part of notes 34 and 45.

We are fortunate in having as a starting point a detailed account of an important trial for treason by the full curia regis at the beginning of the reign of William Rufus. It is manifestly the account of an eyewitness, and we are told by one of the highest authorities upon the character of the historical material of this period that there is no ground on which to question its authenticity.[5] It certainly gives abundant internal evidence of its genuineness. The account is lively, sympathetic, and apparently full, and though plainly written by one of the supporters of the accused, it makes a decided impression of trustworthiness in matters of detail.[6] This is the trial of William of Saint-Calais, bishop of Durham, in 1088.[7]

[5] Professor Felix Liebermann, *Aufsätze dem Andenken an Georg Waitz gewidmet* (1886), p. 159, n. 10; see also the critical study of this account by Professor C. W. David, *E.H.R.*, XXXII, 382-387, who reaches the same conclusion.

[6] The *Chronicon Monasterii de Bello* (*Anglia Christiana Societas*) (1846), pp. 85-104, gives us one other account of a curia regis trial of so detailed a character that it is of peculiar value for comparison and control. This was a case of the early years of Henry II involving the liberties of the abbey, called in question by the claims of the bishop of Chichester. It was first summoned before the great council at St. Edmunds at Pentecost, 1157, but on account of the pressure of business was adjourned to May 24 at Colchester. There it was finally decided by what seems from the names of those present (p. 87) to have been an unusually large small council. See *Origin*, p. 197. On the 24th the king with a few whom he personally selected, in the presence of the abbot but not of the bishop, examined the abbot's written evidences and asked some questions, but the actual trial was not held until the 28th. I shall cite it by reference to the pages of the chronicle. To the action of the king in this case in making a preliminary examination of the evidence for one side, there is an interesting parallel in a suit between the abbot of St. Albans and the bishop of Lincoln. *Gesta Abbatum* (R.S.), I, 150-153. Henry with an earl, a baron, and an archdeacon goes apart to examine the charters submitted by the abbot. The archdeacon of Canterbury comes in while this examination is going on and offers suggestions and the king tells him to go away. In the Battle Abbey case he forbids at the outset anyone to go with him who is not invited. Such a practice does not seem to have been general. It may have been peculiar to Henry II.

[7] *De injusta vexatione Willelmi episcopi primi.* Simeon of Durham (R.S.), I, 170-195; Dugdale, *Monasticon* (1849), I, 244-250. References that follow are made to the Rolls edition of Simeon of Durham.

The circumstances leading to the trial need only the briefest statement. They are fully given in several modern histories, notably in Freeman's *William Rufus.*[8] In the great rebellion of the Norman barons in England against William II at the beginning of his reign, the bishop of Durham after some service to the king suddenly abandoned him, and if he did not join actively in the revolt he at least rendered the king no further service. Even before the rebellion was put down William Rufus, who for some reason seems to have felt more bitter towards the bishop than towards any other of the revolting barons, had begun proceedings against him, seizing his barony and treating it as virtually confiscated in advance of a formal condemnation,[9] a liberty with the strict law frequently allowed themselves by the Norman kings, and indeed hardly to be avoided. Some earlier incidents of a procedural character would be of interest in a

[8] Freeman, *William Rufus,* I, 28 ff. and appendix C.

[9] The bishop in his second letter to the king (p. 174) calls this seizure of his lands ''sine ratione et judicio'' and so it was in strict procedure, but the occupation of the fief of a rebellious vassal in advance of a judicial decision against him was altogether too frequent in the feudal world, except where the vassal was so powerful as to make steps against him partake of the character almost of interstate war, to be regarded as an unwarranted injustice. It is quite possible that it is action of this kind in many cases to which the phrase ''sine judicio'' refers in the baronial complaints, leading perhaps to c. 39 of Magna Carta. William Rufus seems in this case to have gone a step further in making grants from the bishop's lands as if the fief were already legally in his hands by a formal confiscation. Whether so extreme a step was common before a judicial sentence or not I cannot say. It was certainly common in the case of escheats and confiscations legally *in manu,* including ecclesiastical fiefs during vacancies, which might be considered *quasi* wardships. Examples of these last are to be found in the *Red Book of the Exchequer* (R.S.), pp. 210, 211. Both these last cases, it will be noticed, indicate the difficulty which ecclesiastical baronies had in getting a practical benefit of the principle of the law that such grants should not be in permanency. Glanvill, VII, 9. The bishop says (p. 180) that he sees in the assembly former liege men of his who are now holding their lands of the king.

full history of the case, but the formal trial, with which we are here concerned, began on November 2, 1088, in a meeting of the great council at Salisbury.

In regard to the composition of the assembly by which the bishop was tried, we are given no definite information. Incidentally it appears from the narrative that many great nobles and many bishops were present. The statement on the subject made by the writer, at the point at which the bishop first retired in order that the court might pass judgment on the demands which he had made, is not to be taken very seriously.[10] It is certainly not a technical statement, but doubtless indicates in a general way the classes recognized by an eyewitness as present, and seems to have been intended to imply the prejudiced character of the court. Three well marked classes are clearly in the writer's mind as present, bishops, lay nobles, among whom he refers only to those of the rank of earl, and officials.[11] Noticeably there are mentioned

[10] ''Egresso itaque episcopo cum suis, et rege cum suis, episcopis, et consulibus, et vicecomitibus, et praepositis, et venatoribus, aliisque quorumlibet officiorum, in judicio remanente,'' p. 183.

[11] One can hardly fail to think of the composition of the court in another famous trial of a bishop as given in the anonymous life of Thomas Becket: ''rex edicto publico convocavit episcopos et abbates, comites etiam et proceres, et omnes officiales suos, omnesque omnino qui alicujus essent auctoritatis vel nominis, die designato apud Norhamtonam,'' *Materials,* IV, 41. To this should be added the passage in Fitz Stephen's account, *Ibid.*, III, 67, concerning the reinforcement made to the court after the bishop had withdrawn: ''Evocantur quidam vicecomites et secundae dignitatis barones, antiqui dierum, ut addantur eis et assint judicio.'' These words appear to indicate a summons in peculiar circumstances of persons not usually attending. It is interesting that in what is, I think, the first case before the curia regis after the Conquest which has been reported to us (1070), the composition of the court is stated in practically the same terms that are used for two hundred years: ''in consilio, in loco qui vocatur Pedreda celebrato, coram rege ac Doruberniae archiepiscopo Landfranco, et episcopis, abbatibus, comitibus, et primatibus totius Angliae,'' Florence of Worcester, II, 8. See what is said above in Chapter I at notes 9 and 10 of the presence in the assembly of numerous persons who are not members of it.

among the latter, sheriffs, reeves, and huntsmen, but they are not mentioned in such a way as to justify us in inferring the presence here of any persons outside the baronial class, though there is very likely a suggestion intended that some present were not of high rank.[12]

Earlier in the summer, the bishop had twice been formally summoned to answer the charges against him in the king's court, probably by royal writ, "de vestro brevi," he says in his second letter to the king.[13] There had been no trial, however; in the first session of the court, the bishop refused to be tried as a feudal tenant, and the king refused to accept the purgation which the bishop offered. As purgation was a method of meeting charges constantly employed in the ecclesiastical, as well as in the popular courts, the bishop could offer it without stepping outside the limitations which he was trying to put upon the king's right to try him.[14] The king probably saw clearly enough the futility of such a method of proof in this case, and his refusal to accept it indicates that it was not a part of any regular procedure in the great curia regis which could be demanded as customary, but no reason can be given why it should not be used occasionally.[15] That a written summons was sent the bishop for

12 Lanfranc's opinion, expressed on page 191 of Simeon of Durham, that the court could not try the bishop on a new charge because he no longer held anything of the king, though resting upon ground which would certainly not be recognized as sound by the later prerogative courts, shows clearly enough that he regarded the court as distinctly feudal and that the principle of the composition of the feudal curia regis was in mind. It is a rather important statement. The bishop as being no longer a vassal of the king could not be held to answer a charge in that particular court. See note 49.

13 Simeon of Durham, I, 174.

14 P. and M., I, 426.

15 Or it may be merely that the king refused to accept the bishop's oath except by a judgment of his court since the award of the oath, in theory at least, implied a presumption of innocence. In a case before the great council in 1176, Bigelow, *Placita,* p. 223, from John of Brompton in Twys-

the meeting of the curia of November 2 is not stated, but on the day of his arrival at Salisbury he was visited by Urse d'Abetot, who summoned him orally to the presence of the king. In this act Urse could hardly have been acting in any regular official capacity, certainly not as sheriff.[16] His authority was probably a special delegation for the occasion, made to him merely in his capacity as a peer of the court.

This method of summons, through the authority of the court or of the king, was the regular method for the curia regis in all its forms after the Conquest. The original Teutonic method of private summons, served by the complainant or plaintiff himself, which had survived the Saxon age in the popular courts of the hundred and shire, seems never to have been employed in the Norman king's courts.[17] This is sufficiently accounted for by the fact that this method of summons had never been employed even in early times by the Frankish royal courts, and that indeed by the tenth century the official summons of the royal courts, the *bannitio,* had driven the private summons, the

den, *Scriptores,* p. 1109, between the archbishop of York and the bishop of Ely, the latter was allowed to purge himself. Wager of his law by the bishop of Carlisle was ordered by the council and the bishops, *Bracton's Note Book,* pl. 741; Round, *Calendar,* no. 1172; Orderic Vitalis, II, 433. If purgation were excluded the ordeal would be also in the twelfth century, and Roger of Wendover records that under William I at a date not specified Remigius of Fécamp, who was made bishop of Lincoln, was purged of treason by a famulus of his who went to the ordeal for him (ed. Coxe), II, 24; M. Paris (ed. Luard), II, 20. There was nothing in the ordinary feudal law which would lead it to exclude purgation. On the contrary it made use of it constantly. See *Usatici Barchinone Patrie,* c. 168 (In Giraud, *Droit Français,* II, 501); *Libri Feudorum,* I, 4, and cf. the *Compilatio Antiqua,* I, 7, in Lehmann, *Lehnrecht,* p. 89. In the *Libri Feudorum, defensio* constantly means the oath. Not so given in Du Cange, but see *Libri Feud.,* II, 58 (57). The distinction between *probatio* and *defensio* is frequently made in the *Libri Feudorum.*

16 Urse d'Abetot was sheriff of Worcestershire.

17 See Bigelow, *History of Procedure in England,* Chap. VI.

mannitio, out of use in the popular courts of the Empire.[18] Naturally, therefore, the Norman practice would not include it. On the other hand what may be perhaps described as the normal feudal summons, the summons of a peer of the court by one of his fellow peers, or by two peers, seems not to have been exclusively employed in the Anglo-Norman king's court, but this method and the writ were probably both in use with little distinction in rule or practice between them.[19]

18 Brunner, *Schwurgerichte,* pp. 60-63; *Deutsche Rechtsgeschichte* (1906), I, 410; Luchaire, *Institutions Monarchiques* (1891), I, 325-327; Glasson, *Droit de la France,* VI, 477 ff.

19 The question of the method of summons employed in royal and private feudal courts is one of a good deal of difficulty, and probably the only safe conclusion at present is that there was always much variety and no particular method prescribed and necessary. Still I think that the evidence points to the fact that summons by peers, or a peer, of the court was, before the thirteenth century, the more normal and expected method. This seems to be the meaning of the first issue raised in the pleadings of the Countess of Flanders in the famous appeal of default of right brought against her in the court of the king of France in 1224. See Langlois, *Textes relatifs a l'Histoire du Parlement,* no. XXI; Boutaric, *Actes du Parlement,* I, ccciii, c. 2; Martène, *Amplissima Collectio,* I, 1193. The court decides that summons by two knights is sufficient, a decision which rests manifestly upon a different body of evidence from that on which another issue raised in this case is decided, *viz.,* that the officials in the court ought not to be considered as peers of the barons. See *Origin,* p. 270. The decision as to summons is less consistently supported by the evidence and is to be regarded, I think, as a judicial settlement in the interests of the royal courts, just beginning to assert their authority, of a point not definitely settled by the earlier customary law. Parallel to this case is that of the abbot of St. Michael who pleads, some time after the French occupation of Normandy, that summons to the host by a sergeant is not sufficient in the case of a baron of the king, but the court decides against him. Brussel, *Usage des Fiefs,* I, 173. Cases of summons by peers, or a peer, of the court may be found as follows: Langlois, *Textes,* no. XIX; Brussel, *Usage,* I, 337. Beaumanoir (ed. Salmon), I, 43, c. 58, states the principle, and in c. 68, p. 48 the exception in favor of the count who may claim sovereign, or semi-sovereign powers. The principle, in the analogous case of summons to perform feudal services, is still more fully stated in the *Assizes de Jerusalem, Livre de Jean d'Ibelin,* c. 218 (ed. Beugnot), I, 348. Whatever may be thought of the capacity in which Urse

As the narrative goes on to the trial as a whole, one cannot fail to be struck with the informality, the conversational freedom of a large part of the proceedings. There were plainly what seem to be strict rules which were followed when it came to the point of the actual transaction of business, but formal decisions were prepared for by what seems like the impromptu give and take of a debating and deliberating assembly.[20]

d'Abetot is acting in summoning the bishop of Durham at Salisbury, there can be no doubt about the summons by peers of the court served upon him after the trial was over to appear before the court in London at Christmas time, Simeon of Durham, p. 193. When Henry III is preparing to have Hubert de Burgh outlawed, and is taking some pains with the legality of his procedure, he orders him to be summoned by "duos barones regis qui de rege tenent in capite." *Close Rolls, 1231-1234,* p. 161. In a privilege of the Emperor Frederick I for the bishop of Cremona, dated 1159, it was provided that if the vassals summoned "a paribus curiae tuae" did not appear within forty days they should lose their fiefs, Ficker, *Forschungen,* III, 324.

20 This appears very clearly in the detailed account of the case in the *Chron. Mon. de Bello,* pp. 87-104. The king is constantly speaking. He interrupts the bishop's statement of his case three times; Henry of Essex also interrupts three times, Richard de Luci once, and the chancellor speaks to the bishop once. The bishop in turn interrupts the chancellor's speech. The last part of the case is particularly conversational: "Multis igitur super his hinc indeque habitis, tandem silentio inposito Ricardus de Luci surgens regem voce supplici exoravit," and later (p. 97). Free discussion with some disorder is also graphically described in the account of Anselm's trial, particularly in the effort to formulate a judgment against the archbishop. Eadmer, *Hist. Nov.,* p. 58.

The clearly informal character of general discussion which is so evident in these proceedings may very possibly be another evidence of the failure to make any clear distinction between legislative and judicial action. The curia regis was primarily a deliberative body and, while certain things must be done according to formal rules, especially when the final decision of the curia was expressed on any point, its method of reaching such a decision, of finding out the matured opinion of a majority, was that of informal and free discussion. Instances of discussion in political sessions may be found in Matthew Paris, III, 380-384; IV, 185-188; 362-368; V, 423-425, 520, 530. In this last instance besides the political business, Robert de Ros was on trial.

Accounts of trials in the great curia regis from the reign of Henry II are of particular interest because the question inevitably arises whether the

Before the formal opening of the court, but in the presence of the assembly, the bishop had requested to be allowed to take counsel with the other bishops who were present, and this had been refused him.[21] Apparently also before the formal opening[22] he had stated to archbishop Lanfranc that the proceedings must be canonically conducted, and suggested that he appear in his official vestments before the other bishops similarly vested, thus foreshadowing his chief line of defence during the whole trial. Lanfranc evidently saw the point and declared that they would be able to judge between him and the king vested as they were.

On the opening of the court, bishop William did not wait for a formal accusation but took matters into his

new prerogative procedure which was then so rapidly developing, especially in the itinerant justice courts, and in the central court corresponding to them, affected methods of trial in the old central curia regis. That this was not the case is, I think, clearly shown in the cases cited in these notes. Especially interesting is the trial described in the *Chron. Mon. de Bello*, pp. 106-109, for it began with a writ of right, a part of the prerogative procedure, and was afterwards transferred for the actual trial to the curia regis. It should be said that some of the trials referred to in these notes are not great but small council trials. This is true at least of some of the Battle Abbey cases. See the outline of the dispute between the bishop of Chichester and the abbot of Battle in Bigelow's *Placita*, pp. 157-159. There was, however, so far as we can ascertain, no difference of procedure in these two forms of the council. Miss Helen M. Cam has recently published (*E.H.R.*, XXXIX, 568-571) an extract from a chronicle narrating proceedings in a king's county court, or rather in a court of two counties united before a king's justice, towards the end of Stephen's reign. The passage is a chronicle, not a record, and it was plainly written to preserve a precedent for the rights of St. Edmund's, but it bears every mark of trustworthiness and seems to be closely contemporary, or more likely based on a contemporary account. The picture which it gives of proceedings in the court is lively and entertaining and quite in agreement with our other evidence.

21 See below, note 42.

22 In the suit between the abbot of St. Albans and the bishop of Lincoln, *Gesta Abbatum* (R.S.), I, 150-153, the abbot raises a point before the formal opening which apparently the king decides himself, perhaps because he thinks the royal dignity or sovereignty involved.

own hands at once. He rose in his place[23] and demanded that his bishopric which had been taken away from him "sine judicio" should be returned to him. Lanfranc answered, "rege tacente," as if the writer at least expected the answer to be made by the king. Lanfranc denied that his bishopric had ever been taken from him, and the bishop then stated at length how he had been disseised of his "whole bishopric which he had in the county of York," and the lands of the church given away by the king to his own barons as he pleased.[24] Lanfranc again saw the drift of the attempt which the accused was making to confuse bishopric and fief and so to dodge the real issue and reminded him that he was there to do justice to the king; afterwards he might make his own complaints. "Do you say this as counsel or as a judgment," quickly demanded William. Lanfranc was not to be tricked into saying that he gave counsel. "Certainly," he said, "I do not say it as a judgment, but if the king would take my advice he would quickly cause it to be made into a judgment."[25] Then the barons "animati" by these words

[23] This "surgens," which is noted in many cases both before private and royal courts, denotes a certain degree at least of formality. In the bishop of Bath's court the "testes surgentes" and "stantes in medio" give their evidence. Madox, *Exchequer*, I, 111, note 1; in the bishop of Durham's court, H. de Percy "exurgens" speaks, Simeon of Durham, II, 262; in the curia regis, Richard de Luci states the case of the abbot of Battle, "surgens et in medio stans," *Chron. Mon. de Bello* (p. 88), then "eo residente abbas surrexit" and went on with his case (p. 89), and afterwards the bishop "surgens" argued against it (p. 90). See *E.H.R.*, XXXIX, 570.

[24] "Rogerum Paganellum, quem hic video, qui ex praecepto regis me dissaisivit de toto episcopatu meo quem habeo in Eboracensi comitatu" (p. 179). This carefully framed answer indicates that bishop William had clearly in mind the difficulty created by his feudal relationship to the king, by the barony which he held, and was deliberately trying to dodge it. See notes 39 and 44.

[25] " . . . sed si rex mihi crediderit, satis cito faciet inde judicium fieri . . .," a plain enough statement that the king does not make the judgment, notwithstanding his great interest in the case. Cf., in the agreement under which the bishop comes to court, the promise that the trial shall not

"exclamantes dixerunt" that the bishop must first do justice to the king.[26] This was equivalent to a judgment of the court but it seems to have been very informally reached and with some confusion for the narrative goes on: "Laicis vero hæc et alia multa declamantibus et iterantibus, facto silentio dixit episcopus."[27] The position

be delayed beyond the end of September "nisi per consensum episcopi, vel per tales terminos quales judices legales dictis causis inter regem et episcopum juste poni debere decernerent" (p. 178). Very interesting is the evidence of the trial of Anselm upon this point. The king was bitterly determined to condemn the archbishop and tried to drive the court to make the judgment he desired. He said: "Quid placet, si hæc non placent? Dum vivo parem mihi in regno meo utique sustinere nolo. Et sic sciebatis eum tanto in causa sua robore fultum, quare permisistis me incipere placitum istud contra eum? Ite, consiliamini, quia, per Vultum Dei, si vos illum ad voluntatem meam non damnaveritis, ego damnabo vos." Eadmer, *Hist. Nov.*, p. 62. He failed however and was obliged to accept his failure: "Quod ille repressa sustinuit ira, rationi eorum palam ne nimis offenderentur contraire praecavens." Eadmer, p. 64. In the case of Becket, the king says: "Cito facite mihi judicium de illo," and clearly indicates the kind of judgment which he wishes, Roger of Hoveden (R.S.), I, 228, and Fitzstephen says: "Rex exegit judicium," *Materials*, III, 52, and *ibid.*, IV, 42. An interesting instance of the king's asking the advice and judgment of the curia, not in a suit at law, is to be found in the *Chron. Mon. de Bello*, pp. 164-165. On the abbot of Battle's asking that a charter decayed by age be renewed, the king said: "Non hoc, inquit rex, nisi ex judicio curiæ meæ facturus sum." Later "rege super hoc, si faciendum esset necne, judicium procerum requirente, decet, inquit Ricardus de Luci, decet vos si placet domine cartam ecclesiæ de Bello renovare." Evidence that this conforms to the general practice is hardly necessary. Says Beaumanoir, Chap. lxvii (ed. Salmon) c. 1883, . . . "la coustume de Beauvoisins est tele que li seigneur ne jugent pas en leur court, mais leur homme jugent."

26 The writer says it is the laymen who call out but, as the decision was perfectly just, it is likely that some of the bishops besides Lanfranc joined in it.

27 Similar confusion in the court is not infrequently recorded. In the bishop of Bath's court, Madox, *Exchequer*, I, 111, after the evidence was presented and when the court should proceed to judgment some tumult arose, "aliis bona laudantibus, aliis ex adverso tumultuantibus." In the case narrated in the *Chron. Mon. de Bello*, pp. 87-104, the laughter of all at the humor of the king is related, and twice the murmurs of the assembly against the bishop. Similar disorder is also very evident in the trials of Anselm and Becket.

which the accused then took, falling back on what is evidently his carefully prepared line of defence, is that he will not have the lay members of the court as his judges but only the king and the bishops.

At this point the king interposed for the first time and said he had hoped that the bishop would answer the accusation which he made and was astonished that he demanded something different. Upon this Alan of Brittany and Roger Bygod who had pledged themselves to the bishop's safe conduct, spoke up and said that they had brought him there to do justice to the king. "I am ready," cried the bishop, "if it is canonically judged that I ought to respond despoiled, for I will not in this trial transgress the law of my order."[28] Then Roger Bygod[29] turned to the king. "You ought," he said, "to say to the bishop of what you wish to appeal him,[30] and if he answers cause

28 In raising this technical point, the "exceptio spolii," which he very possibly derived from the Pseudo-Isidore, see P. and M., I, 97, the bishop was trying again to confuse the issue. There was no question of his bishopric before the court, nor directly of his fief but, as Hugh de Beaumont makes clear in his detailed statement, the question was whether he had not been unfaithful to his sworn feudal duty. The taking in hand of his fief in advance of the decision of this question was a very different thing from the sort of disseisin which the courts would recognize as giving a right to this exception. Cf. *Bracton's Note Book*, pl. 1113, 1136; M. Paris, VI, 74; *Leges Henrici*, 53, 3-6. In the council in 1139 which considered the attempt of King Stephen to arrest the bishops, his brother, the legate, said: "Rex itaque faciat, quod etiam in forensibus judiciis legitimum est fieri, ut revestiat episcopos de rebus suis: alioquin jure gentium dissaisiti non placitabunt." William of Malmesbury, *Gesta Regum*, II, 553 (c. 474). Cited by P. and M., I, 97, n. 4. In the present case the bishop was called upon to answer before the court in regard to nothing of which he had been despoiled.

29 Father of Hugh, first Earl of Norfolk, who had taken part in the revolt, but, admitted to the king's favor, he appears in the court as one of its members in the trial of his fellow rebel. Freeman, *William Rufus*, I, 36, 98.

30 The word "appeal" is of course a technical word, indicating that a criminal charge was made against the accused by an individual acting in his private capacity. How far we are warranted in regarding it as technical

him to be judged upon his answer, and if he does not answer take counsel with your barons as to what should be done.''[31] Things were thus drifting rapidly against the bishop's contention and he again emphatically repeated his refusal of lay jurisdiction, but Hugh de Beaumont for the king, ''ex præcepto regis,'' rising, made formal accusation stating fully and specifically the king's case.[32]

here, is doubtful. The writer is plainly not careful to use technical language. But see ''rex te appellat'' in the formal opening which follows and other cases of the use of the word. The case certainly is an appeal whether the writer was conscious of the technical meaning of the term or not.

31 This should be the regular and formal opening of the case. That it had been so long deferred, that so much discussion had preceded it, shows how unusual had been the line of action followed by the accused, and also that with the deliberative character of the court such action was entirely possible. A formal opening seems to have been the regular rule, followed by an equally formal reply by the defendant, but there is no trace of any fore-oath, nor of an oath of any kind from the parties. The openings are speeches. In the *Chron. Mon. de Bello,* p. 88, the abbot's case is opened by Richard de Luci; in the case on page 107 two representatives of the abbot speak, ''ex ordine exposuerunt''; in the bishop of Bath's court the prior opens the case. The opening should regularly be followed by a speech from the other side arguing against the case presented, or by a statement of the opposing case. In the first Battle Abbey case cited above, the chancellor called on the bishop to reply; in the case on page 107, the defendant calls attention to the lack of a seal on the charter submitted by the other side, ''ne nihil objicere videretur.'' See *Gesta Regis Henrici,* I, 134.

32 The narrative of this trial is so circumstantial that if the king had personally taken an active part in conducting it, the fact would surely have been noted. The ''ex præcepto regis,'' which introduces Hugh de Beaumont's action, raises the question whether the king was not always represented by some member of the court when he was a party to a suit before it. This seems altogether likely, but the evidence does not permit a positive assertion. The somewhat greater share which William II takes in the trial of Anselm at Rockingham, in a closely parallel case, is clearly that of a party deeply interested in the outcome and seems to be noted as exceptional. Nearly all the cases cited in these notes from the reign of Henry II show that king taking a hand freely in the immediate conduct and direction of proceedings of all kinds, but the fact may be due to his personal character. In political sessions of the curia, it was not infrequent that someone spoke for the king. See M. Paris, III, 380; IV, 185, 187. In 1244 that the king speaks ''ore proprio'' is noted as if it were unusual. *Ibid.*, IV, 362. But later

Again the bishop refused to plead except under the conditions he had stated.[33]

On this a tumult broke out in the assembly, some calling out arguments and others insults, says the writer. In the midst of the confusion apparently, the bishop of Coutances suggested to Lanfranc that the bishops and abbots should retire and with some of the barons and earls should decide whether the bishop's demand that he be reinvested before pleading should be granted or not.[34]

(p. 365), others speak for him, and yet he suddenly appears in person, "rex solus festinanter et ex abrupto advenit."

[33] "Episcopus autem Hugoni respondit: Hugo, dicas quicquid volueris, non tibi tamen hodie respondebo, nec accusationem aliquam recipiam, vel placitum aliquod ingrediar usque quo juste pudicetur quod dispoliatus debeam placitare, vel canonice de episcopatu meo investiar; et postea de quibuscunque rex me appellaverit voluntarie respondebo" (p. 181). The form of the bishop's answer shows how informal were the proceedings at this point.

[34] The proposition of the bishop of Coutances that the point in dispute be decided by a committee of the court was in accordance with a very frequent practice of the feudal courts. They often committed their function of making a judgment to a selected body of their own membership though, as may be seen in the judgments made in the present case, such a proceeding was entirely optional. Instances will be found in Round, *Calendar*, nos. 712, 1190, 1212, 1257, this last in a private court. There the committee is said to be "electi," but it is not said by whom. So also in the *Usatici Barchinone*, c. 80: "Judicium in curia datum, vel datum a judice de curia electo, ab omnibus sit acceptum et omni tempore secutum." In the trial of Thomas Becket in the first judgment against the archbishop, *Materials*, IV, 42, the committee was appointed by the king, "Egrediuntur mox ad judicium quos rex ipse judices ex nomine dessignabat." In the court of the bishop of Bath, Madox, *Exchequer*, I, 111, the judgment was made by a committee "secedentes a turba." On one occasion William I seems to have submitted a case between two monasteries to a committee of bishops and abbots alone who withdrew into a chamber and made a judgment which the king confirmed. Round, *Calendar*, no. 1114. See Liebermann, II, 701, Article "Urteilfinder." A confirmation by the court seems regularly to follow the committee decision. See M. Paris, IV, 362. Some of the cases of consultation apart by members in political meetings of the curia, to which reference is made in note 42 below, may be cases of action by committees. On the possible derivation of the committee system of the later parliament from this early practice, see

"It is not necessary that we should go out," said Lanfranc, "let the bishop and his men go out, and we clerics and laics will judge equitably what we ought justly to do."[35] To this bishop William agreed,[36] but in going he admonished the bishops to do nothing contrary to the canons. "Go on," said Lanfranc, "for we shall do justly whatever we do," and Hugh de Beaumont cried out to the bishop, "If I am not able to judge you and your order today, never shall you and your order judge me further";[37] and the bishop in reply again refused to accept any except canonical judges.[38]

It is very evident that the bishop's refusal to accept the jurisdiction of the court, and the grounds upon which

Holdsworth, as cited in note 4 above. An illustration in the transitional period, in the Parliament of 1305, may be seen in Maitland, *Memoranda de Parliamento* (R.S.), no. 454, and cf. Maitland's comment at page xliv. The committee system is certainly analogous to the practice of the early Teutonic courts from which the *rachimburgi* were derived and the later official *scabini* (*échevins*), and may possibly be directly descended from it.

35 From such evidence as we have it is not possible to say that the accused was required to go out of the court while the judgment was being made, but I am inclined to think that he was. *The Court Baron* (Selden Society), p. 48, gives a case in a private court where the steward asks both plaintiff and defendant to retire while the court takes council and makes the judgment.

36 "Ego, inquit episcopus, libenter egrediar." The bishop's attitude in general towards the court makes it impossible to consider that his *libenter* means that he had really any choice in the matter.

37 A clear enough statement of the position of the bishops in the curia regis on the same footing as the other barons. In Becket's case the bishops say: "Non sedemus hic episcopi, sed barones. Nos barones et vos barones pares hic sumus." *Materials,* III, 52. See "Constitutions of Clarendon," c. XI, and above, Note B at the end of Chapter I.

38 The conclusion to which the air and tone of this whole account conduce, that it was written by an eyewitness, is strengthened also by the fact that no attempt is made to tell what went on in the court while the bishop and his men were out. It seems also to be based on contemporary memoranda, though it may not have been put into the form in which we have it until later. See Simeon of Durham, I, xxv, and Professor David as above in note 5.

he based his refusal, were unexpected, and that the assembly was greatly troubled in consequence.[39] The bishop had taken his position with great skill, probably for the first time in English history, and he had fortified himself with a book of "Christian law"—"quam hic scriptam habeo"—possibly a copy of the Pseudo-Isidore, as has been suggested. Lanfranc, however, met him at every turn. If the point, as pushed home so vigorously, was new in practice, it was logically so clearly involved in earlier cases, as well as in the general claims which the church was making, that the lawyer archbishop of Canterbury had no difficulty in seeing to what conclusions it led, and in providing for them.

The writer says that it was only after long delay that the bishop and his company were called back to the assembly. The judgment which the court had reached was made known to him by the archbishop of York. He said that the archbishop and the curia regis had judged that he must do right to the king before he was reinvested with his fief.[40] Instantly the bishop pitched upon this

39 H. Boehmer, *Kirche u. Staat in England u. in der Normandie*, p. 174, says that the bishop did not understand the distinction which Lanfranc makes between his bishopric and his fief. This opinion will not stand the test of a careful reading of the bishop's case. It is quite evident from the skill with which he chose his line of defence that he had the point clearly in mind from the start and knew that if he allowed a feudal trial on feudal grounds his case was hopeless. Cf. notes 24 and 44. Boehmer remarks (p. 173) that the position which the bishop takes is in agreement with the principles of the Pseudo-Isidore, and this has been also noticed by P. and M., I, 97. Freeman, *William Rufus*, I, 104, note 1, says that he seems to have had a copy of the False Decretals with him. In the trial of Anselm at Rockingham in 1095 he reversed his position. He "was the man who above all others maintained the royal jurisdiction over the bishops." Article "Carilef," *Dict. Nat. Biography*. Eadmer, *Hist. Nov.*, pp. 59-62. The same position as the bishop of Durham was taken by bishops in France. See Luchaire, *Manuel des Inst. Françaises*, p. 559, n. 1, and Vernon Harcourt, *His Grace the Steward*, p. 272.

40 The use of the term curia regis in announcing the two formal judg-

phrase: it was that he might be judged concerning his bishopric that he had gone out. No one had said a word to him before about his fief, nor he to anyone. The judgment means, explained the archbishop, that the bishop is not to be reinvested with anything before he has done justice to the king. The bishop then demanded that the judgment be proved to him to be canonical and just, and Lanfranc said in effect that the judgment was just, and that the bishop knew it and ought to accept it, or make formal answer, *contradicere*. Bishop William then asked to be allowed to take counsel with certain of the bishops and was told by Lanfranc that the bishops were his judges and could not be his counsellors.[41] William appealed directly to the king on the point and was told to consult with his own men, for he could have no aid from the king's, and he went out to advise with them.[42]

ments which were made by the court, should be noticed. The notion that this term was in any way especially connected with the small curia (A. M. Chambers, *Const. Hist. of England*, p. 97) or with any institutional change in the reign of Henry I has no support in the sources. The chroniclers use it not infrequently of William I's time. Orderic Vitalis, II, 263, 264; *Chron. Mon. de Bello*, p. 26.

41 As the accused was an ecclesiastic, this was not a case which could be expected to involve regularly a blood judgment, and therefore it does not come under the exception allowed in the court service of prelates in c. XI of the Constitutions of Clarendon.

42 The right of the accused, or of a party to the case before the court, to go apart and consult with his friends was clearly recognized and of frequent exercise. *Leges Henrici*, 46-48. In 1102 Robert of Bellême took advantage of the custom to escape trial. "Cumque Rodbertus licentiam, ut moris est, eundi ad consilium cum suis postulasset, eademque accepta, egressus purgari se de objectis criminibus non posse agnovisset, equis celeriter ascensis, ad castella sua pavidus et anhelus confugit. Orderic Vitalis, IV, 170. In the bishop of Bath's court the prior spoke for the church, "habito cum fratribus consilio." Madox, *Exchequer*, I, 111. In the case in the *Chron. Mon. de Bello*, p. 108, the king in directing the abbot to go out to take counsel gives him a plain hint as to what he should decide upon. In the case, *ibid.*, p. 97, Richard de Luci makes formal (*surgens*) request that the king will permit the abbot "consilium cum amicis suis secretius habere."

On his return bishop William in a rather long speech formally refused to accept the judgment which the court had just made for the reason which he had already stated, that he could not be canonically judged by a lay tribunal, and closed with a formal appeal to the pope, the final act for which he had no doubt been preparing from the beginning. To this speech Lanfranc replied that he was not judging him as a bishop but concerning his fief, as the bishop of Bayeux had been judged before the king's father, "de feodo suo, nec rex vocabat eum episcopum in

In this case the counsellors are members of the court and the king goes out of the room while they consult. They seem almost like a committee of the court to form a judgment, but the long speech of the chancellor, Thomas, who is chosen as their mouthpiece, when the court resumes, is not a judgment but an argument for the bishop. The same practice in an ecclesiastical court may be seen, *ibid.*, pp. 175-176. The bishops advise both Anselm and Becket to submit to the king, but such counsel is quite different from that desired in the conduct of a case before the court. The bishops definitely refused counsel of that kind to Anselm. Eadmer, *Hist. Nov.*, p. 56; Migne, *Patrologia*, 159, p. 74. The first right of the king to the counsel of his vassal who is at the same time the vassal of another is clearly implied in the statement about Nigel d'Oily, *Chron. Mon. Abingdon*, II, 133. Counsel of the sort asked for by the bishop is different from that of the professional or semi-professional advocate who developed in the course of the thirteenth century. Full provisions in regard to such counsel are given in the Assizes of Jerusalem, *Livre Jean d'Ibelin*, cc. x. ff. The siegneur might assign such duty to any member of his court but no one could plead against his lord or his man without the consent of the seigneur. *Ibid.*, c. xxv. Other thirteenth century codes contain provisions regarding the advocate. The practice of consultation apart in political sessions of the curia regis may be seen in M. Paris, III, 381; IV, 185-188, and 362. This seems to me at least a more probable explanation than that suggested by Ramsay, *Dawn of the Constitution*, p. 80, and to apply also to the other cases there referred to, *Foundations of England*, II, 194, and *Angevin Empire*, p. 46. Consultation by members of a local popular court in a matter political rather than judicial in character is recorded in *Bracton's Note Book*, pl. 1730. A number of citations to the same effect might be added, but there can be no doubt of the custom. Even the king followed it, *Materials Thomas Becket*, I, 35; IV, 46. The proceedings indicate clearly the presence in the court of the attendants of the bishop who were not members of the court, as remarked above in Chapter I.

placito illo, sed fratrem et comitem."[43] After a brief dispute with Lanfranc on this point the bishop said that he did not understand the distinction[44] and asked to be allowed to go to Rome according to his appeal. This demand brought before the court another point upon which judgment must be passed, and the accused was again told to go out, "et rex, cum suis habito consilio, dicet tibi quid sibi placuerit." When the bishop returned, however, it was not the king but Hugh de Beaumont who made known to him the judgment of the court.[45] This had gone beyond a decision of the request which the bishop had made and

[43] This passage suggests the possibility that this particular method of dodging the difficulty presented by the double position of the bishop may have been adopted in the earlier case at Lanfranc's suggestion, as William of Malmesbury asserts, *Gesta Regum*, II, 361. He certainly remembers clearly the exact point. According to Fitz Stephen there was also some allusion to the case of Bishop Odo in the discussions attending the trial of Thomas Becket. *Materials*, III, 65. See above, Chapter I, Note B.

[44] This looks like a deliberate falsehood on the part of the bishop. To one with as keen a mind as his, who had had so much to do with public affairs as he, the double position of the bishop in the feudal state must have been evident and the contradiction clear enough to suggest its advantage for him in his present straits. See above, notes 24 and 39.

[45] This may be the actual *Rechtsgebot*, the final and legalizing pronouncement of the judgment of the court, in which case Hugh de Beaumont was probably directed by the king to make it known. Or it may be the formal announcement by the court of the judgment it had reached, which would become final and binding when the king signified his assent. Such a formal statement by a single member of the court speaking for the rest, probably to make known the judgment to the lord, seems to have been not uncommon. *Gloucester Cartulary*, I, 14; *Bracton's Note Book*, I, 198, pl. 243; in *Chron. Abingd.*, II, 297, Glanvill may be acting as chief justiciar but the principle is the same; in the bishop of Salisbury's court, *Salisbury Charters* (R.S.), p. 19, no. xxi. See also the controversy between the barons and the bishops as to which shall pronounce the judgment of the court in one portion of the case against Thomas Becket. *Materials*, III, 52. On the *Rechtsgebot*, see *Origin*, p. 64, note 7. For a good example of it in a case under Geoffrey in Normandy, see Delisle, *Actes de Henri II*, Introd., p. 138, note 1. It is from this that comes the absolute veto of the king on legislation of the later Parliament.

was in effect a final decision of the case though not upon the merits of the original accusation. The bishop was informed that on account of his refusal to plead and of his appeal to Rome, the court (curia regis) had declared his fief to be forfeited.[46]

This is evidently the technical end of the case, but after some conversation between Hugh de Beaumont and the bishop, going over again some of the points earlier made, the king interfered for the second time, so far as is directly stated in the narrative, and demanded that since the bishop would not accept the judgment of his court, his castle should be surrendered before going to Rome. This demand the bishop resisted, attempting to fall back upon the safe conduct which certain barons had guaranteed him, and there was much conversation on the question, Lanfranc sustaining the king's demand,[47] and finding reason against the bishop's appeal to the safe conduct, but no formal action by the court is stated. The bishop finally yielded to the reiterated declaration of the king that he would not let him out of his hands until his castle was surrendered. Disputes then followed on some minor points, on all of which the bishop was forced to yield to the king.

The case of the bishop being finally finished, William de Merlao, a man of the bishop of Coutances, rose and addressing the king complained that some of the bishop of Durham's men had seized cattle belonging to his lord and that they had not been able to obtain compensation. He prayed the king to secure it for his lord. The king referred the request to the court. "Barons," he said,

[46] Regarding the bishop as a baron, this is in every respect a correct judgment. It has its exact legal parallel in the case of Robert of Bellême. Orderic Vitalis, IV, 170, and in the judgment pronounced against King John in 1202 by Philip II's court declaring his French fiefs forfeited.

[47] And quite rightly. The bishop could find no possible ground on which justly to retain possession of his castle after he had forfeited his fief.

"see if I can justly implead the bishop,"[48] and Lanfranc answered that it could not justly be done, because the bishop no longer held anything of the king,[49] and was entitled to safe conduct. The account follows the bishop to Normandy, but contains nothing further for our purposes.

Two later curia regis trials of great ecclesiastics upon similar charges are fully reported and of special interest, the trial of Anselm in 1095 at Rockingham, and the trial of Thomas Becket at Northampton in 1164. In both cases the charge seems to have been lese-majesty, against Anselm for recognizing Urban as pope without the permission of the king, and against Becket for refusing to obey a royal summons to court, at least this was the charge at the beginning of his case.

The account of the trial of Anselm which is given us by Eadmer[50] is that of an eyewitness, but it is much less objective and impartial than the account which we have been following of the trial of the bishop of Durham, and it is so untechnical in character that it is not easy to use it for the present purpose. Some points, however, are sufficiently clear and have been referred to in the notes. Of the trial of Becket we have important accounts which supplement each other satisfactorily and give us many details.[51] One especially is by an eyewitness who also evi-

48 See above, note 25. This is plain here again and also in the two formal judgments already pronounced by the court.

49 Lanfranc's answer is defensible legally only on the narrowest ground of the strictly feudal jurisdiction of the curia regis, and this is probably what he meant, but it was undoubtedly politic and morally right. See above, note 12.

50 Eadmer, *Hist. Nov.* (R.S.), pp. 53-67.

51 In Robertson, *Materials for the History of Thomas Becket* (R.S.) in seven volumes, as specifically referred to in the preceding notes. The account of Fitz Stephen in Vol. III shows considerable legal knowledge. The description of the appeal of default of justice which is given in one of the accounts of the trial (the Anonymous Author, IV, 40-41) is so incorrect in some

dently had some technical knowledge of the law. References have also been made in the notes to points of interest in this trial bearing upon specific questions of procedure.

Here I wish to indicate the general conclusion that, with two apparent exceptions at most, both of which are in reality doubtful exceptions to any rules of procedure, these two cases are, so far as we are able to decide upon their details, in full agreement with the other cases cited. The exceptions referred to are first, that in both cases the accused seem not to have been present regularly in the formal sessions of the curia, and second, that they seem to have had the counsel of the bishops, either as allowed them by the courts or as thrust upon them by the ecclesiastics themselves. In neither instance, however, do the prelates seem to have given counsel upon points involved in the actual trial, but upon the general conduct of the accused, and upon the carrying out of the sentence of the court. The same thing is to be said of all the cases, French and English, which I have read: while in most cases the record is brief, and clear details of procedure not frequent, when they do appear they are in harmony with those to be found in the more full accounts.[52]

particulars that it creates at first a presumption against the legal accuracy of this account, but in the main the presumption is not justified. The legal details of the Anonymous Author are fairly accurate. Of the appeal, he twice says that it is a new constitution, which of course it was not, as it was universal in the feudal world. It is probable, however, that Henry II introduced by legislation some new details in its operation, especially in the method of proving a default, and that the author is confusing these with the appeal itself. The description of the appeal which the Anonymous gives does not differ materially from the caricature of it which we might expect from an angry baron who felt himself injured by it. It may represent what Archbishop Thomas thought of it.

52 An interesting account of a trial in the great council from the reign of Henry I, which seems to be correct in all points of law and procedure, is contained in a charter of doubtful authenticity in the cartulary of St. John of Colchester, Roxburghe Club, I, 82. In the trial each side states its case.

From the cases which I have been able to bring together in text and notes, it does not seem to me possible to say that any definite procedure, or order of procedure, was required in the great curia regis as formally necessary. We can only say that certain forms or rules were so common, or in the case of some of them perhaps, so universal, that there is a presumption that they were formal and required, of the nature of fixed rules.

There should be a formal opening in which the case of the plaintiff or appellant is stated; to this the defendant, or the accused, should make a formal answer, *contradicere,* or formally abandon his case. In the trial there might be much set argument and explanation addressed to the court by the parties, or their representatives, apparently under no very formal regulations, and evidence oral or written might be produced,[53] and members of the court were free to interrupt by question or objection. Probably both parties, certainly the accused, or the defendant, had the right to retire from the court and take

Then by order of the king the charters of both are read and carefully considered. The king inquires who the donor to Westminster was. The seniors of the curia and the monks declare who he was and what was his relation to the property. Upon this the king takes counsel "cum episcopis ceterisque consiliariis suis" and "in propria persona sententiam protulit," saying that Elward could not grant to anyone what he did not have nor even what he had without the consent and will of the lord of the fee. On the authenticity of this charter see Round in *E.H.R.,* XIV, 726. The objections to the charter do not affect the fact of the trial, which undoubtedly took place. See J. A. Robinson, *Gilbert Crispin,* p. 165, and Farrer, *Itinerary Henry I,* no. 353A. For French cases see Langlois, *Textes,* nos. i-xxi, and Boutaric, *Actes de Parlement de Paris,* nos. 298-299, and see also Rozière, *Cartulaire du Saint Sépulcre de Jérusalem,* no. 89.

53 As the case against the bishop of Durham never came to a trial upon the real issue, there was no opportunity for the introduction of evidence but it is clear from many of the cases cited in the notes that evidence both written and oral might be produced by either party and often in what seems a quite informal way. In the case in the bishop of Bath's court, cited above, note 27, both oral and written evidence was introduced.

counsel with his own men, but he could not have such counsel from the members of the court; they were his judges. The court rendered judgment from time to time, as the suit went on, upon such questions as arose, probably in the absence of the accused, and might even turn a judgment upon a special point into a final judgment upon the case as a whole. We get no evidence of any formal process by which a judgment was reached, by vote or otherwise. The majority opinion of the court plainly made the judgment, but what the opinion of the majority was, seems to have been ascertained by free discussion and indicated often by the more or less disorderly outcries of the members of the court.[54] When it was known, the party who had gone out was recalled and the decision formally announced to him, either by the moderator or by some member of the court designated for the purpose.

[54] With reference to the witenagemot Liebermann maintains, *National Assembly*, p. 52, that a "majority could not possibly decide," emphasizing the "more powerful voice" with which "an archbishop or an earl was sure to speak." It does not seem to me necessary to modify the statement in the text. Undoubtedly some individuals influenced the decision much more than others, but they did this from no right of decision of their own but because their opinions were readily accepted by others. It is unlikely that any formal vote was taken and therefore unlikely that any formal majority was expected, but what decided was the common opinion of the assembly and that was the opinion of a majority however informally obtained. As says the Abingdon chronicle, II, 203, "communi sapientium plurimorum, qui vocati erant, consideratione ostensum est. . . ." It is said of a rather tumultuous assembly in 1191 of "pontifices, comites et barones," surrounded by a great crowd, which considered itself a great council and conducted a "judiciale examen": "Post varias altercationes et consilia multa, tandem communi omnium censura sententia prodiit diffinitiva." Gerald Cambrensis (R.S.), IV, 406. See Shirley, *Royal Letters*, I, 102, an interesting case in a sheriff's county court: "Et ad hoc maxima pars comitatus consensit. Sed quia totus comitatus ad hoc non consensit, neque certus fuit de hoc judicio faciendo, cum ipse [whom the judgment concerned] magnus homo erat et baro domini regis, judicium illud respectatum fuit usque ad alium comitatum, ut interim possent habere super hoc assensum de curia domini regis." On reference to the council, see P. and M., I, 164, note 3.

The part taken by the king, or by the moderator of the court, in the ongoing of an ordinary case, and the amount of indirect influence which he might have on the making of the final decision are left somewhat in doubt. It seems reasonably clear that when the king was a party in the case he took no part, or almost no part, in the proceedings.

When we have, however, taken everything into account which seems to be at all formal, it must still be said that in judicial proceedings before the great curia regis there was much informality and much of the freedom of discussion of a deliberative body. This is only what we should naturally expect at a time when no sharp line was drawn, either in action or in theory, between the legislative and judicial functions of the curia.

CHAPTER III

THE LOCAL KING'S COURT IN THE REIGN OF WILLIAM I[1]

Of the incidents of the reign of William the Conqueror which indicate the attitude of the new government towards Saxon institutions, certain lawsuits held in various counties have long been considered of especial importance,[2] and they are certainly deserving of re-examination in the light of our present knowledge. My special purpose in doing this is to ascertain if these cases give any information on the relation of Saxon and Norman institutions and law to one another during the reign of the Conqueror and of the extent of feudalization in this period, as well as to describe an important feature of the local organization of justice. I shall not follow a chronological order, but begin with a case from the second half of the reign, because our accounts of it are the most detailed and indicate most completely the points of interest in all the cases.

Probably soon after 1079 Wulfstan, bishop of Worcester, brought suit against Walter, abbot of Evesham,[3] for "servitia et consuetudines" withheld.[4] Bearing directly

[1] Reprinted with slight changes from an article in the *Yale Law Journal*, April, 1914, XXIII, 490-510.

[2] See the references from individual cases below.

[3] Freeman, *Norman Conquest*, American edition, V, 509-510; Round in *Domesday Studies*, II, 542-545; *Victoria County History*, *Worcestershire*, pp. 254 ff.

[4] "Consuetudines," though a general word, is to be taken in a connection like this to mean the right to receive payments which may be of various

on this suit we have five separate documents which are in the probable order of date: 1. The original writ by which the suit was opened, issued by the king in Normandy and appointing Geoffrey, bishop of Coutances, commissioner to preside "in meo loco." 2. The king's writ of execution,

kinds. "Servitia et consuetudines" is the subject of the later writ *De consuetudinibus et serviciis* (Glanvill, IX, 9; Bracton, f. 329, ed. Twiss, V, 88; Holdsworth, III, 15-16) and is proper feudal language. So are other expressions of these documents. Both the king and Geoffrey in nos. 2 and 3 speak of the abbot's owing service to the bishop "sicut alii sui feudati . . ." Still more feudal in character is the king's claim to a share in the services due the bishop. In no. 2 some, at least, of the services which the bishop has recovered are "mea servitia ad suum hundredum"; in no. 1, those who hold the bishop's lands should always be ready "in meo servitio et suo." I hardly think, however, that "servitia et consuetudines" can be taken here as evidence of feudalization, and perhaps none of the expressions can be, though of cumulative force with other evidence for which see below. The "servitia et consuetudines" for which the bishop is suing plainly go back into Saxon times and, though some of them, the "expeditiones," for instance, may have been feudally made over, there is nothing in these documents which makes it necessary to suppose that they had been. Nor is it necessary to suppose that feudalization took place everywhere, in all bishoprics for example, at the same date. It is likely that it was carried through comparatively early in the reign. That the language of these documents is consistent with feudal relationships should at any rate not be overlooked. Mr. Round has shown conclusively, I think, that both the bishopric and the abbey lands had been subinfeudated before the Domesday record. See *Feudal England*, pp. 294, 301-306, *V. C. H. Worcestershire*, 256-257. Professor Liebermann has accepted Round's evidence for the feudalization of the Evesham lands: "Dies krönt den Beweis," he says of it, with reference to Round's whole argument on knight service. *Deutsche Zeitschrift für Geschichtswissenschaft*, VII, E. 23. More recently he has expressed a doubt whether the Conqueror would compel a man like Wulfstan to degrade the ownership of his episcopal lands into feudal tenure. *National Assembly*, p. 78. Round's argument from the three knights fees held by the king of the bishop in 1166 and before the Domesday survey seems to me unanswerable as to the fact of subinfeudation. It is impossible to suppose that the service due the bishop could have been imposed on these lands after they passed into the hands of the king, and it is equally difficult to believe that subinfeudation would have been introduced if the bishop had not become the king's vassal. Maitland, *Bracton's Note Book*, pl. 758, shows the ease with which an old Saxon service could be interpreted as feudal. Cf. Vinogradoff, *English Society in the Eleventh Century*, p. 67.

of uncertain date, but probably not long after the suit, addressed to the sheriff of Worcester and others, directing that the judgment of the court be carried into effect. 3. A formal report addressed by Geoffrey of Coutances to the Domesday commissioners for Worcestershire, concerned chiefly with the judgment rendered by the court, and presumably to be dated 1086. 4. The record of a compromise by which was settled a case which had arisen before the Domesday commissioners involving practically the same questions and the same lands. The settlement would be of the date 1086 and the record is very likely of the same date. 5. An historical account of the original suit, calling itself "Commemoratio placiti," written after the death of William I[5] but during the lifetime of many persons present at the trial, and occasioned it would seem by a threat of the abbot's brother to bring the results of that case again into question.[6] While this is the latest of the documents in date, it gives the fullest account of the case, and it will be necessary to use it as if it were contemporary with the suit.[7] These documents fit perfectly together, with the slight discrepancies to be noted below, and constitute a very satisfactory record for so early a date.

William's writ authorizing the trial is quite general in

5 The writ under which the trial was held is "breve et preceptum regis Willelmi senioris." Later it is said that there are many survivors who heard the trial, "et adhuc multi de tempore regis Willelmi idem testificantes." Bigelow, *Placita*, pp. 17 and 18.

6 The witnesses are "parati hoc probare per sacramentum et bellum contra Rannulfum fratrem ejusdem Walteri abbatis, quem ibi viderunt, qui cum fratre suo tenebat illud placitum contra episcopum, si hanc conventionem negare voluerit, factam inter episcopum et abbatem." *Ibid.*, p. 19. See Round, *Feud. Engl.*, p. 302, note.

7 All these documents are printed by Bigelow, the "Commemoratio" and no. 2 in his text, pp. 17-19, from Thorpe, *Diplomatarium*, pp. 440-442, the others in Appendix A. No. 1 is no. 184 in Davis, *Regesta;* no. 2 is Davis, no. 230; and no. 3 is Davis, no. 221.

character. While it is made clear that the case is to be tried in a king's court,[8] the statement of the points in dispute is so vague that almost any question between the two parties might have been tried under it. Still more to the purpose is the fact that no directions whatever were given to Geoffrey as to how he should proceed and no description of the court to be formed. It would seem certain, therefore, that the king knew that Geoffrey would understand what to do and what should be the composition of the court under such a writ. The process was a familiar one to both of them.

[8] The "in meo loco" of the writ implies that the court is one over which the king might naturally preside. It is a court of his. Stubbs, 1897, I, 419. The appointment of commissioners by royal writ in judicial cases is a delegation to them of position and authority belonging to the king. The court so constituted is not limited in membership to the ordinary membership of the local court whose testimony is desired, but may be made to approach more or less nearly to that of a great curia regis. It seemed natural to the writer of the *Acts of Lanfranc* to call the Penenden Heath court a *magnum placitum,* which is a frequent name during the first century for the national assembly. Plummer, *Two Saxon Chronicles,* I, 289; Thorpe, *Anglo-Saxon Chronicle,* I, 387. Cf. Stubbs, I, 301. The same is true of the *conventus magnus* of the "Commemoratio" above. The court in which the sheriff tried a case "per breve regis" was not called, so far as I know, curia regis. (Cf. Liebermann, II, 451, 10 c.) It was the ordinary county court and tried the case by county law (Glanvill, IX, 10; XII, 23), but the function of the sheriff in such cases was clearly distinguished from his ordinary function. He is mentioned always in Glanvill as acting "per breve regis," and see especially Bracton f. 154b (ed. Woodbine, II, 437): "Potest quidem vicecomes facere placita non ex officio vicecomitis, sed vice ipsius regis ex causa necessaria, non sicut vicecomes sed sicut iustitiarius regis . . ." In these cases the court has whatever competence the writ gives it. It is convenient to distinguish this court from the ordinary sheriff's county court by calling it a king's county court. In a charter of confirmation by William de Mandeville, Earl of Essex, of 27 Henry II, he calls curia regis a court which is thus referred to in the grant which he is confirming: "iv carucatas terre in Estwell ex hereditate mea que redidit mihi dominus per breve domini regis ex judicio totius comitatus." This was evidently a writ of right against the lord which constituted the sheriff a justice in case the lord did not act and which was tried in the county court, called therefore here curia regis. Nichols, *History of Leicestershire,* II, 1, App. p. 134. Printed

If we ask our earliest documents what was the composition of the court which tried the case, there seems no doubt about the answer. The king says in no. 2 that the case was tried before certain barons, "testante vicecomitatu" (sheriffdom, county). Geoffrey says in no. 3 that it was tried before certain barons of the king, "judicante et testificante omni vicecomitatu." That is, the county was present in some capacity and took some part in the action, and barons, it would seem from their especial mention not usually forming any part of the county court, were present—a combination strikingly like the later itinerant justice court. The "Commemoratio," however, differs from these earlier statements in two particulars. It says that the court was a "conventus magnus . . . vicinorum comitatuum et baronum," and it makes no mention of any action by the county, saying that the medial judgment, of which it gives a full account and by which the proof was awarded to the bishop, was made by

also by Mr. Round, *Hist. MSS. Comm.* (Rutland MSS.), (1905), IV, 3-6, who did not find these charters in Nichols. Mr. Round reads "mihi deus" in place of "mihi dominus" above, the MS. being apparently less legible than in Nichols's time. The correct reading must be "dominus."

Professor Maitland has warned us (P. and M., I, 132), a warning which we needed, that in speaking of the curia regis we should not forget that "the definite article is not in our documents. Any court held in the king's name by the king's delegates is curia regis." This is very true but it should not lead us to overlook the fact that in the English language, if we use an article at all, as we generally must, it must be "the" curia regis until 1178 at least. Until the court of common pleas is established with a definite purpose and a strictly limited function, there is only one curia regis. Whatever body of men, acting under a summons like a great or small council, or under a writ addressed to some individual, like a king's local court, made a judgment or a ruling on some administrative matter, the action was always that of the curia regis. This is true in a sense after 1178, but very soon after that date, if not before it, men began to distinguish for some purposes between the old central court, which they still called curia regis, and the new "bench" or the king's justices at Westminster. The itinerant justice court was rapidly assimilated to this latter and was distinguished from the older curia regis in a way it was not before.

the barons.[9] I do not think that the variations of this later account are of importance. When we notice the emphasis which the "Commemoratio" places on the baronial element in the court, making no mention of any other, and consider that it would be perfectly regular for the justiciar to summon barons from any county to a king's court of this kind, we are hardly justified in allowing enough weight on these points to the later account to compel us to modify the definite statements of the two earlier documents. It would seem probable that the "conventus vicinorum comitatuum," if accurate at all, refers exclusively to the baronial element and that the county proper which was present was Worcestershire alone. It is probable also that the two earlier documents, though less detailed, should outweigh the later on the point of action by the county, though, even if we could say that the county court was the formally acting body in making the judgment, the "Commemoratio" is no doubt right in emphasizing the great influence which the baronial element in the body would naturally exert.

The "Commemoratio" is the only document which gives any detailed information on the procedure made use of in the case, and as it appeals to the testimony of many living persons and proposes a similar procedure in the prospective suit which it implies, we may accept its statements with confidence. The procedure is that with which we are familiar as common in such cases. Each of the two parties presents his side of the case; the bishop produces his witnesses who had seen in the time of King Edward the services performed which he demands; the abbot is able to bring forward no witnesses. The court then proceeds to award the proof, in this case to the plain-

[9] "Tandem ex precepto justitiae regis et decreto baronum, itum est ad juditium et, quia abbas dixit se testes contra episcopum non habere, judicatum est ab optimatibus quod episcopus . . ." Bigelow, *Placita*, p. 18.

tiff,[10] it is expressly stated, because the defendant has no witnesses, allowing the defendant, however, to choose the relics on which the oath shall be taken.[11] The case is then adjourned to a later session of the court to which Geoffrey summons the barons who were present in the first session.[12] In the second session the abbot attends with his

10 See the last note; *Origin*, p. 118, note; Holdsworth, II, 135; H. Adams, *Essays in Anglo-Saxon Law,* pp. 186, 240; P. and M., II, 632.

11 A privilege to the defendant which would enable him to give to the oath something of the character of an ordeal, and which may have been granted because the proof is here awarded to the plaintiff. Such decisions show some option still left the court in spite of the formalism of procedure. In a Lincolnshire roll of 1202 are three cases in which the appellee is allowed to decide who shall make proof and in all he decides that the appellor shall. In all the appellor withdraws. Maitland, *Select Pleas of the Crown,* p. 10 and n. 3. See a similar case in Normandy in 1213, Delisle, *Jugements de l'Exchiquier,* no. 113, and cf. the award and the result in a case before William in Normandy in 1060-1066, Round, *Calendar,* no. 1172. An offered oath is refused also in *ibid.*, no. 78 (A.D. 1080). In this Worcestershire case, Geoffrey's report (no. 3) seems to imply that the oath was successfully made: "hoc fuit diratiocinatum et juratum coram me," but he may be referring to testimony of the county, given in some way in the case but not recorded, or to the general result of the trial.

12 ". . . et ex precepto Gosfridi episcopi, affuerunt barones qui interfuerant priori placito et juditio" (Bigelow, *Placita,* p. 18), which makes it evident that they were not regular members of the county court. The "conventus magnus . . . vicinorum comitatum et baronum" shows the same fact, which is also more or less clearly implied in other cases here discussed. See notes 21 and 49. When the justiciar was acting as the king's deputy or lieutenant (Stubbs, I, 299, 374) in the absence of the king, there can be no question of his right to issue writs. See Davis, *Regesta,* no. 7 (Round, *Feud. Engl.,* p. 430, note 19). The justiciars in 1075 summoned the rebel earls to the curia regis, "illi vero praeceptis eorum obsecundare contemnunt." Ord. Vital., II, 263. In the reign of John the abbot of St. Albans takes exception to a writ that it was issued in the name of Geoffrey Fitz Peter while the king was in England. *Plac. Abbrev.,* p. 76. See *E.H.R.,* 1924, XXXIX, 79; Madox, *Exch.,* I, 34, note *u;* Gervase of Canterbury (R.S.), I, 376 (Eyton, *Itinerary of Henry* II, 279-280), and below, note 25. That a mere commissioner could himself issue an original writ while the king was in the country is not probable. This consideration may increase somewhat the likelihood that Geoffrey acted as justiciar with Lanfranc and the count of Mortain (Stubbs, I, 375) about the year 1082 and give to this case

relics, but seeing the readiness of the bishop to take the oath, and the whole proof ready to be made, he abandons the case which is then closed by a concord and conventio. As to the method of proof used in the trial and offered in case of a second trial, there can be no doubt but that it was proof by witnesses and not compurgation. The emphasis placed on seeing and hearing alone would indicate that.[13] In the second case, however, it is the Norman

approximately that date. The original writ (no. 1) is addressed to the same persons as two of the Ely documents below (Davis, *Regesta,* nos. 151, 156), Lanfranc and Geoffrey, though the commission to act as justice here is to Geoffrey alone.

13 Adams, *Essays in Anglo-Saxon Law,* pp. 186-188; Liebermann, I, 398, c. 8; *Leis Willelme,* c. 24; in a case before the king in Normandy, 1072-1079, "affuerant etiam antiquissimi homines qui hec viderant et audierant parati probare secundum judicium regis quod nos edisseramus. *Memoires de Antiquaires de Normandie,* XV, 196; Round, *Calendar,* no. 1190. Cf. Brunner, *Schwurgerichte,* p. 54. I have not attempted to draw evidence as to procedure from any continental source except Norman, though it might be done. The Norman evidence is, it seems to me, conclusive of the fact that in the matter of the procedure used in the local courts the parallel between Saxon and Norman was so close that it is almost a matter of indifference whether we say that the Saxon survived or that the Norman took its place. In most particulars no conscious choice between them could have been made by contemporaries. See Brunner, *Schwurgerichte,* Chapters III and IX. While the greater part of the evidence which we have of procedure in the Norman local courts is post Conquest, it is clear that the sources give us no indication of a change at any time towards the ordinary Teutonic forms from something different existing earlier. The only change in Norman procedure of which we know anything is that of the twelfth century and comes, as in England, from the introduction of the inquest process. It seems to me that every student of Norman sources must agree with Brunner's conclusions as to their relation to Frankish sources "mit dem sie die deutschrechtliche Grundlage gemeinsam haben," and that after the settlement of the Northmen "die Fränkischen Institutionen blieben bestehen und wurden hier zum Teil lebenskräftiger erhalten und fortgebildet, als dies sonst im westfränkischen Reiche der Fall war." To Scandinavian influence "ist wenigstens eine mittlebare Einwirkung insofern zuzugeben, als der einfluss der vorhandenen germanischen Rechtselemente auf die Fortbildung des Neutrischen Rechts durch die skandinavische Ansiedlung eine erhebliche Stärkung erfuhr." Brunner, *Geschichte der Englischen Rechtsquellen im Grundriss* (1909), pp. 62-63. Norman and Saxon forms in local procedure are

method of witness proof which is proposed, as is evident from the offer of battle,[14] and presumably this was also the case in the actual trial.[15]

closely akin to one another because they belong to the common Teutonic legal family and, through some slight influences at least, to the Scandinavian subdivision of that family. Norman evidences of local procedure from the twelfth century as surely indicate what it was in the tenth, as do English of the twelfth what was the Saxon of the tenth.

[14] On battle as a feature of the Norman witness proof see Brunner, *l. c.*, pp. 68, 198-199; Thayer, *Evidence at the Common Law*, pp. 17, 40. The capitulary referred to by both and quoted in full in Thayer is now to be found in a later edition by Boretius in the *Monumenta, Capitula Regum Francorum*, I, 282. That churches and clerics should offer battle was not unusual. See Liebermann, II, *Rechtsglossar*, art., ''Zweikampf,'' c. 7 e and g. William interfered in such a case in Normandy (1074) ''ne causa Ecclesie determinaretur humano sanguine.'' Round, *Calendar*, no. 165; Davis, *Regesta*, no. 73. Text from Valin, *Le Duc de Normandie*, p. 198, note. See William's law regarding procedure, Liebermann, I, 483-484, protecting the Englishman against compulsory trial by battle in criminal cases. Above, Chapter I, at note 24. A case which has been often referred to is recorded in *Domesday Book*, I, 44b (Bigelow, *Placita*, p. 38) which seems to include an issue drawn between an older and a newer method, or principle, of proof by witnesses. It would appear from the context that Picot asserts that his *testes*, men of low rank, are of equal value or better than those of higher standing produced by William, and that the court, puzzled perhaps by the emphasis of his assertion, refers the question to the king. ''Sed testes Willelmi nolunt accipere legem nisi regis Edwardi usque dum diffiniatur per regem,'' which implies an admission that the principle of the older practice, on which the testes of William stand, might be overruled by the king. Cf. *Leges Henrici*, 29, 1; Thayer, *Evidence*, pp. 23-24. Freeman, *Norm. Conq.*, V, App. A, I think misunderstood this passage. The question primarily in dispute is one of fact, not of law. It is, who was the antecessor. That being settled, the disposition of the land is settled, as in a hundred other cases in the record. What is peculiar and new, is the character of the proof offered by Picot. The sentence quoted above can hardly bear any wider meaning than that the *testes* of William refuse to yield to a method of proof (*legem*) which they think is not warranted by precedent, until the point is decided by the king. The use of the word *lex* as meaning judicial proof is too well known to need illustration. The following, which occurs not infrequently, is interesting in this connection: ''Consideratum est quod ipsi defendant se xii manu . . . et veniant cum legibus suis a die . . .'' *Bracton's Note Book*, pl. 184.

[15] Bigelow says, citing this case, ''This form of testimony by witnesses, unrestrained by the limits apparently set in the Anglo-Saxon period, was

The case which comes before the Domesday commissioners in 1086 indicates that, though the first case had been decided in the bishop's favor, he had not been able to obtain from Hampton and Bengeworth the services and payments for which he had sued. He lays claim now therefore not to "servitia et consuetudines" but to these lands themselves, to be held by him in domain, a claim which can only mean continued default of service. The commissioners apparently sent to Geoffrey to find out exactly what had been decided in the first case and received in reply document no. 3, which all our evidence indicates to be a very exact statement. With this before them and with the confession of the abbot to the facts established in the first case, and very likely with the testimony of the county,[16] it seemed to them and to the others that the lands should remain in the possession of Evesham, but that the abbot should be obligated to a faithful performance of the services, and to this the abbot consented.

Of the more famous case of Lanfranc against Odo, bishop of Bayeux, commonly known as the Penenden Heath case, we have less satisfactory accounts.[17] Happily these accounts, while differing in some particulars among themselves, agree in those which are essential for our

employed in the time of the Conqueror." *Placita*, p. xxi and note 3. See Brunner, *Schwurgerichte*, pp. 399-400. There is an interesting case in Normandy of the employment of charter witnesses about 1040, in which William is mentioned as acting, in Delisle, *Saint Sauveur-le-Vicomte, pièces*, no. 14, p. 17.

16 Not so stated in the record but in Heming's account of this case in his cartulary, written by direction of Bishop Wulfstan. Quoted in Bigelow, *Placita*, p. 288. It is practically certain that only one county gave testimony in the case in 1086.

17 See Freeman, *Norm. Conq.*, IV, 244-247; Stubbs, I, 300-301. Stubbs says this is "perhaps the best reported trial of the reign," but he does not seem to have known of the evidence bearing on the Worcestershire case. See *ibid.*, I, 299, note 3.

purpose. According to the longer account Bishop Odo,[18] coming to England some years before Lanfranc, was able to seize upon many lands and "consuetudines" belonging to the archbishopric. Soon after Lanfranc became primate, he made diligent inquiry into the matter and, discovering the losses of his church, appealed to the king for redress. Thereupon the king in 1072 issued his writ to Geoffrey of Coutances directing the county to sit upon the case under him as justice.[19] The county came together

[18] Printed in Bigelow, *Placita*, pp. 5-9, from the notes to John Selden's edition of Eadmer (1623), pp. 197-200. For an incomplete but dated copy of the shorter text, together with a discussion of earlier printed copies and of the date, see Dr. W. Levison in the *English Historical Review*, 1912, XXVII, 717-720. The account printed by Dr. Levison, which lacks the historical introduction and some details of the longer account, has more the appearance of a formal record, or the original record but slightly changed. If it be taken as such, the longer account as printed by Bigelow from Selden will show how the later historian with the record before him added details to complete the narrative, and may possibly indicate what was done in other narratives based on a record, as in the "Commemoratio" in the Worcestershire case above, the first Ely case, and the case of Bishop Gundulf against Picot below. Nothing was added by the historian in the Penenden case which affects the points we are considering here, and probably nothing was in the other cases, though the Ely case is badly confused. The writ printed by Bigelow, p. 4 (Davis, *Regesta*, no. 50), upon which he says the trial appears to have been instituted, can hardly have a connection with the case. At a time when the forms of writs were still unsettled, this writ might perhaps have been interpreted, in a second stage of the action it contemplates, as an original writ, but hardly in the Penenden case; it seems rather to be an executive writ. It names among the commissioners Lanfranc, who is plaintiff in the Penenden case, and it concerns domain lands only. Without a good deal of laxity in judicial interpretation, no church could have recovered under it any land which it held "in servitio."

[19] The county met "ex precepto regis." *E.H.R.*, XXVII, 719. "Huic placito interfuerunt Goisfridus episcopus Constantiensis qui in loco regis fuit et justitiam illam tenuit . . ." Bigelow, *Placita*, p. 7. It would be apparent that this was a curia regis held in the county, if from no other evidence, because in it "multa placita . . . et verba . . . ibi surrexerunt et etiam inter consuetudines regales et archiepiscopales" (both texts). This was business in which the king had a direct interest. The same thing is implied by the *Rechtsgebot* of which the closing sentence in Bigelow's text is a good example: "Hujus placiti . . . determinatum finem postquam

at Penenden and, because of the number of questions needing to be settled, was held in session for three days.[20] Besides the ordinary county court there were present barons—*Francigenae*—of the county, who probably would not usually attend, and barons from other counties.[21] The bishop of Chichester is named as having been specially summoned by royal writ, "ex praecepto regis," to give information about the ancient "consuetudines."[22]

rex audivit, laudavit, laudans cum consensu omnium principum suorum confirmavit, et ut deinceps incorruptus perseveraret, firmiter praecepit.'' These words may possibly imply action by the central curia regis, confirming that by the local court, but whether such action was taken or not, the king's action here described would give the decision of the local court the same effect, which indeed it would have in law anyway.

20 Cf. *Magna Carta*, c. 19. This fact implies the presence of the county court.

21 ''. . . et alii multi barones regis et ipsius archiepiscopi atque illorum episcoporum homines multi, et alii aliorum comitatuum homines etiam cum toto isto comitatu multae et magnae auctoritatis viri, Francigenae scilicet et Angli.'' Bigelow, p. 8. There is no evidence of any county court officially present except that of Kent.

22 ''Consuetudines'' here are of the same sort as in the preceding case. Strictly speaking, the bishop was not brought to testify as to the laws of the land or the ancient customs of England (Freeman, *Norm. Conq.*, IV, 245) in the meaning usually given to these terms. In proving, however, to whom the Saxon ''consuetudines'' belonged in order to prove to whom they should belong after the Conquest, it is necessarily implied that the rights remain the same, as is also implied in regard to the royal ''consuetudines'' later in the account of this case. There would be therefore in such cases more truly a carrying over of Saxon legal arrangements than in the mere transfer of land from the old to the new holder, which need imply nothing as to the form or nature of the holding. This is also true of the continuation of *sac* and *soc*, liberties, and immunities. There is an interesting case under Henry II of disputed jurisdiction turning on the question of fact, to whom the Saxon grant had been made, in the chronicle of Jocelin de Brakelonda, p. 37. See also *E.H.R.* XXIV, 417-431, and *Bracton's Note Book*, pl. 1716. All these things differed, however, in principle in nothing from similar arrangements in Normandy and probably very little in detail. See Haskins, *Institutions*, pp. 25-27, 89, n. 21, and below note 35. Grants of the early Norman kings sometimes confirm such grants by their predecessors. Haskins, *Institutions*, p. 90. While it is true that customary payments for land were continued from Saxon into Norman times and evidence from the facts of

In this case we have then, as in the first, a county court reinforced by barons not usually belonging to it, summoned before a royal commissioner who was acting as presiding justice in place of the king, "qui in loco regis fuit et justitiam illam tenuit," a king's county court.

As to the procedure employed, we are given almost no information. That the county had something to do which was considered essential seems to follow from the fact that it was detained for three days, but we get no details of its action. The statement as to the judgment reached implies that barons and county acted together in making it: "Et ab omnibus illis probis et sapientibus hominibus qui affuerunt fuit ita ibi diratiocinatum et etiam a toto comitatu recordatum et judicatum."[23] In regard to the method of trial it is implied only that both witnesses and

Saxon times was often appealed to determine what the payments were, and while it is also true that similar evidence was used to determine what lands belonged to a given Saxon holder and ought therefore to pass to a given Norman, these facts hardly justify the statements which have been based upon them. See Freeman, *Norm. Conq.*, IV, 244-247, and Vinogradoff, *Eleventh Century*, p. 224. The latter statement that these facts "ensured a wholesale reception of Old English land law by the French conquerors" is cited by Holdsworth, II, 168, with approval. These words, if they are to be taken as they would ordinarily be understood, affirm the reception by the Normans from the Saxons of the law controlling the nature of land ownership and the principles of transfer and inheritance. I think it is clear not merely that these things were regulated by feudal law after the Conquest but that the evidence cited does not concern them.

[23] The new version of the shorter account printed by Dr. Levison (*E.H.R.*, XXVII, 719) varies these words slightly: "Et ab omnibus sapientibus, qui affuerant, fuit ibi diracionatum atque judicatum a . . ." Presumably the word "comitatu" should follow. The brief accounts in Eadmer, *Hist. Nov.*, p. 17, and Gervase of Canterbury, (R.S.) II, 369, add nothing to the records used here and are so late in date that they can stand only for the traditional understanding. Eadmer, who relates briefly the same historical circumstances as the longer account, calls the meeting a "conventus principum," but mentions the county and says of the decision that it was "ex communi omnium astipulatione et judicio." Gervase knows nothing of the county and speaks of the suit as "in congregatione illa famosa nobilium Angliae et seniorum quae ex praecepto regis facta est apud Pinindene."

argument, or discussion, were employed. The end was determined "multis testibus multisque rationibus," and in the presence of all "multis et apertissimis rationibus demonstratum fuit." While these statements are unsatisfactory and warrant no more detailed inferences than those made above, they are so far as they go entirely in harmony with the Worcestershire case, and with what we should expect.

The case of the church of Ely presents some peculiar difficulties from the incompleteness of the sources. It is probably impossible with any certainty to arrange chronologically the documents concerning the rights and lands of Ely which belong to the reign of William I.[24] If we place them with reference to the facts which they concern in the order that from internal evidence seems more likely than any other, we have first a document (122) included in the *Liber Eliensis* having some of the forms of a record, but mainly a historical narrative, manifestly written some time after the event and so indefinite and uncertain in character as to be of little value. Two facts only it seems to establish satisfactorily. 1. A case concerning the "liberties" of Ely was tried before a royal commission. Whether the commission was issued to Odo of Bayeux as the presiding justice, or Odo as justiciar himself commissioned the justices upon the king's order, is not apparent.[25] Either proceeding would in general be

[24] These documents are printed in Bigelow, *Placita*, pp. 22-29, from the *Liber Eliensis*, except the last one considered. The numbers in parenthesis in the text are the numbers assigned to the different documents in Davis's *Regesta*. See Freeman, *Norm. Conq.*, IV, 327; Round, *Feud. Engl.*, pp. 459-461.

[25] It has been generally supposed that the presiding justice in this case was the bishop of Bayeux, but the language is what would have been used if the king, absent from England, had issued his writs through Bishop Odo as justiciar: "rex tandem respectu divinae misericordiae instinctus his intendere, principibus circumpositis per Baiocensem episcopum praecepit haec discutere." The historical record (122) is dated April 2, 1080. William

possible. The latter seems from the language more probable in this case. 2. It seemed to the person writing that the court could properly be formed by several counties, or the representatives of several counties, united. What the counties were or how many, or in what way they were united, it is not possible to say.[26] The account at first says three counties were united, but later the number is given as four, and altogether the representatives of at least seven are named. The description is so vague and confused that we can only say that a combination of counties, or representatives of counties, to form a single court seemed possible to the author. The second document (129) appears at first sight to be a writ of execution following this case. It names the same place of trial, and the same subject, the liberties of Ely, established "per pluras scyres ante meos barones," but it names so different a commission before whom the case had been tried, headed by Geoffrey of Coutances, not likely to be forgotten, that the relationship of the two documents must be left in doubt.[27] All we can say is that this relates also to a king's

was in Normandy at that time (Davis, *Regesta*, p. xxii), but we do not know that Odo was justiciar then. See notes 12 and 39 in this chapter, and Stubbs, I, 375. It seems to be implied in no. 129 that Geoffrey of Coutances was the presiding justice.

26 In Davis, *Regesta*, no. 122, this is said to be a "record of an inquest . . . by the oath of the three neighboring shires." The statement is an inference, perhaps probable, but the fact is not directly affirmed in the document. Cf. *ibid.*, p. xxix. Nor is anything more definite said in no. 129. That several counties were united on occasions like this in some capacity admits of no question. See evidence in the cases here following and *V. C. H. Worcester*, p. 254. For evidence of a similar union of several counties in one court in the Frankish state see Waitz, *Deutsche Verf.*, 1885, IV, 411-413; Brunner, *Forschungen*, p. 192. Cf. Round, *Calendar*, no. 737; Stubbs, I, 426, note 3; Stanton, *Early History of Abingdon*, p. 37.

27 When a document like this writ is opposed to a historical account plainly inexact, the normal conclusion would be that the writ is correct, and perhaps there is less difficulty in supposing Geoffrey's presence to have been forgotten than that two trials were held with so many features in common.

local court of more than one shire presided over by a royal commission.

An especially interesting commission is no. 155. It concerns not the liberties but the lands of Ely, once held in domain but now usurped by barons.[28] Referring to an earlier suit on the same subject, it directs all the shires which were present in the former case to be reconvened, and those who can come of the barons who were present before, and those who hold lands of the church.[29] When they are assembled, there are to be selected several of those English who know how the lands of the church were lying on the day on which King Edward died, and what they report is to be attested by oath.[30] Plainly this is the Nor-

This would imply, however, that Odo took no other part in the case and that he was acting as justiciar, or at least that he issued the convoking writs in the king's name. See above n. 25. It is to be noted also that the barons named in the writ as those before whom the case was tried are ten in number, a considerably larger body than the usual commission, and that the writ of Henry I (Dugdale, *Monasticon*, I, 482), which follows his father's in part, names a commission of five, four named in William's writ, and one, Walkelin, bishop of Winchester, an entirely new name.

28 It is therefore, if the language is used strictly, as it is likely to be, not the above case.

29 "Mando vobis et praecipio ut iterum faciatis congregari omnes scyras quae interfuerunt placito habito de terris ecclesiae de Heli, antequam mea conjux in Normanniam novissime veniret. Cum quibus etiam sint de baronibus meis qui competenter adesse poterunt, et praedicto placito interfuerunt, et qui terras ejusdem ecclesiae tenent." Bigelow, p. 24. Those who hold lands of the church are parties interested in the case before the court and are hardly summoned as among the "baronibus meis" who, according to the language usual in these documents, form a part of the court. This is not, I think, a second session of the earlier *placitum* referred to in the same document, for which the writ would surely read differently, but a new trial.

30 Following immediately on the passage quoted in the last note, it is said: "Quibus in unum congregatis, eligantur plures de illis Anglis qui sciunt quomodo terrae jacebant praefatae ecclesiae die qua rex Edwardus obiit, et quod inde dixerint ibidem jurando testentur." This is the same as the arrangement referred to in the record cited in note 36 below from the *Inquisitio Eliensis*: "testimonio hominum rei veritatem cognoscentium." The two *placita* concerned the same subject and employed the same method.

man jury of inquisition, and the directions are especially interesting as an early and clear statement of both the process and the principle of the jury and of its use in a suit at law. It is evidently expected that two classes of lands will be found, one about which there will be no doubt but that they belong to the domain. These lands are to be restored at once unless the holders can make terms with the abbot. The other class is of lands whose holders set up the plea that they received them from the king.[31] Of these the king directs that it shall be signified to him in writing what the lands are and who hold them. It would seem that this document was followed after no long interval by no. 276. In the latter not all the land of either of the classes of the former document has been restored to the church. The domain of the abbot is here distinguished from the domain of the monks, which looks like more careful consideration.[32] Abbot Simeon has probably recently come into office and is not yet in possession of all his "consuetudines," which need not mean, however, a failure to carry out the decision of the court referred to in no. 129. Lanfranc is not named among the commissioners as in most of the other cases, and no directions are given as to the formation of a court, but the assembly is called "istud placitum."

Of the other Ely documents of this immediate group, only no. 154 concerns us.[33] It appoints a commission for

[31] The term "thaneland" is applied in this writ to both these classes of land, to that held of the church as well as to that held of the king.

[32] "Facite simul venire omnes illos qui terras tenent de dominico victu ecclesiae de Heli . . ." See the Ramsey cartulary (R. S.), I, 234.

[33] Nos. 151, 152, and 153 seem almost beyond question to have been issued in that order, as may be seen from the references to the consecration of the abbot, and no. 154 may be placed next because of the reference to Remigius. No. 151 is later, I think, than 155 and 276, because of the reference to the abbot's lands and the "sicut alia vice praecepi." Nos. 156 and 157 are later than 155, but their exact position in the series can hardly be determined. It is quite likely that some of these documents were prac-

the trial of a possible suit concerning "consuetudines" claimed by Bishop Remigius in the island of Ely which are suspected to be new. The king declares that he is unwilling that the bishop should have any rights there except those which his predecessor had on the day of King Edward's death and, if the bishop wishes to go to law about the matter, directs that he shall plead as he would have done in King Edward's time.[34] At first sight these words seem to mean that the bishop must employ the same procedure that he would have done in Edward's time, but if so this is the only time in cases of this kind that William shows any interest in procedure, or any consciousness that procedure had changed, except through the introduction of trial by battle. What William is everywhere anxious to have established is the fact about the Saxon *antecessor*. What was the land which he held? What were the contents of the liberty? What were the rights and "consuetudines"? Nothing further than this.[35] Again if we regard the question from the side of

tically contemporary, that is, certain of them were issued before others had been executed. Several of them vaguely imply that the king was out of the country.

34 "Nolo enim ut ibi habeat nisi illud quod antecessor ejus habebat tempore regis Eadwardi, scilicet qua die ipse rex mortuus est, et si Remigius episcopus inde placitare voluerit, placitet inde sicut fecisset tempore regis Eadwardi . . ." Later in the same writ it is directed that a suit begun by certain barons against the church is to be postponed "si inde placitare noluerint sicut inde placitassent tempore regis Eadwardi." Further on a little indication of procedure is given, in line with what we have had. The abbey is to have its "consuetudines" "sicut abbas per cartes suas et per testes suos eas deplacitare poterit." The meaning of "consuetudines" in these cases is here clearly shown.

35 The question of the manner of holding, the kind of tenure, is not raised. The fact of Saxon ownership is unquestionably used to prove title after the Conquest, but nothing more. (Cf. P. and M., I, 92; Vinogradoff, *Eleventh Century*, p. 224.) There is nothing in such inquiries as this, or in inquiries as to liberties and "consuetudines," as in the Worcestershire case, which implies the impossibility of so much of a revolution in land tenures as would be made necessary by the general introduction of military

procedure, the Saxon and the Norman methods of proof were so nearly identical that it would be impossible to point out any peculiarity of the Saxon, differing from the Norman, which would be a protection to a defendant and which he might wish to have preserved. What is wanted in this case is to find out what rights were exercised by the bishop of Edward's time, and what is demanded is that Remigius should prove his case by evidence which existed in 1066 and by nothing which he could not have used in that year. He must be limited in his pleadings to the facts as they existed in Edward's day.

There is another document relating to the lands of Ely not included in the above list which records the results of a *placitum* held before a royal commission of five, Bishops Geoffrey and Remigius, Earl Waltheof, and Sheriffs Picot and Ilbert.[36] The king's writ besides appointing the

tenure where it had not existed before. I am not taking into account here intra-manorial tenures proper, and also important incidents of landholding are indicated by *sac* and *soc* and "*consuetudines,*" but practically the same things are so closely bound up with landholding in Normandy that their existence in England would assist rather than hinder the introduction of the complete Norman system. Haskins, *Institutions*, pp. 26-39.

[36] Hamilton, *Inquisitio Comitatus Cantabrigiensis*, p. 192; Round, *Feud. Engl.*, pp. 459-461. One is tempted to try to fit this document into the series first named and to guess that it relates to the *placitum* mentioned in no. 155 as held "antequam mea conjux in Normanniam novissime veniret," that the list of lands (Hamilton, *Inq. Cantabr.*, pp. 192-195) was then made out; and that it is the one concerning which the king asks for information in no. 152: "Inquire per episcopum Constatiensem et per episcopum Walchelinum, et per caeteros, qui terris sanctae Ætheldrithae scribi et jurare fecerunt, quomodo juratae fuerunt, et qui eas juraverunt, et qui jurationem audierunt, et quae sunt terrae, et quantae, et quot, et quomodo vocatae, et qui eas tenent." At the date of 152 the king has learned of this list and he wants to know how it was made and practically demands a copy of it. The report called for in 152 is considerably more detailed than that asked for in 155. Then he asked merely for information about the lands said to be held of him: "Illas vero litteris mihi signate, quae sint et qui eas tenent." If Matilda was in England during the absence, or absences, of William, 1075-1080 (see Davis, *Regesta*, no. 189, Bigelow, *Placita*, p. 33), the reference to her in no. 155 would make probable the order here

justices directed the assembling of the county before them. In the court an inquest was held and "testimonio hominum rei veritatem cognoscentium determinaverunt terras que injuste fuerant ablate ab ecclesis . . . quatinus de dominio fuerant, tempore videlicet regis Edwardi." There follows a list of those who had usurped lands of the church with the holdings which they unjustly possessed. The jury of those who know is evident, but no further indication of procedure is given and no evidence that the court included a special baronial element besides the royal justices.

A case interesting in many ways is that between Bishop Gundulf of Rochester and Picot, sheriff of Cambridgeshire, over the land of Fracenham, which Picot claimed was the king's.[37] The county court met to decide the right by their judgment, as directed by the king, under the bishop of Bayeux as king's commissioner. Influenced by fear of the sheriff, they decided against Gundulf. So far as the record goes, it is the county court which makes the judgment, and no baronial element is mentioned besides the king's justice. By what procedure the case was tried is not indicated. The bishop of Bayeux, however, suspected the decision and was unwilling to accept it.[38] He directed the court if they knew they had

suggested for the first two of these documents, and William's absence would account for his not knowing the results of the *placitum*. Round, *Feud. Engl.*, 133 ff., thinks the whole *Inquisitio Eliensis* was drawn up in answer to no. 152 and that the writ refers to the Domesday survey. Davis's date of 1082 is more likely.

[37] Bigelow, *Placita*, p. 34, from *Anglia Sacra*, I, 339; Madox, *Exchequer*, I, 31; Freeman, *Norm. Conq.*, IV, 249; Round, *Feud. Engl.*, p. 121; Holdsworth, II, 171.

[38] There is a commission of Henry I's to a sheriff and three others to view boundaries ". . . et facite recognoscere per probos homines de comitatu. . . . Et si bene eis non credideritis, sacramento confirment quod dixerint." Palgrave, *Commonwealth*, II, 184, n. 84 from Dugdale, *Monasticon*, VI, 1273 (Vol. VIII. ed. 1846). Cited in the same connection, Thayer, *Evidence*, p. 52, n. 1.

spoken the truth, that is, if they wished to maintain their judgment, to choose twelve of their number—''seipsis duodecim eligerent''—who should confirm by an oath what all had said. This they did and here the case rested for a time. It should be noticed that the presiding justice assumes to direct the court to take action supplementary to a decision usually final and such as never would have been taken at that date by an ordinary county court.[39]

Of no other case in the reign of the first Norman king, do we have particularly significant details. If we count, as I think we must, four separate cases in the interest of Ely, with a possible fifth, we have considered above seven cases, and perhaps found an eighth. There are mentioned during the reign seven other cases and a probable eighth.[40]

39 The later portion of the case does not concern our present purpose, as it is carried on not in a local but a more general curia regis. It is interesting to notice, however, that the court, not a great, but a reinforced small council (''multos ex melioribus totius Angliae baronibus''), is summoned to London not by the king but by the bishop of Bayeux; that the jury of the county is put on trial before this court on an accusation of perjury and convicted; and not merely this, but that the judgment of the first court is set aside, contrary to the usual practice, and the land assigned by that judgment to the king is given back to Bishop Gundulf. The whole case is extraordinary in the matter of procedure and is a striking example of how far the new rulers might allow themselves to go in interfering with the older judicial customs, very likely in the interests of justice.

40 There are fewer instances of similar commissions in Normandy during the same reign. A probable case is found in a document of about 1036: ''Quo vero clamore prolato in medio, invenerent, Robertus, sc. archiepiscopus, Odo comes, et Niellus vicecomes aliique seniores justiciam regni obtinentes, quod illas terras . . .'' Delisle, *Histoire du Château et des Sires de Saint-Sauveur-le-Vicomte*, p. 14, no. 13. Not long after 1070 two barons were commissioned to make an inquiry under oath which they were to record, and this was done. *Gallia Christiana*, XI, instr. 65; Brunner, *Schwurgerichte*, pp. 148, note 4, 270; Valin, *Le Duc de Normandie*, p. 201, note 1. In 1076 there is an interesting case, probably not of *missi*, but of the delegation of the authority of the curia ducis to Geoffrey of Coutances (''Gaufredus, Constantiarum presul, est delegatus regali auctoritate discussor et judex hujus disceptationis'') with others who seem to decide the case independently of the rest of the curia. Delisle, *S.-Sauveur*, p. 40, no.

Of these three are referred to in Domesday Book, two in royal writs, two in the Miracles of St. Edmund, and one probable case in the Abingdon Chronicle. In one Domesday reference (I, 175b) it is said that Abbot Walter of Evesham recovered five hides "in iiii sciris coram episcopo Baiocensi et aliis baronibus regis." (Davis, *Regesta,* App. nos. xxiii, xxiv.) In another (I, 2) the case is said to have been decided "judicio baronum regis qui placitum tenuerunt." In the third case (I, 101b) Bishop Osbern is said to have proved his title to a manor "coram baronibus regis." In the first writ case (Davis, *Regesta,* no. 66) King William gives notice that Abbot Scotland had recovered eight prebends in Newington by the testimony of the county of Kent before Lanfranc and three other barons who are named and "ceteris meis optimatibus illius comitatus." In the second case[41] (Davis, no. 213), Bishop Wulfstan, the abbot of Evesham, and Rambald the chancellor, adjudged lands in Worcestershire to be held in domain by the abbot of Westminster. Of the two St. Edmund's cases, one refers to what looks like an *iter,*[42] and the other to a commission to Lan-

36; Round, *Calendar,* no. 712; Davis, *Regesta,* no. 92. About 1080 there is another case very much like the last in which the authority of the curia ducis is again delegated to Geoffrey with three others. Delisle, *S.-Sauveur,* p. 46, no. 42; Round, *Calendar,* no. 1212; Davis, *Regesta,* no. 132. See Haskins, *Institutions,* pp. 56-58. On the pleas of the king of France held throughout the Vexin in 1091, see Round, *Calendar,* no. 3. The fact should not be overlooked that the character and operation of the court seem entirely familiar to all who are called upon to operate it. It is natural, as a result of the disturbance of titles made by the Conquest, that there should be more cases calling for the use of *missi* in the kingdom than in the duchy.

41 The second writ case originally cited here, from Davis, *Regesta,* no. 188, has been conclusively shown by Mr. Round, *E.H.R.,* XXIX, 350, to belong to the reign of Henry I.

42 ". . . praesentibus ejusdem loci majoris aetatis fratribus, sed et accitis illuc ab abbate quibusdam regis primoribus, qui dictante justitia in eadem villa regia tenebant placita." See Round, *Feud. Engl.,* p. 329, and Davis, *Regesta,* p. xxxi.

franc to take the testimony of the county in the case between St. Edmund's and Bishop Herfast.[43] This last case was decided by the witness of the abbot of Ramsey, reaching back to the days of Cnut and supported by the testimony of nine counties, or of the representatives of nine counties. In the Abingdon case no mention is made of royal commissioners, but the details given agree so exactly with the other cases of commissioners that it is probably one of the kind. Under the authorization of a royal writ, by a charter of King Edward's and the witness of the county, Abingdon proves its right to certain "consuetudines" against royal officials.

I believe, if we leave one side the action of the counties before the Domesday commissioners, there is no other clear reference to judicial action by a county court in the reign of the Conqueror.[44] These which have been consid-

[43] For the first St. Edmund's case see *Memorials of St. Edmund's Abbey* (R. S.), p. 63, and Liebermann, *Anglo-Normannische Geschichtsquellen*, p. 253, and for the second, *Memorials*, p. 65, and Liebermann, *l. c.*, p. 254, and cf. Davis, *Regesta*, nos. 138, 139, and Liebermann in *Zeitschrift f. Geschichtswissenschaft*, VII, E, 34. For the Abingdon case see *Chron. Abingd.*, pp. 1-2 (Davis, *Regesta*, no. 49). I have omitted from this list the second case between Odo of Bayeux and Lanfranc because, while it may very likely be another instance of a local royal court, the account is so indefinite that no positive assertion is possible. See Bigelow, *Placita*, p. 10, and Eadmer, *Hist. Nov.*, pp. 17-18. I have also omitted a case "coram regina Mathilde in praesentia iiii vicecomitatuum" (*Domesday Book*, I, 238b; Bigelow, *Placita*, p. 300) for the queen may be thought to represent the king in a more personal way than an ordinary commissioner, though the case is the same in principle. Cf. *Domesday Book*, I, 48b. Matilda may indeed during the king's absence herself have issued the writs convoking the court. On the judicial action of the Domesday commissioners, see *V. C. H., Suffolk*, I, 385, and on other possible commissions, *ibid.*, pp. 386, 379, and the references there given. There is another possible case referred to in the writ printed by Davis, *Regesta*, App. no. xxviii.

[44] In a sense it was the old county or shire court which was acting in these cases, as was the court which met the itinerant justices later, but the additions made to its membership when acting under the king's writ, the presence and authority of the king's justice, and in the particular case the derivation of its authority from the writ, made it institutionally different.

ered all agree among themselves in any details which they give, both as to the general plan in operation and the procedure in the conduct of the cases. Certain minor points only are left in doubt. The one feature in which all the cases agree without exception and with no room for doubt is the presence of the royal commissioners, the king's *missi*.

The Norman origin of the practice of sending a special justice, or justices, by a written order of the king's, to hold a local court for the trial of a specified case, is not likely to be questioned. No case of exactly the sort has been found in Saxon times.[45] If every case, however doubtful, of royal influence on popular courts in the Saxon period be allowed to be a forerunner of this practice, it springs into such sudden and extensive use in the reign of the Conqueror that we should be obliged to reckon it among the instances of the substitution of an institution in an advanced stage of development for one in its faint beginning. But the facts will hardly warrant us in claiming even so much as this for a Saxon forerunner, for there is no case in that period of royal commissioners holding a local court under a king's writ. We are certainly dealing here with a Norman institution, imported by the Conqueror, whose historical antecedents in Normandy and connection with the Carolingian *missi* do

As a judicial institution, it was the forerunner of the itinerant justice court, which was the local court held by the king's *missi* made general and regular.

45 Zinkeisen in the *Political Science Quarterly,* 1895, X, 132 ff., has studied the evidence for Saxon times with negative results. See Liebermann, II, 482, 5a, 6a; Freeman, *Norm. Conq.*, V, 298-299; Stubbs, I, 206. While no case clearly like that of the later *missi* with their specially constructed court is to be found in Saxon times, the king does occasionally send formal directions to the local courts in regard to cases before them. The evidence for this is cited from Kemble, *Codex Diplomaticus,* nos. 693, 929, and more doubtful 755. These documents will be found in H. Adams, *Essays in Anglo-Saxon Law,* pp. 355, 360, and 365, respectively.

not fall within our subject. I believe that the frequency with which the process was put into use and the importance which it must have had as a means of government in the minds of the king and his advisers have never been realized. No comment made upon it and no list of cases drawn up have been at all adequate to indicate the place which it plainly occupied in the government of the time.[46] If among the scanty records of the reign which have been preserved to us, we can discover fourteen undoubted cases in its twenty-one years, we may be sure that this method of bringing royal justice into the localities and of bringing local evidence and local knowledge to bear on royal justice was clearly understood, highly esteemed by those interested in government, and in practically constant employment, a most important new contribution to the institutional life of the state. There is, however, no sign that it was yet regularized or systematized except in the Domesday plan. The cases are unconnected, each arranged and carried through for itself alone. The evidence in one instance that commissioners on an *iter* may be in session relates to one place only and is too incomplete to warrant another conclusion.[47] It is evident, however, that the method is so frequently employed and so well understood that it can easily be made regular and systematic by another generation.[48]

[46] Stubbs, I, 375, 478; P. and M., I, 109, note 2; Davis, *England Under the Normans and Angevins*, Appendix II, and *Regesta*, p. xxix.

[47] Above, note 42.

[48] In one respect, so far as our scanty evidence enables us to judge, the *missus* of William I's time differed from the itinerant justice: he was explicitly commissioned as the personal representative of the king. "In meo loco" the writ says. The later bench of justices who go on the circuits are in place of the small council, not of the king. In a way of course they represent the king because the court they hold is a king's court, and of every king's court in theory the king is the presiding moderator. But this is mere theory with which the practice does not actually concern itself, as may be seen for instance in the reservation of questions for the opinion of

In many of the cases, barons besides those forming the commission were summoned to attend the court from the county in which the court met, or from other counties, or from both, and took part in the action of the court. In a few cases they are not mentioned, but in these nothing precludes their presence. Their attendance would give to the court more obviously to contemporaries the character of a king's court and distinguish it sharply from the ordinary county court.[49] Evidence that the judgment was made by them exclusively is not sufficient to warrant such a conclusion and appears to me of doubtful validity. In exactly what way the judgment was made in the later itinerant justice court, it is very difficult to say, but it is highly probable that both in them and in their ancestors in the time of William I the baronial element in the court exercised an influence upon the decision disproportionate to its numbers, but it seems to me more than likely that the decision was in form an act of the assembly as a whole.[50]

the king which is frequently occurring. The reservation except in a few special cases is really for the council in which the king may or may not be present. The theory comes nearest perhaps to practical expression in the equity jurisdiction of the itinerant justice court, say at the end of the thirteenth century. At least some features of the court's equity work find their easiest explanation in the supposition that the court stands for the king, but even here this is not a necessary explanation. That the court represents the council meets all the requirements of the case. If the *missus* of the first reign was understood to be the personal representative of the king, then he certainly took no part in making the judgment, and the assembly of the county or of the united hundreds was a necessary feature of the institution.

49 In the itinerant justice system of the twelfth and the first part of the thirteenth centuries, barons from the country, not attending the ordinary county court, were required to attend personally or by representatives, but, so far as I know, barons from other counties were not summoned in addition to the commissioners, though there was nothing in the ideas or practices of that time which would make a summons to them seem unwarranted.

50 See above Chapter II, note 54.

In many of these cases the county is mentioned, or a group of counties, as attending the commissioners and taking some part in the action of the court, and in places where there is no such reference, its presence should probably be assumed. The county which attends is probably the county court which meets the sheriff in its ordinary sessions. The language of the documents in most of the cases would be satisfied if we supposed attendance to be confined to a county jury which speaks for the county in giving testimony, as the hundred juries do for the hundred in Domesday Book. This may be the case in those instances where several counties meet, except for the one county forming the court, but the later itinerant justices certainly met a full county court, and it is difficult to see how such a practice could have developed out of one in which juries only attended. The natural development would be the other way. The case of Bishop Gundulf against Picot seems also to imply, though not necessarily, the formation of a jury from an assembly on the spot.[51] As to the action of the county in making the judgment, nothing further need be said except to call attention again to Geoffrey's "judicante" in document no. 3 in the Worcestershire case.[52]

We have then in formation of the court, first, the king's writ, the creative, constitutive fact, without which the court would have no existence; second, the justice or justices, who represent the king, "in meo loco," and who preside over and direct the action of the court. These two points together determine not merely the existence but the character of the court. They make it a king's court, differing from a great curia only in numbers and in the absence of the king. Its judgment is equivalent to a judgment of the great curia and is so accepted and pro-

[51] See above at note 38.

[52] See above at note 9.

claimed by the king. Third, there is present a specifically summoned baronial element, also a distinguishing mark of the court and emphasizing its royal character, but apparently not a necessity; and fourth, as the local foundation of the court, that which brings the local into contact with the royal, is the county court, undoubtedly the old Saxon shire court. The purpose for which this court is summoned is, however, not to constitute the court. A local curia regis could unquestionably be constituted for the same purpose without its presence. It is needed to bring the local evidence and the local testimony to bear upon the case in the simplest and most natural way. The institution is essentially Norman in its constitution and in its place in government as a whole, that is, it belongs to the central, not to the local government. These cases should, therefore, not be cited as meetings of the original Saxon shire court, though they are evidence of its continued existence, but of this there is of course abundant other evidence.

As to procedure but little can be said, and that little of a general character. We have here no definite information of anything except the oath, witness proof and the jury or inquisition. The last is Norman, the second in the case most fully given shows Norman characteristics. This is to be said of procedure, however, that all the methods of trial in use in Saxon England, compurgation, witness proof, charter proof, the ordeal, were familiar to the Normans in their own courts in addition to battle and long continued to be.[53] Procedure in local courts is distinctly one of those cases where Norman and English

[53] This statement hardly needs proof, but on the ordeal of the hot iron, see Davis, *Regesta*, no. 146a (Appendix, no. xvi), dated 5 September, 1082. For a case of its use in the time of William I, in what was probably the great curia of the duchy, see Orderic Vitalis, II, 433. See above note 13.

methods were so closely alike that they easily and imperceptibly ran together into one, and such slight innovations as the Normans may have made could hardly have seemed significant. Even battle which appears to have been unpopular was not out of harmony with Saxon methods. The king's local court and the jury were more decided innovations, but neither was revolutionary and both were adjusted easily to the older local organizations of justice.

CHAPTER IV

THE AGE OF HENRY I

During the first half of the twelfth century no change occurred in councils or curia which appears to be anything more than the natural growth which would take place under the pressure of increasing business. The small council comes into sight more clearly in the form of the exchequer, exercising an administrative and financial function in what seem to be separate sessions of the council held for this purpose, but they are not sessions from which other business of the council was excluded.[1] The king's local curia under a specially commissioned *missus*, or *missi*, appears to be developing into a regular and systematized judicial institution, but in institutional character it is not different from the courts of *missi* under William I. Some faint indications in the general atmosphere of the sources, really perhaps only the relative frequency of cases, lead us to suspect that a change in the emphasis placed upon council functions is beginning like that which is apparent in the first half of the thirteenth century.[2] For the time being at least, the function of advising upon questions of governmental policy and the function of trying suit at law as a court seem to be coming into greater prominence than before. But the change, if there really is a change, can hardly be called permanent. These are the

[1] See below, Chapter VIII at notes 47 and following. Cf. Luchaire, *Manuel*, pp. 500-502. There is always danger that the emergence of an activity or of a function for the first time in the sources as we have them may be taken as evidence of a new beginning. It is clearly not adequate proof.

[2] See below, Chapter X at note 32.

only lines of development during this second period which are promising enough to lead us to expect institutional change, and there is nothing that can be found in them beyond the signs of natural growth.

In regard to the topics chiefly discussed in Chapter I, the composition of the great council and its legislative activity, much the same thing is to be said. With the exception of one point concerning composition, no information is given us which adds to or changes what we learn from the first period. There is evidence of greater activity.[3] The reign of Henry I is a period of almost identical length with the first two Norman reigns but the number of meetings of the great council in it of which we have information is considerably larger, and the same thing is true of the number of meetings which we can be confident are those of the small council, at least when we include its judicial business. The legislative result, however, is not

[3] See note A at the end of the chapter. The appearance of greater activity does not seem to be entirely due to the greater abundance and fullness of the original sources from which we obtain information, though it is perhaps in part. It should be noted that there is no evidence that the judicial development of the reign was brought about by legislation as it was under Henry II. Nor is there any indication that the composition or procedure of the council was varied at all to suit different functions. Both forms of the council passed from one kind of business to another in the same session with no apparent consciousness that any change of significance had been made. The following instances may be cited of sessions in which a variety of business was done, the first in Normandy. Mid October, 1106, Orderic Vitalis, IV, 233-234. Whitsuntide, 1108, Eadmer, *Hist. Nov.*, pp. 193-194; *Gloucester Cartulary*, I, 13-14. 13 June, 1109, *A. S. Chron.*, II, 210; Eadmer, p. 207. 2 February, 1123, *A. S. Chron.*, II, 217-219. 25 December, 1126, to January, 1127, see Farrer, *Itinerary Henry I*, in *E.H.R.*, XXXIV, p. 539 and references there. Interesting examples from the reign of Henry II may be found in *Gesta Regis Henrici*, I, 4-6, 132-136, and 144-156. The identity of the curia in all functions is also true of France. "Si le Parlement de Paris se trouva mêlé souvent à des affaires extrajudiciaires de l'ordre diplomatique, législatif ou politique, c'est que les rois n'avaient jamais fait *formellement* la distinction de leur *Curia* judiciaire et de leur *Curia* générale." Langlois, *Revue Historique*, XLII, 91.

great. The settlement after the Conquest created an unusual number of problems which had to be solved and, when they were once disposed of, feudal society returned to its normal state in which new law was made by the natural evolution of custom rather than by conscious enactment. In this way much new law was made in the second period which will be considered in its proper place,[4] and it will also be seen in this chapter, I think, that the legislation of the time was a trifle more important than sometimes has been thought.

In the matter of composition there is a rather more frequent use of the phrases like "clero et populo" which have already been noticed but in no connection which gives them a new significance or makes necessary any revision of what has been said above.[5] The increased fre-

4 See below, Chapter V.

5 In the twelfth century and especially in the second half of it, the term "sapientes" for members of the council is used more frequently than before. This has been considered by some to imply a reminiscence of the use of "witan" in Saxon times. In the legal writings of Henry I's day there are some cases where it is used as a translation of witan, but the term is so natural a one to use to designate members of the council and the usage on the continent both in meaning and in frequency of occurrence is so closely parallel to that in English writers, that it ought not to be held to denote any general tradition from the Anglo-Saxon period. See Round, *Peerage and Pedigree,* I, 332, commenting on Freeman, *Norman Conquest,* Am. ed., V, 276, 587, and contrariwise Liebermann, *National Assembly,* p. 75. There seems to have been something like a common fashion in language, words, phrases, and terms, technical and colloquial, between the writers of England and France during these centuries. It is therefore not surprising when we notice an increase in the use of such terms as "sapientes" and of phrases which indicate the presence of the minor elements in the councils, like "cleri et populi," in the English sources from about the middle of the twelfth century on, to find the same increased frequency in the French sources also. See Froideraux, *De Regiis Conciliis,* Cap. X. Both Freeman and Liebermann cite the sources of Henry II's time as if they were of the same value in this connection as those of Henry I's reign, which is hardly the case. The use of the word "sapientes" in c. 80 of the *Usatici Barchinone* towards the close of the eleventh century, cited above in note A at the end of Chapter I, is interesting. The passage is stating the composition of the court of one

quency is not evidence that an objective fact is occurring more often than before, but that the writers are using more regularly a formal vocabulary which is not, however, the normal vocabulary of English institutions. The one exceptional fact which does throw some light on the institutional situation is the share attributed by the chroniclers to the Londoners in the acceptance of Stephen as king in December, 1135, and in his deposition in April, 1141.

What occurred at Stephen's accession to the throne need occupy us only briefly. Several writers of the twelfth century in narrating the event use the word "electus," and we are strongly tempted to put into the meaning of that word the sense which it has today and to suppose that some kind of formal act is described.[6] There is, however, not the slightest evidence of the exercise of

who was strictly speaking a mesne lord. Such a use is also found in *Chron. Abingdon*, I, 128, 184.

I do not think that the peculiar reference to the share of the generality of his subjects in a great council decision which is contained in Stephen's charter granting the bishopric of Bath to Robert of Lewes (Rymer, *Foedera*, I, 16; Madox, *Exchequer*, I, 13, note *s*) has been noticed. He says he has granted the bishopric to Robert "canonica prius electione praecedente et communi vestro consilio voto et favore prosequente." "Vestro" refers back to the address at the beginning of the charter which is: "Stephanus Rex Anglorum, archiepiscopis, episcopis, abbatibus, comitibus, vicecomitibus, baronibus, et omnibus fidelibus suis per totam Angliam constitutis, salutem." This is the Easter meeting of 1136 which undoubtedly was continued in the Oxford meeting at which the king's second "charter of liberties," the charter to the church, was granted. In that he says that he has been "electus . . . assensu cleri et populi." No specific significance is to be attached to either expression. Probably the conjunction was produced in the Bath charter by pure carelessness. Certainly there was at that time no theory of representation by which "omnes fideles" could be considered to be constructively present in the council. See Round, *Geoffrey de Mandeville*, pp. 16-24.

[6] Gervase of Canterbury (R.S.), I, 94; *Gesta Stephani*, *Chronicles of Stephen, Henry II, and Richard I* (R.S.), III, 5; Stephen's second charter, Stubbs, *S.C.*, p. 143. See Freeman, *Norm. Conq.*, V, App. DD; Stubbs, I, 345; Round, *Geoffrey de Mand.*, pp. 2-6.

anything which can be called a constitutional function nor of any action which is made to conform to a traditional and established standard. No great council met until just after Stephen's consecration and the evidence seems clear that only a few barons had part in the decision by which he was made king.[7] The accounts of what took place, written then or not long afterwards, are of a kind which would certainly have indicated the presence of a strong representation of the baronage if there had been one. The part of the Londoners is made clear and that of the church, but nothing is said of the share of the baronage. Indeed the unusual emphasis upon London's share seems to prove that the barons did not play their ordinary part on this occasion. They seem plainly to be described as accepting an accomplished fact. The "audacious"[8] claim of the Londoners, "Id quoque sui esse juris, suique specialiter privilegii, ut si rex ipsorum quoquomodo obiret, alius suo proviso in regnum substituendus e vestigio succederet,"[9] may be dismissed as having no more foundation in fact than the similar claim for the clergy advanced by Henry of Winchester. "Ventilata est hesterno die causa secreto coram majori parte cleri Angliae, ad cujus jus potissimum spectat principem eligere simulque ordinare."[10] No men and no body of men had in the modern sense a constitutional right of election, as is shown clearly by what happens at the time of every undisputed succession, as then no evidence of election is to be found. When the succession is disputed, somebody must decide among the candidates, and who it is that makes the decision is determined by who may happen to be present at the spot and moment when the decision can

[7] Hugh Bigod is the only one assigned by name a prominent part.

[8] Round, *Geoffrey de Mandeville*, p. 2, note 3.

[9] *Gesta Stephani*, p. 5.

[10] William of Malmesbury, *Gesta Regum*, II, 576.

be made. In 1100 it was the barons who were present at Winchester. In 1135 it was undoubtedly the Londoners[11] and the church, which acted mainly through Stephen's brother Henry, with a few barons who were present. In the case of John it was done by careful preparation and a show of military force in the absence of any effective opposition. Once the fact was accomplished, it was itself sufficient to bring in the absent and the doubtful.

We may say then of the events of Stephen's accession that they give us no information about either composition or functions of the great council. From the events of April, 1141, however, we learn indirectly a fact of considerable importance. No great council it is true was held at that time. Stephen's brother Henry, bishop of Winchester and papal legate, who had been greatly outraged by Stephen's arrest of the bishops at Oxford and who recognized the opportunity offered by the severe defeat of Stephen at Lincoln, which had left him a prisoner in the hands of Matilda's party, called together a council of the English church. This has sometimes been spoken of as if it were a great council,[12] but it can be considered no more than a great ecclesiastical assembly or one of the whole kingdom, if it was even that. It certainly was not a great council of the realm and, as an ecclesiastical assembly, was not imposing enough to attract the notice of more than one chronicler. Bishop Henry apparently had

[11] Freeman, *Norman Conquest,* V, App., Note DD, compares the position of the Londoners on this occasion to their share in the "irregular body by which William of Orange was first called upon to undertake the provisional administration of the government" at the end of December, 1688, and, so far as constitutional position is concerned, the comparison seems exact.

[12] Liebermann, *National Assembly,* p. 87, and cf. p. 80. Stubbs, I, 356, says of the bishop that as legate he "held a great council at Winchester in April, and in it the empress was solemnly chosen as lady of England." He may mean no more than a large council of the church.

entire control of its proceedings and determinations.[13] He divided the members into three groups according to their ecclesiastical rank and consulted with each separately, one guesses in order to make sure of his control and of getting the answer upon which he was determined.

On 8 April, the second day of the council, in a speech which the legate made to the whole assembly, occurs the statement which is of special interest.[14] He says that he has invited the Londoners by his messengers to meet with the council and that he expects them immediately. "Londonienses," he says, "qui sunt quasi optimates, pro magnitudine civitatis, in Angliae"; and the next day in refusing their request for the release of Stephen, he speaks of them as "Londonienses qui praecipui habebantur in Anglia sicut proceres." It is evident that the bishop recognizes that his act in sending for the Londoners is extraordinary and in need of explanation and defence. His defence is that they occupy a place in England of such importance that they may be considered "quasi optimates," "sicut proceres," using two of the common terms for the members of the great council but making it clear that they are "quasi" and "sicut," not really "optimates" or "proceres." The conclusion is unavoidable that the Londoners as such had no standing in the great council.[15] The bishop would have asserted that if it had been possible to do so. Its members are "optimates" and "proceres," which the Londoners are not; they are "quasi," not members by regular and expected practice like the "proceres." Their position in the country, however, from the greatness of their city is such that their wishes are of weight and should be considered. This I believe to be an

13 This fact is made quite clear by William of Malmesbury who was present. II, 574-577.

14 W. Malm., II, 576.

15 Otherwise Liebermann, as above, note 12.

exact statement of the constitutional place of London through the whole of its history. The city as such, the citizens as such, had no place in the great council; they had no special right in the choice of a king; but their influence was a very essential factor in making up the national decision upon any difficult question.

In the use of names for the councils there is some slight indication of a change which may be important and at least deserves notice. In no case of which the record or account is clearly of the first two reigns was any name or descriptive term used which indicates a conscious distinction between the great and the small council. Soon after the opening of the twelfth century descriptive terms begin to be used which seem to imply that men have begun to notice a distinction of size or completeness, and their use slowly increases in frequency. "Magnum placitum" or "magnum concilium" is, until it becomes technical, too purely descriptive and indefinite a term to be taken to indicate a conscious comparison.[16] It may mean only that a particular meeting was a large one whether a great council technically or a reinforced small council. "Universale concilium," "generale concilium," though undoubtedly borrowed from the vocabulary of the church, are more definite and are not likely to have been used without a sense of comparison. Their use, however, can hardly be placed before the middle of the reign of Henry I. The earliest forms of expression which seem to imply that a distinction is in the mind of the writer are such as "omnes regni primores," "tota nobilitas regni," "conventus omnium episcoporum, abbatum, et procerum regni," with which occur such qualified phrases as

[16] Indeed all the expressions by which the assembly was characterized by contemporaries, and even those used in formal records, retain a certain degree of vagueness throughout the period, that is, they are to a great extent consciously descriptive and not technical.

"ferme totius regni nobilitas," "presente magno procerum conventus," implying a consciousness that the assembly was not universal. Apparently the earliest use of phrases of this kind is to be found in Eadmer in accounts of meetings held in the preceding period but not written until a few years after 1100.[17] From the date of his writings on their use becomes increasingly common. The evidence from these phrases that contemporaries were beginning to be conscious of a fact about the councils not before observed is slight and must not be pressed to a dogmatic conclusion, but it is worth noting, and it may at least be said that the beginning of a conscious distinction, so far as our evidence shows, does not go back of the first decade of Henry's reign.

Any study of the various forms of the council must begin with a clear recognition of the two extremes: first, the formally summoned great council intended to include all who owed court service as tenants-in-chief[18] and there-

[17] Henry I in his coronation charter of 1100 says that he has been crowned "communi consilio baronum totius regni Angliae" (Stubbs, *S.C.*, p. 117), but there was no great council held to which he can refer. Early in the reign of William I the pope directed that the question of the primacy between Canterbury and York should be decided "tocius regni episcoporum et abbatum testimonio et judicio" (above, Chapter I, note B), but here again there is no reference to a great council, though the origin of such phrases may be indicated. The *Latin Acts of Lanfranc,* which call an ecclesiastical synod "generale concilium" and the Penenden Heath assembly "magnum placitum" (Plummer, *Two Chronicles,* I, 288, 289), may have been written before the close of the eleventh century but the language is clerical. See above, Chapter III, at note 17.

[18] The difference between an assembly to which all the magnates and one to which only a part had been summoned was sometimes noted in the thirteenth century. In December, 1284, Edward I returning from Wales held his Christmas court at Bristol. "Quo expleto, convocatis quibusdam de magnatibus, singulare non generale tenuit parliamentum." *Ann. Osney.* Or as it was put by Wykes: "celebratisque solemniis et habito ibidem cum quibusdam regni sui magnatibus non universali seu generali sed tanquam particulari et speciali parliamento . . . secessit Londoniam." Both in *Annales Monastici* (R.S.), IV, 300. Cited Stubbs, 1875, II, 117, note 4. The only

fore a "concilium universale"; and second, the purely administrative small council composed of those administrative officers only who were concerned with the business of the particular session and therefore containing no members specially summoned for the occasion or attending as members on their own initiative. An example of this extreme form would be the council at the exchequer for exchequer business only. Such a session might conceivably contain others but would be complete without them. Between these two extremes, which theoretically are clearly marked, there may be innumerable intermediate forms, according as the smallest body is reinforced by other persons summoned for some special or general reason or who attend because they are with the king when the meeting is held or because they have business of their own which they wish to bring before the council. If we are to distinguish between these various forms as the men of the Norman and early Angevin ages distinguished between them, we must recognize a difference of size only. There are numerous indications that contemporaries did recognize differences of size but none that they felt any distinction in function or field of action or competence or power. That is, the men of that time recognized only one body. They saw that it was not always composed of the same men nor of the same number of men and they noted the fact, but always they noted it incidentally as a fact of no great importance. Institutionally they knew of only one body, always the same in competence whatever its external form.

If we attempt for our own convenience to set up a technical distinction between great councils and small councils, where contemporaries recognized none, we meet a

difference noted, however, is one of size. On the general question of the difference between the two forms of the council, see *Origin*, Chapter IV, note B, pp. 196-198.

practical difficulty at once. No institutional difference existed. We must make a technical distinction out of a difference which is superficial, which does not touch the nature itself of the council. I think we are narrowed down to saying that the only great councils which we can positively affirm to be such are those which can be described as above, that is, those which are intended to include all tenants-in-chief who owe court service and are therefore intended to be universal.[19] In practice this distinction cannot be based upon the summons to individual barons because, when we reach a date when this point can be tested, we find that to councils which are plainly great councils the same individual barons are sometimes summoned and sometimes not. That a baron had been summoned to one great council did not imply that he would be to the next. I

[19] No doubt others were in practice great councils though we may be able to find no exact test by which to mark them as such. Stubbs, I, 605 ff., distinguishes, in addition to the small council, three kinds or grades of great councils according as they are composed of the magnates only, of all tenants-in-chief, or of all freemen. His instances of the last are the assembly at Salisbury for the general oath of allegiance in 1086 and the assembly of 1116 for the homage of all tenants to William, son of Henry I. Bigelow, *Procedure,* p. 21, gives a series of tests for distinguishing between the great and small councils, calling the latter ''the King's Court as distinguished from the Witenagemot.'' He regards the witenagemot as including the Norman great council. It should be noted that a general summons to all tenants-in-chief, in the sense of Magna Carta, c. 14, would apply to those only from whom service in the king's court was due by the terms of their tenure. See note A at the end of Chapter X. Of the beginning of the fourteenth century Maitland says, referring to Stubbs, sec. 230, ''As yet any meeting of the king's council that has been solemnly summoned for general business seems to be a parliament.'' *Memoranda de Parliamento* (R.S.), p. lxvii. Professor Baldwin, stating that ''only for purposes of taxation, according to Magna Carta, art. 14, was it stated that all the barons should be summoned and how they should be summoned,'' adds: ''For other functions there was no standard of size, how large the council should be, or as to formality, in what manner it should be assembled. Often it was small, but from its narrowest circle it expanded to its widest through every degree of dimensions.'' A. H. R., XX, 332-333. Whatever one may think of the first sentence quoted, the second is surely correct and well put.

have no doubt that instances existed in which, tested by the personal summonses to barons, council meetings which were not intended to be universal did not differ from those which were intended to be. One thing only can prove beyond a doubt the intention to hold a "concilium universale"—the general summons to all tenants-in-chief of the counties through the sheriffs.[20] Such a summons must necessarily include all barons whose individual summonses to earlier great councils were not renewed in the given case. There is no reason to suppose that practice in regard to the personal summons in the twelfth century differed from that in the thirteenth.

A distinction between two organized bodies which is based on no functional difference but merely upon size, or completeness of attendance, may be said to be a distinction of no practical value. In a certain sense that is true for the first Anglo-Norman century at least. It looks to the future as the germ of a differentiation which becomes real in the thirteenth century only in the rise of an official council. Still it is highly probable that, if there was no difference of function, there was from the beginning in practice a difference of fields. The humdrum, everyday details of government and administration were no doubt exclusively supervised by the small council in the narrow sense, unreinforced or reinforced more by accident than intention by barons happening to be with the king. If a question of difficulty or of especial importance had to be considered, others were summoned to act with

[20] By this I do not mean that other meetings were not to all intents and purposes great councils and used to do a great council's business. What I mean is that we cannot now be certain that they were intended to be, and were regarded by contemporaries as being great councils. There is in fact sufficient precedent from 1066 on for meetings in which only a part of the great council do the business of the whole to justify anything in the way of partial assemblies in the time of Edward I. And also, it may be added, of meetings uniting diverse, and some non-feudal, elements.

the group which was doing the daily business, their number depending on the importance of the question and the convenience of time and place, up to what would be to all practical intents a great council, though not one universally summoned. It is impossible to resist the impression that some councils to which there had been a partial summons only were employed as great councils, and there was no reason why they should not be, since great and small were alike in function though we may be able to find no test which allows us to distinguish with certainty between them and reinforced small councils. The regularly summoned great council would have for its field the most important trials and those questions which were of national importance, though it undoubtedly settled others also. It is, however, of far greater value historically to insist upon the unity of function of the council in all its forms than upon any distinction between them, apparent or latent, because the process of differentiation, which begins so soon after the reign of Henry I, is a labyrinthine tangle to one who is not alive to this unity and to all that it logically implies.

While it seems to me clear that the general summons through the sheriff is the only test by which we may determine with certainty that any particular meeting was intended to be technically a great council, the exceedingly scanty information which we have through all the early generations about the general summons makes it a test which for these centuries is of no practical value. We must use other tests and be content that our conclusions are therefore only probable. If an assembly at the time of one of the three chief religious festivals,[21] when the

21 Great councils were not held at every occurrence of the chief festivals. See Farrer, *Itinerary,* pp. 339, 362, 363, 371. The difference in incidence between a summons of the *servitium debitum* and a summons to a great council, made very near to each other, may be seen in the summonses of February, 1177. *Gesta Regis Henrici,* I, 138-139.

great social court met, does business which it belongs to the council to do, I have believed that it could be called a great council with a high degree of probability. When at other dates a council is described as *generale* or *universale* or is said to bring together the barons or "proceres" "totius regni," I have considered the probability, though less than under the conditions just stated, sufficient to justify calling it a great council. On these grounds and neglecting councils held in Normandy, we may reckon 27 great councils held during Henry's reign.[22] In view of the fact that the sources which have survived to us from which we may expect to obtain evidence of great council meetings are not very numerous, this is a notable number and may be added to the judicial and administrative facts which we know to support our judgment of the extraordinary governmental activity of the reign—extraordinary when we consider the date and the character of feudal government in other countries of the time. If we remember that Henry I had no model to follow, as his more conspicuous grandson had, and that he was laying in the dark the foundations of a strong national government with only the exceedingly simple feudal machinery and a few undeveloped survivals from the Carolingian monarchy to work with,[23] we can only wonder at the perma-

[22] See note A at the end of the chapter.

[23] I use the term Carolingian because these institutions had then reached their highest point of development in the Frankish kingdom and show most completely their relationship to the institutions brought into England by the Normans. They go back of course for their origins into Merovingian, and very likely into Roman, times. The most interesting account of them as they existed under the Carolingian monarchy is to be found in Fustel de Coulanges, *Les Transformations de la Royauté*, Livre III, Chaps. VI, VIII, and IX. M. Fustel's peculiar views affect the account in these chapters scarcely at all, and many suggestions will be found in them of the sources from which Norman institutions came. On the development of the administrative system, see "The Sheriffs and the Administrative System of Henry I" by Professor W. A. Morris, *E.H.R.* XXXVII, 161-172; Tout, *Administrative History*, I, 76-92.

nent improvements which he introduced into practical government and conclude that our admiration of his political genius is well founded.[24]

I am convinced we have a right to say that the small council must have been in practically constant session. It must have been in practice, though it is not yet so called, a perpetual or continual council. It is hardly possible that the government could have been carried on without the constant presence with the king of a small nucleus of permanent councillors[25] who could be called upon at any moment for the advice or decision of the curia regis. Naturally the attention of contemporary chroniclers and of later historians has been attracted most by the council as national assembly, that is, as the great council, composed of the great men of church and state from the

24 Apparently William Rufus was seeking the same result as Henry, a strong central power, constitutional in character and vested in the king, but he was doing it with much less skill and, so far as we can now tell, with nothing to rely upon except feudal principles pushed to an extreme. It is not an unwarranted guess that Henry profited decidedly by a study of his brother's attempt. He certainly relied greatly on his development of the Carolingian survivals and he did obtain the feudal results which his brother had sought for and which he had himself promised in his coronation charter not to continue.

25 Professor Liebermann, *National Assembly*, pp. 17-18, uses the same fact from which to infer the existence of the small council in the Anglo-Saxon state, and it undoubtedly suggests that conclusion. Standing alone, however, it seems to me hardly sufficient proof. See above, Introduction, at note 13. All evidence which tends to show the existence of the exchequer in the eleventh century is necessarily evidence for the existence of the small council and, with less certainty perhaps but with great probability, evidence which reveals the traces of definite financial organization, that is, which goes to show that the management of the finances of the kingdom, or of the duchy of Normandy, was according to a considered plan. Unhappily the evidence, as we now have it, does nothing more than suggest. It is rather stronger for the early financial organization than for the early existence of the exchequer. See Haskins, *Institutions*, pp. 39-45, 84, 88-89, 175-176; Tout, *Administrative History*, I, 13, 93 ff.; Poole, *The Exchequer in the Twelfth Century*, especially pp. 42-69; Round, "The Origin of the Exchequer," in *The Commune of London*, pp. 62-96.

whole country. But considered as the instrument of general government, the council was something more than national assembly or great council. An assembly which brought together at a single meeting place all the men of a given rank from the whole kingdom could manifestly be held only a few times in the course of a year. The difficulties of travel and the pressure of local interests and duties would not permit of more than that. But the business of government had to be carried on in the intervals; ordinary administrative operations, general and local, had to be supervised; financial business especially was continuous; questions of policy were constantly arising whose decision could not be deferred; some suits at law even might press for immediate hearing and more or less legal business of other sorts, grants, permissions and confirmations, had to be determined. In those days, as will be noted later, much business which was really legislative was comprised under one or the other of these heads. There must be in continuous existence, unbroken by the intervals between the meetings of the national assembly, some institution possessing the powers and performing the functions of the great council. Otherwise the general government, as yet undifferentiated into different institutions for different functions, would tend to break into pieces and anarchy to prevail.

We are shut up, however, almost entirely to inference for our knowledge of the small council and its activities, but there are some things of a negative sort that can be said about it and some fewer of a positive sort. There were as yet no councillors who can be distinguished as technically members of the council while others of the court are not.[26] No one was yet appointed to the council

[26] Florence of Worcester, II, 57, under date of 1107, mentions the death of seven prelates and barons and calls them "regis consiliatores." "Regii consiliarii" are referred to in *Chron. Mon. de Bello*, p. 50 (Bigelow, *Placita*,

as to a differentiated office. There was no councillor's oath to be taken as creating a special responsibility. At least no trace of any of these things is to be found during this period. So far as we can see the sole ground of special obligation on which the performance of this duty could be required, apart from the general bond of allegiance, which was made use of only rarely, was the tenant-in-chief's obligation of court service. Officials of the king's household had a peculiar duty in respect to certain administrative details, enforced probably by a special oath of fealty as a member of the household,[27] but this position gave them no peculiar standing or right in the council. Any tenant-in-chief might be asked to attend and would be then upon the same footing in the council as chancellor or treasurer. Certain officials were, it is true, coming to be recognized as having special duties and special functions to be performed in certain lines of government activity, but there is no evidence that they possessed as yet

p. 123), and in 1178 the *servitium debitum,* summoned to Winchester for service abroad, does the business of a council and is called ''consiliarii regis.'' *Gesta Regis Henrici,* I, 178. Cited Stubbs, I, 606, note 1.

27 See above, Chapter I, note 12. There is room to doubt whether contemporaries, when they were thinking specifically of the composition of the great council, thought of the household officers as an element in it to be distinguished from the baronial element. None of the formal statements contains any mention of them, though they are mentioned in informal enumerations of classes present. See above, Chapter II, notes 10 and 11. Magna Carta c. 14 is a full statement of the composition of the great council for one of the most important of its functions. It contains no mention of household officers. The reference by Henry I to the aid ''quod barones mihi dederunt'' (*Chron. Abingd.,* II, 113) shows that early in the twelfth century the same function was performed in the same way. Both passages show that a purely feudal assembly was regarded as the normal assembly, not in this case for a trial, but for one of the acts of a legislative body which is in all states considered of the highest importance. The grant then made was no doubt a grant by a single class, or estate, but it was by the estate which at the moment was the only one having any share, however limited that may have been, in the conduct of public affairs. See Professor A. F. Pollard in *History,* III, 162-164.

peculiar rights of membership. The idea of membership as office had not yet arisen.

In records and chronicles the ordinary everyday business of the council would leave no impression. It is only by what seems like accident or when something unusual happens in the course of its business that we can find traces of its action, or when its business is of a sort that may need to be referred to in the future and therefore is put into a permanent record or a chronicle account. A permanent record is naturally most often desired of the judicial action of the council, and it is in this line of its business that we find the evidences of its meetings most numerous.[28] It is impossible to pretend that a list of the cases coming before the small council as a court of law during the reign and remaining to us in surviving record has been made complete, but one can be made which will give some idea of the amount of this kind of business which it had to transact. I have noticed the undermentioned cases, including a few in Normandy.[29]

In deciding what court is trying a case of which we have a record, it is to be noted that at this time the only curia regis trying cases apart from the council was the court of the king's commissioner, either of the *missus* or of the sheriff specially commissioned for the case. There was as yet no bench of judges acting as a central court. The bench set up in 1178 was plainly a new creation. Com-

[28] It will be understood that this chapter, and indeed this whole book, proceeds upon the supposition that curia regis when acting as a court of law and when acting in any other capacity, are identical bodies. There is, I believe, no evidence to show that any difference in composition, organization, or procedure was made to suit different functions. All the evidence that can be found goes to show that the council or the curia regis was in all cases one and the same. In the thirteenth century that evidence is overwhelming, and there is no trace of any change in this respect in the interval. See above, note 3.

[29] See note A at the end of the chapter.

mon pleas cases were tried in the exchequer but it was clearly the council that was acting, not a separate court.[30] If the record indicates that the case was tried before a group of judges, barons, magnates, *proceres,* or what not, not *missi*, it may safely be called a council case. There was no other group or bench of justices trying cases in Henry's reign.[31]

There are a number of instances of advice offered the king by the council during this period, of which perhaps the most interesting is that recorded by Henry of Huntingdon, p. 252, of the great council of 8 September, 1131, concerning the return of Matilda to Geoffrey of Anjou, but they present no unusual features, and this function of the council has been sufficiently illustrated. Perhaps Eadmer's idea of the function of the council should be noticed:[32] "In sequenti autem mense Augusto, cum de statu regni acturus rex episcopos, abbates et quosque regni proceres in unum praecepti sui sanctione egisset et dispositis iis quae adunationis illorum causae fuerant . . . Anselmus . . . rogavit regem . . ."; and again, "Admirati ergo episcopi, abbates et nobiles quique Lundoniae adunati sunt, super his et quibusdam aliis, praesente regina, communi consilio tractaturi." *Tractare* becomes in time almost a technical word in formal summonses, denoting the business to be done by the council,[33] but we cannot say that it was so in this period.

30 See below, Chapter VIII, notes 47-49.

31 Of course neither "bench" nor "justices" in a technical sense can properly be applied to the council in the twelfth century. I use these terms as the simplest way to make the meaning clear.

32 *Hist. Nov.*, pp. 80 and 239 respectively. Cf. Davis, *Regesta,* no. 77 (Orderic Vitalis, V, 158); *ibid.*, IV, 329.

33 Early instances of the use of the word in summonses, or in what seem to be quotations from them, are: *Gesta Regis Henrici,* I, 160 (1177); Ralph de Diceto (R.S.), II, 98 (1191); *Ann. S. Edmundi,* in Liebermann, *Anglo-Normannische Geschichtsquellen,* p. 143 (1204). Later instances in summonses given in Stubbs, *Select Charters.*

Of the legislation of Henry I there are traces enough remaining to lead us to suspect a considerably greater activity than we can prove.[34] Especially interesting, as asserting the claim of the council to a share in legislation, is the evidence that King Henry by an *edictum* had modified the ancient law of wreck to the disadvantage of those who had profited by it. The question was brought before the council in the next reign by an accusation that the abbot of Battle had broken this new law. The abbot's defence was that the king could make new law by edict which would be binding during his lifetime but not beyond "except by the common consent of the barons of the kingdom."[35] The council refused a post-mortem sanction of the law and judged the plea sufficient. Henry's legislation against counterfeiters and false money is equally interesting in another way. His earliest legislation on the subject, made known to us in a single copy of the writ[36] sent to the counties, of the date of Christmas day 1100, seemed so clearly to assign the duty of enforcing the law to the royal authority that the fears of some at least of the holders of liberties were excited. Gerard, archbishop of York, obtained shortly from the king a charter to protect his court from interference and providing that what

34 Liebermann, *Ueber Leges Henrici,* p. 22.

35 He says the king is able "pro libitu antiqua patriae jura mutare in diebus suis . . . sed non nisi communi baronum regni consensu in posterum rata fore." *Chron. Mon. de Bello,* p. 66 (Bigelow, *Placita,* p. 145); Liebermann, *ibid.,* p. 22, note 1, citing Gerald Cambr., VIII, 119 and III, 136; *E.H.R.,* XXIX, 434. The illustration of the effect of legislation to modify the existing common or customary law should be noticed. Henry makes the new law "hanc abhorrens consuetudinem." The council by their judgment in favor of the abbot, deciding that the ordinance was not binding after Henry's death, virtually decided that it was binding during his lifetime, and also by plain inference that, if it had been regularly made by the legislative body, the great council, it would have been permanently binding.

36 Rymer, *Foedera,* I, 12; Liebermann, I, 523. On the date see Liebermann III, 299; *E.H.R.,* XXVIII, 426.

the law required should be done by his own justice though he must act according to the statue.[37] In 1108 this legislation seems to have been practically repeated with an addition against thieves and robbers, if that had not been a part of the original legislation, and in 1125 there was another reform of the currency.[38] Drastic and successful reforms in the conduct of the members of the royal court towards the common people checked serious abuses existing for some time and are likely to have been adopted early in the reign.[39] The *Constitutio domus regis,* what-

[37] Farrer, *Early Yorkshire Charters,* 1914, I, 31. This charter was offered in pleadings in *quo warranto* proceedings against the archbishop in 8 Edward I. *Placita de Quo Warranto,* p. 198, where in the address the initial O. of the sheriff of Yorkshire is wrongly extended Odo instead of Osbert. An exemplification of this *quo warranto* record was granted the then archbishop in 12 Edward III and the record was copied on the patent roll of that year. *Calendar of Patent Rolls, 1338-1340,* p. 166. It will be noticed that in this charter the legislation is said to concern ''placita latronum'' as well as of makers of false money, and that in the writ itself there is no reference to robbers. In this respect the charter seems to refer more exactly to the legislation of 1108 (Flor. Worc., II, p. 57) and that date is given it by Professor Haskins. *Norman Institutions,* p. 86, note 9. The reference can hardly be to that legislation, however, because the archbishop would then have had no opportunity to become aware of the effect of the new law and to secure the charter protecting his courts. The legislation of 1108 was adopted at the Easter meeting of the great council, 5 April, and archbishop Gerard died on 21 May while on his way to attend the council of London. Farrer thinks this charter to the archbishop may refer to the provision in regard to false money in Henry's coronation charter, but the connection with the writ of Christmas, 1100, is too specific to admit of question. Farrer dates the charter between Gerard's becoming archbishop and 18 April, 1102, but see his *Itinerary,* of Henry I, 1919, no. 208, where it is dated 1108.

[38] *Anglo-Saxon Chron.,* II, 221; Flor. Worc., II, 79; *Dialogus de Scaccario,* Oxford ed., p. 38.

[39] Eadmer (*Hist. Nov.,* pp. 192-194) prefaces his account of the legislation against false coiners of 1108 and of the acts of the council of London of the same year with an account of the legislation against the excesses of the courtiers, as if it were of the same date, and begins the paragraph ''inter ista,'' as if he recalled a multiplicity of acts. There is a presumption, though the conclusion is not a necessary one, that there was legislation on the subject at least before the death of Anselm, for Eadmer says categori-

ever its date may be, was probably based on regulations for the organization and compensation of the members of the royal household fixed by the king.[40] Other legislative reforms are attributed to Henry of the times and circumstances of which we know little or nothing: changes in the form and payment of the county farms and in the assaying of money at the exchequer, this last said to be a reform of Roger of Salisbury's, "habito super hoc ipso regis consilio constitutum est";[41] legislation about measures,[42] to substitute the liability of the hundred for the murder fine in place of that of the vill,[43] and perhaps there should be added the feudal and forest reforms of the coronation charter.[44] The important legislation in Normandy in regard to the Truce of God[45] does not seem to have been repeated in England.[46]

Upon the topics discussed in this chapter nothing further is to be noted from the reign of Stephen. The chief advance of that period concerns formal law, mainly procedure, and will be considered elsewhere.

cally that it was adopted "per consilium Anselmi et procerum regni." See Haskins, *Norman Institutions*, p. 114. There may have been legislation on the subject at more than one time and at a different time still upon the *Constitutio domus regis.* William of Malmesbury, *Gesta Regum,* II, 476, 487, also brings together the legislation on coiners and courtiers in a description of the vigor of Henry's government, but he wrote a good deal of his history with Eadmer before him and he may have got the impression from him.

40 Haskins, *Norman Institutions*, pp. 114 ff.; Poole, *The Exchequer in the Twelfth Century,* pp. 94 ff.; Round, *The King's Serjeants and Officers of State,* pp. 54 ff.; Tout, *Administrative History,* I, 83-86.

41 *Dial. de Scacc.*, I, vii, Oxford ed., p. 91, and cf. p. 32.

42 William of Malm., *Gesta Regum,* II, 487.

43 *Leges Edw. Conf.*, c. 15, 4; Liebermann, I, 641.

44 Liebermann, *National Assembly,* p. 84.

45 *Très Anc. Cout.*, c. LXXI; Haskins, *Norman Institutions,* p. 120; Liebermann, I, 628, note *e;* III, 343.

46 On Henry's legislation in general see P. and M., I, 73-74. There seems to be a trace of legislation about burials in the Gloucester cartulary, I, 14.

NOTE A

MEETINGS OF THE COUNCIL

In this bare catalogue of instances reference is made only to Farrer's *Itinerary of Henry I* as printed in the *English Historical Review,* Vol. XXXIV, pp. 305-382, 505-579 (also separately printed), where the authorities will be found, unless it seems desirable to add a reference for some special reason. The references to Farrer, when not otherwise specified, are to the pages of the *Review*. Passing over the question of a great council at the time of Henry's coronation and other doubtful cases, the first to be noted is in 1102, probably 29 September, "omnes principes regni," Flor. Worc., II, 51. At the same time or immediately after, Anselm held a council of the English church with the king's consent and that of the great council: "communi consensu episcoporum et abbatum et principum totius regni," and at Anselm's request of the king "primates regni" attended this council, Eadmer, *Hist. Nov.*, pp. 141-142; Farrer, p. 318. The Easter assembly, 29 March, 1103, at Winchester, Flor. Worc., II, 52; Farrer, 322. May 3, 1106, "omnes barones meos," Farrer, 338; cf. M. Paris, II, 131. 14 April, 1107, the Easter court at Windsor, H. Hunt., p. 236; Farrer, 342. 1 August, 1107, at London, W. Malm., II, 493; *Chron. Mon. de Bello,* p. 51; Farrer, 345. 5 April, 1108, the Easter assembly at Winchester, Farrer, 348-349. A great council and national synod at London, 24 May, 1108, Whitsuntide, Farrer, 349-350; Flor. Worc., II, 58. 13 June, Whitsuntide, 1109, Farrer, 353. 17 October, at Nottingham, Farrer, 354. The Christmas court of 1109 at Westminster was probably a great council, Farrer, 356. Probably also another was held, 23 February, 1110, Farrer, 357. The Whitsuntide assembly at Windsor, 29 May, 1110, Farrer, 358-359. On Farrer no. 262, cf. *E.H.R.,* XXXV, 392, and XXXVI, 304. A great council at Windsor, April, 1114, to consider filling the archbishopric of Canterbury, Farrer, 371. All the bishops and barons "totius regni" were called to Westminster, 16 September, 1115, Farrer, 376. The Christmas court of 1115 was held at St. Albans, Farrer, 379. 19 March, 1116, homage was done to the king's son William at

Salisbury, Farrer, 380; Flor. Worc., II, 69; Gerv. of Cant., I, 92. August, 1116, at London, Farrer, 382. Two great councils seem to have been held in January, 1121, about the king's second marriage: on 6 January, at London, the marriage plan was announced and on 29 January, at Windsor, the marriage took place, Farrer, 514-515; cf. Round, *Geof. de Mand.*, 428-429. The meeting at Westminster at Whitsuntide, 29 May, 1121, seems to have been a great council but there is no record of council business done, *A. S. Chron.;* Farrer, 519. The Christmas meeting of 1122 was held at Dunstable whence the king went to Woodstock, where apparently council business was done either by the great council or, more likely, by the small council continuation of the Christmas curia. Then writs were issued for a great council on February 2 at Gloucester where considerable business was done, cf. *A. S. Chron.*, with Sim. of Durham, II, 267-268; Farrer, 528. The Easter court of the year, April 15, met at Winchester, and then was probably issued the confirmation charter, Farrer, no. 491; cf. Round, *Feud. Engl.*, pp. 482-487. The council activities of this year since Christmas no doubt indicate the normal amount of business of this portion of the reign. At the end of 1126 we have again the double curia, the Christmas court meeting at Windsor and then going to London for January first, this time apparently the whole great council, the chief business being the settlement of the succession upon Matilda, W. of Malm., II, 528; Farrer, 539. The meeting held at London at the time of, or just before, the ecclesiastical council which the archbishop of Canterbury convened 13-16 May was probably a great council, Flor. Worc., II, 86; Farrer, 540-541; cf. Stubbs, I, 404, note 4. The Easter curia of 1130 was probably a great council, Farrer, 554, as was certainly that of 8 September, 1131, at Northampton, while that of 29 April, 1132, was probably not, Farrer, 563 and 567.

During the first two reigns of Anglo-Norman history the existence of the small council in England is not clearly revealed in the sources and must be found by a process of inference, partly from the necessities of the case and partly from indirect evidence in the material at our command. In a large proportion of the cases we have no means of deciding which one of the two bodies is acting except from some indication of the number of persons present or other incidental evidence. In composition the small council so closely duplicates the great council in the classes of which it is made up, officials, ecclesiastical and non-official barons, that characterizations attached to the names of the persons present do not help us. While it is true, as shown above, that the occurrence of a name in the list of witnesses of a document which records council action cannot be safely taken to prove the membership of the given person in the council, names of those whom we know on other grounds to be rightfully council members may indicate to us whether at a given date a large or a small number of barons had been brought together. When the chronicler in referring to the curia assembled by Bishop Odo to review the findings in the case of Bishop Gundulf against Picot says "fecit venire multos ex melioribus totius Angliae baronibus," we may be reasonably sure that we do not have to do with a great council, but that there was held a small council reinforced by specially summoned barons. Above, Chapter III, note 39; Bigelow, *Placita,* p. 36. On the other hand attendance at a great council was probably never complete. Eadmer notes that to a very important great council to which all had been summoned (episcopis, abbatibus, cunctisque regni principibus) not all came ("ex regia sanctione ferme totius regni nobilitas . . . apud Rochingeham coit"), recalling perhaps absences which had been noticeable to him. Eadmer, *Hist. Nov.,* p. 53. I add a catalogue of council meetings of the reign of Henry I which are probably those of the small council.

Early in September, 1101, various business of a legal and conciliar character was done at Windsor in an unusually large assembly which may possibly have been a great council. Farrer, nos. 25, 26, 28. At Salisbury 13 January, 1103, similar business was done in what was probably a small council continuation of a Christmas great council of which we have no record. Farrer, no. 59. In February or March probably, 1105, a suit was tried "coram me et baronibus meis" and other business done. Farrer, nos. 114, 115; cf. *Liber Eliensis,* p. 298; Bigelow, *Placita,* p. 124. In 1108 the king uses of a case the remarkable words "per dirationamentum regni mei et curiae," which may possibly indicate a great council trial. Farrer, no. 221; Bigelow, *Placita,* p. 98. 1109-1116, "ante me et barones meos." Farrer, no. 242; Bigelow, *Placita,* p. 310. 1110-1116, "ante me et barones meos." Farrer, no. 331; Bigelow, *Placita,* p. 137. 1110, "in praesentia mea redidit." Farrer, no. 250. A probable instance, May 15-18, 1110, at London. Farrer, no. 261; Bigelow, *Placita,* p. 108. Between August, 1111, and July, 1113, the well known case "apud Wintoniam in thesauro." Farrer, no. 323; Bigelow, *Placita,* p. 100. In September, 1114, at Westbourne "coram me et baronibus meis" and probably "consilio episcoporum et principum suorum." Eadmer, *Hist. Nov.,* p. 224; Farrer, p. 373 "Sept." and no. 334. A probable case in the presence of the king and certain bishops, earls and others occurs somewhere between August, 1115, and the end of 1121. Farrer, no. 353A; *E.H.R.,* XVI, 726. The accession of a new abbot of Abingdon gives us a glimpse of what is undoubtedly the enlarged small council which continues in session for a time after the great council has broken up. See Chapter X. In this case the great council was of the end of January, 1121, and had assembled for Henry's second marriage. See above in this note. *Chron. Abingdon,* II, 161; Farrer, p. 515. A claim of the monks of Durham to the church of Tynemouth gives us a chronicle account of an assembly on April 13 of the same year, plainly a large one of northern barons but not a great council, though it was in Easter week. They presented their claim "coram magno conventu principalium virorum qui tunc forte propter negotia quaedam illuc confluxerunt scilicet Rodbertus de Brys . . . aliique quamplures." No judicial action was taken on the claim. Simeon of Durham, II, 261; Farrer, p. 516. In 1123 the king, "habito cum suis apud Wdestoc . . . consilio," sends a military force to Normandy. Simeon of Durham, II, 267. According to the order of events in Simeon of Durham this was before the great council meeting of February 2 at Gloucester. Farrer, p. 528. See above in this note. At Winchester in 1227 "in curiam meam venerunt coram me . . . de placito . . ." Farrer, no. 542. In 1127 apparently begins the suit of Urban, bishop of Llandaff, against Bernard, bishop of St. Davids, concerning the rights of his see, Flor. Worc., II, 90; Farrer, pp. 540-541, of which we hear again just after Easter, 1132, and February 8 and May 1, 1133. H. Hunt., p. 253; W. Malm., II, p. 535; Farrer, p. 567. Probably no one of these meetings was a great council, but that in 1132 looks like a small council continuation of a great council. The notification probably of 1130, Farrer, no. 615, may be of a great council case, but the small council is more likely. Cases tried in Normandy would add a few instances to this list.

I add the criminal cases affecting barons which I have noted, whether before the great or the small council. At this date any serious criminal charge against persons of baronial rank would be a council case, either great or small, and would be tried *coram rege*. The prosecution of Robert of Bellême in 1102 is well known. Farrer, p. 316; Bigelow, *Placita,* pp. 83-84. The condemnation and exile of William Giffard, elect of Winchester, probably just preceded the Easter curia of 1103. Eadmer, *Hist. Nov.,* p. 146. The trial of Robert de Montfort in 1107 may have been in Normandy. Orderic Vitalis, IV, 239; Bigelow, *Placita,* p. 94. Three barons were disinherited at the Pentecost great council of 1110. Farrer, p. 358. The final condemnation of Robert of Bellême occurred in Normandy in November, 1112. Farrer, p. 365. In Normandy also was the trial of the captured rebels after Easter, 1124, which is especially interesting because of the objection of the count of Flanders to the punishments inflicted upon rear vassals captured in the service of their lords and the defence which the chronicler puts into the mouth of the king, based upon their oath of fealty to him. Orderic Vitalis, IV, 460. An accusation of treason was made against Geoffrey de Clinton at Easter, 1130, in what was almost certainly a great council. Farrer, p. 554. See Luchaire, *Institutions,* II, 327-334, for a list of cases brought before the French curia regis between 1137 and 1180, 85 in number.

The author of the *Gesta Regis Henrici* under date of 1170 (I, 4) says of Henry II that he "tenuit curiam suam in sollemnitate Paschali apud Winleshoveres," and there were present almost all ("fere omnes") the nobles of England, bishops, earls and barons. And then, the Easter celebration being finished, he went to London and "ibi magnum celebravit concilium" concerning the coronation of his son Henry "et de statutis regni sui." This indicates what was probably a frequent relationship between the social curia and the business meeting. The one is finished before the other begins, and the two are not necessarily held in the same place. The second is also sometimes, it would seem, the small council, usually enlarged, continuing the great council meeting.

CHAPTER V

THE ORIGIN OF THE COMMON LAW[1]

The leap forward which was taken in the development of the law and of the judicial system in England from the reign of Henry I to the end of Henry II's is to us surprising in every respect and in some almost incredible. From the death of Henry I to the writing of the book which we call Glanvill was almost exactly half a century. Of what was going on in the way of judicial change in the second half of this period, from 1160 to 1185, we have many and instructive glimpses. Of the first half, the period of Stephen's reign and of Henry's bringing England into order, we know practically nothing and yet the impression that we get is strong that the growth which begins to be evident soon after 1160 starts considerably in advance of the point which had been reached in 1135.

The stage of development in law and judicial institutions reached by the changes under Henry II is made abundantly clear to us in the remarkable and enlightening book of Glanvill. There is nothing which sums up in the same way the progress under Henry I. To find out what was done in his time we are shut up to a study of the rather scanty remainder of material from his reign, and to understand the relation of the facts this material gives us to the general evolution of which it probably is a part, we must study it in the light of the results attained in the last half of the century. Does it show that

[1] Published originally in the *Yale Law Journal* for December, 1924, XXX, 115-128. Republished here without change, except in annotations.

whatever movement we can detect was going on in a direction naturally leading to the results which occurred? To answer this question we have first a body of legal literature exceptional in amount for so early a date; second, a body of institutional material in writs and charters, smaller than we could desire, but greatly increased over the preceding period; and third, a single financial document from the end of the reign, the pipe roll of 1130, especially valuable from the close connection existing then between judicial and financial administration.

In beginning our study it is necessary first of all to recall the fact, indicated by the studies of the foregoing chapters, that the changes in the judicial system which form the great constitutional advance of Henry II's reign were the natural and gradual culmination of a series of changes which began with the Norman Conquest. As has been before shown, the first instance of the use of the new judicial processes out of which Henry's reforms grew falls within half a dozen years of the battle of Hastings.[2] From 1072 on they never dropped out of use and, although we can trace them only at intervals, it is already to be seen in the evidence which we do have that their use was increasing and that they were growing more and more into a judicial system. Indefinite they certainly were and unfixed as yet, but still a complete judicial system was taking shape over against the older system of the popular courts as an alternative which might be used in many cases. A study of the writs of Henry I's reign, of which there is a great number, not as yet critically edited or dated, but brought together in Bigelow's *Placita Anglo-Normannica* of 1881, with many later additions now possible,[3] will show clearly both that they are a natu-

[2] See Chapter III at note 18.

[3] These may be noted from William Farrer's "An Outline Itinerary of King Henry the First," *E.H.R.*, pp. 303-382, 505-579; also published sepa-

ral outgrowth of what was begun by William I and also that the development was already under way which was to result in the advance made by Henry II.[4] If further we consider the development which goes on in Normandy under the father of Henry II,[5] as we must, as an epoch in the growth of English institutions, then it becomes manifest how natural is the continuation of that growth under Henry II, and how broad a foundation had been laid in the past for his work.

Looking forward instead of backward, we are compelled to say that there is scarcely to be found in history a group of changes which make so little innovation upon what had gone before, and yet were followed by so wide reaching and profound results. This is true whether we consider them as individual institutions or in their united constitutional effects. Not merely do our judicial institutions and processes, writ and jury, the judge and his relation to the trial, the system of courts, and equity and the common law, come directly from these changes, but it was as a reaction against the strict centralization which they produced in the constitution, the transformation of the practical absolutism of the Normans into a constitutional absolutism, when that came to be expressed in the sort of despotism to which the character of John gave rise, that the Great Charter was demanded and the foundation of free constitutional government was laid down.[6]

rately. This itinerary serves admirably as a general index to the documentary material of Henry's reign, with more careful dating than before, but hardly takes the place of critical *regesta*.

4 See below, note 25.

5 See Haskins, *Institutions*, pp. 123-155.

6 It must be understood that to deny a reactionary character to c. 39 of Magna Carta, as is now often done (See below, Chapter IX, note 19), is not to deny the reactionary character of the whole movement of which Magna Carta is a result. The enduring centralizing effects of the Carolingian constitution, from which these institutions came, and especially of the *missi*, the Anglo-Norman itinerant justices, are admirably described by Brunner:

When we study these changes as they occurred under Henry II, we are studying law, but we understand only half their significance if we regard merely their judicial and legal results. I imagine it is possible to have our free constitution without our judicial system or our common law, but without the incidental results of the processes by which they were brought into existence under Henry II and extended in principle to administration under Richard I, it is doubtful if we should have had, it is difficult at least to see how we could have had, our present constitutional government as it was historically formed. Whether so much as this is true or not, it is at least true that, though we are studying in Henry's time judicial and legal institutions, we are really studying the history of our constitution in one of the most important periods of its growth.

The expansion of earlier practices in the reign of Henry to which we may attribute these results concerns not so much the actual content of the law, regulating conduct and business, substantive law, as it does the administration and enforcement of the law through the judicial system and processes. They were primarily and in their character institutional rather than legal changes and were accomplished through new regulations in regard to the writs, the jury and the system of courts. Combined to-

"Schärfer als jede andere Einrichtung kennzeichnet das missatische Institut den Geist der karolingischen Verfassung. Als des Königs unmittelbare Stellvertreter brachten die Missi in Staat und Kirche die Reformgedanken des Königtums zur Geltung und machten sie eine Centralisation der Verwaltung möglich, wie sie kein germanischer Staat des Mittelalters aufzuweisen hat, mit Ausnahme der normannischen Staatsbildung, die auf fränkischer Grundlage erwuchsen. Die lange daurende Nachwirkung, welche die fränkische Rechtsentwicklung nach Auflösung der Monarchie in den daraus hervorgegangenen Reichen hinterliess, beruht zum guten Teile auf dem tiefgreifenden Einflusse, den der fränkische König durch seine Missi auf die Provinzialverwaltung ausübte." *Deutsche Rechtsgeschichte* II, p. 195.

gether and regarding strictly the institutional and not the constitutional results, they gave rise to the English common law, which also took up into itself a body of pre-existing substantive law which had not been affected by these changes. Regarded from this point of view, as giving rise to the common law, these institutional changes established three things which may be stated in this way: first, new courts of more extensive and summary powers; second, a new method of getting the defendant or the accused before the court; and third, a new method of proof. In other words these are again: the itinerant justice and common pleas courts, the writs, and the jury in their later forms, including the assizes, and these were only extended applications of the courts of the king's commissioner or *missus,* the writs, the jury and the recognitions of William I's time.[7]

Plainly these changes concerned procedure and, putting them together, it can readily be seen that they furnished a nearly complete substitute for the old judicial system in which procedure was as strongly emphasized as in the new. But it is equally clear that they furnished no substitute for the old substantive law and scarcely any addition to it. At the end of the reign of Henry II it was possible to try a case to judgment and execution with hardly any use of the old procedure;[8] but it was not possible to try it without constant recourse to the old sub-

7 See above, Chapter III.

8 It should be said by way of qualification that the old method of making judgment by the decision of the body of suitors who formed the court had not changed. See Chapter II at note 54. In *Bracton's Note Book* (1887), pl. 67, of the year 1219, in the case before the itinerant justices, it is plainly the county which makes the judgment. The justices are fined, not because they made the judgment, but because they did not instruct the county that the evidence was insufficient and the verdict of the jury incomplete. The division of functions is clear. The justices declare the law; the assembly makes the judgment. The Carolingian *missus* asks the assembly or the *scabini* to form the judgment. Brunner, *Forschungen* (1894), p. 242; see note 16.

stantive law as defining and determining rights and obligations. Upon such subjects as the holding, transfer, renting and inheritance of land, the property, inheritance and dower rights of women, debts, contracts and distraint, personal status, the obligations of the warrantor, the right of advowson, and many such topics of substantive law, the new law had nothing to say. It might be true that there was here and there during the period some modification of the law of these things, made generally by special enactment,[9] but such modifications were by the way, of minor importance, and they were not necessary parts of the new whole. That provided new courts and new remedies but not new definitions of right.[10]

It is clear then that the new common law considered as a whole comes from two different sources; its substantive law from one source and its adjective law from another. Its adjective law as made a part of the national judicial system was new; its substantive law as defining rights and obligations was old, that is, it was old as compared with the new judicial system which could now be used to enforce it. It belonged in the time of the old judicial system of the popular courts which was now beginning to be pushed out of use. But it was not itself pushed out of use with the old system to which it originally belonged. Taken up by the new system, it formed nearly the whole

[9] See some of the instances enumerated below in note 33.

[10] It is desirable to hold in mind the fact that for a long time the new system was only an alternative one. No one was in any way obliged to make use of it who did not wish to do so. See *Origin*, p. 146. The old courts and the old processes still remained open and were indeed in constant use during most of the thirteenth century and in occasional use still later. In the king's council, great and small, the head and summit of the popular courts, the new procedure did not establish itself, and their representatives today, the house of lords and the privy council, in important particulars still use the old.

of the body of substantive law which was enforced by the courts, at least until the first great legislative age of English history, which was opened by the statute of Marlborough in 1267.

By general consent Glanvill's *Tractatus de Legibus et Consuetudinibus Angliae,* written probably between 1185 and 1190, is regarded as the first in the series of great books on the English common law. There was, however, an earlier period which may be considered roughly the first quarter of the twelfth century when there was a remarkable activity in writing books about English law. In that time or only slightly outside its limits, seven books were composed, or collections put together, purporting to give contemporary law. They were, as now entitled: *Hic intimatur; Leis Willelmi; Quadripartitus; Leges Henrici; Instituta Cnuti; Consiliatio Cnuti;* and *Leges Edwardi Confessoris.*[11]

The general presumption which these books create is that they were designed to give the contemporary law actually in force; or that it was thought they would be useful books for those who for any reason needed to know what the law was by which the courts of the time were guided. In one of them, the *Leges Henrici,* this intention is so plainly implied as to be more than a presumption.[12] When we come to examine them in detail, however, we find that without exception what they record is either Anglo-Saxon law or law purporting to be made or accepted by William I. At the date when they were written, especially at the date when the longest and most instructive of them, the *Leges Henrici* and the *Leges Edwardi Confessoris,* were written, there had been a very

[11] Liebermann, I, 486-619, 627-671.

[12] Cf. *Leges Henrici,* c. 8, 7; Liebermann, I, 554, and Liebermann, *Ueber Leges Henrici* (1901) p. 44, notes 5-9.

considerable development of the new prerogative justice. The writ as a judicial process was in frequent use and was beginning to show signs of growth upon its formal side;[13] inquisition by a jury to establish facts in litigation was not uncommon; iters by royal justices to hold the new courts in the counties were probably not yet made the regular rule but they were common enough to show that such a step was near;[14] and royal commissioners to hold local king's courts were frequently appointed.[15] The new justice was far from being a fixed part of the constitutional system, far from being a substitute for the older judicial organization, but it seems to us as if it were already so prevalent on every side of legal administration that it could not escape the notice and remark of any contemporary interested in practical legal matters, especially not of a king's justice. When we add that all the writers of Henry I's time show themselves to be more interested in adjective than in substantive law, the fact that in them all there is scarcely a reference to the new

[13] See below, note 24.

[14] Bishop Stubbs's argument, *Lectures on Early English History* (1906), pp. 154, 155, based upon *Leges Henrici*, 10, 4, and 19, 1 (Liebermann, I, 556, 559) for the activities of the itinerant justices under Henry I, must be given up, since these clauses are dealing not with jurisdiction but with revenue. Liebermann, III, 318. They do not mean that the king's pleas shall not be heard by the sheriffs *ex officio*, but that the proceeds of these pleas are not to be reckoned in the sheriff's farm unless there has been a special agreement that they shall be. The king's pleas were at this time unquestionably heard by the sheriffs *ex officio*. They go back, though not the whole list of them, into a time when there were no itinerant justices and no royal commissioners hearing pleas of any kind and they would naturally pass with other functions of the sheriff into the Norman period. For the approach to regularity of the iters of the justices, compare the entries concerning them in the pipe roll of 1130 with similar entries in the pipe rolls of Henry II, 1160 to 1170.

[15] See an interesting chronicle account of one of these courts, of the last part of the reign of Stephen, strikingly like those of the time of William I, published by Miss Helen M. Cam in *E.H.R.*, XXXIX, 568-571.

prerogative justice in any of its particulars becomes significant.[16]

It becomes exceedingly significant when we consider the case of the *Leges Henrici.* If there is among these writers anyone who could contest with Glanvill the honor of opening the series of great writers on the English common law, it is the author of the *Leges Henrici.* His book with all its limitations is a most interesting one. It is of about the same length as Glanvill; it fits into the same general framework of things; it deals with many of the same topics; it has, like that book, much feudal law and much non-feudal mingled together; it is by a justice of the curia regis and emphasizes the superiority of the king's law; it deals at length with the boundary line between private jurisdiction and the royal jurisdiction; and it occupies in regard to all these topics much the same point of view as Glanvill. The book also clearly reveals

[16] There are unconnected references in the *Leges Henrici* to single features of the new procedure. Summons by writ is barely mentioned, 41, 6. The justice summons to his county court and whoever so summoned does not attend is guilty of contempt of the king, 53, 1; cf. 42, 2; 52, 1. The king's justice is referred to often, sometimes the specially appointed, probably itinerant, justice, 66, 9, more often doubtless the sheriff commissioned as justice, but only two passages are of real significance. In 31, 2 we are told that when opinion is divided among those who make the judgment (*judices,* the assembly or the committee standing for the assembly, 29, 1*b*) "the opinion of the better shall prevail, that which seems more satisfactory to the justice," clearly even if it is that of minority—a very welcome indication of the function of the royal justice before he acquires the power of making the judgment. Certainly in case the opinion is that of a minority, it must be the justice who decides that a judgment has been reached. In a certain case of doubtful evidence, a jury is to be chosen from the better men, chosen probably by a king's justice, since the jury is still a royal process only, and apparently by virtue of his general commission without a special writ, 42, 2*a*. This is the only reference to the jury in the book. The reference to the use of juries by William I to compile the old laws of England in the unhistorical introduction to the *Leges Edwardi Confessoris* is evidence that the writer was familiar with such a use to which the jury might be put, but is hardly evidence of that use of the jury in judicial procedure in which we are here interested.

the high ambitions of its author. He had read some books of canon law and had been interested in the discussion he found in them of the ultimate principles of jurisprudence. He had reflected upon the English law which he had administered as a king's justice.[17] He had a dim conception of the philosophy of law, and the ideal which he held up before himself was a scientific treatise on the English law in which he should show its relation to the fundamental principles of jurisprudence and as a practical matter should classify its actions. He hoped to accomplish something like what Bracton attempted nearly a century and a half later under happier auspices. But the task was too great for him and the fault was not entirely his. The undeveloped and transitional character of the law of his day, the lack of unity in it as a whole, the contradictions in it as he found it even in details, though he may not have been quite conscious of these defects, affected the training to be derived from its study and inevitably limited the possibilities of the mind which derived its material from reflection upon it. It was too difficult a task to bring into scientific order a body of law which was an inharmonious mixture of two or three different legal systems and, as it was written down at least, of more than one stage in the development of the same system.[18]

When we compare these books with Glanvill's *Treatise* these characteristics of the best of the writings of Henry

[17] Liebermann, *Ueber Leges Henrici*, pp. 44-45.

[18] The payments in kind for various ranks under the name of "relief," specifically provided for in *Leges Henrici*, c. 14, belong to a stage in the development of feudalism far in the past of the Norman feudalism of the writer's own time, which he faithfully depicts elsewhere. William II's writ for the collection of relief in the bishopric of Worcester, of 1095 (Round, *Feudal England*, pp. 308-311, cf. Hubert Hall, *Engl. Hist. Documents* (1908), p. 269, note 1, shows the practice of money payments well established. This writ was printed by Bigelow, *Placita*, p. xliii, with comment on it in relation to the relief and to Flambard's system. The payment of re-

I's time stand out still more clearly. Two inferences are especially important for our present purpose. One is that in the earlier period the new prerogative justice had not yet reached a point where it gave any indication of what its future was to be or even impressed itself as a matter of interest upon students of the law who were engaged in its practical enforcement and deeply interested in procedure. The men most likely to understand what these innovations would mean and to describe them in the books they were writing gave no indication that they were conscious of their existence. The other inference is that in the half century or a little more before the writing of Glanvill's book the advance in the development of these institutions must have been exceedingly rapid. The new justice was as entirely the only justice for Glanvill as the old was for the author of the *Leges Henrici* or of the *Leges Edwardi Confessoris*. Further, the law which Glanvill writes is no longer an inharmonious mixture thrown together unblended, from different sources and different stages of the history of the same source. Glanvill's law, while it can be analyzed to show clearly enough the different sources from which it comes, impresses us as we read it as a wholly consistent and homogeneous body of law grown into one organic whole as if from the hand of a single legislator.[19] These two things have happened in

lief in horses and arms, as recorded in the *Leges Henrici* and Cnut, from whom the passage is mainly borrowed, is quite consistent with a feudalism which had developed out of the comitatus side only of feudal origins, but not with Norman feudalism.

19 The book came from the hand of a writer to whom the law was not a mass of detached fragments still bearing the marks of their distinct origins, nor framed of separate pieces still showing joints however cunningly carpentered together, as it was in general to the writer of the *Leges Henrici*, but from one who has come to feel the law as a consistent unity with no consciousness of the sources from which it has come. It is interesting to note that in this characteristic of organic combination into a unified whole the first part of the Norman *Très Ancien Coutumier* (Tardif, *Coutumiers de*

the half century: the new justice has become the ruling judicial system of the kingdom and the law which it enforces has been fused into a whole, unified and self-consistent.

When we come to raise the question whether we can determine exactly how these two results were accomplished in that half century before Glanvill, that book is again our guide to the answer. First as a matter of historical explanation it cannot be too strongly emphasized that the book, if it was written by Glanvill,[20] reveals clearly the fact that a king's justice, a chief justiciar of the kingdom even, in the last quarter of the twelfth century was mainly interested in procedure. The book is first and foremost a book of procedure. Whoever wrote it, the essential fact is the same, for beyond doubt it was written, if not by Glanvill himself, at least with his sanction and probably with his guidance and advice. The inference from these facts is, I think, not to be questioned. Procedure was the one chief interest, and it attracted chief interest to itself because it was the impelling and formative influence which had made the book possible. The book which records the result of the great transformation of the preceding generation in the supremacy of the new justice shows unmistakably that the transformation which had been wrought was a transformation of procedure. The new justice was new on its procedural side. Almost the whole of its substantive law was old.

If now we analyze Glanvill in search of an especially impelling and creative element of procedure, it becomes instantly apparent that what claims the writer's first and constant interest is the writ. The book is primarily a book

Normandie, Vol. I) which is a little later in date than Glanvill, and the Lombard *Libri Feudorum* (Lehmann, *Das Langobardische Lehnrecht,* 1896) of the next century plainly reveal the patching together of material of various origins not yet merged into a common unity. P. and M., I, 146.

[20] P. and M., I, 142-143.

of writs. The active agent in it is the writ. Whatever departure from the old system of justice is to be made, whatever innovation is to be introduced, or has been in the past, whatever thing of any kind is to be done, the writ is the instrument by which it is accomplished.[21] Further Glanvill implies that this process of change by which the system he describes has been built up may go on indefinitely by means of new writs which are easy of formation.[22] Glanvill leaves no doubt that it was the writ which was the compelling force by which the new justice was made the ruling judicial system at the end of the twelfth century. How that was done, it is not necessary to show here by the history of specific writs like the writ of right or the writ *praecipe*. Their operation in extending the jurisdiction of the prerogative courts is well enough known.[23] What I wish to do rather is to emphasize the fact that in transforming the judicial system of the kingdom from the Saxon system of nationally unorganized popular courts into the closely organized and even centralized system of later times the active agent which was used to bring the change about was the writ.

Originally the writ was any written command of the king addressed to anyone, official or non-official, directing him to do any kind of thing. There is no evidence that at first fixed forms were used in the composition of the writ. Each new one was written to fit the occasion, seemingly as if no one had ever been drawn up before.[24] No

21 See P. and M., I, 130, and *Origin*, p. 111, and note 4.

22 Glanvill, II, 13; XII, 3; XIII, 34.

23 I have endeavored in *The Origin of the English Constitution*, pp. 77-83, to make the operation and effect of these writs clear to one who reads without technical knowledge.

24 Reference here is not to the diplomatic forms which distinguish the writ from the charter. These are fairly well fixed in the time of William I, though there is in them also no fixity of language. The command which follows the greeting is given in a considerable variety of words, and *precipio*

classification of the early writs is possible. If we say that a given writ of William I's is the ancestor of a class of later writs, we do so because the business it initiates belongs to that class of writs, not because the formula peculiar to the class is used. Though in the phrases used some later formulae are foreshadowed, yet they were not used as formulae at that time. There had not yet been experience enough in their use to suggest that the writ should be made more specific in form and that permanence of form would be a convenience. In the next reign phrases begin to be repeated in the way of formulae, but it is the reign of Henry I that is the period of real progress in fixing the form of writs and so of preparing the way for an arrangement into classes.

The development of writ forms and writ classification is slow,[25] but from the very beginning the compelling and

has as yet gained no lead over *volo* and *mando*. The reference is to the formulae which later denote the purpose of the writ like those of the writ of right or of novel disseisin. The formula so frequent in later writs of right, "ne amplius clamorem audiam pro defectu justicie," occurs in briefer form in one writ of William I's. Davis, *Regesta*, App. no. XXIX. In this occurrence it is probably a Frankish reminiscence and is hardly used like a formula with a specific intention. See an example of a writ of right of Stephen's in informal, almost conversational, shape. *Gloucester Cartulary*, pp. 96-97. See Maitland, *Forms of Action* (1909), p. 315.

[25] A good instance of the development of the writ, indicating and no doubt following an increasing clearness of purpose, is that of the writ of novel disseisin. Compare (1) LXVI and LXVII of Davis's *Regesta*, App. (Round in *E.H.R.*, XXIX, 349), which show, so far as language goes, prerogative reseisin after recent disseisin with no provision for a trial. See Davis, App. LXIII, and *Ramsey Cartulary*, I, no. 157. (2) A writ of Henry I's, *Gloucester Cartulary*, no. 202 (Bigelow, *Placita*, p. 128), which shows a distinct advance in form and does provide for a trial. (3) A writ of Stephen's printed by Round, *Commune of London*, p. 114, note 3, less satisfactory in form but providing for a trial and another, *ibid.*, p. 114, less advanced. (4) Two Abingdon writs of early Henry II, *Abingdon Chronicle*, pp. 222, 223 (Bigelow, *Placita*, 169, 170) which show some advance especially in clearness. Bigelow says, at p. 173, that this is the "first appearance of the perfect, or nearly perfect, writ of novel disseisin."

To compare with these writs is an interesting judgment of a baronial

directing force which is behind the writ is evident. It is the royal authority, the king's absolute power. The writ is the one formal instrument which, in advance of the formation of the constitutional absolutism which was to result from its use, was employed by the king as the instrument of his authority. It was a serious matter to disobey the king's formal mandate. "Contemptus brevium" was a king's plea, added to the Saxon pleas, after the analogy of the "dispectus litterarum regis" of the Frankish law and putting the offender "in misericordia regis."[26] In the writ *praecipe,* which was the weapon of the most formidable attack of the twelfth century upon the independence of the baronial jurisdiction, the legal justification for setting the baron's court aside was found in the obligation of every man to obey the king's command. If the defendant does not do justice as directed, the sheriff is commanded to summon him to come before the king or his justices "ostensurus quare non fecerit," to explain his disobedience. If it is well known that he will not do the act of justice called for in the first part of the writ and that, when he appears before the king's justices, he will not in form explain his disobedience but answer in regular pleadings in a civil suit, these things do not obscure the legal right upon which the king's action rests. The writ, the instrument from the beginning of the king's absolute prerogative, was the active agent by which the whole structure of prerogative justice was built

court in France of about 1132, Langlois, *Textes Relatifs a l'Histoire du Parlement* (1888), no. VII, p. 13, pronouncing a restoration of seisin, leaving the question of *jus* to be settled by a later action, which seems also to be the implication in some of the writs cited above. Of equal interest is a writ of Geoffrey de Mandeville's of Stephen's time directing in plain terms a recognition to be made of an alleged disseisin. Howlett, *Chronicles of Stephen, Henry II and Richard I,* III, xxxvii, and see Howlett's text. This writ is also in Bigelow, *Placita,* p. 160, and Madox, *Exchequer,* II, 108, note *k.*

26 Brunner, *Schwurgerichte,* p. 77.

up into a national system of justice, taking the place of the old system of the Saxon popular courts.

But if the writ was agent and process, it had very substantial materials with which to work in building up a new judicial system. The court of the king's commissioner held in any locality of the kingdom was a curia regis, that is, it was not subject to the defects and limitations of the popular county court. The court which met the commissioner was the old ideal county court; all exemptions and liberties which cut into the assembly of the sheriff's ordinary court were suspended.[27] The law which the court applied and enforced, while it was the old local law,[28] was that local law supplemented and possibly overruled in some particulars by the superior and uniform king's law. When the presiding justice was a commissioner specially sent for the purpose, like the itinerant

[27] Very likely it was considered that as the new courts and processes were not an outgrowth of the older judicial system but came from a wholly different origin, arising from an exercise of the king's prerogative, nothing in an earlier grant of liberty released from them. The suspension of the liberty was no violation of the grant. The suspension is indicated in Henry I's writ regarding the local courts, Stubbs, *S.C.*, p. 122; in *Leges Henrici*, cc. 7, 2; 29; 31, 3; and in the "Assize of Clarendon," cc. 5, 8; 9; 11; cf. *Très Ancien Coutumier*, c. XLIV. Quite naturally in an age of special privileges the principle was not maintained. New exemptions began at once to be granted which did relieve from attendance on the new courts and from service on assizes and juries, and continued to be freely granted during the century which followed Henry II. See the "Petition of the Barons," 1258, c. 28, for the effect of these exemptions on the business of the county court. Stubbs, *S.C.*, p. 378.

[28] Glanvill, XII, 23. Glanvill recognizes clearly enough the fact that the king's court accepts and acts upon the local law, if there is no overruling legislation. In XII, 5 and 6, he necessarily implies that judgment of the Lord's court in a writ of right case rendered "secundum rationabiles consuetudines ipsarum curiarum" will be valid, though the local customs vary so greatly that he despairs of getting them into writing. In IX, 10, he notes that amercements in certain cases due the sheriff differ in amount in the different counties according to local custom, but suggests that they might have been made uniform by a general assize. See XIV, 8.

justice, he stood distinctly, sometimes in early writs by explicit declaration in his commission, in the place of the king and enjoyed extensive powers in issuing summary processes and in guidance concerning the law.[29] In the jury was provided a method of proof by getting at the knowledge of the locality about the exact facts at issue in place of the older methods of compurgation, which at best merely got the opinion of the community concerning the credibility of the parties, or of the ordeal as an appeal to heaven in which even in the twelfth century men were beginning to lose faith. The jury accounts for what popular support there was for the new justice and explains the current which began to set out of the old courts into the new, for in that more primitive period the man who was confident that he had a good case was anxious to get a jury trial if he could. So it is to be remembered that the new judicial system was not built up by the prerogative power alone, but by that power reinforced by better law, a better court, more summary processes, and a superior method of proof.

But the importance of these facts in themselves and as historical explanation should not lead us to forget that procedure is after all only the practical method by which the law is applied and enforced. It is not the real substance of the law. It is not substantive law. The new procedure was the one great interest of the time, but the growth of the new procedure into a national system made possible another transformation in the end of even deeper significance, the bringing of Saxon and Norman substantive law together into a unified national law, as they appear in Glanvill. To understand how this was brought about we turn again to the adjective side of law. It was

29 See the powers assumed by the justice in the case of Bishop Gundulf against Picot, above, Chapter III at note 38, and on the duty of the justice to instruct the court in the law, see above, note 8.

in the prerogative courts that this process of unification was accomplished.

For the ordinary sheriff's county court the normal law was the Saxon. According to that law would be determined all cases naturally falling in that court. The feudal law, or the new Norman law, would come into the county court probably not at all or rarely, and then it would not be into the ordinary county court but into the court of a king's commissioner using the machinery of the county court to hold a local curia regis.[30] All the usual cases under feudal law, which would include practically all cases relating to land, were provided for in the private courts of the lords or directly, if important enough or involving a question of title held from the king, in the great or small curia regis as the king's court for the whole kingdom. In this way it is highly probable that, without saying anything about it, the Norman conquest made a division of jurisdiction from the beginning. The law regulating the ownership of land ceased to be Saxon; it became feudal.[31] All cases regarding it would fall naturally into the feudal courts, royal or private, and, while not in any formal way withdrawn from the old local courts, would appear there no more.[32] Such a practical separation of courts and of law we suspect from the pecu-

30 As in a case arising between the vassals of two different lords, or one of default of right on the part of the lord. See note A at the end of the Chapter.

31 See, for a discussion of this question, above in Chapter III at note 34.

32 The baronial court is a local court, coordinate, for the cases falling in it, with the county court though not in the same system of justice. See below, Chapter VI, especially at note 18. The court rolls of the next century show that a good deal of litigation concerning land took place in county courts, but they give no evidence that it came into them as courts of first instance. Much the larger proportion of such cases plainly appears in these courts through the operation of writs of right and there is a clear presumption that in all cases the county court is the king's, not the sheriff's. The writ of right of course indicates an original baronial jurisdiction.

liarities of the *Leges Henrici,* and such a separation of jurisdiction and of law would continue with no progress towards a unification of the two systems, so long as each set of courts confined itself to its own business, and no courts arose trying at once and on the same footing both kinds of cases. It is the increasing frequency of the use of the court of the king's commissioner or *missus* which brings about the union. Primarily in the Norman state this was a feudal court for feudal cases and, so far as we can now see, it was pressure from increasing business of this feudal kind that forced the development forward, but this justice court, as a king's court, was just as normally a national court for all kinds of cases under any kind of law locally recognized. In the curia regis, general or local, there was no ground on which a distinction of jurisdiction, feudal or non-feudal, or of law, Saxon or Norman, could be maintained. In the king's court, under the king's justice, the two systems melt into one homogeneous whole for that court and, because that court appears everywhere, for the whole kingdom. That is, it becomes the common law.

There were united then in Glanvill streams from two sources of substantive law, Saxon and Norman, to form the greater stream of English common law which flows from this point on without an interruption. To these sources must be added a third whose contribution was just beginning to be received, legislation,[33] for although

[33] Glanvill knows a considerable body of legislation and is well aware of its effect. In II, 7 is the well known passage in praise of the grand assize which is stated in correct technical phrase to have been granted "de consilio procerum," as if the writer had a copy of the document before him, like the ordinance of William I on the ecclesiastical courts, or was familiar with its language. In the same ordinance apparently, the penalty of those jurors who swear falsely in the assize "ordinata est." II, 19, 1. To this assize had been added, at another time it would seem, "quedam constitutio" to limit the number of possible essoins. II, 12, 2. Still another question had arisen,

the early statutes were in their practical effect in the courts like those of today statutes and not common or customary law, that is, they overruled all other law, the important ones of this period all became in the process of interpretation and application absorbed into and indistinguishable parts of the thirteenth century common law. In other words the new body of law which appears thus formed in Glanvill was from its birth, to change the fig-

evidently in the experience of the writer with the assize, which could be, but had not been, settled. II, 21. ''Statutum est etiam in regno domini Regis'' that those clerks who had been presented to churches by those who had usurped the right of advowson during time of war should hold them during their lives. IV, 10, 2. Undoubtedly this ''statutum'' would constitute a perfect defence in any court against a claimant. By assize, ''de consilio regni inde factam,'' record in the king's courts had been granted to minor courts in several specified cases. VIII, 8, 3. A ''general assize'' might have been made to equalize through all the counties the amercement falling to the sheriff in a certain case. That is, a statute would override the differences of the local laws. But none has yet been made on the subject. IX, 10. The court Christian has been forbidden to hear pleas of lay debts or tenements on the ground of faith pledged. X, 12, 1. The other forms of jury trial to which the name assize became permanently attached, besides the grand assize, the three possessory assizes, and the assize *utrum,* are discussed in Book XIII and their legislative character recognized, ''ex beneficio constitutionis regni,'' but it is evident that the distinction which was later made between them and the recognitions called for by a new issue raised in the course of the pleadings, which were called *jurata* to distinguish them from the assizes, was not yet sharply made. Glanvill seems to class them all together in XIII, 2, and in XIII, 13, he calls one of them *assisa.* Perhaps it was still fresh in mind in Glanvill's time that all uses of the jury had been granted by a legislative act. XIII, 11, 11 is an exception which must have been made such in the legislation creating the assize, or added to it later, and it would probably be later in date than the great rebellion of 1173-1174. XIII, 11, 12 states that the assize also will not lie in case of a burgage tenement ''per aliam assisam ex causa majoris utilitatis in regno constitutam.'' According to XIII, 32 the time within which a disseisin must have taken place to come within the assize had more than once been fixed ''a domino rege de consilio procerum.'' The use of the jury of accusation, as provided for in the Assize of Clarendon, is not clearly referred to by Glanvill except in the passage concerning the punishment of usurers, VII, 16, 3, and its legislative character is not mentioned, unless it be indirectly referred to in XIV, 2. A reference should be added to XIV, 3, 2.

ure, a living thing. It began at once to grow in the two ways by which it has ever since continued to grow, by the power of natural expansion from within through judgments rendered and precedents established and by accretion from without by legislation. By a date hardly more than a century after Glanvill its natural growth had so changed the body of the law that both the great elements of which it had originally been composed, as they appeared in Glanvill, had almost disappeared from sight. The Saxon had disappeared more completely than the feudal or more accurately perhaps survived in less conspicuous features of the law. But the feudal was hardly less changed for, while it is true for example that the feudal is clearly enough the foundation of our land law, it is also true that the feudalism of the great land statutes of Edward I's reign would have been thought in Glanvill's time a strange feudalism, a distinctly emasculated feudalism. Glanvill marks the beginning of the common law upon its substantive side by the union of earlier elements and reveals clearly the sources from which they came, but it was a living not a dead law which he recorded, and the rapid life of the thirteenth century soon left his book behind and his law in the form in which he wrote it. His adjective law, which formed the other great side of the common law, changed less from what he wrote, as is natural perhaps in matters of form, and many of Glanvill's writs though divided and subdivided may be recognized in common usage down to our own time.[34] If it were possible for Glanvill to attend the session of a common pleas court in any English-speaking country of the present day, except perhaps in those few places where the Roman law prevails, he would see and hear much that would make him feel at home.

[34] Compare the medieval and the modern writs in Holdsworth, I, App.

NOTE A

THE KING'S COUNTY COURT

One must hesitate to maintain a difference of opinion from a scholar so fortified in the knowledge of Anglo-Saxon law as Professor Liebermann, but in the following subjects of discussion we are in a Norman and feudal, not in a Saxon, period and in the midst of the development of a new system of justice which we should naturally expect to give some evidence of itself in contemporary documents.

I confess that I have not been convinced that the references to the county court in *Leges Henrici*, cc. 7, 29, and 31 refer to the ordinary county court only. Liebermann, I, 553, 563, 564, partly quoted in Stubbs, *S.C.*, 125-126. The "judices regis" of c. 29 seems to me an insuperable objection to that view. They are those who make the judgment when the court is the king's. Else why the "regis"? See the case referred to above in Chapter III, note 14, where "villani et viles plebes," the "viles et inopes persone" of c. 29, are objected to, not indeed as *judices* but as compurgators, in a case before the royal commissioners, that is, in a king's county court. C. 31 seems to me equally conclusive, where use is made again of the same passage in Cnut as in c. 7. The whole of c. 31 I believe to refer to the same court, as very likely is not the case with c. 7. It is called curia regis in 31, 4, and its character as a court of record emphasized. The prerogative assigned the justice in 31, 2, see above, note 16, I can interpret only as belonging to the new judicial system. It might possibly be exercised by the sheriff commissioned to hold a local curia regis but that does not seem likely. The prerogative certainly belongs to the new system, not to the sheriff's powers in the ordinary county court, and it is much more likely that it would be exercised by a special king's *missus* than by a sheriff naturally carrying over into the unaccustomed position reminiscences of his limitations in the ordinary court. That the statement about those who compose the court is taken directly from II Cnut is not an objection to this interpretation. The king's county court was a restoration of the old Saxon court, of the ideal county court, through a suspension of all exemptions, and the statement of its composition in Cnut, which may in its own time have been more or less an ideal, would be wholly appropriate to it, in fact almost required.

Professor Liebermann also holds (III, 301) that the clause in the charter of Henry I in regard to local courts (*ibid.*, I, 524; Stubbs, *S.C.*, 122), which provides that a case arising between the vassals of two different lords shall go into the county court, refers to the ordinary county court under the sheriff in his ordinary capacity. He supposes that here the feudal law, in spite of its general prevalence, "gives way to the state and its local officer, the sheriff," though shortly afterwards, in *Leges Henrici* 25, 2, the feudal law is shown controlling on the same point. I prefer to maintain the interpretation which some time ago I suggested (*A.H.R.*, 1903, VIII, 488; *Origin*, p. 380) as much simpler, requiring no unusual explanation and strictly in accordance with the principles of feudal law and with all the evidence. This interpretation is that the sheriff is acting in this instance not in his ordinary capacity but as a royal commissioner, or as Glanvill expresses it "per breve regis" (see the exactly parallel case in Glanvill, XII, 8, which the writer says "ex necessitate itur ad comitatum"), so that the court becomes a curia regis, a king's county court, and is therefore competent to hear the case as the court of the suzerain of both lords. That the sheriff is in one sense in every capacity a king's justice and the county court a king's court, is undoubtedly true, but distinctly not so in the sense of the new prerogative justice. That in the king's court Anglo-Saxon law might be applied where it bore upon the case does not affect the character of the court. It was so applied in every king's court, including the highest, so long as it had application. The question here, however, is not one of substantive law and does not involve any rivalry between feudal and old local law. It is merely a question of what court has jurisdiction and on that the feudal law, which was then the only ruling law as to land ownership and which as between vassals and their lords would also unquestionably be the ruling law, was perfectly clear.

Glanvill, XII, 8, from which a quotation is made above, is so significant regarding this and related questions as to deserve detailed notice. It concerns the problem arising when the plaintiff in a writ of right claims to hold of one lord and the tenant holds of another. "Of course (*equidem*)," says Glanvill, "in that case the lord of the plaintiff, to whom the writ is directed, is not able to hold the plea because he cannot disseise another, unjustly and without judgment, of the court which he is known to possess [his baronial court for his vassals' cases]." "Ex necessitate itur inde ad commitatum et ibi procedit placitum vel in capitali curia," that is, in the central court of common pleas. The sheriff's ordinary county court had no jurisdiction, no existing court had in fact, over the case of a holding in dispute between the vassals of two different lords, except the court of a common suzerain, usually a curia regis, into which it would be transferred by the king's writ. This was the effect of the *nisi feceris* clause contained in practically every writ of right. It is only because the county court thus becomes the court of his suzerain in the new Norman-feudal system of justice that the lord of whom the tenant holds is not disseised of his court. The principle is precisely the same as in Henry I's charter for the local courts and in the proceedings regarding default of right. The fact should not be overlooked that the passage cited above from Glanvill, "vel in capitali curia," puts the sheriff's court of the county in this case on a par in jurisdiction with the central court of common pleas, which would be absurd if the ordinary county court is what is meant. Glanvill disavows treating of the business of the ordinary county court in either civil or criminal matters. XII, 23; XIV, 8.

CHAPTER VI

PRIVATE JURISDICTION[1]

To estimate the full significance of the changes which date from the reign of Henry II, especially upon the constitutional side, requires an understanding of the private jurisdiction of the time. It is essential to see clearly how great its share was in carrying on the judicial business of the state and how large was the amount of private litigation which it subtracted from the national courts.

It has long been recognized in theory that there were three distinct kinds of private jurisdiction in the English state of the feudal age: the jurisdiction which the lord had over the tenants of the manor; the jurisdiction of the public hundred court which had passed, very probably with additional powers, into the hands of some private lord, sometimes over the whole hundred and sometimes over only a portion of its territory or only a portion of its jurisdiction; and third, the jurisdiction of the baron over the military and some of the other free tenants of his barony.[2] While these distinctions are clear enough in

1 This chapter is based upon the outline sketch published in the *American Historical Review,* April, 1918, XXIII, 596-602, and upon the more detailed study by Professor Warren O. Ault, *Private Jurisdiction in England* (Yale Historical Publications), 1923, where evidence from many sources will be found brought together. Soon after the present book appears, Professor Ault's volume of court rolls of the abbey of Ramsey and the honor of Clare, chiefly of the thirteenth century, now ready for the press, will be published. In that book will be found further evidence of the same kind.

2 The common freeholder held by a tenure which was of course historically not feudal, that is not military, but he and his holding were everywhere attracted into the predominant system. He was made to owe suit to the pri-

theory, it has also long been observed that in practice there seems to have been no such clear-cut separation of the jurisdictions of the private courts. The court of the manor often does business which belongs properly to the hundred court; the hundred court sometimes does the business of the manor; the baronial court occasionally acts in the capacity of either one of the other courts; and in later times, which are sometimes supposed to indicate earlier conditions, a court baron for freemen is attached to a manor court. The question therefore at once naturally arises whether a distinction which does not seem to be maintained in the practical operation of the courts should be insisted upon by the historian. A more careful examination, however, of the facts of private jurisdiction shows that the mixture of jurisdictions which took place in practice was for the sake of economy and convenience, and that those who made the mixture understood what they were doing.[3] A careful study also of the history of private jurisdiction and of its relation in different periods to the public jurisdiction of the state, on the lines of that which follows briefly in this chapter, will show that neither private jurisdiction itself, nor the details of the development by which the practically exclu-

vate courts, both domanial and baronial; they passed upon questions regarding his holding, each regarding it from its own peculiar point of view; and the feudal incidents, homage, relief, and in some cases even the payment of scutage (See Ault, *Private Jurisdiction*, pp. 61-62, 180-181, 213-215), were attached to it, and he with his land became as completely incorporated in the feudal machine as the vassal or the villein. In some cases it is altogether probable that the tenure actually became feudal but in most certainly, notwithstanding its subjection to feudal forms, it remained distinguishable as a common freehold. Besides these semi-feudal common freeholds, there are others which remained outside the sphere of the feudal influence and so under the jurisdiction of the normal hundred and county courts. See Gloucester Cartulary, I, 172-173. There are many such records but it is not in all cases certain that the hundred court may not be doing the business of the lord's baronial court.

[3] Ault, *Private Jurisdiction*, pp. 323-344.

sive authority of the public courts was built up, can be understood unless these distinctions are at all times carefully maintained.

One difficulty for the present day historian which is not easy to overcome has been created by this apparent confusion in the facts—a difficulty in the assignment of technical names to the different jurisdictions which shall be at the same time accurate and sufficiently distinguishing. It was natural for the historian who had no need to go below the surface appearance of things to call all kinds of private jurisdiction "manorial,"[4] because every kind seems at one time or another to be connected with a manor. But a mixture of terms must be avoided if possible because it is certain to confuse the understanding of the reader, even if it does not mean a confusion of the writer's own understanding.

The term "manorial," which is the obvious name for the jurisdiction which belongs to the manor, must, I think, be dropped entirely. There is so long a history of confusion associated with it that no one can use it now with any certainty that his meaning will be clear. It is, however, so convenient an adjective that one can hardly help using it in places where its meaning will not be misunderstood, but as a technical term of jurisdiction it must be given up. The best term to use in its place is probably "domanial."[5] The court of a manor is always the court

[4] Bigelow, *History of Procedure, passim.* One is likely to be led into the same temptation if he begins to suppose that the facts of private jurisdiction as they are found in the late fourteenth or the fifteenth century may be used to explain what they were in the twelfth or thirteenth. The twelfth century is the great age of baronial jurisdiction in England. It must be studied mainly, however, in incidental allusions and scattered references in charters and other sources whose immediate subject is something different.

[5] "J'emploierai dans les pages suivantes les mots de 'juridiction domaniale' et de 'droit domanial' pour designer la juridiction et le droit que les érudits allemands appellent *Hofrecht.* On ne peut employer dans ce sens ni l'expression de 'juridiction seigneuriale' qui dit trop, ni celle de 'juri-

of a domain manor; the business of the court is domain business; it is, not wholly but mostly, of the same kind as that which makes the manor a domain manor—economic. It is the business of the cultivation of the domain and of the tenures and the services by which they are held, and these are economic. The term is no doubt clumsy and perhaps a better one can be suggested, but it will be used in this book for the court whose sphere of jurisdiction is the manor. The public jurisdiction of a hundred court which has passed into private hands is held by virtue of a franchise created by a grant from the king, that is, if it is held by a strictly legal title. This jurisdiction, public in private hands, may therefore properly be called "franchisal,"[6] and with no danger of confusion since neither a manor nor a barony was in itself a franchise. The jurisdiction of the feudal baron over the military and free tenants of his barony may obviously be called "baronial," and there ought to be little danger of confusion in the use of this term, but as a matter of fact it has been used for all the kinds of private jurisdiction indis-

diction domestique,' qui dit trop peu." Pirenne, *Revue Historique*, 1893, LIII, 56, note 4. A beautiful example of this jurisdiction is to be found in no. 46 of the returns to the Inquest of Sheriffs (1170), printed in the *Red Book of the Exchequer*, II, cclxxvii, in the midst of returns which for the most part illustrate the baronial jurisdiction. A stupid steward interpreted the "per judicium" requirement of the inquiry as including the domanial court, although these merely economic returns were clearly not called for.

6 "But very often a lord has other and greater powers than the feudal principle would give him; in particular he has the view of frankpledge and the police justice that the view of frankpledge implies. All such powers must in theory have their origin in grants made by the king; they are franchises. With feudal justice therefore we contrast 'franchisal' justice." Maitland, *Domesday Book and Beyond*, p. 80. This jurisdiction is sometimes called in the original sources "curia baronis," which means, I take it, a court belonging to a baron. The Gloucester cartulary, III, 221-222, contains a very interesting set of articles of the frankpledge without date. They clearly relate to a view in private hands and they give the impression of having been drawn up by the lord. The last eleven items imply a supervision of the manorial court by the view.

criminately and, if any term free from that confusion were to be found, it would be better to drop this one.[7] But "feudal" and "seigneurial" are open to the same objection and "vassalic," which some have used in France, does not quite cover the facts. One is for the present rather shut up to the use of the term "baronial" in the hope that the correct meaning of it is so obvious that it will not be misunderstood.

The baronial jurisdiction is the special subject of this chapter. For the purposes of this book the domanial jurisdiction may be passed over entirely. The state during this age had no interest in it. It was not created by any grant from the state. It was an outgrowth of the nature of the manor itself—the local regulation by a little community, shut in upon itself, of its own interests, disputes and offences, which concerned in truth no one outside the manor[8] and which were for all the business of the state

[7] The use of the term "baronial" for the other two kinds of private jurisdiction is by no means so common as the use of "manorial" for all kinds, and the attempt to reform its use is not quite so hopeless. The court designated by the later term "court baron" was a degenerate descendant of the baronial court, reduced to a more or less formal existence after the lord's real interest in a baronial court had disappeared and closely associated with a domanial court. It was employed mainly for certain technical matters where the decision of a court composed of freemen was formally necessary. P. and M., I, 516; Hearnshaw, *Leet Jurisdiction in England,* 1908 (Southampton Record Soc.), p. 78.

[8] The formal law writers, since they are dealing with the law and the courts of the state, have practically nothing to say about it. The writer of the *Leges Henrici* seems to know of its existence. He knows the hallmoot having sac and soc, that is franchisal jurisdiction, attached and the hallmoot without. Cc. 9, 4; 20; 57, 8. But he really does no more than mention its existence. Neither Glanvill nor Bracton pay any attention to it. Liebermann, II, 2, 489, "Hallengericht," c. 5, expresses dissent from Maitland's opinion, *Domesday Book and Beyond,* p. 82, that every lord will hold a hallmoot for his *villani* and exercise that jurisdiction "which does not infringe the royal preserves." Maitland is, I believe, correct and indeed, it may be added, every freeman who gets together economic dependents enough will be likely to hold a court for their common affairs, whether he hold a manor or not. See *The Estate Book of Henry de Bray* (Royal Hist. Soc.), 1916, p.

insignificant. There was no infringement of the state's jurisdiction, except possibly in the case of some minor police offences. As the state did not create it nor authorize its existence, so it never attacked it. It survived all other forms of private jurisdiction[9] and died a natural death after the close of the middle ages. The state was also very little concerned in the twelfth century with franchisal jurisdiction. The reforms of Henry did cut into it in one or two particulars, more fully noticed later, but the deliberate attack upon it which checked its interference with public justice belongs to the end of the thirteenth century, after the reforms of the twelfth century had been fully realized in the centralization of the state under a strong government. The legal doctrines also upon which that attack was based were developed, as principles clearly held, in the course of the thirteenth century.[10] The

xv. Other instances in Ault, *Private Jurisdiction*, cf. p. 235. It seems to me clear that Maitland is also right in supposing that the term ''sac and soc'' as commonly used does not include this jurisdiction. Sac and soc I believe to be generally the public jurisdiction which is conveyed in the grant of a liberty and that it does not include the jurisdictions which are derived from the nature of the manor itself or of the barony, though it does seem exceptionally to include the latter.

9 The survival of the leet court in some boroughs is not an exception to this statement because the borough was really a public unit and its leet court really a public local court and not a private jurisdiction in the sense of the feudal age. It perhaps ought to be added that in some purely formal legal phrases and expressions the baronial jurisdiction survived to modern times. See Blackstone's *Commentaries*, III, App., Writ no. 1, ed. Cooley, p. 1199; Holdsworth, I, App., p. 653, writ to ''the Lord of the Land.''

10 That the right to exercise a jurisdiction of this kind must be proved by definite legal evidence, that it could not be transferred, that it could not be divided, that if it was not exercised it lapsed, and that if it was not proved before the itinerant justices whenever they came into the county it lapsed (*Placita de Quo Warranto, passim*), are all thirteenth century principles unknown to the twelfth and indeed to the early thirteenth.

The different interests of the twelfth and thirteenth centuries in this respect are well illustrated by the corresponding differences between Glanvill and Bracton. Glanvill has scarcely a reference to the franchisal jurisdiction of the lord but much to say of his baronial. Bracton naturally has to say

weight of Henry II's changes, considered as interference with private jurisdiction, fell upon the baronial court.

Baronial jurisdiction in its origin, in the conditions which developed and maintained it and in its character, presents a considerable likeness to domanial jurisdiction. The feudal barony like the manor formed in early feudalism a little community by itself of the lord and his vassals, united by various rights and obligations among themselves with which no one outside the community was concerned, not even the state, for the state, certainly during the early and formative stages of feudalism, looked to the lord for the services and duties which should be performed for his land and did not ask by what internal

some of the same things about baronial jurisdiction as Glanvill, since the writ of right is the same thing in his time as in the earlier and the baronial jurisdiction has as yet scarcely begun to show the effects of its decay, but he puts his main emphasis on the franchisal. See note A at the end of the Chapter. The liberties granted to Bury St. Edmunds are studied in detail by H. W. C. Davis in *E.H.R.*, XXIV, 417-431. It can be seen clearly in the documents there printed that the contents of the liberty do not include the jurisdiction of a baronial court, and this is apparent in many other charters of liberties. In *Bracton's Note Book*, pll. 775, 1110, the jurisdiction belonging to a franchisal court, to a hundred court in private hands, is distinguished from the normal jurisdiction of the sheriff as representing the public authority. So long as the chief dependence for the punishment of crime was on the local courts, it is likely that the liberty was not felt to be a serious interference with public justice. The private hundred court probably functioned as well as the hundred court still independent. It was only when the central government began to feel its responsibility for the repression of crime and had devised a new method of detection and trial, and even then not until time had demonstrated the superiority of the new system and accustomed men to its operation, that the recovery of public justice from private possession could be felt to be necessary and be seriously undertaken. The attempt was begun under Henry III but it does not become a main business of the government until the reign of Edward I. The king himself, as landlord, exercised this jurisdiction. See *Bracton's Note Book*, pl. 824. The expression "in curia Domini Regis de Wyndesores" indicates clearly that the court is not a public curia regis. The court hears an appeal of larceny and a duel is adjudged and pledged. Windsor had been a possession of the king's since the Conquest and it had belonged to King Edward before.

arrangements he got them.[11] As a territorial unit the barony did not form, any more than did the manor, a subdivision of the state in its political geography, but it was a territorial unit and what land was included in it was as well known and as easily ascertained as for the hundred. In it centered interests, rights and obligations as closely limited to its own membership and as quickly and sharply defined and enforced by custom as those belonging within the hundred or the manor.[12] But they were different rights and obligations; the interests concerned were different; and the men to whom those interests belonged stood upon a different footing in the community. They were not merely free men; they were the emphatically free men of the time. They were men of rank and wealth, and formed the nobility of the new states which grew up among the ruins of the Roman Empire. For the defining and enforcing of those political obligations which they had assumed as rent for the fiefs they had received from the baron their lord, they could not be subjected to the local court of the hundred or to the villein, or half villein, court of the manor. On the other hand the state had, at first at least, no concern in the enforcement of those obligations to their lord nor in what varieties of local custom might grow up in their definition. With reference to the details of the law and the regulation of their holdings, each one of these military communities of the lord and his vassals was a unit shut in to itself as truly

11 From this fact arise the numerous local variations in feudal law. And from this comes also the fact that these variations when investigated prove to be in most cases about minor and not very important details, that is, not important when regarded as parts of the whole system of feudal law, however important they may have been to the individual lord or vassal concerned, or as a variation in local feudal law. The general feudal law which deals with the larger matters of character and structure of the feudalism of western Europe and the Latin Orient is surprisingly uniform when we consider how it was formed.

12 *Leges Henrici,* cc. 55, 56.

as was the manor. So arose by natural growth, without concern of the state,[13] owing nothing to a royal grant,[14] the private court of the barony for the settlement of the questions coming up in regard to its internal arrangement of those interests and obligations, and this constitutes the sphere of its jurisdiction.

The baronial court was thus as distinct in origin, in the territory included, in the rights defined and in the law created from both the other forms of private jurisdiction as they were from each other. In name and theory the court was that of a barony or of an honor. And so it probably was in origin, and so it continued to be when the lands held by the lord and his vassals form a single unit as he held them from his lord or from the king. But in later feudal days, at least, a barony was not necessary to the formation of a baronial court. If a lord had vassals

[13] Liebermann, I, 575, note *a*. The provision of the law stated in *Leges Henrici*, c. 55, 1*a*, would not hold of a franchisal court. On the right of the lord to take a duel out of the honor "ad suam capitalem mansionem," see Howlett, *Chronicles*, IV, 333, no. 10 (Round, *Calendar*, p. 267). *Select Civil Pleas* (Selden Soc.), no. 104 is a different matter. It concerns a franchisal court and a manor owing suit to it. Interesting is the first sentence of the answer of the prior of Merton in *Placita de Quo Warranto*, p. 313: ". . . dicit quod hujusmodi curia non est libertas nec regale per quod dicit quod ipse non debet domino Regi inde ad hoc breve respondere." Just what he means is not clear for he seems to be exercising a franchise, but the answer is noteworthy. Perhaps he means that he is exercising his franchise in a baronial court and so need not answer so far as the court is concerned. If this is what he means, the answer is quite correct. The king's representative presses the question in regard to the contents of the franchise but not as to the court.

[14] P. and M., I, 558, 567, 572. Professor Maitland does not hold the different jurisdictions strictly apart. What he has to say on p. 567 as a matter of fact does apply to both domanial and baronial jurisdiction but as based upon grounds so different as to make them entirely distinct. The "general words" do "describe rights which the donor would have though no such words were employed," and they do point in one case to "feudal," and in one to "manorial," jurisdiction, but in the former the right rests upon a contract and in the latter upon such a state of economic dependence that contract is impossible.

enough to form a court, no matter if he held each knight's fee as a separate fief from his lord, or even from a variety of lords, he could unite his knights in a baronial court of his own. Distinct baronies, however, held by the same lord, were not so united; each had its own distinct court.

The sphere of this baronial jurisdiction in its larger outline is easily marked out. The lord had from the nature of the case jurisdiction over all questions concerning the tenures of his vassals and those growing out of their duties and relations to him and to one another. It was a civil not a criminal jurisdiction.[15] The possession of a baronial court never relieved the lord, nor membership in it the vassal, from responsibility to some public tribunal for any crimes they might commit. But as a civil jurisdiction so far as the land held by these tenures was concerned, the court was omnicompetent: right and title,

[15] Regarded solely as a matter of theory, it is possible that a baronial court might in some cases exercise an ordinary criminal jurisdiction, coordinate with that of the hundred or even of the itinerant justice court. If a rear vassal was accused of crime, he was entitled to the judgment of his peers. But his peers in the strict sense were the other vassals of the same lord, who might therefore claim his court and try his man for whatever crime in his baronial, not his franchisal, court. See the case of two knights accused of treason against King Stephen, where the lord claims his court. Cited by Howlett, *Chronicles,* III, xxxv-xxxvi, from Bloomfield, *History of Norfolk,* III, 28, a case not entirely clear in the account which Bloomfield quotes. This is the only example which I have found in English sources, and such jurisdiction must in the main be regarded as merely theoretical.

I leave this note as it was originally written for the recent publication by Miss Helen M. Cam (*E.H.R.,* XXXIX, 568-571) of Bloomfield's source, an extract from a chronicle narrative, while it clears up some questions, leaves the point made here still in doubt. It suggests the possible explanation, by inference, not by direct statement, that the trial, or reconciliation, took place in the abbot's court before a king's justice, or possibly before the king himself, with barons of the king acting with the barons of the abbey. This would be an entirely normal arrangement, but the narrative represents the abbot as being the active agent in bringing about a concord, though this does not necessarily mean as presiding over the court.

seisin, inheritance, transfer, establishment of boundaries, infringements of rights or boundaries, and the proper treatment and maintenance in value of the holding,[16] formed the normal field of its general jurisdiction. It also decided and enforced the obligations of the tenants towards the lord. Services, rights, relief, homage, investiture, wardship and marriage, and everything covered by the idea of loyalty, were its concern.[17] These terms all covered something more than mere ceremony. If the lord refused to accept the relief and homage of one who claimed the right of paying them, he challenged him to prove his right of inheritance, and suits in the baronial court were common to compel the lord to accept homage, and the common defence to such a suit seems to have been that the claimant's right to be heir is doubtful. This was naturally a question of great importance and it is one of the first items of the baron's jurisdiction in which the state shows an interest when it begins to enlarge its own operations.[18]

16 See Esmein, *Cours Élémentaire d'Histoire du Droit Français*, 1921, pp. 255-257.

17 Including forinsec service. Madox, *Exchequer*, I, 112, note *n*.

18 See P. and M., I, 290-292. The subject of inheritance and relief occupies considerable space in Glanvill. See Books VII and IX. The state by the time he wrote had gone far towards establishing its right to protect the inheritance of the rear vassal. It seems reasonably clear, however, that it had done it, as it did in other similar cases, by the use of the evocatory writs, especially *praecipe*. Glanvill, IX, 5. These writs practically make the king's court a court of first instance, though they do not do so in form. C. 4 of the Assize of Northampton, which is framed to remedy evils complained of against private lords, does not have the air of entirely new legislation.

The old Saxon county court entertained freely cases involving the title (*jus*) to land. No tenant of land by a military tenure, however, could in strict feudal law sue or be sued concerning his title to that land in the Anglo-Norman sheriff's county court as a court of first instance. His tenure obliged him to take such cases into his lord's court, or the court of the defendant's lord, and the right to try them was an important part of the reserved property of the lord in his vassal's fief. Even the king had no right to take such cases out of the lord's court into his own except on the ground

Another question of the same kind was seisin. We are naturally inclined to think that it would always be considered that the duty of protecting its citizens in the possession of their property lay first of all upon the state. But that was not the idea of the feudal age, and nothing shows more clearly than this how the baron's court had taken its full share in the parcelling out of the natural jurisdiction of the state. This is to be seen in the fact that the question of the protection of seisin is one of the most frequent questions raised between the king's court and the baron's, as soon as the new prerogative procedure becomes well established, and continues to be until the decided decline of baronial jurisdiction in the last half of the thirteenth century. For example: confiscation remains theoretically through the whole period the lord's right against the tenant who withholds the services due from the land he holds. And this is the penalty regularly enforced by the judgment of the baronial court. Thereupon the tenant who wishes the protection of the new justice brings a royal writ of *novel disseisin* against his lord. The lord must then appear in the king's court and plead to this writ. The writ alleges that the complainant has been disseised "injuste et sine judicio," and the lord's plea in answer is that the confiscation was by the regular judgment of his court for default of service, and he produces the record of his court. Apparently if all forms have been complied with and the record is clearly proved correct, the plea is judged sufficient and the parties are returned to the baron's court, but, the record

of failure of justice. If he interfered more directly with the baronial jurisdiction of the lord by means of the writ *praecipe,* he did it on the ground of a right which overshadowed the feudal law. *Origin,* pp. 80-82. When the king transferred a case in this way into the county court, that court was no longer the old county court of the sheriff but became the new king's court under the sheriff as a special commissioner, that is, it was a feudal court, the court of the feudal suzerain. See above, Chapter V at note 32.

often says, with an admonition to the lord to treat his tenant "reasonably." This evidently means to restore his seisin on satisfactory security for the arrears and future performance of the service.[19]

The baronial court was also the normal tribunal for the enforcement of the lord's obligations to his tenant. These obligations may be stated in general terms as protection and warranty—protection being broadly interpreted to include not merely military but moral protection and warranty the protection of the tenant's title against an adverse claim. These rights could all be demanded and secured in the lord's own court under the well known principle that the judgment was made by the suitors of the court and not by the lord. As a matter of fact in the practical operation of the system these cases were often brought to judgment in the court of the next higher lord, either as a court of first instance or by an appeal of de-

[19] See the cases cited in note A at the end of the Chapter. A most interesting and peculiar case is to be found in *C.R.R.*, I, 320-321. The plaintiff says that by judgment of his court for default of service he took the dower land of J., "donec illa vi eum ejecit." Therefore he brings a writ of *novel disseisin* to recover. Judgment: "Consideratum est quod ipse non fuit seisitus inde ut de libero tenemento suo quia illud tenementum erat Juete," the defendant. If this record is taken as it stands and given the most natural interpretation, it declares that a baronial court cannot give the lord seisin "ut de libero tenemento suo" for default of service, that is, cannot pronounce confiscation, a judgment which goes much farther than any other in the line of precedents before and for a long time at least afterwards.

It should not be overlooked that these precedents in the royal courts are really establishing a decided change in the feudal law. In the early days of feudalism confiscation for default of service was, and must have been, real. The system could not otherwise have been maintained under a weak central government. But the effect of the cases here cited is to reduce confiscation from a penalty to an extreme form of distraint, so that the original penalty is no longer enforced. Fundamentally they mean of course that the tenant is coming to be regarded in reality as owner, though still in theory tenant. That is, the tenant is coming to be considered as having permanent rights in his holding of which he cannot be deprived, even for default of service. His tenement is his "of right and inheritance." See P. and M., I, 335 and note.

fault of right. The early assertion in England of the principle that the appeal of default of right was a king's plea was one of the first extensions there of royal power at the expense of feudal independence, but the assertion of the principle did not establish the fact.[20] In a case of this kind the extreme penalty of confiscation, when imposed upon the lord, meant the cutting out of the fief which his tenant held from the fiefs immediately held of him and its transfer to the group of fiefs immediately held of the next higher suzerain. The injured vassal ceased to be the vassal of the offending lord and became a vassal of the next higher lord coordinate with him, that is, his peer in the next higher court.

The ladder of baronial courts rising, as implied in the last paragraph, one above another was closed at the top by the king's council, great or small, which was the king's baronial court for all his military and feudal tenants-in-chief, as was that of each baron in the ascending ladder for his tenants.[21] The king's baronial court differed in no respect from theirs, not in the extent of its

[20] Given in the list of king's pleas in *Leges Henrici*, cc. 10, 10, 1; 59, 19. Given by Glanvill among the pleas belonging to the sheriff ''per breve regis.'' I, 4; cf. XII, 7; *Très Anc. Coutumier*, c. XXX. The English practice differed from the general feudal only in some details of method which may have been parts of Henry's legislation. *Materials Thomas Becket*, IV, 40-41; Hoveden, I, 225. On the general practice, see Flach, *Origines*, III, 367 ff.; Beaumanoir, ed. Salmon, c. 1740; Esmein, *Cours Élémentaire*, pp. 259-260. There is an interesting case of the appeal going from the county to the court of the higher suzerain instead of to the king in *R.C.R.*, I, 356-357 (*Plac. Abbr.*, pp. 54, 45 b). On the frequency of the intervention of the higher suzerain, see the Petition of the Barons, 1258, c. 29. Apparently the lord was sometimes allowed to recover the right to try the case. *Chron. Abingdon*, II, 226 (Bigelow, *Placita*, p. 198). See the discussion of the subject by Maitland in *Manorial Courts*, pp. lviiif.

[21] In this Chapter the point of view is that of the baronial court and the feudal law. That the great and small curia regis served other purposes as well goes without saying. They were, as said in the last Chapter, also the head of the popular court system and, through their hospitality to both, Saxon law and Norman law became united in the common law.

jurisdiction, in the law which it interpreted, nor in the procedure which it used. It should be added that it never ceased to be in this sense a baronial court. Although it became in course of time a court of errors for the prerogative courts and threw off also new off-shoots which became other prerogative courts, it never became itself a part of the prerogative court system, open only to those who had obtained the right to use it by the purchase of a writ.

Such was the situation when Henry II came to the throne. Large portions of what would normally be districts under the jurisdiction of public local courts had passed into the hands of lords as their private jurisdictions. Measured territorially, the enforcement of ordinary criminal law in a large part of the kindom was, from the growth of the franchises, not a public but a private responsibility. Measured by the number of cases to be tried, most of the enforcement of civil law in regard to the largest property interest of the time, land, was also a private matter. Of the two historical public courts of the localities, the county and the hundred courts, many of the hundred courts were no longer public in the original sense, and the jurisdiction of the county courts, quantitatively considered, had been seriously cut into by the baronial courts. On the other hand Henry had at his service a fully equipped prerogative judicial system whose organization and processes had been greatly improved by the work of his grandfather and father, though it was still almost without modification the king's private machine, not as yet really public or national. The use of the writ in judicial matters had been greatly increased and systematized; if a regularly recurring system of national courts acting in the localities had not been actually set up, the way to do it had been so clearly shown that the final step was plain; and the jury trial, increasingly familiar in use, had been opened by the assizes in Normandy to anyone who might care to use it in several classes of land cases of frequent occurrence. The means had at last been provided by which the state could recover its judicial authority and function from the private hands into which the conditions of the feudal age had been necessarily obliged to put it, could recover it not for the old system of public courts but for the new royal machinery which would thus become constitutional. To accomplish this, to form a permanent judicial system and to give to it certain definite rights in both civil and criminal questions, was the work which Henry II did.

In doing this he made no direct attack on private jurisdiction. A century later his great-grandson Edward I openly challenged in direct attack the right of the lords to their franchisal jurisdiction and forced them to prove their title to it by legal evidence. But Henry II did nothing of that sort. He accomplished his purposes by indirect methods. He called upon no man to prove his right and in form he took no man's right away.[22] He set up an alterna-

[22] The *praecipe* writ did not do this. It accomplished its purpose by introducing a new issue into the case. So Glanvill, XII, 25 merely introduces a new formality. But if the rule which is here laid down by Glanvill, that no man need answer in the court of his lord concerning his free tenement without the king's writ, was established by Henry II, it was in that aspect an interference with private jurisdiction which had no justification in existing law. But it interfered with the method of its exercise only; the jurisdiction was clearly recognized in the writ. See the note on Glanvill XII, 25 in *Origin*, pp. 96-105. To the evidence cited in that note that this principle came to be regarded as law should be added certain cases from the records, the earliest of which was in 1194, less than ten years after Glanvill was written. The demandant refused to put himself upon an assize in the court of the bishop of Coventry "nec voluit intrare in placitum de libero tenemento suo sine precepto domino Regis vel Justiciis ejus." *R.C.R.*, I, 62 (also in *Staff. Hist. Coll.*, III, 27). In 1199: "Et Reginaldus dicit quod nunquam habuit inde summonitionem in curia illa et aliquod breve non fuit inde de recto." *R.C.R.*, I, 448. In 1 John: "G. . . . defendit jus suum et petit videre et audire breve per quod in placitum trahitur et non est inventum." *Ibid.*, II, 4. As the thirteenth century goes on, cases appear

tive, competing system, giving better methods and results, to which he gave certain rights of supervision, but all this left the old jurisdictions as they were, with their competence in civil cases unchanged. Any case which they could try before, they could still try, and no litigants were obliged to abandon them for the king's new courts unless one or the other of the parties chose to do so.

That choice was, however, offered without reserve to one or the other of the parties in practically all the cases named above upon payment of the required fees. The writs in the four assizes of *novel disseisin, morte d'ancestor, darrein presentment* and *utrum* all granted a jury trial and when obtained by the plaintiff they therefore forced the defendant to appear and answer before the king or his justices. The writ of right to be sure did go upon the theory that the case was the lord's to try if he would try it, but it provided that, if the lord refused to do so, the plaintiff could get it transferred into a king's court.[23] If the lord did set out to try it, the grand assize

more frequently in the records. There can be, I think, no question of the fact that the principle is law in the thirteenth century. I have found no evidence of the recognition of it before Glanvill's dictum. There are cases in which the king's writ appears in the baronial court before that date, but in no one of them is there any evidence that the writ was necessary to the trial. See, Farrer, *Yorks. Charters*, II, no. 804; *Charts. and Docs. of Salisbury* (R.S.), p. 19; Madox, *Exch.*, I, 110, note *l*; *Bracton's Note Book*, pl. 386, a case probably early in the episcopate of Robert, bishop of Bath, which was from 1135 to 1166; *Chron. Mon. de Bello*, pp. 106-107 (Bigelow, *Placita*, p. 175); *Chron. Abingd.*, II, 184; cf. the payment of H.f.R., Pipe Roll Soc., XVI, 109 (Madox, *Exch.* I, 429, note *r*). See also Davis, *Regesta*, App., no. 62, a grant by William II: "Et nolo ut alicui quicquam respondeat inde nisi ego precipio vel abbas dominus suus." Here the same right is allowed the lord which the king claims. This grant is of the nature of those, rather frequent at the time and a little later, of exemption from trial in any courts but those of the king. Brunner suggests that it was from these privileges that Glanvill's dictum was derived. *Schwurgerichte*, p. 410, and cf. Maitland, *Manorial Courts*, p. liv.

23 As an appeal of default of right. But it is to be noticed that, if the case is thus transferred directly into a king's court, the rights of all the

allowed the defendant to throw the case into a king's court, as soon as issue was joined for proof, by a demand that proof should take the form of the verdict of a jury. Only if the case had gone so far that a judicial duel, the normal method of proof of the old procedure, had been pledged, then the alternative proof allowed by the grand assize could not be chosen. By these provisions practically any case concerning land could be taken out of the old and transferred to the courts of the new system, but the transfer was not compelled by the law; it lay wholly in the choice of the individual. But the attraction of the new was so strong that it might almost as well have been compulsory and by the end of a century the baronial court as a real rival of the state's jurisdiction had disappeared with no further effort of the state against it.

NOTE A

THE BARONIAL JURISDICTION

It is possible to collect a large number of cases illustrating the baronial jurisdiction over the subjects mentioned in the text, as well as the way in which the new royal courts were beginning to interfere with that jurisdiction. The following references are only selections from the evidence at hand but they are enough to show that these courts were very lively competitors of the state courts for the possession of the civil jurisdiction over the land before the new prerogative courts were opened to general use and for some time afterwards. Before the prerogative courts were opened, the baronial court served, as has already been implied, all the purposes of a local court for such cases and its position in

intermediate lords are passed over without notice, into whose courts under normal feudal practice the appeal would naturally fall before it could reach a king's court. See above, note 20.

the scheme of courts then existing was probably coordinate with the county court, that is, coordinate in the kinds and character of business disposed of. There was of course no national judicial organization in which they were recognized as coordinate members. In the rebuilding of a national jurisdiction which follows the changes made by Henry II, the old county courts recover nothing and their decline, as is well known, was as rapid as that of the baronial courts and coincident in time. In the references which follow no case is cited which is later than the early part of John's reign unless for some special reason which is indicated. Down to that time the changes made by Henry II would not greatly affect the baronial courts, indeed they affected at any time not the character but the amount of their business. I have considered it allowable to add a few instances from Normandy because the conditions are so closely parallel, and in this period it was not unusual for the same baron to hold courts of the same kind on both sides of the channel with the same vassals as suitors, or a part of the suitors, of both courts.

Examples of the writ of right in baronial courts: See Maitland's analysis of cases, Pipe Roll Soc., XIV, xxxix; *R.C.R.*, I, 34 (64); *ibid.*, II, 55 (Pipe Roll Soc., XIV, 119); *Plac. Abbr.*, p. 32b; *Select Civil Pleas*, nos. 22 (30), 34, 169; Farrer, *Yorks. Charters*, no. 804; *Chron. Abingd.*, II, 184 (Bigelow, *Placita*, 168); *Chron. Mon. de Bello*, 175. See also many of the references below. The writ of *tolt* testified into modern times, though as a matter of form only, to the unwillingness of the feudal lord to try the case as directed by the writ of right. See Blackstone, III, App. 1; Holdsworth, I, 425.

Illustrations of seisin and of confiscation for default of service: Pipe Roll Soc., XIV, 43, 69, 134; *R.C.R.*, I, 48, 62, 174, 366, 447; *ibid.*, II, 22-23, 58, 91, 94, 117; *Plac. Abbr.*, pp. 5, 25, 73, 95b; *Select Civil Pleas*, no. 191; *Charts. and Docs. of Salisbury*, p. 19, no. 21; Yorks. Arch. Soc., XLIV, 13; Madox, *Exch.*, I, 112, note *n*; Round, *Calendar*, no. 1205 (A.D. 1095). See *Bracton's Note Book*, pl. 1767 for what is probably meant by treating the tenant reasonably in relation to default of service. Cf. the entry in the Pipe Roll of 31 Henry I, p. 134: "R. . . . de

Rullos debet i markam auri ut juste tractetur in curia domini sui."

Examples of concords made in baronial courts: see Glanvill, VIII, 3, and with it compare the entry in the Pipe Roll of 30 Henry II, p. 8 (Pipe Roll Soc.); on what is probably the private court of Geoffrey Fitzpeter, see *R.C.R.*, I, 436; *R.C.R.*, I, 40; *ibid.*, II, 269; *Plac. Abbr.*, 1-2, 7, 59b; *Select Civil Pleas*, no. 30; Som. Rec. Soc., XI, no. 8; *Cart. St. John of Colchester*, II, 514, 643; Farrer, *Yorks. Charters*, III, 211, 213.

Examples of transfers of land in baronial courts: *R.C.R.*, I, 341, 436; Farrer, *Yorks. Charters*, nos. 1226, 1686; *Select Civil Pleas*, no. 26; *Cart. Glouc.*, I, 219; *Cart. Rames.*, I, 131; *Charts. and Docs. of Salisbury*, no. 20; Pipe Roll Soc., XXXIV, 75; Farrer, *Lancashire Pipe Rolls*, p. 440; *Cart. St. John of Colchester*, II, 644. Many grants of barons stating that they were made "consilio baronum meorum," or with similar phrases, show the existence of a baronial court: *Cart. Glouc.*, II, 84, 118; *Cart. Rames.*, I, 142, 153; Round, *Calendar*, nos. 358, 567; *Cart. Bath.* (Som. Rec. Soc. VII), 39, 63; *Chron. Mon. Abingd.*, II, 21, 110, 136; Orderic Vitalis, V, 179, 188, 190; *British Museum Charters*, I, no. 31; Madox, *Exchequer*, I, 198 *e*.

The following miscellaneous references are added as of special interest or illustrating in the particular case more than one of the preceding points: *R.C.R.*, I, 44, 313, 376, 430 (II, 262), 356 (*Plac. Abbr.*, p. 54) a very interesting case; *ibid.*, II, 36; *Plac. Abbr.*, pp. 27, 28, 45, 95; Pipe Roll Soc., XIV, 26, 40; *ibid.*, XXIV, 239-240; *ibid.*, XXXIV, 48, 75, 186; *Magnus Rotulus, 31 Henry I*, pp. 94, 110; *Rotuli de Oblatis*, p. 105; *Cart. Glouc.*, I, 35-36; *Cart. Eynsham*, I, no. 595; Round, *Calendar*, nos. 232, 1205, 1257; Farrer, *Yorks. Charters*, no. 1125; Nichols, *Hist. Leicestershire*, I, 2, App., p. 12; *Chron. Joc. de Brak.*, 20-21; *Red Book of the Exch.*, I, 186, 220, 239, 288, 351; *Close Rolls, 1231-1234*, p. 164 (a new baronial court established).

Nearly all cases on the court rolls during this period where the baron "petit curiam suam" are instances of this jurisdiction, not of the franchisal. Glanvill, XII, 7; see the claim of B. de S. Walerico, Haskins, *Institutions*, p. 187, in note 179, and cf. *Leges*

Henrici, c. 57, 5, and Brunner, *Schwurgerichte*, p. 408. *R.C.R.*, 13, 324, 326, 386, 429; *ibid.*, II, 13; *Plac. Abbr.*, 2b, 32; *Select Pleas of the Crown*, no. 98, concerns a franchisal court.

The court of an ecclesiastical baron often, perhaps usually, was partly formed of clerics, naturally because the chapter or the convent had important rights of ownership. Madox, *Exch.*, I, 198, *e* (Bigelow, *Placita*, p. 147); *Chron. Abingd.*, II, 136, 234; *Chron. Joc. de Brak.*, 19-20; Farrer, *Yorks. Charters*, no. 1125; *Cart. Rames.*, I, no. 145 (Davis, *Regesta*, no. 177, who misses the point of the last sentence, cf. *Cart. Rames.*, I, no. 169.)

If franchisal jurisdiction over a considerable part or all of his lands were added to the natural civil jurisdiction of the baron over his vassals and other free tenants, he might well feel a certain degree of political independence even in England, especially under a king like Stephen. In choosing illustrations of baronial assumption of something like a royal style and of the right to use royal processes, I have omitted those which refer merely to the use of the writ, because in the nature of the case every baron would have need to use the writ and its ordinary use means nothing as to the baron's position. Nor are the palatinates referred to because there the use of royal processes was legitimate. The special point here is not so much the borrowing of royal processes as the aspect of an independent and vigorous judicial system which these instances permit us to see. There is more evidence of this sort before Henry II than after. The effort to prevent the use of these processes in other than royal courts was not long maintained. Howlett, *Chronicles*, III, xxxii, xl; *Cart. Eynsham*, I, no. 15a; Madox, *Exch.*, I, 108, *k*, 120, *h;* Nichols, *Hist. Leicestershire*, II, App., pp. 22, 134; *Charts. and Docs. of Salisbury*, no. 209; *Cart. St. John of Colchester*, I, 176; *Cart. Glouc.*, II, no. 757; *R.C.R.*, I, 61-62; Madox, *Exchequer*, I, 98, *l*, an assize of *mort d'ancestor* in a private court by permission. On charters see Maitland, *Domesday Book and Beyond*, p. 265, n. 1.

The baronial court holds a large place in Glanvill's book. I have noted here only the references to it which are of some significance. They amount really to official recognition of its place and right in carrying on the ordinary business of the state, as indeed we should expect. Books, II, 8, 9; VI, 6; VIII, 3, 8, 10; IX, 1, 8, 9, 11, 12, 13; X, 8; XII, *passim;* XIII, 11. Especially significant is VIII, 10, concerning the reference of doubtful questions from the baron's court to the king's for solution, "et hoc debet dominus Rex de jure baronibus suis," and after the difficulty is settled the return of the case to the baronial court for final decision. There is a passing reference in Bk. I, 2, to the franchisal jurisdiction of the barons in the matter of the pleas that belong to the sheriff "per defectum dominorum." Notwithstanding the steady decline in importance of the baronial court during the first half of the thirteenth century, it was still a recognized element in the judicial system when Bracton wrote. It is much less in evidence in the court rolls of the middle of the century than in those of the beginning, and Bracton, although he clearly recognizes its existence and its rights, refers to it in only a few places and all merely by the way. Relatively considered the place which it takes in his book is much less important than in Glanvill's. See Bracton, f. 98 (ed. Woodbine, II, 281); note that the bond between the suitor and the lord's court is the bond of homage. Ff. 105-105b (Woodbine, II, 300); f. 330b (ed. Twiss, V, 98-100). On the writ of right and the lord's court: ff. 328-329b (Twiss, V, 80-90); f. 401 (Twiss, VI, 162); f. 411b (Twiss, VI, 246). On the lord's right of distress: f. 156 (Woodbine, II, 439 ff.); f. 205 (Twiss, III, 352); f. 217b (Twiss, III, 450). The lord's right of distress for service withheld and the king's plea of *vetitum namii* form one of the points where these two jurisdictions touch one another very closely. On the other hand, the lord's franchisal jurisdiction occupies a larger place in Bracton than in Glanvill, though it also is treated as secondary and subordinate to the royal jurisdiction. On the franchisal jurisdiction see (ed. Woodbine) ff. 14, 55b-57, 122b, 154b; (ed. Twiss), ff. 396, 412, 424, 442-442b. On its delegated character see in addition to the above f. 37 (Woodbine, II, 117) an old *addicio* confirmed as to the delegation of jurisdiction by f. 333b (Twiss, V, 124) a part of Bracton's text.

It is no doubt true that with the growing competence of the national courts to deal with disorder and local crime, to say nothing of the financial motive, the attention of the government was more and more attracted to the barons' liberties. It is interesting to note the decidedly greater frequency of the entry "exceptis libertatibus" in relation to communal amercements in the Pipe Roll of 1242 (ed. Cannon) than in those of Henry II. The position of the liberties in such matters was attracting increased attention. Cf. *Ann. Dunstable,* p. 270. Bracton's attitude, however, towards the liberty is not hostile but he makes it clear that it is a delegated jurisdiction. He seems even in places to go so far as to imply that the right to try a writ of right is a delegated power and that it may form one of the elements of a liberty. F. 56 (Woodbine, II, 167), f. 98 (Woodbine, II, 281), f. 328b (Twiss, V, 84). "Soke" in the writ in this last passage may mean no more than "any private jurisdiction." See P. and M., I, 566. If Bracton really held this doctrine, he doubtless derived it from the principle of Glanvill, XII, 25, now firmly established, of which it would be only a natural extension. See below in this note.

One very noticeable difference between Glanvill and Bracton in their attitude towards private jurisdiction is to be found in the difference of their emphasis on the evocatory character of the royal processes. For Glanvill this is one of the most fundamental matters. His treatise starts out with it as the first assertion about the new justice (I, 5), as if he were to say: We are going to build up a royal judicial system. We have got to do it in the teeth of private jurisdictions which occupy in civil cases a very important part, almost the whole, of the field. We therefore lay down at the outset the fundamental principle that, on petition of the complainant, by the writ *praecipe,* the king may draw into his court any plea he wishes concerning land feudally held or any free tenement. This I believe may be regarded as a fair interpretation of the tautological phrase Glanvill uses—"de feodo aut de libero tenemento suo." He seems to wish to draw attention to the fact that the land of the vassal, subject normally to baronial jurisdiction, is included. Then he proceeds in eleven of his fourteen books to treat of the use of the writ *praecipe* and the questions of law and procedure which grow out of it. See

XII, 1. That is, all this, the major portion of his book, deals with evocation. Book XII, treating of the ordinary writ of right, is really a continuation of the same subject, leaving the assizes to be treated in Book XIII, a rather long book, and criminal procedure in Book XIV, a short book. I do not mean to assert that we are justified in saying that we know what Glanvill's primary purpose was in writing his book and that it was to explain the way in which it was proposed to build up a national jurisdiction in cases concerning land at the expense of private jurisdiction. But it is not too much to say that, if this had been his purpose, he must have written very much as he did. There are other things in the treatise; a good deal of substantive law for instance. But these other things are by the way. The continuous theme is the royal jurisdiction over land and similar questions of permanent right and how it is to be made effective. Bracton is wholly different. There is not, I think, in his whole long treatise a single reference to the evocatory character of the prerogative processes. The writ *praecipe* has lost its importance. There are a few references to it but all subordinate. The writ of right itself receives nothing like the relative emphasis that it did in Glanvill. Bracton makes clear enough his understanding that the writ of right is logically superior to the assizes (f. 413, *e.g.*), but as a practical matter his chief interest seems to be in the assizes, especially in the assize of *novel disseisin.* This change of emphasis since Henry II is not due to Magna Carta, c. 34. The effect of that had been overcome by indirect methods. Emphasis has changed rather because all the conditions in which general judicial operations take place have changed. The royal jurisdiction was now firmly established. Cases concerning title to land and seisin of land went naturally into the king's courts. Not that the barons had lost their jurisdiction, but they had ceased to be greatly interested in it. The evocatory formulae, still retained in the writs, vitally of the essence of the writ in Glanvill's time, were now hardly more than common form. The lords no longer attempted to protect their jurisdiction of this kind. *Hengham Magna,* a few years after Bracton, states what is undoubtedly the real reason. It no longer paid (*cap.* 3, from P. and M., I, 575, note 2), and why it did not pay is partly explained by the great difficulty the lords had in enforcing suits to their courts as shown in the provisions of Westminster of 1259 as well as in the court rolls.

Writers on early legal history tell us that the hundred court did not entertain pleas concerning the title to land. P. and M., I, 544. How long this remained the case it is hardly possible to say. Certainly after the prerogative processes became common land cases appeared in hundred courts "per breve regis." See *e.g.* the recognition in the hundred of Meldon referred to in a writ of Stephen's printed in Howlett, *Chronicles,* III, xxxviii, and *Cart. Glouc.,* I, no. 45. Probably, however, prerogative cases are always exceptional and should not be considered as making an enlargement of the normal jurisdiction of the hundred court. But such a limitation of jurisdiction would, I think, almost necessarily be abandoned when the hundred court became the private court of a baron by virtue of a franchise. It would be abandoned, at least to all appearance, so far as we can distinguish, when the lord was led as a matter of convenience, or from any motive, to use the court of his liberty to do the business of a baronial court. The writ of right would appear frequently in such a court and, by a natural extension of the principle of Glanvill, XII, 25, as said above, the trial of cases under a writ of right might finally appear among the contents of a liberty, and it might begin to be said, as it is in Bracton, that the right to try such cases rests on a royal grant. See above, in this note. This is analogous to the fact that while in Glanvill the lord's right to bring suit in his own court to enforce payment of services from his tenant with no reference to the king is recognized, in Bracton it is said that the king's writ is necessary in certain of these cases because they may lead to the loss of the freehold. Bracton, ff. 156-156b, 157b (Woodbine, I, 441, 444), and cf. *Origin,* p. 101. I have found only one case in which an actual grant analogous to this is contained in any charter of a liberty. This is in the charter granted 3 July, 1233, to the bishop of Ely, printed in *Cart. Rames.,* I, 112, and in abstract in *Charter Rolls,* I, 183. The bishop claimed this liberty under Edward I. *P.Q.W.,* p. 307. Cf. *Bracton's Note Book,* pl. 655. The normal jurisdiction of the hundred court was also enlarged by other grants in the franchises when the actual trial of king's pleas, like the plea *vetitum namii,* was granted. The hundred court was sometimes certainly treated as having the same jurisdiction as the county court. A writ of 1234, *Close Rolls, 1231-1234,* p. 572, directs the sheriff, because the defendant cannot be moved on account of illness, to cause the hundred court to sit at Grenested in Sussex, where he lies, "et loquelam illam que est in comitatu inter eos in eodem hundredo teneri facias de die in diem quousque loquela illa inter eos terminetur, vel saltem quousque idem W. attornatum suum ibi fecerit in predicta presentia secundum consuetudinem comitatus." The suit was one "de captione et detentione averiorum."

In a valuable article in the *English Historical Review,* XXXV, 161-199, entitled "Barony and Thanage," Dr. Rachel Reid presents a view of the baron's jurisdiction which differs from that here set forth. She believes that barony is an office and that the baron holds his court as a part of the state's official machinery. I do not see how this view can be maintained. I can here notice only the fact that it is supported in part by arguments which do not distinguish between the baronial and franchisal jurisdictions and treat them as if they rested upon the same principle of right, as for example in the comparison of Glanvill's treatment of the baron's jurisdiction with Bracton's, *E.H.R., l.c.,* p. 177. A careful comparison, however, of the details named in the accounts which Glanvill gives of the jurisdiction he is describing with those which Bracton gives in the passage which Miss Reid cites (f. 154b), will show that they have nothing in common. Bracton's species of jurisdiction Miss Reid correctly describes as "the rights of public justice," p. 178, that is, franchisal. Of these Glanvill has nothing to say except in I, 2, as referred to above. The only detail common to the two lists is debt, and Glanvill makes it entirely clear that he is concerned with debt "per breve regis" (X, 1) and Bracton that he is referring to debt without the king's writ (ff. 154b, 156). For jurisdiction over debts "que exiguntur sine brevi regis," see *Bracton's Note Book,* pl. 1110.

It is no doubt somewhat presumptuous to imagine that a problem so difficult and so long discussed as the meaning of tenure "per baroniam" can be solved by a simple and long known formula. The more I have studied the problem, however, the stronger has grown my impression that tenure "per baroniam" is nothing more than the tenure of a group of fees as a unit, a unit tenure. If three knights' fees are held as three separate units, though by the same man, with the service regarded separately each by itself and with a distinct homage and relief for each, there is no barony in this sense. If a group of three fees is held as one unit with one specification of service, not parcelled out among the three, but "held by the service of three knights," and with one homage and relief, the tenure is "per baroniam," there is a barony. Here it becomes necessary to point out that in discussing tenure "per baroniam" care must be taken to exclude from the study certain of the uses of the terms barony and baron. Primarily, as is well known, baron means man and in the feudal sense "the man of another," and barony means the holding, the fee, of any tenant-in-chief by military service. Both terms continue to be used in this sense at least until the end of the thirteenth century. This usage must be especially familiar to every reader of feudal sources in reference to the tenants of tenants-in-chief, particularly in documents relating to their baronial courts. A barony is held of the earls of Leicester, *Gesta Regis Henrici*, I, 133-134; the barons of the earl of Warwick act as witnesses, *Chron. Abingd.*, II, 21; King Henry I addresses the barons of the abbey of Abingdon, *ibid.*, p. 90; the barons of the church of Ramsey form its court, *Cart. Rames.*, I, 124, 142, 153; one who is not himself a great baron has his barons, *Cart. Glouc.*, II, 118-119; *Chron. Abingd.*, II, 110. In such instances there is no thought of the character of the tenure and they can throw no light upon it. Pains must be taken to make sure that the examples chosen for study refer clearly to barony by tenure and not to barony as a mere holding of any kind, otherwise there will certainly be a confused result. It is especially important to maintain this distinction when small holdings are considered, the holdings of "minor barons," most of whom do not hold "per baroniam.'' Still it certainly is conceivable that a group of knights' fees might be granted as a unit for the service of one knight, and I have noted cases that I think may be of that kind. This would be unusual, however, and every supposed instance should be carefully scrutinized. If the king or a lord wished to confer a favor of that sort upon a vassal, he would be more likely to make the grant of a serjeanty, and the presumption is that when a small holding of the service of one knight or less is called a barony the meaning is no more than that it is a tenure-in-chief. But there are undeniable instances of baronies held upon the service of two knights, both immediate and rear baronies. If this suggestion is correct, a group of fees can be made a barony by uniting them in a single specification of service and a single homage. A body of non-feudalized land can be made a barony by attaching to it as a unit a multiple service and a single homage. Interesting is the creation of a barony by William I by the union of two knights' fees—''baroniam unam constituit.'' Haskins, *Institutions,* pp. 11-12. There is one difficulty which should be noted. In all other cases a difference of tenure is a difference in service, in the kind of service to be rendered. Tenure by knight service, serjeanty, socage, and fee farm are thus distinguished, but in tenure ''per baroniam'' the service is knight service. Magna Carta, c. 2. The cases are, however, numerous enough in which the term ''per baroniam'' is best interpreted in that meaning to make it practically certain that some characteristic of tenure as tenure was referred to, not some characteristic of the land as land or as a holding like size, or immediacy, or territorial situation. In this sense tenure ''per baroniam'' was group tenure. It was a tenure which held in one grasp several units which the feudal world usually distinguished each from the others as a separate unit, the normal feudal unit, and made of them a new unit to which now attached the service, that is, the payment for the tenure, and to which also attached normally the principle of indivisibility, which nevertheless could not be maintained in practice. I am not prepared to say that this suggested explanation is correct, but only that it does simplify the problem and fit the facts more nearly than any other which I have seen.

CHAPTER VII

THE ORIGIN AND CONTINUITY OF ENGLISH EQUITY[1]

A good deal of light has been thrown within recent years by various publications upon the early history of equity and its relation to the common law courts in the twelfth and thirteenth centuries. The most important of these publications are the *Eyre of Kent, 1313-1314,* in four volumes (especially valuable is the Introduction to Volume II), and *Select Bills in Eyre, 1229-1333,* both works edited by Mr. W. C. Bolland and published by the Selden Society between 1910 and 1914. The review of the latter book by Professor F. M. Powicke in the *English Historical Review,* Vol. XXX, 330-336, is also a material contribution to the subject, and equally important is the paper on the "Early History of English Equity," by Dr. H. D. Hazeltine, published in *Essays in Legal History read before the Congress of Historical Studies in 1913,* edited by Professor Vinogradoff. To these studies should be added Chapter IX of Professor Baldwin's *The King's Council,* in which early equity procedure in the exchequer is discussed. Attention should also be called to an earlier study, to the discussion of certain writs, issued by William the Conqueror and later kings down to Glanvill's time, which give evidence of "the exercise of equity powers by the superior courts of the Norman period," in Bigelow's *Procedure,* pp. 192-196 (1880). This passage in

[1] "The Origin of English Equity" was printed first in the *Columbia Law Review,* XVI, 87-98, February, 1916.

all probability has never received the attention which it deserved because it has not been possible to see that these cases were anything more than rudimentary beginnings leading to no perceptible results, or to connect them in any way with the beginning of equity proper.

The paper of Dr. Hazeltine referred to above adds a considerable number of instances of equity procedure in the early common law courts to those cited by Mr. Bigelow and carries the period of such a common law jurisdiction well into the fourteenth century.[2] It is, however, to Mr. Bolland's discovery of the bills in eyre that we owe an understanding of the importance of this jurisdiction, and of the great extent to which it was employed in the eyre courts at the end of the thirteenth century and the beginning of the fourteenth.[3] The bills in eyre are in form and purport so nearly like the later chancery bills that both Sir Frederick Pollock and Dr. Hazeltine are inclined to regard the chancery bills as descended from them.[4] They are petitions praying remedy of grace and favor, "for God's sake and your own soul's sake"; "for your charity"; "for the love of Christ and the soul of the Queen."[5] They concern a great variety of matters, both

[2] *Bracton's Note Book*, pl. 391, is interesting in this connection. A suit, opening with a petition against the king, was brought in the central court of common pleas by the bishop of Norwich and, though it did not go to judgment, no question arose of the competence of the court. We should expect such a suit by a person of episcopal rank to be brought, at that date (1230), before the council, *i.e., coram rege.* See the petition against the king concerning the earldom of Huntingdon before the council in 21 Henry III, *Bracton's Note Book*, pl. 1221; *Plac. Abbr.*, p. 105.

[3] See especially *Eyre of Kent*, II, xxi-xxx, and *Bills in Eyre*, pp. xv-xix. Also described by Sir Frederick Pollock in *Essays in Legal History*, pp. 290-292.

[4] See respectively *Essays in Legal History*, pp. 291 and 262. Mr. Bolland says, *Eyre of Kent*, II, xxix, that he has "no doubt that these bills are the very beginning of the equitable jurisdiction." The statement is not repeated in *Bills in Eyre.* See note C at the end of Chapter X.

[5] These are citations from actual bills. See *Eyre of Kent*, II, xxv.

outside and within the common law jurisdiction of that day, and make evident the extensive employment of this procedure.[6]

The evidence brought together in the writings referred to above has been considered by the authors with reference to the history of equity only, not with reference to the history of common law. The two are, however, I venture to assert, inseparably bound together; more than this, it is clear, I think, that this union, or this identity rather, is the natural and logical fact in that early age, whether looked at from the side of procedure or from the side of the courts in which the procedure was employed. In other words, we have now reached a stage of this inquiry where we may confidently assert that equity and common law originated in one and the same procedure, that during the first two hundred years of their history they were not distinguished from one another, and that if we now distinguish between them during that period, we do it artificially, by the application of tests impossible to contemporaries. The bearing of this fact upon constitutional, as well as upon legal, history should not be overlooked, for it makes clear upon one side, as has already been done upon others, the wholly undifferentiated character not merely of institutions, but of functions also, during the first age of our constitutional his-

[6] Mr. Bolland notices the wide range of cases covered by these bills, and says they "embody complaints of infractions of almost every kind of personal right." *Eyre of Kent,* II, xxiii; *Bills in Eyre,* p. xl. It is interesting to add that the Frankish ancestors of the *praecipe* writ seem to have provided for an equally wide range of cases. See the following from the form book of Marculf (I, 29): "Ille rex, vir inlustris, illo. Fidelis noster ille ad presentiam nostram veniens nobis suggessit, quasi vos eum, nulla manenti causa, in via adsallisetis et graviter livorassetis et rauba sua in solidos tantos eidum tullesetis vel post vos reteneatis indebitae, et nulla justicia ex hoc aput vos consequer possit." *Mon. Germ. Hist., Formulæ,* ed. Zeumer, p. 60. No. 80, *Bills in Eyre,* p. 53, is a case of highway robbery with violence.

tory. It is well on in the fourteenth century before we get any clear distinction between equity and common law, and it is in that century also that we find contemporaries beginning clearly to differentiate in numerous cases between functions and between institutions, though the beginnings of more or less vague distinction and separation may be traced back into the thirteenth century.

The common law originated, to summarize what has gone before, in new procedure and new judicial machinery brought into England at the Norman Conquest.[7] Its growth as a continuous development was due to the rapid expansion in character and extension in application which was given in England to old Frankish forms and institutions which had existed in a somnolent condition for many generations. In this new legal evolution, the following principle is fundamental from the very beginning: the new procedure and the new machinery are the king's private property; they are no part of the public machinery of the state to which any individual may appeal in his personal need as he might to the shire or hundred court. This principle applied just as truly to the case of the baron who was bound to the king by the tie of feudal vassalage, and consequently a member of the central curia regis, as of the common freeman, or of the knight who was a rear-vassal only; he could not use the new procedure as a matter of right, for this was no part of the procedure of the curia regis, and was never used by it, nor by any form of council court, during the first hundred and fifty years unless by a special commission of the king's.

This fundamental principle immediately revealed in two particulars the control which it exerted over the

[7] Such portions of the older law and procedure as survived for any considerable time, did so in the end because they were taken up into, or originally formed a part of, this newer system.

whole development. 1. If an individual wished the use of the king's procedure, he must first get the king's permission. 2. If he used the king's procedure, he must do it by means of the king's machinery. If a private person, for example, wished the use of a local jury in order to get the facts of his case before the court, he must get the king's permission, because the jury procedure was a private possession of the king's used for administrative cases or for cases in which the king was directly concerned;[8] and if he actually made use of it, he must do so in a king's local court before a royal commissioner specially appointed for that purpose, because the commissioner represented the king and stood in his place, "in meo loco," as William I told the bishop of Coutance in one of the most important and instructive cases of his reign.[9] In a sense which probably seemed more real to that age than it would to ours, the king in such a case was operating his own machinery.

If we look at the matter institutionally rather than from the side of the practical motive, the fundamental principle which has just been stated was the reason for the establishment of the itinerant justice system and all that it developed into. If the jury was to be used in the

[8] This statement is not to be modified by the fact that cases were begun before the itinerant justices without a writ, or tried by the old procedure, or that in cases begun without a writ recourse was had to a jury. See note C at the end of Chapter X. The new procedure and competence were added to the old, not substituted for it. The old procedure was the natural one for the curia regis in all its branches, and its use in an itinerant justice court would be entirely normal, even apart from the fact that the court was a county court as well as a king's court. Recourse to a jury in a case begun without a writ would not be beyond the competence of the justices as representing the king, and in the same way they would be competent to refuse an assize called for by a writ. See Round, *Calendar*, p. 147, no. 438. And upon this same principle rests also the fact which Mr. Bolland notes that "not even the king's prerogative will avail a man before the Justices in Eyre." *Bills in Eyre*, p. xviii, referring to a case in *Eyre of Kent*, I, 54.

[9] Above, Chapter III at note 5.

counties in the detection of crime, or in inquiry into the conduct of the sheriff, or in the trial of suits at law between private persons, it must be taken there and operated by a commissioner, or commissioners, who stood in the place of the king and held a local king's court.[10] It would not seem possible to the twelfth century to do it in any other way.

With the fundamental principle already stated, there was from the very beginning combined another which linked this purely judicial growth with the broader constitutional development which was at the same time going on. This is the conception of the function of the king in the life of the community which had come down to the feudal age as an inheritance from the past. The king was not a mere feudal suzerain, not merely the lord paramount of the realm, though often he might seem to be nothing more than that. He owed a duty to the community at large to preserve order, to see that justice was done to rich and poor alike, which might at any moment override his feudal duty as the lord of vassals, and must override it, if the two came into irreconcilable collision.[11] The Anglo-Norman kings found this fundamental principle, generally recognized in their time, of invaluable assistance in their attempt, whether consciously or unconsciously made, to embody their practical absolutism in constitutional forms, but in so doing they laid down the

[10] In an interesting case of 20 Edward I, specially cited by both Sir Frederick Pollock (*l.c.*, p. 292) and Mr. Bolland (*Eyre of Kent*, II, xxiii), the petitioner addresses the justice: "Dear Sir, I cry mercy of you who are put in the place of our lord the King to do right to poor and to rich." The case is no. 11, p. 6, *Bills in Eyre*.

[11] The primary duty of the king to make justice prevail is frequently expressed in the charters. Mr. Bolland refers to ". . . the immemorial belief that inherent in the King are the right and the power to remedy all wrongs independently of common law or statute law and even in the teeth of these." *Eyre of Kent*, II, xxviii.

road along which our equity and common law came to us.

Common law and equity originated together as one undifferentiated system in the effort of the king to carry out his duty of furnishing security and justice to all in the community by making use of his prerogative power through his prerogative machinery. The identity of the two systems at the beginning, their origin in the same prerogative action, can be clearly seen in this: the essential characteristic of equity procedure of a later date is that it begins with a petition asking the king to interfere to secure justice where it would not be secured by the ordinary and existing processes of law. But it was the essential characteristic of all common law actions in the eleventh and twelfth centuries that they began with a petition asking the king to interfere to secure justice where it would not be secured by the ordinary and existing processes of law. In some form, it does not matter in what, because forms were not yet fixed nor the following of a definite form regarded as a matter of importance, the man who wished to have the advantage of the king's prerogative procedure and the use of the king's machinery, that is, who desired a remedy not provided him by the ordinary judicial system, must ask for it and obtain permission to use it; and the permission must be granted in so demonstrable a way as to authorize or command the royal officials to act in the case. This authorization and command is the original writ in an action. Indeed in one sense, this has remained the fact in common law practice to the present day. The original writ in an action at common law must be sought and asked for however perfectly it may have become *de cursu*.[12]

Of the first actual case in which this new procedure was used of which we have any knowledge, the case of Arch-

12 This is not the case in some of the United States in which the old common law pleading has been replaced by code pleading.

bishop Lanfranc against Odo the king's brother, in 1070, we are told in the historical account that Lanfranc, after learning of the losses which the archbishopric had suffered, petitioned the king as quickly as possible and with insistence concerning it and the king directed that a court should be formed to try the case.[13] It is characteristic of all these early instances, upon whichever side of the later division between equity and common law they would fall, that the fact of a petition to the king is not directly stated in the writ which authorizes the action. The fact is, however, often stated in the accounts of trials given by the chroniclers;[14] nor should we overlook the phrase so common in varying forms from the time of the earliest writs: "ne audiam inde clamorem amplius pro penuria recti et justiciæ."[15] Indeed the fact of the petition is almost directly stated in the famous writ *praecipe,* the ancestor of many common law writs, when it commands A to restore to B a measure of land "unde idem B queritur quod predictus A ei deforciat."

The examples of equity cases in the common law courts which have been collected by Messrs. Bigelow and Hazeltine are of writs which would fall in the later classification upon the equity side, and therefore they show, as these writers indicate, that no distinction of courts was then made for cases of this kind. But the converse of this is equally true that there was no difference of procedure in these cases, for it is evident that this common law writ *praecipe,* if we regard it as of the time when the first book on the common law was written, fails in none of the tests

[13] ". . . diligenter inquisita et bene cognita veritate, regem quam citius potuit et non pigre inde requisivit. Praecepit ergo rex comitatum totum absque mora considere . . ." Bigelow, *Placita,* p. 6.

[14] See for example, *Chron. Abingd.,* II, 29 (Bigelow, *Placita,* p. 64); Orderic Vitalis, III, 407 (Bigelow, p. 67).

[15] *E.g.,* Bigelow, *l.c.,* p. 91—a writ of Henry I's of about 1106, from *Chron. Abingd.,* II, 77; Davis, *Regesta,* App. no. xxix, a writ of William I's.

later employed to distinguish equity from common law. It issues upon the petition of the complainant, "in the teeth of"[16] the ordinary existing law under which the case would come, by the prerogative action of the king on the ground of general justice, and provides a remedy, the use of a court and its procedure, which the ordinary law could not furnish.[17] We must not overlook the fact that at the accession of Henry II the system of justice which grew into the common law was as much outside of, and in violation of, the ordinary system of justice which prevailed throughout the Anglo-Norman state, as ever equity was at any later time in relation to the common law system. No equity process of the fourteenth century was more clearly in the teeth of the ordinary law than was this *praecipe* writ in 1187.[18]

Let us look at the writ in detail: "Rex vicecomiti salutem. Precipe A. quod juste et sine dilatione reddat B. unam hidam terre in villa illa, unde idem B, queritur, quod predictus A. ei deforciat; et nisi fecerit, summone eum per bonos summonitores, quod sit ibi coram me vel Justiciis meis in crastino post octabis clausi pasche apud locum illum, ostensurus quare non fecerit."[19] Notice first the petition of the complainant implied in the words "unde idem B. queritur," as referred to above. Second, "quod juste reddat B. unam hidam terre": the justice of the plaintiff's case is assumed and on that ground the command is issued. Third, it is a direct command to the defendant to do justice, that is, it is a prerogative action of the king's based on his duty and right to secure justice for all. Fourth, if the defendant does not obey, he is

16 Bolland, *Eyre of Kent*, II, xxviii, as in note 11 above.

17 The writ removed the action from the court of a baron where it would normally have been tried according to the old procedure by the ordinary feudal law.

18 See Bigelow, *Procedure*, pp. 76-79; *Origin*, pp. 96-105.

19 Glanvill, Bk. I, c. 6.

under obligation to explain to the king why he has not done so, and this obligation it is which brings the case into the king's court and gives to the plaintiff the advantage of its procedure.[20] Had this writ had its origin in the fourteenth century, when the common law and its courts formed the normal system from which the case must be evoked to the special justice of the king, then it would have been necessarily an equity writ, if it could be so called.[21] This is an impossible supposition, but that is exactly the situation with reference to this writ in Henry II's time and states accurately the relation in which it stood in the twelfth century to the older courts and procedure. It is a commonplace of knowledge that the opposition of the feudal courts to it was so strong, because of its violation of their rights, as recognized in the existing organization of justice in which it interfered, that its further use was forbidden by c. 34 of Magna Carta.

The same facts may be shown to be only a little less plainly true of the writ of right. Indeed the identity of equity and common law in the twelfth century appears in every feature of the common law of that time, or of the

20 An interesting writ of William I's, not exactly of the *praecipe* type, states rather plainly the alternative: "Facite abbatem de Heli resaisire de istis terris quas isti tenant . . . si ipse abbas poterit ostendere supradictas terras esse de dominio suæ ecclesiæ et si supradicti homines non poterint ostendere ut eas terras habuissent de dono meo." Bigelow, *Placita,* p. 26. A writ of Henry I's reads: "Praecipio tibi ut sine mora facias habere ecclesiae Sanctae Mariae de Abbendonia terram quam . . . si illa terra est de dominio praedictæ ecclesiae." *Ibid.,* p. 96. The Frankish ancestor of the *praecipe* writ states the fact of petition more clearly than Glanvill, see note 6 *ante,* and the alternative to obedience in much the same way as the writs just quoted: "Certe si nolueretis, et aliquid contra hoc habueretis quod opponere, non aliter fiat, nisi vosmet ipsi per hunc indecolum commoneti Kalendas illas proximas ad nostram veniatis presentiam eidem ob hoc integrum et legalem dare responso." Zeumer, *u.s.* Cf. the mandate, no. 18, Zeumer, p. 120.

21 The equitable character of the *praecipe* writ is seen even more clearly in the form used to enforce the payment of a debt, Glanvill, X, 2.

system which developed later into the common law, so much so that, if we wished to assign to either a precedence in time, we must say not that equity originated in common law, but that common law originated in equity,[22] not in the system of doctrines later known as equity, but in the fundamental principle upon which the whole development rested, in the desire to secure justice for all more surely than existing law would do it, to establish an equitable procedure and to furnish equitable remedies,[23] and in the procedure by which this was accomplished.

When we go on into the thirteenth century, we pass into a time when the older system of law and courts was rapidly falling into insignificance before the advance of the newer system, and when this latter, the common law system, was coming to be looked upon as the normal and prevailing law of the community. It is a time also when differentiation was slowly but steadily taking place in the judicial system. A new central court, the later common

22 Or it may be put in this way: The changes in which the common law originated represent the first stage historically of an attempt to improve the older system of law by giving it more flexibility and freedom through the intervention of the royal prerogative. This first attempt was not permanently successful because its results themselves became hardened into a fixed system, so that flexibility must be sought again through the continued use of the prerogative, and from this second stage came the final equity system.

23 There is no reference in Bracton to a technical equity system. A passage in f. 12b comes nearest to such a reference, but here as elsewhere the word is used in its general, philosophical sense, and the passage and its context show that Bracton understood that the equitable remedy which should be granted was to be granted in the common law court. This passage reads as follows in Woodbine's Bracton, II, 53-54: "Et si idem C. primo feoffatus eundem B. firmarium eicere non possit incontinenti vel post intervallum, competit ei assisa novæ disseisinæ, tam super feoffatorem suum quam super firmarium, et quo casu cum per assisam recuperaverit versus ipsum B. firmarium, de æquitate et per officium iustitiarii tenebitur donator eidem B. firmario ad excambium propter fraudem." The passage on equity on f. 23b is a marginal addition, probably not made by Bracton. See Woodbine's Bracton, I, 375. See also II, 67, 83, 228.

pleas court, had early been found to be a necessary adjunct of the itinerant justice system and it took from the middle of the reign of Henry II a distinct and fairly well defined position.[24] The reservation of difficult cases from this court, or from the itinerant justice courts, to the council, or small curia regis, forced by degrees upon that body, as the common law became more and more technical in character, an increasing amount of technical, or professional, judicial work. This body of work was further increased by the tendency to regard some portion of what was original conciliar judicial work from the technical or professional point of view.[25] By slow degrees, scarcely perceptible in the thirteenth century,[26] this tendency created a distinct court, the *coram rege,* or king's bench court.[27] Meantime the exchequer, as another phase of the council, or small curia, gradually becoming distinct both from council and from *coram rege,* had continued its judicial function, its power to try cases as a court of original jurisdiction and, as in the thirteenth century the advantages of the common law procedure had become so evident as to make it now the prevailing system, the exchequer showed a tendency to assume a common law jurisdiction or, to put it in terms which are appropriate to the thirteenth century, to adopt a common law procedure. The natural effect of these developments was to bring

24 *Origin,* pp. 136-141.

25 That is, coming before the council as a court of original jurisdiction.

26 Because in this body, which was gradually becoming professional, there were so frequent reversions to primitive type, that is, to an administrative council, to a conciliar, non-professional body, which is only to say in other words that the differentiation was still incomplete.

27 See below, Chapter VIII, and note A to Chapter III in *The Origin of the English Constitution.* In this connection Mr. Bolland has, I think, in one place slightly misinterpreted his evidence. In the passage cited in *Bills in Eyre,* p. xvii, "Our Justices at Westminster" and "Our Justices in Bank" both refer to the Bench, or central court of common pleas, and "by the order of Ourselves" is not *coram rege,* but the king's mandate.

forward as never before, probably not into very clear consciousness but as a practical matter, the question of jurisdiction, of boundary lines and fields of action.[28]

As parallel to this tendency there must also be noticed another affecting the history of the writ. It is the increasing attitude of suspicion from before the middle of the century which the community at large adopted towards the growing number of writs and the power of chancery to make new writs at will. Growing out of this are various attempts at the middle of the century and later to regulate and limit the issuing of writs.[29] If we recall the principle which had been early established in the common law that the action as developed before the court must not be different from that foreshadowed in the writ,[30] and the consequent fact that the multiplication of writs which characterized the first century of the common law was a process of the multiplying and classifying of actions, it will be clear that a limitation upon the making of new writs was a marking out of the field of common law to a certain extent and a setting of boundaries to it.

The effect of both these tendencies, to mark out for the courts the boundaries of their jurisdiction and also the boundaries of the law which they applied, was the same. The common law was becoming a hard and fast system with certain clearly defined things which it could do and with equally clearly defined things which it could not do.[31] I do not intend to assert that this point in the de-

28 This fact is indicated in various ways: by the first steps in the development of a procedure in error; by instances of pleading to jurisdiction, as in *Bracton's Note Book*, pll. 1213 and 1220 (Madox, *Exchequer*, I, 102, note *f.*, and *Plac. Abbr.*, p. 105); and by the possibility of such a statement of the difference between the courts as that in Bracton, f. 108.

29 Matthew Paris, (R.S.), IV, 363, 367; *Annales Monastici, Burton* (R.S.), 448; Holdsworth, I, 196, II, 291 and references; Bigelow, *Procedure*, pp. 14, 197.

30 Glanvill, Bk. XII, c. 24; *Select Civil Pleas*, nos. 16, 23, 31, 76, 91.

31 The hardening process was undoubtedly for another reason a natural

velopment was reached at the end of the thirteenth century. It is very evident that it was not, though considerable approach had been made towards it. When the fourteenth century opened, boundary lines still seem now and then vague, fields overlap, content is still variable, the same body will do things that are later regarded as quite distinct, two different bodies will do the same thing,[32] but as compared with the beginning of the thirteenth century great progress had been made towards definition and exclusion. It is possible to say, I think, that this progress had gone much farther in the case of judicial institutions than it had in those which afterwards formed, or were then forming, the legislative, administrative, and conciliar systems, the council and parliament.

It is in this situation, as carried on into the fourteenth century, that we must find the origin of equity as a separate system and by which we must account for its late origin as compared with the common law. So long as the common law remained a flexible system, its field undefined, its power of inclusion unlimited, its organs undifferentiated, there was no reason for distinguishing be-

and normal one, because the new system did not remain as it had begun supplementary to the general body of the law in which it intervened by direct action of the prerogative to improve its processes and to insure a more certain justice. The new prerogative system absorbed the old wholly and became itself the one ruling body of national law. As such it was inevitable that it should be definite, that it should be considered a body of fixed rules and procedure. The law of everyday relations and business must be at any given moment something fixed and certain. The office of arbitrary prerogative was not to build up and constitute the body of the law but to modify its harshness and supplement the remedies which it offered. See Holdsworth, I, 447.

32 See the varying reference of petitions in Maitland's *Memoranda de Parliamento;* Holdsworth, II, 308 at note 7; J. C. Davies, *Baronial Opposition to Edward II,* p. 249; Plucknett, *Statutes and their Interpretation in the Fourteenth Century,* pp. 10-25. Plucknett explains the facts as a "fusion of powers." They are caused not by a fusion of powers but, if one may so speak, by an un-fusion of powers, by a differentiation which is in progress and incomplete.

tween it and equity, and all that was later done by equity could still be done in the field of the common law. Such a distinction between them was indeed impossible. All acts of the king in opening his prerogative procedure to the community were alike in the teeth of the existing system, furnishing unusual remedies, and founded upon his duty to secure justice to all. There was no ground upon which they could be divided into two great classes by the later tests which distinguished equity and the common law. It is only as the common law became a hard and fast system, as men began to ask themselves about boundaries of action and limitations upon the new, that a new field was found for the action of the royal prerogative in securing general justice not specially provided for in the ordinary way. Strictly speaking, it was not new, for this duty and this function still remained to the king, and it remained in constant exercise.

The seat of this action was in a place where it had always existed, in an organ which had come to be more and more recognized, as definition and differentiation increased, as being the special organ of the king's prerogative, in the council. In the early years of the fourteenth century, we find the itinerant justice court exercising a true equity jurisdiction and acting upon petitions for grace and mercy upon a rather extensive scale. This was manifestly a survival, maintaining itself no doubt because in a peculiar degree as royal commissioners the justices stood in the place of the king, but destined soon to disappear.[33] At the same time we find similar petitions acted upon by the council in parliament.[34] In the spirit of the

33 And possibly because this jurisdiction in the itinerant justice courts served still a very useful purpose for the poorer people, who would find it a more formidable matter to petition the council, which might in any case not trouble itself with their small concerns.

34 On how large a scale is clearly shown in Maitland, *Memoranda de Parliamento,* in both Introduction and text.

differentiation which was then under way, this was the normal and natural place for them. It was the original organ for this action and it was the organ in which still resided all those general and undefined functions and powers of the crown which had not been diminished or changed, even when a given function had obtained special organic expression. The relation of the king to the law had not as yet been modified by the development of the common law or of the common law courts, as his relation to legislation was not to be modified for a long time after the development of a special legislative organ.

As the organ of the king's prerogative, the council was the natural place for the exercise of his equitable powers in interference in the field of the common law, and it is therefore under the council that the modern system of equity developed. The ancestor of the bill in equity is to be found, not in the bills in eyre, but in the petitions to the council, which may be read in Maitland's *Memoranda de Parliamento*. It may be of interest to add that when the later bill in chancery begins to assume formal character, the same process of differentiation and limitation was beginning in equity which had earlier occurred in the common law.[35]

The discussion of the relation of early equity and common law to one another, presented in the foregoing paper as originally printed, was continued in an article contributed by Dr. W. S. Holdsworth, now Vinerian professor of law in Oxford University, to the *Yale Law Journal*, of November, 1916, entitled: "The Relation of the Equity Administered by the Common Law Judges to the Equity administered by the Chancellor."[36]

[35] The following part of this Chapter was first printed in nearly its present form in the *Yale Law Journal*, XXVI, 550-563, May, 1917, under the title: "The Continuity of English Equity."

[36] Vol. XXVI, 1-23.

Strictly interpreted the subject discussed by Dr. Holdsworth was not quite the same as that proposed in my article. He was primarily interested in the question: Did the technical procedure and doctrines of the historical equity system of England derive in direct descent from the equity administered by the common law judges of the twelfth and thirteenth centuries? "The cases in the common-law courts of the thirteenth century in which appeal is made to equitable considerations and doctrines are known to be so numerous that 'they raise the important question whether the equity which the common-law judges administered in these cases can be regarded as the beginnings of the system of equity developed by the chancellor; or whether these early equitable doctrines so completely died out that we must regard the chancellor's equity as a new and a different development.'[37] His conclusion that we must is stated in these words: 'Whether we look at the court which administered it, at the procedure which that court employed, at the theory upon which equity was based, or at the contents of the equitable rules, we see a striking contrast between these two phases in the administration of equity. It is so striking that we must conclude that our modern system of equity created by the chancellor is, not a continuation of the equity administered by the common-law courts, but a new, a distinct, and an independent development.' "[38]

With Dr. Holdsworth's conclusion, stated as I should prefer to state it, I have no contention. I believe it to be beyond question that our modern system of equity, looked at as the court which administered it, or the procedure which that court employed, or the contents of the

[37] From "The Continuity of English Equity," p. 551.

[38] From Dr. Holdsworth's article, p. 23. In his *History of English Law*, II, 347, ed. 3, he repeats: "It is a new, a distinct, and an independent development."

equitable rules, did not develop from the equity administered by the common law courts of the twelfth and thirteenth centuries. If we interpret strictly the words "the common law courts of the twelfth and thirteenth centuries," nothing whatever in the way of equity developed from them. The words exclude the equity system which was in full operation at the same time with the equity administered by the common law courts, that is, the equity administered by the council, from which the modern system did develop. I must submit, however, that the words used in stating this conclusion in its positive form: the equity administered by the chancellor is "a new, a distinct, and an independent development," obscure, or even seem to deny, the essential fact which is the key to the whole process of the differentiation of institutions down even to modern times—the fact that, when the council throws off a separate institution for the exercise of a particular function, it continues to retain in itself the power to exercise that function as before and does so without hesitation if occasion demands.[39] The exercise of an equity function by the common law courts did not extinguish the action in equity of the council,[40] and the

39 Had the equity administered by the common law courts suddenly ceased at the end of the thirteenth century, leaving for the moment no institution through which equity was administered, or had been in the past, then a problem would have been created something like this, if it could have been consciously framed: where is it going to be possible to find a principle or an institution by which interference with formal law in the interest of general justice can be continued? This would have meant that a new beginning of equity must sooner or later be made. Fortunately this was not what happened. Equity in the common law courts ceased very gradually, and its place was as gradually taken by the same kind of equity, founded upon the same principle, as it was then, and had long been, administered by the council. But a cataclysm of this sort is logically implied by the words quoted above.

40 Nor, because the common law courts gradually ceased to administer equity, did the council gradually assume a jurisdiction which it had not before possessed. There was offered it an opportunity for expansion of

chancellor also, when he began to branch off from the council and to exercise a jurisdiction outside the council, neither extinguished the equity jurisdiction of the council nor created a new jurisdiction. He was assuming to exercise personally in chancery and without troubling the council about it a jurisdiction which belonged to the council, which it had exercised from the Conquest,[41] and from which came to the chancellor's separated equity system the fundamental principle upon which it rested, and always continued to rest, the duty of the king to make justice prevail through the exercise of his prerogative powers.

The question of the continuity of English equity, which necessarily involves the question of its origin, is so important in our institutional and legal history that it should be considered anew and the endeavor made to show if possible in what respects the history of equity is continuous, not into the thirteenth century merely but into the sixteenth. In such a study there is, I think, no question as to the facts. The question is as to the interpretation of the facts.

In a discussion of this kind there is one preliminary consideration which is important. While Dr. Holdsworth

which it could take advantage because it was already in occupation of a part of the field. The petitions acted upon by the council in 1305 show how it was then administering equity at a time when similar petitions were still being presented in large numbers to the justices in eyre. See Maitland, *Memoranda de Parliamento, passim.*

41 See the cases from the time of William I discussed above in Chapter III. They are all cases resting upon the same principle as does the common beginning of equity and common law under Henry II; the delegations made are all, strictly considered, from the council; the jurisdiction employed is that of the council; if the judgment receives confirmation, it is that of the council as in the Penenden Heath case; and if the action of the local court needs to be supplemented, as in the case of Bishop Gundulf against Picot, the supplementary action is that of the council. The same jurisdiction in equity belonged to the Norman curia ducis. Brunner, *Schwurgerichte,* p. 147 at note 5.

does not overlook the development of the institutional side of later equity, the relation of equity for instance to the council, and especially does not in his *History of English Law,*[42] the main interest of his treatment is in the body of doctrines and equitable considerations upon the principles of which the system was administered.[43] If one is considering the content of equity as distinguished from the common law that is a highly important, indeed the necessary matter to be studied. For a student of the history of law, regarded as a body of ideas and doctrines, of precepts and fundamental principles, the question when and from what source these elements entered into the historical current of the law, and what changes they made in the then existing body of law, is the essential thing to be studied. Such a study will include also the way in which these new considerations modified or rendered obsolete existing procedure, or introduced new and supplementary forms. I hardly think it is likely, however,

[42] Holdsworth, I, 339 ff., 477 ff.

[43] See the passage cited at note 38. "Thus the equitable principles which we can discern in the common law right down to the beginning of the fourteenth century gradually evaporated. It was this fact which made the intervention of the chancellor necessary." Holdsworth, II, 346; *Yale Law Journal,* XXVI, 22. These sentences may very likely have been hastily written and express more than was intended, but as they stand one can only record dissent. The equitable principles upon which the common law was founded in the twelfth and thirteenth centuries did not evaporate. There was no action on the part of the chancellor which should be called an intervention in the sense that he stepped in to take the place of a failing system. He merely kept on in his natural course, adding to the principles upon which he had been acting, the principles which had been earlier the foundation of the common law, and which were still, as earlier, the foundation of equity, certain others whose broadening effect seemed desirable. Equity as administered in the common law courts and equity as administered in the council had a common origin in prerogative interference in the common law, especially active under Henry II, and they continued to develop on lines parallel to one another for more than a century, when equity in the common law courts gradually died out leaving equity in the council to go on as it had been doing since its beginning.

that any student of legal history will maintain that the study of these matters constitutes the whole of the history of law. Legal history regarded as a whole is a history of institutions as well as of doctrines, and it cannot be complete until the influence of each of these two factors in producing the common product is shown in its due proportion. Law can act upon practical affairs only through institutions, and these two sides are indeed so closely connected that it is impossible for any student whose main interest is in one side to give an account of his subject without treating more or less fully of the other.

As I have implied above, the main interest of Dr. Holdsworth's article is in the content of equity, the sources of the considerations and doctrines which have developed or changed its content and in some cases its practices as well. Among these new doctrines those which attempt to state the grounds on which equity rests its right to act must unquestionably be regarded as distinctly fundamental, clearly indicating contemporary ideas and decisive in influence on the future. It should be said that Dr. Holdsworth has shown that considerations of this character entered the history of equity at a date later than the thirteenth century and profoundly affected the development from that time on, so that we must say that the equity of the Tudor age justified its right to act in part at least upon grounds which would not have been advanced in the twelfth and thirteenth centuries. It is an important part of the present question whether these fundamental considerations so profoundly affected the nature and character of the existing system into which they came as to mark the beginning of a new and independent development back of which we cannot trace the history of modern equity, even as a system of doctrines. This is, however, only one portion of the question and our decision as to the continuous history of equity from the twelfth century can only be made when the whole of that which is developing together is taken into the account.

Upon the institutional side I think we are compelled by virtue of facts which are familiar enough to say that there is no break in the continuity of the development. There is no point after the beginning in the twelfth century where there originates a new and independent institutional development. The differentiation of the chancellor's jurisdiction from the council is not a new beginning.[44] It is merely an ordinary case of differentiation, slowly brought about, with no conscious intention, exactly like the earlier differentiations of exchequer and king's bench from the council.[45] So homogeneous and consistent within itself is the entire process of growth that it is possible to represent it graphically in a rough chart. Although such a representation is mechanical, it should be clearly seen that the process which it depicts was not mechanical. It was a living growth in which at no moment were contemporaries conscious that any radical or

[44] The only change the chancellor made was that he began to do outside the council what he had been doing inside it and this change, except in one or two particulars, was so gradual as to be unnoticed.

[45] There is of course one difference in the fact that the jurisdiction of the chancellor as an equity judge he himself had never exercised alone in the council. His jurisdiction as the sole judge of a court never existed anywhere but outside the council. This is not true of the body of barons and justices who by degrees formed the separate courts of exchequer and king's bench. There is in the history of each of these institutions a period where a specialized body of council members, still practically within the council, performed the functions soon to be differentiated into new institutions. The same thing is true of the court of star chamber and of the present house of lords as a supreme court. But this peculiarity of the differentiation of the chancellor's jurisdiction is not of importance from the present point of view. It is important, however, to notice that the court of common pleas differed in that it was never council. It represented the royal prerogative by virtue of a delegation, not as the exchequer did because it was council. That is, equity in exchequer and king's bench was not really equity in common law courts but equity in the council.

revolutionary change had occurred. Each stage in the development, each differentiation, came about so gradually, by such minute and natural changes, that they were wholly unsuspected. The changes indeed, measured after long lapse of time, are seen to have worked no greater transformation than those wrought in similar periods in the history of the English language, and like these no man in the line seemed to himself to be doing a different thing from his father.

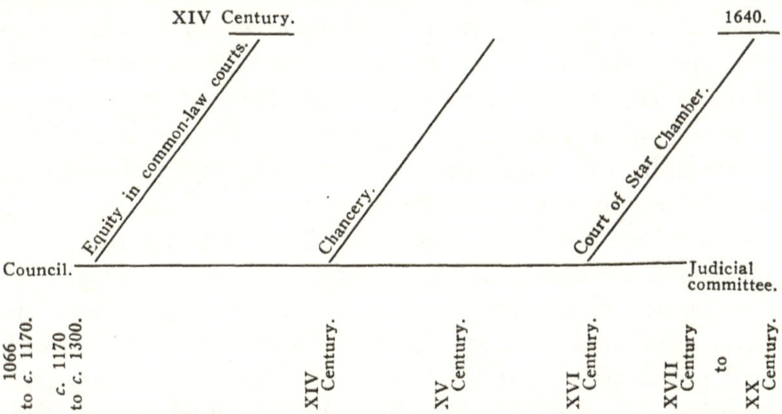

The first period, 1066 to *c.* 1170, is the period of equity as prerogative action, not yet distinguished from other prerogative action, and not yet looked at theoretically, administered by the council, great[46] and small; that is, by

[46] It will be understood of course that the mention of the great council means no more than that the same powers were possessed and the same functions could be exercised by the great as by the small council. As a matter of fact it is almost always the small council that is acting in the cases that we know, and it is always from it that the differentiations upon the judicial side take place. It is true also that neither great nor small council, exactly considered, made use of the new prerogative procedure of the common law courts, though it would be difficult to say why not, and though the council as *coram rege* seems to have done so in a limited way. See Pike, *House of Lords,* p. 280.

the curia regis, or by royal commissioners appointed for special cases, who hold a local curia regis. The action of the court is occasional only and by special permission. The second period, from *c.* 1170 to *c.* 1300, is that introduced by the judicial changes of Henry II. New royal courts were created specially to administer the prerogative interference with the ordinary procedure on equitable grounds. These were the itinerant justice courts and the central court of common pleas. Prerogative action was still the special function of the council and, by reason of that fact, the operation of these new courts was under the supervision of the council, to which important and difficult cases were reserved[47] and which during the period began a jurisdiction in error.[48] The action of the council in this connection came soon to be known as *coram rege* and was the germ of the future king's bench court, which can hardly however be said to be differentiated as a distinct court till near the close of this period. The equity procedure which in the preceding period had been occasional and special only, was now opened to all and regularized, but the forms by which it was regularized tended rapidly to become fixed and hardened, so that the free and untrammelled operation which was general earlier was gradually left to the council only. This process of fixing and hardening was that by which the body of the common law with its courts became distinguished from equity proper, which remained the function of the council. This is the state of things which characterized the next period, the fourteenth century. Equity could still occasionally be administered by the common law courts, especially by the general eyre, but this was a survival

47 *Gesta Regis Henrici Secundi,* I, 207.

48 *Patent Rolls, 1232-1247,* 162; Bracton, f. 108. The justices of the bench seem sometimes to have corrected the itinerant justices. See *Bracton's Note Book,* pl. 1445.

only and ceased before the close of the century. The true line of the development of modern equity in this age is to be found in the action of the council, great and small, at the beginning still in function undistinguished from each other,[49] upon petition and still clearly based upon prerogative. This equitable jurisdiction of the council rapidly increased in importance during the fourteenth and fifteenth centuries, and somewhere in the fourteenth the chancellor began imperceptibly to relieve the council of some of this work[50] and so by degrees to draw off more and more of this equity jurisdiction until what we know as equity proper had been withdrawn from the council. The chancellor's court had become distinct from the council before the end of the fifteenth century.[51] It is along the line of this court that the great body of equitable doctrine and practice came down to us. But if the technical equity system was now dissociated from the history of the council, that body did not cease to be the

[49] While equitable action seems to have been primarily the function of the small council, as indicated for instance by the address of the majority of the petitions, the fact of the absorption of the small council in the great at the time of a meeting of parliament is more clearly indicated to us in the records of the time of Edward I than before. See Chapter X, note 39. This is the meaning of the phrase *consilium in parliamento,* which made its appearance as a common phrase about this time, in which *consilium* means the small council, as it practically always does down to this date. The expression would seem to indicate that the relation between the two councils, or perhaps the difference between them, is more consciously regarded than it had been earlier. For this reason I have said in the text that it was in function that they were still undistinguished. On the jurisdiction of the council at this time see Maitland, *Memoranda de Parliamento,* pp. lxxix-lxxxix, especially lxxxv.

[50] Possibly the first impulse to this differentiation came from the statutes of 8 and 21 Edward I, in regard to the classification of petitions and their disposition. See Holdsworth, I, 354, 401.

[51] The chancellor sat alone as a judge as early as the reign of Richard II; Baildon, *Select Cases in Chancery* (Selden Soc.), p. xvi; but the chancery was hardly a distinct court until near the end of the fifteenth century, *ibid.,* p. xix; Holdsworth, I, 404.

organ of the king's prerogative in its superior function of correcting and supplementing the ordinary law, the same function from which equity had originally grown. In exercising that function it continued to be a court. Both these facts are clearly to be seen in the preliminaries which led to the court of star chamber and in the history of that body.[52] The progressive separation of the court of star chamber from the council is more closely parallel to that of the exchequer and of the king's bench than to any of the other cases of differentiation,[53] and the court is for a long time rather the council itself, or a special body of the councillors acting in a particular capacity, than a distinct court. This is perhaps the reason why the changes of 1640 left hardly any of the old judicial functions remaining in the council. The abuses of which Parliament complained seemed quite as much those of the council as of the star chamber. Its appellate jurisdiction, however, survived and it is in that particular that it has come down to its modern form, the judicial committee of the privy council, constituting a court of appeals rather than one of original jurisdiction. The judicial committee is however the direct lineal descendant of the council from which the star chamber separated in the sixteenth cen-

[52] See Holdsworth, I, 495 ff.

[53] The analogy between star chamber, king's bench and exchequer at one point in the process of their differentiation and the present position of the house of lords as a court of law is very close and especially instructive because the differentiation of the house of lords as a court has been arrested in mid-process. It now appears stationary in the position where the court is composed of a special body of members of the large body acting alone for this particular function, but clearly as being in theory the larger body, and themselves remaining members of the larger body for all purposes. This was exactly the case with the star chamber under Henry VII and with the king's bench in Bracton's time, and the exchequer a generation earlier, except that these were differentiations from the small council and for some time and in special cases acted as the council itself. See A. F. Pollard, *E.H.R.*, XXXVII, 337 ff., 516 ff.

tury, the chancellor's equity court in the fifteenth, and the common-law courts in the thirteenth. As Dr. Holdsworth says: "The act of the crown in allowing or dismissing an appeal, according to the advice contained in the report of the Judicial Committee, is the lineal descendant of the judgment given by the king in person in the Curia Regis."[54]

There is no escape from the conclusion that institutionally the modern system of equity has come down to us in a continuous and unbroken growth from the system of prerogative action of the first Anglo-Norman kings, which was started upon a new development by the reforms of Henry II. There is no point between 1066 and the twentieth century where there occurs such a break that we cannot easily see the passage of the institutions which were administering equity through and beyond it. In fact there is no break at all. The institutional history of equity is as continuous as the history of the English language from the same date.

What we have now to consider is whether, into this line of institutional development, there entered at any point new doctrines and theories so fundamentally changing the character of the body of equity which was accumulating from stage to stage as to constitute, in spite of the institutional continuity, a new, distinct, and independent development, marking thus a date before which modern equity was not beginning to form.

In the first place, it should be noted that any peculiar developments in equitable considerations or procedure appearing in the common law courts of the thirteenth and early fourteenth centuries can hardly be expected to affect the later development of equity proper.[55] They lie

54 Holdsworth, I, 520.

55 In studying the cases of Bracton's time with reference to their possible later use as precedents, it would be important to distinguish those

clearly outside the line of continuous growth. If they do affect later equity, it can only be because they have been borrowed, not because the later doctrines or procedure have come out of them by a natural process of growth. The natural process of growth does not follow that line. The common law line of equitable practices and doctrines alike is doomed to early and complete extinction. It has no natural descendants. It is a distinct advantage to have it clearly shown, upon the side of doctrines, that no such connection exists; that even borrowing did not take place; but, except as to borrowing, the same assertion could be made, a somewhat *a priori* assertion perhaps, from a study of the line of institutional descent.[56]

cases which are really common law cases from those which are council, or *coram rege* cases, if it were possible to do so. In some cases it is possible but not in all. The headings of the rolls cannot be taken as final evidence. I think there can be no doubt but that a councilman of Edward I's time would have regarded a true *coram rege* case of Bracton's period as distinctly in the line of council precedents. And there was as yet very little reason why it should not be so considered. They would undoubtedly be reckoned as king's bench precedents also. Bracton could hardly have thought of king's bench and council as two courts staffed by the same men. Holdsworth, I, 447. They were to him only one court acting sometimes in one way and sometimes in another, sometimes with a larger and sometimes with a smaller and more special staff. The reason why such common law features as enter into *coram rege* cases in Bracton's time (and they are much fewer than would appear in a careless reading of the records) do not affect later council development, is not because *coram rege* is then something different from the council, but because the distinction between common law action and council action is not yet quite clear but is becoming from Bracton's time on and in the whole situation rapidly sharper and clearer. As the common law system becomes more and more a fixed system, the more free and unrestricted possibilities of action by the council as the organ of prerogative, stand out more clearly.

[56] If A represents a continuous line of development from which B at some early point branched off, we should expect B to continue to show for some time characteristics which belonged to the original line before the separation. But we should not expect A to owe anything to B, either to B's independent development of the characteristics which had belonged to the undivided line, or to the distinct developments which it had brought in as

In the second place, it should be noted that the original foundation upon which the right of equitable interference rested, the supreme duty of the king to secure justice to all, as carried out by the royal prerogative, continued as the chief justification of equitable interference by the council proper so long as that interference continued.[57] Such action by the council undoubtedly survived two great crises in its history, one at the point where the common law courts were differentiated,[58] and one where the chancellor's court was differentiated. It apparently succumbed in the next crisis of its history when the court of star chamber was destroyed. But so long as it survived, its justification was always found in the royal prerogative, in the supreme function of the king in the state.

For two reasons it seems more difficult to believe that this fact is also characteristic of equity as administered by the chancellor. One is because the chancellor's jurisdiction branches off from the council at so early a date,

original additions since the separation. Direct borrowing from one line might indeed affect the other, but there could be no cross influence of the forces of natural growth. These have been split and separated into two channels by the differentiation. This reasoning applies as well to tribunals and procedure as to doctrines. Forms of procedure developed in the chancellor's court after the separation which could not have been derived from the equity procedure of the common law courts are precisely what should be expected.

57 Holdsworth, I, 506.

58 I hardly think it will be thought by anyone that the differentiation of the common law courts with their equitable powers brought to an end the equitable jurisdiction of the central curia regis, that is of the great or small council, so that it would have to be revived again after the new common law courts had proved, from the hardening of their procedure, inadequate. There is too large a mass of evidence of the continuance of this council jurisdiction throughout the thirteenth century to permit such a supposition. Interesting cases are: *Bracton's Note Book,* pll. 857, 1106, 1133, 1221, 1235; *Patent Rolls, 1225-1232,* p. 131; *Red Book of the Exchequer,* p. 1013; see above notes 2 and 34. The number of cases illustrating the general as well as the equitable jurisdiction of the council in the thirteenth century is large.

beginning while the common law courts were still acting as equity courts, so that it is easy to believe that the chancellor's equity is something different. The other is because such important developments in practice and in doctrine took place in the history of equity under the chancellor that it is easy to believe that they must have modified even the foundations. The essential fact characterizing the whole development, however, is not the petition to the king which opens the proceedings, that is merely a method of setting the machinery at work, though a significant one; nor is it the fact that the remedies provided are an interference with the ordinary system of justice, that is a characteristic of the result though it would seem to be an inseparable characteristic, expressed or latent. The essential fact is the existence of the king's prerogative; that is, of a power recognized as above the ordinary everyday machinery of the state, whatever that may be at any given time, and free therefore from the rules and regulations which condition the running of that machinery. For this reason it is at liberty to act, or it assumes to act, as above the law to secure any sufficiently important object: the furnishing of justice to all, the enforcement of the rule of conscience, the establishment of a system of criminal equity, the suspension of a statute for a special purpose, the creation of a new offence by proclamation, or the pardoning of a convicted criminal.

If there was introduced into the history of equity a new doctrine explanatory of its right to act so fundamental as to constitute a new beginning, back of which we cannot trace the history of modern equity, the introduction must have taken place at some point after the line of the development of equity proper had parted from the line of the development of the council's jurisdiction.

In the latter line the original explanation continues unchanged to the end.

That is what occurred, I take it, as indicated by the facts presented in Dr. Holdsworth's article. It is directly in the line of the development of the equity system proper, which in the end passes under the jurisdiction of the chancellor, that the new doctrine entered and the new results occurred. The new doctrine is that it falls within the function of the equity court to enforce the rules of reason and of conscience. This new doctrine assured a broader function than that of securing justice to all.[59] It enabled the equity court to insist that faith should be kept in cases where the common law courts could not act from lack of some condition which they regarded as essential, as of a formal agreement, or of some other necessary evidence. It enabled equity to insist that unjust advantage should not be taken of ignorance or folly; that fraud should not succeed because mere forms were on its side, or because the common law had not provided an exact remedy.[60] To most if not all of these cases the older

[59] This new development should hardly be represented as implying that a new fundamental principle had been added to the old. What really happened is that a new test had been found for the application of the old principle. It did not now become the business of equity to secure general justice plus what conscience declared to be right, but it remained its business to secure justice, as it was in the past, but what was justice could now be determined in a new range of cases by what conscience declared ought to be done.

[60] The attitude of counsel towards the new doctrine and how the common law court would act are significantly shown in a case cited by Maitland from a manuscript "Year Book of Edward II." *Year Books of Edward II* (Selden Soc.), I, xix: "Once in the name of good faith he [Bereford, C. J.] urged the defendant's counsel to admit a fact that had not been proved. Back came the retort: 'You must not allow conscience to prevent your doing law.' " References to conscience as a guide of action begin early in the history of the law. Bracton says, speaking of the jury: "Si autem nec adhuc sciri possit veritas, tunc discere oportebit de credulitate et de conscientia ad minus. Et in quo casu non committunt perjuriam, quia contra conscientiam non vadunt, ut infra plenius dicetur de convictionibus." Bracton, f. 186.

principle that justice must be secured, if stated barely and alone, did not seem to be of immediate application. It might at least be plausibly said by the counsel for the defendant that the prerogative of justice had no ground on which to interfere. If the feoffee to uses converted to his own use the property which had been conveyed to him to the use of another, justice, as that was interpreted at least by the rules of the common law, was satisfied. The forms under which the conveyance had been made legally permitted such action by the feoffee to uses. If the confiding *cestui que use* supposed his interests would be safe, he had himself to thank for his loss. This was at least a plausible argument and, if nothing of more direct application than a bare appeal to justice could be adduced as ground of interference, the equity judge might well hesitate. Here entered the rule of conscience, that faith ought to be kept, and the equity judge found it no long step, a simple and obvious step indeed, to say that the function of his court already established and widely developed to secure justice, rightly enabled him to enforce good faith and to prevent injustice through a fraudulent use of legal forms. Conscience was not asserted as a substitute for the prerogative of justice, that is, as an independent basis of interference, but as proof that in a peculiar set of cases prerogative had the right to interfere.[61] In other words the rule of conscience made

[61] The relation of the duty of the king to the development of the system of equity jurisprudence is different from that of the rule of reason and conscience; the first is creative; the second is defining, guiding, directing. Reason and conscience alone could never have created the equity system because they alone could have furnished no ground upon which to interfere with the ruling system of the common law. What created equity was the continuous action of the council as the organ of the king's prerogative action in the endeavor to secure justice against prevailing forms from the Norman Conquest on without a break. When in the fifteenth century the chancellor gets the idea of appealing to reason and conscience to determine whether the justice which he has been and is administering cannot be more

it clear that here was a case that called for the action of the prerogative court because only in that way could justice be secured. The duty to secure justice was still the foundation upon which the new extension rested.[62]

In this explanation I am carrying only slightly, if indeed any, farther a suggestion derived from a paper read by Professor Vinogradoff before the Berlin Historical Congress in 1908 and printed in the *Law Quarterly Review*.[63] In that paper Professor Vinogradoff is primarily concerned to show the source from which the doctrine of conscience was derived and through what intermediaries it made its way into the system of English equity. In developing this subject he distinguishes at one point between those portions of equity in which the new doctrine found application and those in which it was not needed. He says: "The lawyers and ecclesiastics employed in framing equity jurisprudence in the light of conscience were primarily concerned with the application of three doctrines: equitable remedies had to be provided for those who had not understood how to avail themselves of their legal rights; transactions based on confidence should be protected; promises of parties to contracts

widely applied, the development becomes so broad and rapid that it seems like a new and independent beginning, instead of what it really is, an auxiliary reinforcement to a development already long going on.

62 What was to be secured may indeed not improperly be directly called justice. Says Professor Ames: "In most of these cases [after enumeration of certain classes of cases] it will be seen, the plaintiff is seeking restitution from the defendant, who is trying to enrich himself unconscionably at the expense of the plaintiff. Certainly in these instances of early English Equity, Chancery was giving effect to an enlightened sense of justice." *Harv. L. Rev.*, XXI, 262.

"The spectacle of feoffees retaining for themselves land which they had received upon the faith of their dealing with it for the benefit of others was too repugnant to the sense of justice of the community to be endured." *Ibid.*, 265. This article on the origin of Uses and Trusts is reprinted in *Select Essays in Anglo-American Legal History*, Vol. II.

63 *Law Quart. Rev.*, XXIV, 373-384.

should be enforced in certain cases, even if the ordinary legal formalities had not been complied with. There are other points about the equity jurisdiction of the chancery, for example the greater laxity as to certainty of claims, the putting down of maintenance, discovery in procedure, etc., but they proceeded from other points of view than that of conscience and it is to the latter only that we have to attend." That is to say, there was at the time of the introduction of the new doctrine a considerable portion of equitable jurisprudence, developed during its past history, in which no application of the new doctrine was made, because it was not needed, and this continued to be an essential portion of equity jurisprudence. It is into this indeed that the new results, however wide their reach, were incorporated. They formed no new and independent body of jurisprudence distinct from the rest of equity.

A special case cited by Professor Vinogradoff shows how the new principle was introduced in the portion of equity to which it was applied. "In a case tried in Chancery in 1467 (Y. B. P. 8 Edw. IV. f. 4, 11pl.) Genney, counsel for the defendant, tried to argue that the plaintiff had not taken care to follow prescribed rules as to covenants, and, if he suffered thereby, it was his own folly. The Chancellor, Bishop Stillington, granted a subpoena and justified his action in the matter by a characteristic maxim: *Deus est procurator fatuorum*. . . . God acts as attorney to foolish people. The maxim bears the stamp of rough and ready mediaeval clericalism, and it opened the way for the Chancery to look behind the external regularity of all sorts of transactions with a view to the redress of wrongs committed by skillful miscreants who had taken advantage of weakness of intellect, insufficient knowledge, or casual negligence." This is a special case but undoubtedly it did not stand alone and it shows clearly how the rulings of the chancellor would introduce the new doctrine into the body of equity.

The change in equity which resulted from the introduction of the rule of conscience has been, I think, in outline correctly described in the above sketch. The change was made in a line of development already going on, and continuing to go on, the line of practices and doctrines, not now of institutions. It was made not as a revolutionary or destructive change, cutting off the past, but as adding new life and power of growth in harmony with the past. Such a result is also what we should normally expect from the institutional continuity of the equity system. The growing complexity of the business life of the community, especially the wide extension of the practice of uses, created new legal needs which equity supplied by corresponding extensions of its fundamental principles, extensions always in harmony with the old, though made by the help of doctrines borrowed from without and leading into new and larger fields of action. There is no more a break of continuity in doctrines than in courts. Keeping in mind the difference between common law and equity, the change, both in process and in result, is analogous to that which was made in the common law by the introduction and extension of the writs of entry and of trespass.[64] Even if the new doctrine had come to be in the course of time the sole basis of modern equity by the disappearance of the classes of cases to which there had been originally no need to apply it, nothing more than this could be said historically. Large new fields were opened but they were added to the old, not put in the place of them, and both old and new have continued to be diligently cultivated together to the present day.

64 That is, keeping in mind the fact that in such expansion what the common law needs is not new justification of action but new forms, and what equity needs is not new forms of action but new justification.

CHAPTER VIII

THE ORIGIN OF THE COURTS OF COMMON LAW[1]

It has seemed to all scholars necessary to regard the event recorded of the year 1178 by a contemporary chronicler as the beginning of a new epoch in the history of English judicial institutions. The chronicler says that King Henry II, after an investigation of the matter, "when he learned that the land and the men of the land were burdened by so great a number of justices, for there were eighteen, chose with the counsel of the wise men of his kingdom five only,[2] two clerks and three laymen, all of his private family [household], and decreed that these five should hear all complaints of the kingdom and should do right [declare right in each case] and should not depart from the king's court but should remain there to hear the complaints of men, with this understanding that, if there should come up among them any question which could not be brought to a conclusion by them, it should be presented to a royal hearing and be determined by the king and the wiser men of the kingdom."[3]

1 Originally published in the *Yale Law Journal,* June, 1921, XXX, 798-813.

2 Much has still to be done with regard to the personnel of the new court, but it seems fairly certain that the limitation to five justices was not permanent.

3 "Itaque dominus rex moram faciens in Anglia quaesivit de Justitiis quos in Anglia constituerat, si bene et modeste tractaverunt homines regni; et cum didicisset quod terra et homines terrae nimis gravati essent ex tanta Justitiarum multitudine, quia octodecim erant numero, per consilium sapientium regni sui quinque tantum elegit, duos scilicet clericos et tres

It is impossible to interpret this account otherwise than as the establishment in the judicial organization of the kingdom of a new court, of a court which in that form did not exist before, and it has been universally so interpreted. The opinion about it which prevailed until a generation ago may best be outlined from the account in Stubbs's *Constitutional History of England.*[4] He held, in agreement with the view then regarded as settled, that it was the court of king's bench which was established in 1178 "as a separate committee of the Curia Regis," holding sessions *in banco* in the curia regis "nominally but not actually *coram rege.*" The court of common pleas as a distinct court owed its existence according to this explanation to c. 17 of Magna Carta by which the common pleas were "separated from the other pleas which came before this court," and at the beginning of the reign of Henry III the three common law courts were in existence with practically the same distinctions in jurisdiction as those which were finally considered to separate them in theory.

No departure was made from this interpretation until the appearance of the first volume published by the Selden Society, *Select Pleas of the Crown,* in 1888. In the introduction to that volume[5] Professor Maitland made two decided modifications of the older explanation. He was of the opinion that the new court established in 1178 was the later court of common pleas,[6] but he regarded it

laicos, et erant omnes de privata familia sua. Et statuit quod illi quinque audirent omnes clamores regni, et rectum facerent, et quod a curia regis non recederent, sed ibi ad audiendum clamores hominum remanerent; ita ut si aliqua quaestio inter eos veniret, quae per eos ad finem duci non posset, auditui regio praesentaretur, et sicut ei et sapientoribus regni placeret terminaretur." *Gesta Regis Henrici,* I, 207; Stubbs, *S.C.,* p. 155.

4 Secs. 145, 163, and 233. No change was made in the edition of Volume I, which was published in 1897.

5 Pp. xi-xvii; cf. Maitland, *Bracton's Note Book,* I, 56-58.

6 The name, court of common pleas, was not used until some generations

still as a differentiation from the earlier curia regis; and he held that in this court there appeared after a time and by gradual degrees a split, or secondary differentiation, by which in the end the court of king's bench was formed. That is, the new court contained in itself, as yet undifferentiated, both the later courts, and it was by the natural development resulting from its use that, a generation or two later, probably in the reign of John, it began to separate into the two courts of common pleas and king's bench, the latter thus not an immediate differentiation from the small curia regis or council but a division formed in the new court of justices and not as yet known technically as king's bench but only as *coram rege*. The division between the two, however, was not as yet sharply made. In 1893 Maitland carried farther the history of these courts with especial reference to the judicial organization at the end of the thirteenth century,[7] but without change of the original explanation. In 1894 Mr. L. O. Pike in his *Constitutional History of the House of Lords* elaborated this explanation of what was done in 1178,[8] without making reference to Maitland's discussion but with considerable new evidence, and since that date it may be regarded as the current explanation.[9] Pollock and

after the founding of the court. Glanvill, who was already a royal justice in 1178 and chief justiciar in 1180, speaks of it in common with other courts as curia regis (I, 3, 5), often apparently not thinking it necessary to be exact or to distinguish between different courts. It is referred to frequently in the writs in his book as "coram justiciis meis apud Westmonasterium," or "coram justiciis in banco sedentibus" (II, 6), or "residentibus" (VIII, 1; XI, 1). The official title of the justices was "the justices of our Lord the King of the Bench." In this Chapter the court is referred to as the court of common pleas, the central court at Westminster, the common bench, and the bench.

7 Maitland, *Memoranda de Parliamento*, pp. lxxix-lxxxv.

8 Pp. 33-43.

9 See Holdsworth, I, 195 ff.; Poole, *The Exchequer in the Twelfth Century*, pp. 180, 182; McKechnie, *Magna Carta* (2d ed. 1914), p. 263. See note A at the end of the Chapter.

Maitland's *History of English Law* which appeared in 1895 adds nothing to the conclusions already reached.

In a note to Chapter III of my *Origin of the English Constitution* of 1912 entitled "The Origin of the Court of Common Pleas,"[10] it was tentatively suggested that a further considerable modification of the current explanation should possibly be made. It was said that if the account of the chronicler quoted above be interpreted as record evidence would be, it would imply that the new court was not a natural differentiation from the existing curia regis, or council, like the exchequer court, but was created all at once by an act of legislation as a result of the experience which had been gained in working the itinerant justice system. The new royal prerogative procedure, the procedure of writs and juries, which it had been one especial function of the itinerant justices to render accessible to litigants generally, had proved popular, and apparently there had arisen a demand that it should be at all times obtainable and not be at the service of the public only when the special royal commissioners were going their circuits through the counties.[11] The new court was a

[10] Pp. 136-143. This explanation of the origin of the court of common pleas was accepted by Professor James F. Baldwin, together with a further outline of the general differentiation of the curia regis during the period covered by the present Chapter, not then in print but communicated by letter, and was developed in the early chapters of his *The King's Council* (1913). See p. 47, note 3 of that work, with reference to the court of common pleas.

[11] If we may trust the evidence of the pipe rolls in their listing of judicial amercements under the various courts which made them, almost the only records of the time which may be called judicial, then no change in actual practice was made by the legislation of 1178. The pipe roll headings are the same after as before that date. These rolls do, however, suggest an explanation of what took place which is at least worth consideration. The "placita ad scaccarium" and part at least of the "placita curie" seem to imply that the itinerant justices after their return from their iters still continued to sit at Westminster, continuing or completing their unfinished business. See, for example, Pipe Roll Society (1176-1177), XXVI, 7, 14, 28,

permanent itinerant justice court, held at a central point, in session between the iters of the justices and accessible to anyone from any part of the kingdom, if he obtained

39, 45, 62, 130, 131, and all volumes immediately before and after 1178. The business under these headings is plainly itinerant justice court business. If this explanation is correct, and it can only be suggested for study, each group of itinerant justices after returning from its iter sat as a bench for a time doing the same kind of business, new or continued. There would thus be as many central courts as there had been circuits formed. Possibly this may explain the complaint of the number of justices and indicate that the legislation of 1178 was a recognition of the necessity of this practice in some form and an attempt to regulate it by combining all continued itinerant justice business in one comparatively small central court before a single bench. There is, I think, both in and out of the pipe rolls, especially in the "fines," evidence to show that it was some time before the new court settled into distinct and definite form. The subject deserves further investigation and, as intimated, there is some material, not yet thoroughly sifted, from which considerable light may be gained through a comparative study of the personnel of the courts, the justices presiding in them, in the reigns of Henry II, Richard and John. The final concords give lists of the justices before whom they were made, sometimes itinerant justices, sometimes justices of the central court, or of a central court. The pipe rolls give other lists, and there is evidence to be obtained at least by inference from the court rolls after they begin. Preliminary study of these sources seems to me to indicate that they do not agree among themselves on this matter, or that the personnel of the courts was not fixed. Mr. Round believes (*Feudal England*, p. 576) that there were four "archijustitiarii regni," Glanvill and the three bishops of Winchester, Ely and Norwich, who held "a position severed from that of the other justices, of whom some act with them at one time and some at another." This seems fairly true of the time of Henry II, if not insisted upon too literally, but not beyond that time. Professor Maitland, relying also upon the fines for evidence, thinks (*Select Pleas of the Crown*, p. xv) that the justiciar sat regularly with the justices of the bench, but the impression made by the court rolls certainly is that he did so very seldom. He is constantly ending his writ to the justices for different purposes, to direct or to postpone action, to announce the making of an attorney, and to give other information. The first impression of the evidence when compared together is that to the early bench, perhaps to as late a point as the end of John's reign, there was no fixed assignment of justices, except possibly of a small central nucleus, but that any justice who had been commissioned for an iter was qualified to serve if needed, and that the actual choice was a matter of convenience. At any rate here is material not yet thoroughly studied which may throw further light on the questions discussed in this Chapter.

the necessary permission, that is, the necessary writ. It was also said that, if this explanation is correct, the court established in 1178 did not divide into two by a later differentiation, but that the court of king's bench was formed some time afterwards by a normal differentiation from the small curia regis or council. Since this explanation was published, further study of the material tends only to confirm the view then expressed, which is here repeated with more full evidence not as a tentative suggestion, but as an explanation which it is believed will stand the test of investigation.

If this explanation is correct, it should be evident in the facts that the new central court, which becomes in time the court of common pleas, was never at any time regarded as the small curia regis, or council. It should never be found performing the general functions of the council. It was not the council, nor an offshoot or committee of the council; it was the creature of the council and this seems to be what the facts imply, though the facts which bear on the question are not so numerous as we could wish.[12] The jurisdiction of the court was a delegated jurisdiction strictly limited by the purposes for which the court was created.[13] Its jurisdiction was indeed less wide than that of the itinerant justices, though it was in one sense a permanent session of their court.[14] The

[12] The historian may sometimes perhaps feel sure enough of the general principles which he believes to be controlling the development which he is studying to predict, as some astronomers have done, though probably not with quite the same confident assurance, that the facts which are still to be uncovered by future investigators will confirm the conclusions which he has reached.

[13] "Habet etiam curiam et justitiarios in banco residentes, qui cogniscunt de omnibus placitis de quibus authoritatem habent cognoscendi, et sine warranto jurisdictionem non habent nec coertionem." Bracton, f. 105b. This could not have been said in Bracton's time of any court which was a direct offshoot of the council. See also ff. 108, 108b.

[14] This court does hear *querelae* or complaints of individuals, apparently

new central court performed no administrative function;[15] it developed no equity jurisdiction, a fact which is decidedly significant and would seem an impossible limitation of any court which was a real differentiation from the council, instead of a legislative creation, at least before the middle or last part of the thirteenth century, that is, before the distinction between equity and common law began to be consciously made. The itinerant justice court carried the council into the counties, not as by itself council, but under a commission which conferred that authority and which limited the range of council action, but was intentionally wide enough to serve other needs of government than merely the rendering of justice. On the other hand the permanent itinerant justice court at Westminster was plainly intended to confine itself to judicial business—the *clamores* of the people.[16] And it did do so. Even king's pleas as introduced by the new procedure, the procedure of the Assize of Clarendon, which it was a special function of the itinerant justice courts to try, do not appear on its rolls, though it is hard to say

as cases under the old procedure, without a clear expression of the equity idea so plain in the bills in eyre, which may in part have developed from these complaints. See *Curia Regis Rolls,* I, 392-393, 405, 408, 425, 434, 469, and note C at the end of Chapter X.

15 Professor Powicke in his review of *Curia Regis Rolls,* Vol. I (see the last paragraph but one of note A at the end of this Chapter), points out some instances of administrative work in the court of the justices travelling with the king, but the cases are few and are probably to be explained by a stronger tendency of this division of the common pleas court to act as an itinerant justice court, travelling as it is with the king, than of the other division forming the central court residing more permanently at Westminster. I have noticed no instances of administrative work by the latter, but if found they would tend to confirm the position here assigned that court as an itinerant justice court permanently in session.

16 *Clamor* is a word of more frequent use in Normandy than in England and was there used of criminal appeals or complaints. Tardif, *Coutumiers de Normandie,* Vol. II, Index. I know of no reason why it should not be so used, since appeals were in the same way as civil cases suits of one individual against another, but such a use in England was certainly rare.

theoretically why they should not. Also criminal appeals, which strictly are *clamores*, that is, are civil suits on the complaint of individuals, are rather uncommon, and seem in some cases at least to involve points of difficulty which may account for their appearance in the court. Nearly all the business of the court is the trial of civil suits and nearly though not quite always by the new procedure.[17]

[17] On the mixture of procedure in the courts of this time see below, Chapter IX, note 38. Cases of old procedure alone or of mixed new and old are: Pipe Roll Soc., XIV, 21-22; *Ibid.*, XXIV, 240-241; Palgrave, *R.C.R.*, II, 41, 51, 58; *Placitorum Abbreviatio*, pp. 38, 59b, 68b; *Bracton's Note Book*, pll. 390, 396. An appeal is presumably always a case of the old procedure, and many are so tried throughout, but in some a jury is asked for and granted, showing that no inconsistency or hesitation was felt in passing from one to the other. *Select Pleas of the Crown*, no. 104; Palgrave, *R.C.R.*, II, 30-31, 244. *Bracton's Note Book*, pl. 1600 is the record of an interesting case. Recourse is had in an appeal to what is practically the inquest procedure of the Assize of Clarendon, not however to find out who is suspected of the crime as in the Assize, but to furnish proof for or against the accused since the normal method of proof, the duel, cannot be used because the appellant is a woman. (Cf. also pl. 824.) By this date, 1223, however, the jury was being used to furnish proof in a number of different ways. From the other side, apparently the only concern of the presentment jury of the Assize of Clarendon with appeals is to report to the itinerant justices that they have been brought that the justices may see to it that they are tried. While Glanvill is pre-eminently a book of the new procedure, the considerable place which the old procedure takes in it should not be overlooked. More significant than the essoin from our point of view is the discussion of the duel (II, 3) and the cases in which "per verba placitabitur et terminabitur" (II, 6; III, 1; IV, 6; VI, 8).

From the gradual character of the process of differentiation, from the overlapping of old and new in the cases before the same court and appearing on the same rolls, and from the retention and exercise by the council of the functions which it had in one form thrown off to the newly differentiated institutions, arises also the confusion which on the surface seems to characterize the facts as we study them. This apparent confusion is sure to reappear in the account of the modern historian unless the key which is furnished by the character of the differentiation is kept in constant use. The mixture of facts in the records is capable of a simple explanation when the course of the differentiation is followed. It is not easy, however, to get rid of the preconception that the development was tangled and confused. I

The fact that the central court at Westminster is not the council, nor any differentiation from the council,[18] is still more strikingly seen in two facts that appear in the judicial history of the thirteenth and fourteenth centuries. One is the treatment of its errors. In the original legislation which established the court, it was provided that questions of difficulty arising in the court should be referred to the king and the council for their decision.[18] This was nothing more than the natural rule for an institution of delegated jurisdiction.[19] Its formal expression, however, undoubtedly made more easy, what was also in a short time evidently felt to be a natural inference, that the council should assume the power, or more correctly exercise the power (for it would belong to the council normally), of correcting errors which it made, to which attention might be called by the complaint of the parties

have been accused of explaining too many facts and of making the institutional progress too simple!

18 It is hardly possible to regard the distinction between *sapientes* and *sapientiores* in the chronicler's account of the legislation of 1178 as otherwise than intended. "Per consilium sapientium regni sui" unquestionably means the great council. *Sapientiores* means a smaller, selected body. In practice the reference from the bench was to the council. See the instructions to the justices of 1218, *Rotuli Litterarum Clausarum,* I, 383; Madox, *Exchequer,* I, 529, *o.* On the use of *sapientes* for members of the council, see above, Chapter IV, note 5. The reference of difficult questions arising in the course of a trial in the court to the council for its decision is virtually, but no doubt unconsciously, a recognition of the fact that the judicial decision may have a legislative effect in defining the application of the law in new cases. It is interesting that the "self-developing" character of the common law appears conspicuously at its very inception.

19 At the beginning apparently the justices of the bench were as individual justices members of the council, as were also at the beginning the itinerant justices. This is probably the meaning of the phrase "et erant omnes de privata familia sua" in the legislation of 1178. See above, note 3. But they could not by themselves in their capacity as a court act as council. As a body by themselves, they were commissioned to act in a delegated capacity, as was the case when one of them was made a sheriff. As sheriff he was not a member of the council, but as an individual he was.

affected. This right, manifestly a right of superior jurisdiction as exercised by the court from which the authority of the lower court was derived, was firmly established in the course of the thirteenth century, was indeed never questioned, and was continued in natural course in the court of king's bench.

Equally striking is the distinction set up between the courts in the operation of the principle which had been emphasized by Magna Carta c. 21 that barons should be amerced by their peers only. Pike and Vernon Harcourt have shown clearly that this principle was interpreted to exclude the itinerant justice court from the right of amercement and, by inference at least, the central court at Westminster also.[20] Certainly the argument from silence would seem to be here of valid force, for in all the judicial material of the thirteenth century no evidence has yet been discovered to show that in looking for a court to "afeer" the amercements of barons any effort was made to use the central court. The argument from silence becomes morally conclusive when we add to the silence of the records Bracton's positive statement of the courts that may afeer—exchequer and council only,[21] exchequer still exercising the functions of the council and *coram rege,* the later king's bench, not yet sufficiently dif-

20 Pike, *House of Lords,* pp. 255 ff.; L. W. Vernon Harcourt, *His Grace the Steward,* pp. 289 ff., and *E.H.R.,* XXII, 733 ff. Pike shows the practice to have been older than the Great Charter. See McKechnie, *Magna Carta,* pp. 295 ff. The objection was not that individual justices were not the peers of barons (Pike, *op. cit.,* p. 255), but that the courts which they formed were not courts of peers because they were not forms of the council. The same justices in the exchequer or the council were the peers of barons because they were then members of the council. The barons never had any objection to the trial of their civil cases in the new courts and appear constantly on the rolls as plaintiffs as well as defendants.

21 "Comites vero vel barones non sunt amerciandi nisi per pares suos et secundum modum delicti, et hoc per barones de scaccario vel coram ipso rege." Bracton, f. 116b.

ferentiated from the council to be thought of as a separate court in this connection. Thus the judicial development of the thirteenth century draws a clear line of distinction between *coram rege* and exchequer on one side, as continuing functions of the council because they are natural outgrowths of it, and the court of common pleas on the other, as inheriting no council functions, because it was not an outgrowth but a creature of the council.

In sharp contrast with the relationship which the facts of thirteenth century judicial history show between the council and the exchequer on one side and the court of common pleas on the other, is the relationship which they show between the latter and the itinerant justice courts. Here the relationship is clearly one of practical identity. Each treats the other as if it were itself. All through the early history of these courts, down certainly to the end of the minority of Henry III, cases begun in one are freely transferred to the other, not for retrial or review but to complete the trial; and this is done, so far as the records show, by the simple act of the justices without writ or mandate of any higher authority.[22] By this I do not mean merely the assignment of a day for trial in another court. That is a process which assumes no identity between the courts concerned. I refer rather for example to the numerous cases in which, the trial being held in one or the other of these two courts, a day is assigned the parties to hear their judgment in the other. The trial is

[22] The writ *pone* was apparently sometimes used by one of the parties in a case, not by the court, to transfer the case from a county court meeting before the itinerant justices to the bench, never *vice versa,* but these instances, in which the court is clearly that of the itinerant justices and not the king's county court before the sheriff, are rare. See *Bracton's Note Book,* pl. 92. It was used in the same way to bring a case from the sheriff's county court into the itinerant justice court. Somerset Record Society, XI, no. 730; *Bracton's Note Book,* pl. 1776.

held in one court and the judgment on that trial is rendered in the other, as if the two courts were really one.[23] The rolls give us other cases in which assizes or trials of other forms begun in one court and carried only partly to judgment are finished in the other. That in most of these cases the trial goes from the itinerant justice to the central court, is not material because that would be natural and almost necessary, since a future iter of the justices would be of uncertain date, while the parties could always be assigned a day at the central court as holding regular terms.[24] There is no evidence in these assignments that the central court was regarded as a superior court. There are one or two cases in which the central court does indeed correct the errors of the itinerant

23 The earliest court roll which has been preserved to us is a roll of the bench for the Trinity term of 1194. It has been edited by Maitland in *Three Rolls of the King's Court,* Pipe Roll Soc., XIV, 1-59. So clear does this record make it that the bench treats sessions of the itinerant justices, which are evidently about to be held throughout the country, as if they were sessions of itself, making adjournments and assignments to them as it would to subsequent sessions of the bench, that the evidence of identity is equivalent to demonstration. This iter took place in September, 1194 (Hoveden, III, 262; Stubbs, *S.C.*, p. 215), and the evidence in the roll that it is about to occur may be added to the proofs assembled by Maitland that it should be dated in that year. See adjournments by the bench to hear judgment in the itinerant justice court, pp. 6 (two cases), 13, 14, 29, 47, 52 (two cases); assizes and other cases to be finished, pp. 2, 4, 5, 7, 11 (two cases), 13, 17, 38, several in essoins 51-58. Further examples may be found throughout the period. See Bracton f. 368: "Et eodem modo excusat consimile auditorium vel aequale, ut si justiciarii de banco suo nomine scripserint justiciariis itinerantibus, vel e contrario; licet par in parem non habeat imperium."

24 That this could not always be done with certainty even in case of the bench is shown by the practice of giving days at the Tower of London, especially when a distant day is set as in some essoins. Bracton gives as the reason for giving days at the Tower "quia justiciarii non semper continue per annum in banco sunt residentes," f. 353b. As examples of days set at the Tower, see Pipe Roll Soc., XIV, 22, 52; Palgrave, *R.C.R.*, I, 400; Som. Rec. Soc., XI, no. 1376.

justices,[25] but not even then as a court of superior jurisdiction as that phrase is commonly interpreted, but rather as a court of the justices united in a full bench, on the principle of the later court of exchequer chamber.[26]

The identity of these two courts is indicated even more obviously by the *nisi prius* relationship which seems to have existed from the beginning, or at least from a very early date, and which is probably implied in c. 2 of the itinerant justice commission of 1194.[27] The cases on the calendar of the central court not yet reached for trial when the justices go into the counties are transferred there to be tried by them. That is, a trial of the case before the itinerant justices is the same as a trial before the bench. The *nisi prius* reservation had become common form in the assignment of days in the bench as early as 1200, and it appears in plain terms in the writ for the iter of 1218. Of course it is not implied that jurisdiction at *nisi prius* or the *nisi prius* clause in the writs of sum-

[25] The court of review formed in 1219 as recorded in plea 67 of *Bracton's Note Book* is very like the later exchequer chamber. Instances of the bench acting as a court of errors are *ibid.*, pll. 243, 530, 564, 1445. The last only concerns the itinerant justices. On the limitations of the court in this respect and in others which find their explanation in its origin, see Holdsworth, I, at pp. 200-202.

[26] Holdsworth, I, 243.

[27] The justices are to try all pleas summoned before them by writ "vel a capitali curia regis coram eis missis." Stubbs, *S.C.*, p. 253. This provision undoubtedly is to be interpreted in the sense of a record of 1220: "et posita fuerunt coram eis [the itinerant justices] omnia placita in eodem statu quo fuerunt apud Westmonasterium." *Bracton's Note Book*, pl. 1412. The "capitalis curia regis" of the commission of 1194 was as in Glanvill the new central court. Glanvill, XII, 23; cf. the case of *Stephen v. Robert* (1194) Pipe Roll Soc., XIV, 16. See the *nisi prius* condition fully stated in 1199: "nisi justiciarii interim venerint in partes illas." Palgrave, *R.C.R.*, I, p. 453; cf. *ibid.*, 421, and Bracton f. 110. As common form see *Select Civil Pleas*, nos. 6, 10; *Staffordshire Historical Collections*, III, 145. The practice is clearly defined in the writ to the sheriff for the iter of 1218, in form as it remains in Bracton. *Rot. Litt. Claus.*, I, 380; Bracton f. 109; cf. the writ for 1231 in Stubbs, *S.C.*, p. 354.

mons had yet been worked out as they came to be by the end of the century,[28] but only that here was the foundation on which the later development rested, existing from the beginning in the relationship of the two courts. This identification of the two courts came to be expressed most completely in the entire suppression of the jurisdiction of the bench for the county in which the justices of the eyre were holding their court.[29] That the two courts are one could hardly be more clearly assumed.

It may be added that the character of the court of common pleas as a legislative creation rather than as a natural outgrowth of the council is reflected in the fact that it undergoes no historical development in the organization or jurisdiction or relationships. The procedure which is employed in its business develops rapidly and the amount of work which falls to it increases greatly and is shared with other courts, but as itself a court institutionally considered it remains to the end what it was at the beginning. Of the other two common law courts this is not true, but throughout the whole thirteenth century the natural growth within the council in which they had their origin continues and changes progressively their jurisdiction and relationships.

From the provision in the legislation of 1178 requiring the reference of difficult questions to a royal hearing ("auditui regio") originated the court of king's bench. With the rapid expansion of common pleas business after the new procedure came into use, many new and difficult questions arose upon which the justices, itinerant and *capitales*,[30] desired the opinion of the highest authority,

28 Holdsworth, I, 278 ff.; G. J. Turner, *Year Books Edward II* (Selden Soc.), IV, xxiv; *Encyc. Laws of England*, III, 78.

29 P. and M., I, 180; *Eyre of Kent*, pp. xviii, xxxiii.

30 On the "justiciarii capitales" as the central court, see note 27 above. Add to the reference to Glanvill there given, VIII, 5, 4. Bracton's designation of the court is the same as Glanvill's: "ut autem de capitalibus

and the reference provided for was clearly to the highest authority, to the king and the *sapientiores,* that is, to the council,[31] to the authority which had created these courts and their procedure, from which were derived their powers and the regulations under which they acted. The meaning of this reference is to be seen in the form which it takes during the absence of the king from England, when it becomes a reference to the justiciar, *coram archiepiscopo,* or to the council direct as frequently during the minority of Henry III.[32]

The first effect of the frequency of reference under this provision was upon the phrase *coram rege.* This phrase had been in common use since the Conquest but in a general and untechnical sense.[33] In Glanvill, a book written

justiciariis in banco residentibus ad presens taceamus,'' f. 108b. In 1194 a case stopped before the itinerant justices by a charter permitting trial only ''coram rege vel capitali justiciario'' goes on in the central court of common pleas.

31 See note 18 above.

32 Palgrave, *R.C.R.,* I, 14, 87; Pipe Roll Soc., XIV, 14; *Bracton's Note Book,* pll. 12, 1306; *Rot. Litt. Claus.,* 383, I, as in note 18 above.

33 In earlier times and until some time after the organization of the new court in 1178, the phrase *coram rege* was used chiefly in two connections: in reference to an actual trial, as in Glanvill, and in grants relieving the donee from pleading in any except a royal court. This grant seems to have been desired in order to escape from the local and baronial courts and, unless unusually specific, seems to have been satisfied by a trial in the great or small council or in a court of any royal commissioner above the rank of sheriff. When the bodily presence of the king is plainly insisted upon, the emphasis indicates the exceptional case. As examples may be cited (in some instances *ante regem*): (William I) Davis, *Regesta,* no. 36; *ibid.,* Appendix, xiv, xvi; cf. no. 183a, and Round, *Calendar,* no. 116; Davis, *Regesta,* no. 63; Haskins, *Norman Institutions,* pp. 21-22; *Domesday Book,* I, 58b; *coram regina, Domesday,* I, 48b, 238b. (William II) Davis, *Regesta,* no. 429. (Henry I) *Chron. Mon. de Abingdon,* II, 164; *Cart. Glouc.,* I, 236; Dugdale, *Monasticon,* VI, 1043; Madox, *Exchequer,* I, 93, *w;* Rymer, *Foedera,* I, 12; ''coram me vel coram proprio justiciario qui super omnes alios vice mea justitiam tenet,'' *Gallia Christiana,* XI, Instr., 156, from Valin, *Duc de Normandie,* p. 109, n. 2. (Stephen) *Chron. Mon. Abingd., II,* 181; *Chron. Mon. de Bello,* p. 66. These references give all the instances I have noted from the reign

after the legislation of 1178, and dealing with almost nothing but the business and procedure of the new courts of delegated jurisdiction, the phrase *coram me,* that is, *coram rege,* is in constant use with reference to these courts.[34] This untechnical use of *coram rege,* this use of the words even for the common pleas court at Westminster, and constantly for the division of that court travelling with the king, continued at least to the end of John's

of William I, but no attempt has been made to complete later reigns. After the accession of Henry II, and especially after the opening of the royal procedure to the public, cases of this untechnical use become very numerous. Madox, *Exchequer,* I, 116-121; Round, *Calendar,* nos. 45, 57, 100, 101, 108, 109, 129, 267, 483, 574, 700, 1280, 1398. Some of these are of special interest. See the formulae given in Brunner, *Schwurgerichte,* pp. 243, 409, and "nisi in presencia mea corporali," *Cal. Charter Rolls,* II, 320. It is, I think, certain that the words *coram rege,* when standing alone, never meant in any period of their history, early or late, "in the bodily presence of the king." See "coram rege in curia sua apud Dublin," *Cal. Close Rolls, 1227-1231,* 344.

34 Every writ of summons in Glanvill, except those which constitute the sheriff a justice, is "coram me vel justiciis meis," and this is so often explained as "apud Westmonasterium" that there can be no doubt the reference is to the new central court. In Book VIII the "in curia Westmonasterii" of c. 3 is plainly the "in banco" of c. 1. There is no evidence in Glanvill that the frequent *coram rege* refers to anything but the Westminster court. Pike, *House of Lords,* p. 37 at note 16, holds otherwise. In Bracton's time writs summoning cases before the bench still used the same form, f. 149. Of course there is no contention that such a writ might not be satisfied by an actual appearance before the king, if the parties could manage it, but the point is that they were satisfied, and were intended to be, by an appearance in the bench. Undoubtedly this early use of *coram me* is an expression of the theory upon which the new procedure goes that it is the king's processes and forms which are being used. The idea is not *coram me* in person, as distinguished from a court in which the king is not present, or that he is more truly present in one court than another. It is rather that the whole thing, courts and procedure, courts in which the procedure may be used, is the king's. Glanvill was written so soon after the founding of the Westminster court that distinctions between it and an especially *coram rege* court had not begun to be thought of. The constant *coram me* in Glanvill is very likely what suggested to early students of the subject that it was the court of king's bench which was founded in 1178. See above at note 4.

reign.[35] It is a survival of the older situation before the increasing development led to the making of distinctions. Meantime there was growing a tendency to regard *coram rege* as having a limited and therefore a more technical meaning.[36] This tendency was not merely due to the ref-

[35] Here belongs the familiar case of the abbot of Leicester who was told in 1200 by the court "that all pleas holden by the justices of the bench were deemed to be holden before the king or his chief justiciar." Maitland, *Select Pleas of the Crown*, I, xiv, from *Plac. Abbr.*, p. 32. Cases in which *coram rege* is satisfied in the bench are: *Plac. Abbr.*, pp. 67, 69b (two cases), 74, 76, 86b; *Select Pleas of the Crown*, no. 115, a case which concerned the person of the king and in which one party appears actually before the king and the other at Westminster; Palgrave, *R.C.R.*, II, 156, 158, 175-176 (these are along with cases where the distinction seems to be made, pp. 159, 167, 173); *Bracton's Note Book*, pl. 243 (A.D. 1227). Days given *coram rege* to a regular bench term, of which there are a good many, probably belong here at this date. *Staff. Hist. Coll.*, III, 69-70, 145. The records published in *Curia Regis Rolls*, Volume I, indicate that the justices with the king, who really were common pleas justices, kept the same terms as those at Westminster.

[36] In the cases cited in this note, except when the council is found acting, *coram rege* must be given the meaning which it is shown in note A at the end of the Chapter to have in the reign of John, that is, the court of the justices travelling with the king. The abbot of Leicester's case was not the only one in which a special grant was pleaded in bar of a suit in the bench, though the judgment of the court is not always recorded. *Plac. Abbr.*, p. 39b; Palgrave, *R.C.R.*, II, p. 41; a day finally given in the bench, *ibid.*, p. 54b; decision apparently against the bench, *ibid.*, pp. 163, 176; cases in which the bench is a second choice in a *coram rege* process, *Select Civil Pleas*, no. 40; Palgrave, *R.C.R.*, II, 182; *Staff. Hist. Coll.*, III, 132; Yorks. Archaeol. Soc., XLIV, 5; cases really *coram rege* by intervention of the king, Palgrave, *R.C.R.*, II, 45, 185, 188; *Select Pleas of the Crown*, no. 83; *Plac. Abbr.*, pp. 50b, 65, 66b (two cases). Other cases really *coram rege*, Palgrave, *R.C.R.*, II, 95, 173; *Staff. Hist. Coll.*, III, 156. Some cases of John's reign do show the council acting as a court, *Select Civil Pleas*, no. 190; *Plac. Abbr.*, p. 95, an interesting case: the king consults "super hoc illos qui tunc cum illo erant, etc., et posuit diem, etc., quando dominus archiepiscopus et alii viri magnates et sapientes terre interesse possent." See Chapter X, note 33. See the cases from John's reign cited in Madox, *Exchequer*, I, 790f. None of the cases cited in this and the last note is later than the reign of John except the one noted above. No effort has been made to collect all the cases. Something has been made in this connection of the mention of courts in the judicial fines of the period (*Select Pleas of the*

erence of difficult questions to the council but it was also a part of the rapidly growing technicality of the whole common law system. It shows itself in an effort to make the phrase more emphatic and specific. It becomes "coram ipso rege," or "coram rege ubicumque fuerit in Anglia,"[37] and in general statements we hear of pleas which follow the king. What the use of such phrases indicates is that a distinction is growing in the thought of the time which had not before been noticed and which there is need to express in a new way because the old seems inexact. *Coram rege* in technical use soon, though not so far as we can yet prove in the reign of John, comes to mean one distinct thing, and that is, the council acting in its judicial capacity.

This second stage in the development of the court of king's bench lasted at least until after Bracton had finished his treatise on the law and customs of England. He does indeed in one part of his book show us that he was conscious of the fact that this judicial business of the council was practically in the hands of a body of justices, who it is highly probable really did all the work.[38] He was

Crown, p. xiv), but a comparison of the lists of the justices given in these shows certain difficulties which cannot yet be overcome. See above, note 11.

[37] This becomes the technical designation of the king's bench in summonses; in judgments it called itself "the court of the Lord King now here." (*Select Pleas of the Crown,* p. xii.) See the declaration of Shareshull, C.J., 27 Edward III, on the three meanings of *coram nobis, Bills in Eyre,* p. xvi. These phrases come into use while the reference is still untechnical, that is, to the common pleas justices who travel with the king, indicating emphasis on the place of trial rather than on the character of the case or of the court. Whether the more technical use begins clearly in the reign of John can only be determined by a study of the rolls of his later years.

[38] Bracton, f. 105b, and f. 108, clearly distinguishes the "justiciarios capitales qui proprias causas regis terminant" from the "justiciariis in banco residentibus," but he does not distinguish the former from the "aula regis." Fleta at the end of the century describes the king's bench accurately enough in a short paragraph (II, 2, 5) as if distinct from the "aula regis"

himself in fact one of these justices.[39] But he nowhere shows any suspicion that this body in truth constituted a court distinct from the council. For him the justices in action are the council. He knows of no court exercising this jurisdiction but the council.[40] The same thing is true of *Bracton's Note Book*, the collection of cases from the judicial rolls which was beyond question that which was made for Bracton's use in writing his treatise. And the same thing is true of the records of the courts, so far at least as these are accessible in print.[41] There is no evi-

(II, 2, 2), but nothing further is said about it, while the ''aula regis'' is described at length. Britton uses a few more words but adds nothing to the statement of Fleta (I, 1, 4 and 11). The evidence that Robert de Brus is to be reckoned the first chief justice of the king's bench, because he was appointed in 1268 ''capitalis justiciarius ad placita coram rege tenenda,'' when compared with the language cited above, hardly seems convincing. The same words would probably be used of any justice of the court, and the date is too early. Fleta says that the king's seneschal ''in aula sua jam tenet locum capitalis justiciarii regis.'' Holdsworth, I, 204f.

39 *Bracton's Note Book*, I, pp. 18 ff.

40 Both the great law books of our earliest legal history are books of the court of common pleas. Glanvill's main theme is that court. It is his ''capitalis curia'' (VI, 8). Its justices are his ''capitales justiciarii.'' See note 30 above. The same thing is still in the main true of Bracton. Now and then he lets it appear in a brief passage that he was aware of the existence of a court in closer relation with the king, having justices of its own, and twice he calls them ''capitales justiciarios'' (note 38 above). He nowhere, however, describes this court at length, and he gives no details of its procedure nor of its relation to other courts beyond the single fact of its superior jurisdiction. Elsewhere in many places he calls the justices of the common bench ''capitales,'' *e.g.*, f. 108b, 411b.

41 Sharp technical distinction between the courts of common pleas and *coram rege* during the whole period, while it was undoubtedly forming, was still not invariably the rule. Though it is difficult, from the way in which the records upon the rolls were made up (uniting as they do in some cases into one record the whole trial of the case in whatever courts held or at whatever dates), to be sure that the whole process as it stands recorded actually took place in the court whose roll we have in hand, there can still be little doubt that the roll fairly represents the business of the court. From the *coram rege* roll of 1234-1235, considered the first of the continuous series, *Bracton's Note Book* excerpts twenty-seven pleas, pll. 1106-1132 incl. Of

dence down at least to the time of the Barons' War that contemporaries were conscious that a new judicial body, a new court, had been thrown off from the council.

Meantime another kind of distinction had been growing up which had an influence upon the final differentiation. Magna Carta c. 17 provided that common pleas should not follow the king but should be held in some certain place.[42] Civil pleas were no longer felt to be, as in

these, ten, 1107-15-16-18-20-25-26-28-29-31, show no clear reason why they should be on this roll. Certainly they could be paralleled by cases of the same period from the rolls of the common bench. I think the same thing can be shown of every *coram rege* roll before 1260 and perhaps later. An interesting roll as showing the character of these records is that extensively drawn upon by the compiler of the *Placitorum Abbreviatio*, pp. 106ff. It shows clearly that the roll is not made up of cases coming *coram rege* in any one place or in any sessional terms or before a court of uniform composition. This is exactly what we should expect of a council court at this date. Compare the court on 109a with that on 110b. See also the roll of 1242-1243, *ibid.*, 118-120. I have no doubt that cases technically *coram rege* began, probably before 1250, to be decided by a bench of two or three justices in attendance on the king, but I have not found a clear instance of the fact in any record which I have read. I am leaving out of account the question of the use of the new prerogative procedure *coram rege*, which is too large a subject to enter upon here, but it may be useful to note in regard to it, as well as to the main subject of this note, that the court of king's bench, which was by the end of the century a naturally formed offshoot of the council, was finally recognized as possessing an original jurisdiction in certain matters which had at first belonged to the common bench, *e.g.*, criminal appeals, trespass, and others in which the king was thought to have an interest. The appearance of cases which seem to be ordinary common pleas on the *coram rege* rolls may sometimes be accounted for, even where the fact is not evident in the record, by the king's prerogative right of ordering any case he pleased *coram rege* or by the original jurisdiction of the council, with which nothing had as yet interfered. Also it was by no means infrequent that one or the other party to a suit fined with the king for permission to have the case tried before this court.

42 It seems to me practically certain that this chapter of the Great Charter made no change in the central court at Westminster established by the legislation of 1178. While that court did on rare occasions hold sessions in other places than Westminster, the practice from the beginning seems to have been general, almost universal, that the bench sat at Westminster. In Glanvill and in the early rolls and fines it is constantly spoken of as "apud

Glanvill's time, all of one kind, but "communia placita" could be distinguished from others which were different, and it was felt that it was not right that they should be compelled to follow the king in his journeyings about the country. Other pleas, those, it comes very quickly to be said, in which the king has a personal interest, those which affect his royal dignity or rights, may properly do so. This was not, as was at one time thought, a new distinction of courts; that had already begun in another way. It was a classification of business, but it necessarily involved an assignment of it by classes to the different courts which had already begun to be distinguished. It undoubtedly assisted in that process of distinction, and in one sense it may be said to be the beginning of an original jurisdiction for the later court of king's bench. It was probably along this line that the criminal jurisdiction of the king's bench was obtained.[43] But the very im-

Westmonasterium," and the original official designation of it seems to have been "the court of our Lord the King before the justices at Westminster" or "the court of our Lord the King at Westminster." As relating to the business of the court, Magna Carta should normally have had an effect to put an end to the trial of common pleas by justices travelling with the king. Whether it did this or not, it is evident from the rolls of later date that it did not concentrate all common pleas business at Westminster. See the note last above. In this connection it is possible that we should regard c. 17 less as affecting the central court at Westminster than as an attempt to put a limitation upon the original jurisdiction of the council or of the court *coram rege*.

43 This suggestion as a subject of investigation of considerable importance can here only be indicated. It is certain that there was in the first half of the thirteenth century a growth of the feeling that certain pleas, which in the twelfth century had been common pleas without question, should be more immediately *coram rege* as affecting the king's person, dignity, or interests. These are criminal cases, those involving a charter of the king's or, sometimes at least, a tenant in chief, certain ecclesiastical cases, and trespass. See Glanvill, I, 32, 5; *Bracton's Note Book,* pll. 12, 1220; *Staff. Hist. Coll.,* III, 124, 127-128; *Plac. Abbr.,* pp. 144a-b; *Close Rolls, 1242-1247,* p. 353; *C.R.R.,* I, 463. The development of trespass from 1194 on is particularly interesting, as is *Bracton's Note Book,* pl. 1121: "Et

portant fact should not be overlooked that the council, which was the only court *coram rege* as yet, had a very extensive original jurisdiction entirely independent of and much earlier than this development.[44]

It is not proposed to follow here this differentiation into the time beyond the age of Bracton when the king's bench became a distinct court, recognized as an independent institution separate from the council,[45] because the final stage of its differentiation is so interwoven with a wider process of the same kind, affecting the whole position of the council, that far too much space would be required. When the fact becomes clear that the *coram rege* business of the council is settling into the hands of a specific body of justices, and that fact is clear from Bracton's statements, the final differentiation is only a question of time. It may be repeated as one anticipation of the later history that the reference of difficult questions to the *sapientiores* for decision led inevitably to the development of a jurisdiction in error, a superior jurisdiction because that of the council[46] and therefore over

Henricus dicit . . . quod blada ita fuerunt asportata et vi et armis et de nocte et hoc pertinet ad Dominum Regem.''

44 In the period before the prerogative courts were regularly established, nearly all the cases brought before the council were instances of its original jurisdiction. See Valin, *Le Duc de Normandie,* pp. 106f., 108. The case in the time of William I before ''multos ex melioribus totius Anglie baronibus'' (Bigelow, *Placita,* p. 36) is not the same as that which had just been tried before the bishop of Bayeux. See above, Chapter III, note 39. Also *Domesday Book,* I, 101b; Davis, *Regesta,* no. 370; Haskins, *Norman Institutions,* pp. 88, note 18, 91 (two cases). Of the cases cited from *Bracton's Note Book* in note 41 above as not clearly *coram rege* cases, the following may well be instances of original jurisdiction: pll. 1118-20-25-27-28-29.

45 See note 38 above.

46 Early cases where the action of the council is clear are: *Rot. Litt. Claus.,* I, 406, 549b; *Bracton's Note Book,* pll. 67, 1166; *Cal. Pat. Rolls, 1247-1258,* p. 431; cf. Bracton's justices ''a latere regis residentes, qui omnium aliorum corrigere tenentur injurias et errores,'' f. 108. Special commissions appointed to correct errors of subordinate courts are interesting, *Cal. Pat. Rolls, 1232-1247,* pp. 162, 192; *Arch. Cambrensis,* Series IV,

the bench itself as well as over the itinerant justices. This passed on into the later centuries when the king's bench is to superficial appearance merely another common law court co-ordinate with the common bench, but, though the historical reason was forgotten, the superior jurisdiction was never questioned.

As an institution apparently distinct, or distinguished, from the small curia regis and in its separate capacity trying cases, even *clamores* or what would later be classed as common pleas, the exchequer is the oldest of the three common law courts.[47] Its action in such a capacity, while in process of differentiation from the council, is of course what is normally to be expected, since the differentiation was incomplete and even hardly felt to be going on. It can be traced continuously from the reign of Henry I.[48] As the earliest of the institutions so differentiated, it is natural that the period of the process, before it was clearly recognized that a new institution had

II, 243. The case in *Plac. Abbr.*, p. 138, cited in Baldwin, *King's Council*, p. 57, as an instance of a writ of error, is the ordinary appeal of false judgment.

47 P. and M., pp. 189 ff.; Poole, *Exchequer*, p. 180.

48 As Mr. Poole says, *loc. cit.*, "there is abundant evidence of common law suits being heard at the Exchequer." Madox, *Exchequer*, I, 209 ff. The best known early case is that recorded in a charter printed in *Chron. Mon. Abingd.*, II, 116, before a rather full small council "in thesauro." Others are: Madox, *Exchequer*, I, 209 *a; Plac. Abbr.*, p. 84b; Haskins, *op. cit.*, p. 88, at note 18; cf. Round, *Calendar*, p. xliv; Bigelow, *Procedure*, p. 123. It is well known that the exchequer in Normandy became the general court of common pleas for the duchy, standing in the same relation to the courts of the itinerant justices as the court of common pleas in England and passing upon the same class of cases. It possessed a jurisdiction somewhat superior to that of the common pleas in England, because the transfer of sovereignty to the crown of France prevented any further development of the *curia ducis* in Normandy. See L. Delisle, *Recueil de Judgments de l'Echiquier de Normandie.* It is a natural conjecture that the exchequer came to occupy this place in the Norman judicial system because no court of common pleas was formed there, and that the English exchequer was well on the way to take the same place when its evolution in this direction was checked by the legislation of 1178.

been formed, should be the longest of any.[49] From early in the twelfth to the end or near the end of the thirteenth century,[50] the separation was going on, and during all

49 As the early process of differentiation is not an easy one to be understood clearly, nor our understanding easy to be logically applied to the facts, I should like to emphasize what appears to me the mark and test, almost infallible, of a differentiation from the council. It is that for a considerable period of time the new special organ which is thrown off continues to be regarded, not as an entirely separate institution, but as council as well. It is a form of the council to which a special line of business is entrusted, and it continues now and again to act as council while developing the special business of its new position. Almost certainly when the differentiation begins, it is due to a classification of business, not to a setting apart of special councillors to do the business. It is a session of the council in which a definite line of business is to have the right of way. As this particular business increases in amount and importance, certain members of the council who are peculiarly fitted for it from their knowledge of that special line of business or because of their official position are assumed to have a special responsibility for carrying it on as council business, and other council members less, but the special session is still a session of the council. As time goes on the special responsibility of these men is still further emphasized, the general responsibility of the others in this particular weakened, until they cease to attend, and the offshoot is complete. A new institution has come into existence but it still retains in many ways rights, prerogatives, functions, formal procedure, and indefinite possibilities, which have descended to it from the council and which bear evidence to the fact that it was itself once council. I have referred above, Chapter VII, note 53, to the history of the house of lords as a court of law as illustrating this process. It is a particularly good illustration because the process has gone on in comparatively recent times and is not yet completed.

50 If it were necessary, many instances of the exchequer acting as a court of law during the thirteenth century could be added to those cited in Madox, *Exchequer*, II, 10 f., 26 f., 77 ff., 118 ff. Of special interest are: *Rot. Litt. Claus.*, I, 608; *Close Rolls, 1227-1231,* p. 504; *Liber de Antiquis Legibus* (Camden Soc.), p. 33; *Red Book of the Exchequer*, p. 842. See also cases in which the barons of the exchequer and the justices of the bench act together: *Close Rolls, ibid.*, p. 503; *ibid., 1234-1237,* p. 383; *ibid., 1237-1242,* p. 69; *Chronicon Petroburgense* (Camden Soc.), p. 141; cf. *Liber de Antiquis Legibus*, p. 84, and *Annales Monastici,* III, 278. The phrase "ad scaccarium," which is rather frequent in the judicial documents of the twelfth and thirteenth centuries, is generally interpreted to mean the place at which the court sat, and not the court which was sitting, and therefore as not necessarily implying the exchequer court. That this interpretation is correct

this time the exchequer acted sometimes as if it were a separate organ of the council for a special kind of business, and sometimes as if it were the council taking advantage of a meeting under a special form to do ordinary council business.[51] This action as council continued, indeed, after it was recognized that there had been a differentiation,[52] and in some respects it may be said not to have ceased until the era of modern judicial reforms.

In two particulars the exchequer court bore into the nineteenth century the marks of its origin in a long process of unconscious differentiation from the council. One is its independent equity jurisdiction, which we need not here consider in detail,[53] but which was an inevitable result of its action as council throughout the twelfth and

in many places cannot be questioned. It is clear, however, in some instances that the barons of the exchequer were the court acting, or formed a part of it, where this phrase is used, and one may suspect that this was true in many instances where the fact is not clearly indicated. See *Bracton's Note Book*, pl. 1095, p. 113; Valin, *Duc de Normandie*, p. 278, no. 25; compare two cases in *Placita de Quo Warranto*, p. 294. Interesting are two strikingly similar accounts, *Chron. Mon. de Bello*, p. 111, and *Chron. Mon. Abingd.*, II, p. 297, and see the story cited in Madox, *Exchequer*, I, 214 *x* from M. Paris, II, 506. It is clear also that in many of these cases, indicated by such phrases as "per consilium domini regis ad scaccarium," "coram rege ad scaccarium," or "ad scaccarium coram consilio nostro," we have an exact parallel to the council later acting in chancery, many instances of which have been noted. Pike, *House of Lords*, p. 54, note 2; Baldwin, *King's Council*, pp. 239-240; Davies, *Baronial Opposition*, p. 261; and cf. pp. 266-278; Baldwin, *Select Cases before the King's Council, 1243-1482* (Selden Soc.), p. xxiii; Vinogradoff, *Oxford Studies*, VI, 2, 168-169, and compare the phrase "before our council in our chancery." In both sets of facts alike the council is acting with one of its offshoots, but acting as council, not as the derivative institution.

51 Baldwin, *King's Council*, pp. 41 ff.; Madox, *Exchequer*, I, 219 f.; *ibid.*, II, 26 ff.; Hovenden, III, 141; *Rot. Litt. Claus.*, I, 361, 438b; compare two cases, *ibid.*, 406a and b; *Cal. Pat. Rolls, 1225-1232*, p. 342; *Chron. Petrob.*, pp. 137-138.

52 See the record quoted in Madox, *Exchequer*, I, p. 423 *z*, and Davies, *Baronial Opposition*, pp. 245 ff.

53 Baldwin, *King's Council*, pp. 223 ff.; above, Chapter VII.

early thirteenth centuries when equity was not yet distinguished from the common law, or when, it would be more accurate to say, all administration of the law through the royal courts was based upon the fundamental principles which were later recognized as those belonging peculiarly to equity. It should be repeated, however, that this jurisdiction is strong evidence that the exchequer was regarded as council, since it exercised a jurisdiction belonging peculiarly to the council, while the common bench was not so recognized.

The second mark of its origin is the treatment of its errors. In the fourteenth century when the court of king's bench, secure in its jurisdiction in error over the common bench, attempted to establish a similar jurisdiction over the exchequer as a court of common law, the exchequer successfully resisted.[54] It based its resistance upon an argument which was historically an incomplete statement of its case, but which was nevertheless historically accurate so far as it went. It declared that it was not a common law court. That was quite true, but it would have been a more complete and effective answer if the whole truth had been stated: that, if the king's bench corrected the errors of the common bench because it was itself an offshoot of the council at one time indistinguishable from it, while the common bench was its creature, then the king's bench could have no corresponding jurisdiction over the exchequer court because this was of the same origin and history as the former, a co-ordinate differentiation from the council and therefore of co-ordinate rank and authority. The argument in the form in which it was put means the same as this and is historically accurate, because, as a court trying cases in the first part of the thirteenth century, the exchequer was not a

[54] Pike, *House of Lords*, pp. 293 f., Y. B. 14 Edw. III, pp. xxi ff.; Baldwin, *King's Council*, pp. 232 ff.

court of the new procedure, of the common law procedure, but in reality the council. It had later gained a share practically in common law jurisdiction by usurpation, by the use of a fiction, the "quo minus" process, which transformed the case from an ordinary "communium placitum" into a case falling under its original jurisdiction as financial organ of the council. That is, common pleas tried in the exchequer were not technically common pleas or cases at common law. This argument was accepted as good law in the fourteenth century. We must accept it as good history, but we must not overlook the fact that it is practically a demonstration that the court of common pleas, as it came to be called, had an institutional origin decidedly different from king's bench and exchequer.

NOTE A

COMMON BENCH AND COUNCIL

In the new edition of his *History of English Law* (I, 51-53, 195-196), Professor Holdsworth repeats the explanation of the origin of the court of common pleas given in his first edition, referring in a footnote to the account of the matter which I gave in the *Origin of the English Constitution,* but not to this more detailed statement as published later. He does not accept my explanation of what was done in 1178, putting emphasis on the fact that the new court was a curia regis, thereby substituting a point of no particular importance for the real point. It certainly was a curia regis in one sense, and that I have clearly said (*Origin,* p. 137), as was the itinerant justice court, and every court held by the sheriff under a royal writ, and by assize justices appointed to take a single assize. But no one of these was curia regis in quite the same sense in which was the council, great or small. No court of delegated and limited jurisdiction can be quite the same as the court from which the delegation is made. The point has, however, no especial importance; it is merely a corollary from the fact of difference of origin. The real point is the difference of origin. The new court was not the council, nor any outgrowth or differentiation from it, as were the exchequer and the king's bench. It was the creature of the council, which is a quite different matter. It should be noticed that I here class the itinerant justice court without reservation with the other courts of commissioners as was not done in the earlier account.

Maitland's explanation is also the one adopted in the first volume of the curia regis rolls of the reigns of Richard I and John published by the Deputy Keeper of the Records at the end of 1922. The volume contains distinct rolls of 2 John of even date in that year, one set recording pleas which were plainly tried *coram rege,* as the term was then used, and the other set pleas which were with equal certainty tried at Westminster. In commenting upon this fact, the editor, Mr. C. T. Flower, says of the first of these rolls in accordance with Maitland's suggestion: "It is therefore probable . . . that the roll now under consideration is an early example of the bifurcation of the legal business of the court into *Placita Coram Rege* and *Placita de Banco." Curia Regis Rolls,* I, 254, note 1. On the contrary I believe that careful comparison of the pleas recorded in these rolls will furnish decisive confirmation of the explanation given in this chapter of the origin of the court *coram rege* which develops into the court of king's bench, and that neither of these two contemporaneous courts of common pleas is its ancestor.

The first result of a comparison is to show that the character of the pleas before the two courts of 2 John is identical. No line of distinction can be drawn between them. There is no differentiation of business. We should expect, for example, questions directly concerning the king to be tried *coram rege,* as was done later when the real *coram rege* had formed. But they are tried at Westminster with no question raised. *Curia Regis Rolls,* I, 279, 281, 287, 463. Here belongs also the well known case of the abbot of Leicester, referred to in note 35 above, printed again in full, p. 462. See also the *Amerciamenta de Itinere Regis* under

John and Henry III cited by Madox, *Exchequer,* I, 150-152. They relate to ordinary common pleas or itinerant justice court business. That a differentiation from the council in some form is the origin of the king's bench can hardly be questioned, but there is in these rolls no evidence of the existence of a council except the doubtful reference on p. 392 where we should probably translate "counsel," and the one noted below from p. 382. The pleas are not tried in the physical presence of the king but by a bench of justices as at Westminster, pp. 258, 265, 396, 398. Writs are sent to this court as to the court at Westminster, p. 255, and the king sends word to the justices, p. 374. Reference of uncertain points to the king is made in the same way, pp. 376, 377, 423, 464-465. This fact is of importance because a reference to the king is in all except rare cases a reference to the council, as provided in 1178 and as is shown in the later records (Madox, *Exchequer,* II, 10, *x.* So said by Bracton, f. 1b, Stubbs, *S.C.,* p. 412), and these references indicate clearly that the justices with the king do not assume to be the council nor any direct emanation of the council, otherwise they would feel themselves competent in nearly all cases to decide such points themselves without the king. In the case from a *coram rege* roll of 25 Henry III printed in the *Placitorum Abbreviatio,* p. 107a (Madox, *Exchequer,* I, 120 *g*), and cited by Maitland as a case of the council's waiting for the king, clearly judgment would have been rendered without the king if a larger number of the council had been in attendance, as it would also have been if the king had been present with the few who were there (See P. and M., I, 499 at note 4). The same fact is indicated in *Bracton's Note Book,* pl. 1273. Various cases in these rolls show the equality of these two common pleas courts. *Curia Regis Rolls,* I, 279, 406, 408. There is no evidence to show that any case is put *coram rege* because of any incompetence of the justices at Westminster to try it, though they may be willing to dodge a difficulty as below, and there is no evidence to be found to explain why a case goes originally into one court rather than the other. The "sin autum apud Westmonasterium" of p. 279, if pressed to extremes, seems to imply that, unlike the council *coram rege* court, the common pleas *coram rege* does not exist if the king is not in England.

The editor cites in a note on p. 254 one specific case from the record on m. 8 of roll 21 (p. 382) in which the king takes action "motus misericordia et per consilium" as "a striking proof that this is the record of a court over which he presided in person." The opinion is due I think to the fact that the editor has not read the entire history of the case as we have it. To get this history it is necessary to add the records printed in Volume III of the *Staffordshire Historical Collections* to those in the *Curia Regis Rolls,* Volume I. This is worth doing, I think, because of its interest apart from the particular question, for we cannot often follow so completely the steps of a case through the courts and the facts have some bearing on the chronology of the rolls. It appears, putting the records in the logical order of date, that the plaintiff brought suit in the itinerant justice court (*S.H.C.,* p. 54). The defendants essoined themselves and were given a day at Westminster five weeks after Michaelmas (*S.H.C.,* p. 37). They appeared at that time and essoined themselves the second time and were given a day in the next Hillary term (*S.H.C.,* p. 31). There all the parties appeared, except the husband of the defendant, and the pleadings are recorded (*S.H.C.,* p. 66; *C.R.R.,* I, 153). These bring out the difficulty in the case, which is that the wife asks for the grand assize without her husband. (Bracton, f. 203; Holdsworth, II, 246.) Evidently the Westminster bench is unwilling to take the responsibility of solving this difficulty and they send the parties "ad audiendum judicium suum," that is, upon this difficulty (see the record), to the justices travelling with the king, assigning November 21 (*S.H.C.,* p. 69; *C.R.R.,* I, 363). On that date at Lincoln these justices also hesitate to take the responsibility and they defer judgment to the octave of St. Hillary and refer the question to the king (*S.H.C.,* p. 70). It follows that the king was not present in their court or judgment would not have been deferred. The king "motus misericordia et per consilium" decides for the defendant, but the decision is not of the origiñal issue between the parties but only of the question raised by the demand of the grand assize. Even on that question the case goes back for the formal judgment to the justices and is recorded on their roll: "Habeat magnam assisam,'' and a day for electing the knights is assigned by them (*S.H.C.*, p. 71; *C.R.R.*, I, 382), and that election is duly held and recorded (*S.H.C.*, p. 72; *C.R.R.*, I, 429). That the pleadings are again entered upon the roll of the justices at the point where the king's decision is recorded does not imply any trial before the king. The facts were undoubtedly explained to him. The ''motus misericordia'' is accounted for by the facts which were stated by the defendant in her pleadings. If also the ''per consilium'' means action by the council, as it very possibly does, the facts were probably formally stated but not as parts of a regular trial. Such a repetition of the record of the pleadings in similar circumstances is to be found on the rolls in many cases. It certainly follows, I think conclusively, that the justices who were with the king at Lincoln on September 21 were not the council or they would have been entirely competent to solve the difficulty without an adjournment of the case, and therefore also their court was not the ancestor of the king's bench.

To me at least these rolls furnish demonstration of the fact, so nearly as any fact of history can be demonstrated, that we have not a ''bifurcation of the business of the court'' but a duplication of the court. The king is journeying about the country with judges in his train, as Maitland said, and they are trying the same kind of cases, by the same procedure in all respects, as the justices of the bench at Westminster. See the interesting account of this situation by Maitland in *Select Pleas of the Crown* (Selden Society), pp. xii-xvi, which should be modified only to imply not a beginning differentiation of the court into two but a duplication of a single court in two places at once, as a general iter of the justices multiplied it by six or eight. It is evident also that the term *coram rege* is not used in these rolls in the later technical sense but as Glanvill used it. See *C.R.R.*, I, 375, ''coram eo vel capitali justiciario suo,'' which is exact Glanvill language. It may be added that probably in these *coram rege* rolls we have recorded the common pleas business following the king which Magna Carta c. 17 tried to transfer to the Westminster court, not with complete success, so far at least as the trial of pleas is concerned. See Maitland, *Select Pleas of the Crown*, p. xviii.

The facts tending to show the identity of the two common pleas courts have sometimes been clearly enough recognized without leading to the probable inference: "In the reigns of Richard and John, when the king was absent, most of the judicial business seems to be done by the Bench. But when the king was present it is difficult to distinguish the Bench from the court held coram rege. Both were in fact curia regis—division of the king's court. Whether the court will be the Bench or the court held coram rege would almost seem to depend on the accident of the king's presence." Holdsworth, I, 52.

While it seems clear from the evidence we now have that the group or bench of judges travelling with the king and called in the early years of John *coram rege* was not the *antecessor* of the technical *coram rege* court which became the king's bench, it cannot be said with any confidence, until we have entire rolls of the later years, whether or not the real germ of that court appears before the close of the reign; nor can we say in what relationship that beginning stands to the common pleas court of the justices journeying with the king. We can only say that action by the council like the later *coram rege* seems so far developed in the minority of Henry III that it probably will be found appearing in the records of John's time. The case of which we have the record in the *Placitorum Abbreviatio,* p. 95, cited above in note 36 from John's time, is a typical council case, and it would be very strange if there were not many such scattered through the records. The incident noted by Eyton, *Itinerary of Henry II,* p. 194, note 2 (Pipe Roll Soc., XXV, 107), of three justices holding a session of the curia regis at York while the king was there and while the itinerant justices were holding their court at the same place, is probably an instance of the justices travelling with the king. This was in 1175, before the establishment of the court of common pleas.

Since the above note was written the *English Historical Review* has published (April, 1924, XXXIX, 264-272) a review of *Curia Regis Rolls,* Volume I, by Professor F. M. Powicke. His view of the relationship of the roll of pleas before the king is the same as that of their editor. "The most striking fact which can be deduced from the rolls of John published by Mr. Flower is that, long before the time when Henry III began to hold pleas in person and the two series of plea rolls regularly appear [1234], the cases which came before the king were recorded on a separate roll'' (p. 265). This roll is in the direct line of the *coram rege* rolls of Henry III. ''There was no change of policy in 1234.'' Of the series beginning in that year ''this roll of 2 John is the earliest example hitherto discovered'' (p. 266). The review makes no comparison in details of character with the later *coram rege* rolls and does not discuss the relation of the court to the council. Prof. Powicke does name (p. 266) a number of differences which seem to him to distinguish the court *coram rege* from that of the justices at Westminster. Of these the only one that could constitute an institutional difference is that the court with the king ''combines administration with judicial practice.'' This combination is certainly a characteristic of the later council *coram rege* court. But an examination of the three cases referred to (pp. 262, 387-389, and 414) shows that the administrative work recorded is not like that of the council, legislative and directive, but like that of the itinerant justice court, looking after the interests of the king in details. Cf. the administrative directions in the justices' commission of 1194. Stubbs, *S.C.*, pp. 252-257. This is administrative work of the sort which we should expect in a court which is a central itinerant justice court permanently in session. That is, the examples cited rather go to show that the court of the justices travelling with the king is institutionally the same as that of the justices at Westminster than different from it. See above, note 15.

Let us put the matter in this way. There was an evolution taking place in the courts of the thirteenth century which it seems to me rather difficult to explain on the supposition that the *coram rege* court of 2 John is the ancestor of the king's bench. In the first place that court is a common pleas court. Its roll—roll 21 in *C.R.R.*—shows no connection with the council. It seems plainly on the same footing as the central court at Westminster, a court of delegated jurisdiction. But at the same time when the cases recorded on this roll are being heard, the council is deciding judicial questions, some of them referred to it by this same common pleas court. See above. In the second place, the later *coram rege* court of Henry III's time is clearly a council court. Such common pleas jurisdiction as it has is that which has always belonged to the council. It does not act by delegated powers but speaks with final authority. In some cases it plainly is the council. Now to suppose that the council *coram rege* court of the later date was developed by natural growth out of the common pleas *coram rege* court of 2 John is to suppose a process of revolution, not of evolution. It seems unnecessary to assume so violent a jump across the natural lines of development when in c. 17 of Magna Carta we have an historical explanation of the disappearance of the court of 2 John which is plausible at least—a disappearance which leaves a place for the natural development of the council *coram rege* court into what it later became. See below, Chapter X.

NOTE B

THE COURTS AND THE AMERCEMENT OF BARONS

The following note, written for another purpose, I have decided to insert here because, though dealing with familiar material, it presents in more full detail the rather important argument which is very briefly stated in the text at note 21 above.

As is known to all, the provision that is made in c. 21 of Magna Carta ("Comites et barones non amercientur nisi per pares suos") is the application to a particular set of facts of a fundamental principle of feudalism which was many generations old at the date of the Charter. The principle is the right of the baron to a judgment by his peers. The most famous statement of this principle, apart from Magna Carta c. 39, and one that is almost in the words of that clause, is that in the constitution of the emperor Conrad II, of 1037, *Mon. Ger. Hist., Legum,* Sec. IV, T. I, p. 90, cited in Stubbs, I, 578, note 1. See *The Origin of the English Constitution,* p. 266. This principle was regarded throughout the feudal world as far more important in cases involving punishment, or something akin to punishment, than in questions of property merely. Many cases may be found in the printed court records of this period in which earls and barons appear as plaintiffs and defendants in the new prerogative courts, raising no question of peerage. In 1220 in the court of common pleas, the earl of Pembroke brings suit against Fawkes de Breauté. *Bracton's Note Book,* pl. 102; Bracton, f. 433. The situation to which the principle is applied in c. 21 is one which clearly involved something akin to punishment, even though some of the offences for which the barons were amerced were merely formal, as when one lost a suit brought in a king's court. The barons were certainly within their legal rights in the provision. It has been proved also that the clause made no change in the law as it already existed in England. Pike, *House of Lords,* pp. 254-256; Vernon Harcourt, *Steward,* p. 308, and *E.H.R.,* XXII, 733. It is probable also that as much light has now been thrown upon the way in which this provision was carried into effect in the courts during the thirteenth century as can ever be done from the records as we have them. See Pike and Vernon Harcourt as next above and McKechnie, *Magna Carta,* pp. 295-298. I am here interested rather in the light thrown by this material on the nature of the courts and their differentiation during the century.

The facts which we must regard are these: In the reign of Richard I (the cases in evidence are all cited in full from the records by Vernon Harcourt, *l.c.,* and for Richard I see also Pike, *l.c.*), it is clear that the itinerant justice court, although it was called and called itself curia regis, did not assume to assess the fines to be paid by barons in cases coming before it but referred the matter to the exchequer for final disposition. While no earlier evidence than this can be cited, there is nothing to lead us to suspect that the practice was new. It is not unreasonable to believe that the later cases indicate what had been done in like instances ever since the itinerant justices had been employed. It is obvious that contemporaries, whether they were feudal barons or official justices, were consciously making a distinction, recognizing a difference in competence, between two courts each called curia regis, and it is something more than probable that they were making it for reasons which they fully understood.

From the reign of John before 1215 we have further evidence to the same effect, with two important pieces of additional information. First that the baron, instead of being referred to the exchequer for the assessment of his fine, might be referred *coram rege*. Vernon Harcourt, *Steward,* p. 308, and *E.H.R.*, XXII, 733. And second that the central court of common pleas did not amerce the baron. Vernon Harcourt, *l.c.,* and also in *Plac Abbr.*, p. 24 and Palgrave, *R.C.R.,* II, 187. That is to say, contemporaries declared that the same distinction existed between the bench and the other forms of curia regis which they saw to exist in the case of the itinerant justice court, while the phrase *coram rege* was applied to some court having the same competence in this respect as the exchequer.

From the reign of Henry III there are two further pieces of evidence, both well known but of great value in their bearing on the question of the relation of the courts to one another. The first is from 3 Henry III, a mandate to the itinerate justices in Kent. *Rot. Litt. Claus.,* I, 383b; Madox, *Exchequer,* I, 529, *o.* They are directed to amerce all who fall in mercy before them "exceptis comitibus et baronibus qui coram consilio nostro amerciandi sunt." That is, we are informed by what is equivalent to record evidence that the council may be added to the exchequer and *coram rege* as having the same competence in this particular, or as a synonym for one or both of them. The other piece of evidence from this reign is from its source entitled also to be regarded as of equal weight with record evidence. It is Bracton's statement in his *Treatise* about the amercement of barons. Bracton, f. 116b, ed. Woodbine, II, 330. He says: "Comites vero vel barones non sunt amerciandi nisi per pares suos et secundum modum delicti et hoc per barones de scaccario vel coram ipso rege." This is an unqualified statement from one who knew both the law and the practice of the reign of Henry III as thoroughly as Bracton did that exchequer and *coram rege* were identical in this function, while it seems clear that in his mind the common bench had no such competence. Earlier evidence cited above identifies council, *coram rege* and exchequer in this particular, indicating plainly the origin of the two latter and why they have alike this competence, leaving it necessary to suppose a different origin for the court of common pleas.

CHAPTER IX

MAGNA CARTA

The place which it seems to me the Great Charter of King John holds in English constitutional history was explained in *The Origin of the English Constitution* published in 1912.[1] Since that date there has appeared one

[1] The most important objection urged against the place in English history assigned the Charter in the first edition of *The Origin* has been fully noticed in Chapter VIII, added in the second edition of that book, and first published as an article in the *American Historical Review*, July, 1915, XX, 744-760. Various objections have been made to points of detail but, as these either are not germane to the purpose of the present book or serve to bring out somewhat clearly the differences between the more traditional views of English institutions and those which I have proposed, they need not be here discussed. See especially the kindly review of *The Origin* by Professor Felix Liebermann in the *Historische Zeitschrift*, 1914, CXII, 407-412, and also, in rather more frequent agreement, the second edition of Professor McKechnie's *Magna Carta, passim.* To these references should be added one to J. Conway Davies, *The Baronial Opposition to Edward II*, 1918, which, without making specific reference to *The Origin*, follows a course very closely parallel to the argument of that book in treating of the constitutional development of the thirteenth and early fourteenth centuries.

One specific criticism of a statement of mine concerning the Charter I should like to notice because of its general bearing. In the *Outline Sketch of English Constitutional History*, 1918, p. 49 (repeated in *A Constitutional History of England*, 1921, p. 138), I said that c. 61 of Magna Carta was "the first attempt ever made in history to put into constitutional form the principle that the government must obey the fundamental laws of the state." On this passage a reviewer in *History*, III, p. 188, remarked: "How would a thirteenth-century publicist have translated into language he could understand 'the fundamental laws of the State'?" There has been of late years too much of such undiscriminating application of a principle which is right enough in itself—the principle that the results of later progress should not be carried back into a more primitive time when they could not exist. Modern taxation and the representative system should not be read into cc. 12 and 14 of Magna Carta nor trial by jury into c. 39. But the

general discussion of the Charter which attributes to it a quite different effect, or practically no effect at all of the sort supposed, and which also has a decided bearing on the meaning which ought to be given to its judicial clauses. This is the interpretation of the Charter proposed by Professor A. F. Pollard in *History,* II, 171, and V, 34-36, and in various places in his *Evolution of Parliament,* 1920, especially in Chapter V. This interpretation is based upon the fact that the Charter was commonly called in the middle ages the "charter of liberties" and, insisting upon the legal meaning of the word "liberty" in the thirteenth century, it declares the Charter to be an exemplification and protection of the liberties of the barons in the technical sense in which these are referred to in cc. 52, 56 and 59 of the Charter and in the addition which was made in c. 32 of the reissue of 1217 to c. 39 of John's charter.[2] In *History,* II, 171, it is said: "the 'libertas' of

quotation from my book criticized above is not of that sort. It is, I think, an accurate statement of the facts. Whatever the men of 1215 might have been able to say, or not say, about it, whether they understood, or did not understand, what they were about, in actual fact what they were trying to do was "to put into constitutional form the principle that the government must obey the fundamental laws of the state," and Magna Carta is the first document in history in which anything of the kind was done. I do not deny that passages like that cited from my book carry back into an earlier time something not possible to that time. But what is carried back is no essential thing or fact to form a part of an historical situation in which it could not exist. What is carried back is explanation, description and name, quite a different matter; though these also may be things very likely beyond the horizon of the age into which they are taken, they may nevertheless be accurate in application to what did exist. The work of the scholar in isolating, explaining and naming phenomena long existing but not understood is a large part of advancing civilization. In the field of science no one thinks of denying the right to apply the names and descriptions later evolved to the corresponding facts where they are recognized to exist in earlier times. The historian should claim the same right.

[2] The barons in this reissue made the "dissaisiatur" portion of the clause read: "aut dissaisietur de libero tenemento suo vel libertatibus vel liberis consuetudinibus suis." Stubbs, *S.C.,* p. 343. It is evident that the

Magna Carta is as little like our modern notion of liberty as the monarchy of John was like that of George V. . . . A 'liberty' was a concrete, individual thing, a local and personal monopoly of jurisdiction;[3] it consisted commonly in the unchecked power which the lord exercised over his tenants in the manorial courts, and the object of Magna Carta was largely to prevent the royal judges from encroaching on these private preserves and drawing jurisdiction into the national courts of justice. The servitude of his villeins was the principal element in the liberty of the lord." On page 10 of the *Evolution of Parliament* it is asserted that the liberties against which the commons petitioned in 1348 were the liberties granted in Magna Carta and it is said that "the chief claim of Magna Carta is that those who possess these franchises shall be exempt from the royal or national interference,"

barons did not regard c. 39 as it originally stood as sufficiently protecting their "liberties." The following may be added to the passage cited from *History,* II, 171. "Magna Carta guaranteed extensive liberties, amounting to arbitrary power over the mass of the people, to a small minority consisting mainly of greater and lesser barons. So far as it was effective, it checked rather than hastened the growth of general liberty."

[3] To say that a "liberty" in the technical sense was "a concrete, individual thing, a local and personal monopoly of jurisdiction" is correct enough if it is made to apply to one only of the three kinds of private jurisdiction existing at the time, the franchisal. It is hardly possible to agree with any other statement in the passage cited, but this is not the place to show how they should be modified. There is no reference, direct or implied, in the Charter of 1215 to the "barons' liberties" except the reference to the franchises as to other property in cc. 52, 56 and 59. The Charter has nothing to say about the contents of the liberties or franchises and certainly does not confirm them, nor does it offer them any other protection than it does property in general. One source of error in this interpretation is the belief that c. 34 in forbidding the writ *praecipe* protected that jurisdiction of a baron which was granted in a franchise. See *Evolution of Parliament,* p. 27. The clause refers of course to his baronial, not to his franchisal, jurisdiction; nor has it anything more to do with his relation to his villeins than with his franchise. Down to the end of John's reign no attempt had been made to encroach on the private preserves granted in any liberty nor to draw jurisdiction from them into the royal courts of justice.

and on page 173 we are told that "the destruction of these liberties was the great service rendered by the Tudors to the cause of English liberty."

It is undoubtedly true that in form the Charter consists of the grant of what may be called special privileges, belonging in many cases not to the whole nation, if the whole population be considered to form the nation, but to particular classes, though most existing classes were included in one place or another. It could not have been put in any other way than that in 1215. But the essential point to be regarded in the interpretation of the Charter is not that of special privilege; it is rather the fact that the privileges which seem to be granted are really, with very few exceptions, parts of the existing law and belong of right to the class which then constituted the nation, the baronage, lay and ecclesiastical. What the king really granted was not the privilege.[4] That existed as a right before he was born and in many cases far beyond the bounds of England. What he granted was his pledge to keep the law in the future in the given particular.[5] And that is the permanent contribution which Magna Carta made to the development of the constitution: the introduction of the rule of law as a fundamental principle underlying all special conflicts between king

[4] There is no specific grant in Magna Carta of any privilege which constitutes a part of a baron's liberty and, though it is no doubt true that the grant of any sort of privilege might be termed in the middle ages the grant of a liberty, and such privileges when granted be termed liberties, this fact should not confuse our minds to such an extent as to blind us to the really important facts that Magna Carta concerns the ruling general law of the time and that by definitely introducing the rule of law it began and was a long step towards the establishment of political liberty in the modern sense, constitutional free government. Comment upon some of Professor Pollard's interpretations of particular clauses of the Charter will be made in connection with the constitutional topics which they concern.

[5] "Ibi [in the charter] quoque jura sua baronibus, et aliis de quibus indubitantur constabat quod eis competebant, rex restituit." Ralph of Coggeshall (R.S.), p. 172.

and nation at any later date, the establishment of the principle that the king must keep the existing law and may be compelled to do so if he refuses.

In the development of English liberty that which has been the one continuous interest, the unifying effort alike in every age, is the attempt to limit the arbitrary action of the king and to subject him to the rule of law. What determines the special features of any age and creates what may be made perhaps to seem vital differences between one generation and another[6] is the fact that from time to time the point of attack varies, or the effort of the king to retain or increase his power affects a different constitutional matter. But the necessary point to be regarded is that the continuous and unifying effort of the whole history is to make arbitrary action impossible for the king. The special points concerning which his arbitrary action is peculiarly forbidden, the interests in whose favor freedom from arbitrary power is particularly emphasized, may and do differ from age to age. But it is not therefore possible to say that liberty itself varies from age to age, since liberty consists not in the things protected but in the protection, in the freedom from arbitrary interference, and this has remained constant as a principle and as an accumulating total.

Clause 39,[7] if we consider it as a combination of both

6 See Pollard, *Evolution of Parliament*, pp. 166-167.

7 Nullus liber homo capiatur vel imprisonetur, aut disseisiatur, aut utlagetur, aut exuletur, aut aliquo modo destruatur, nec super eum ibimus, nec super eum mittemus, nisi per legale judicium parium suorum vel per legem terre.

No freeman shall be taken or [and] imprisoned or disseised or exiled, or in any way destroyed, nor will we go upon him nor send upon him, except by the lawful judgment of his peers or [and] by the law of the land.

Text and translation from McKechnie, *Magna Carta* (2d ed.) 375. This comment on c. 39 was originally published in the *Yale Law Journal*, March, 1919, Vol. XXVIII, 450-462.

judicial and constitutional provisions and have special regard to the permanence of their influence, is next to clause 61 the most important single clause of the Charter. This clause is also, because of the later meaning given to it, one of the most famous clauses of the Charter, and it is one of the most difficult to interpret, if we wish to be sure that our interpretation is the same as that of the barons who extorted the Charter from the king. Two of the writers of the *Magna Carta Commemoration Essays* published by the Royal Historical Society in 1917 in celebration of the seven hundredth anniversary of the Charter,[8] Sir Paul Vinogradoff and Professor F. M. Powicke, deal with this clause, and it was the matter chiefly interesting the reviewer of the volume, Professor Tait of Manchester, in the *English Historical Review*.[9] All three comment to some extent, and the two last named to a large extent, upon the views expressed in note D to Chapter V of my *Origin of the English Constitution*, pp. 262-274. One feels a natural temptation not to rest satisfied with even the best results in the interpretation of so important and difficult a passage, and, when also one's own ideas have been misunderstood and misstated, no doubt because of some obscurity in the original statement, the temptation becomes irresistible.[10]

[8] *Magna Carta Commemoration Essays.* With a Preface by the Rt. Hon. Viscount Bryce, O.M. Edited by Henry Elliot Malden, M.A. For the Royal Historical Society. 1917.

[9] *English Historical Review,* 1918, XXXIII, 261-266.

[10] Clause 61 is not directly germane to c. 39, but Professor Tait (*E.H.R., l.c.,* 264) makes so tempting a suggestion—that the pope may have found in that clause a legal right to interfere as suzerain and annul the Charter—that it can not be passed over. The suggestion can hardly be accepted in view of the principle on which c. 61 rests. In the clause the barons were demanding nothing outside the feudal law, no grant of new principle, nor any addition to the rights which were recognized throughout the feudal world as belonging to the vassal. On the contrary what they were really doing was to put limitations on their right; they were agreeing not to exer-

In the interpretation of the clause, there are two points which exceed in importance all others and occasion the most serious differences of opinion: the classes to be included in the words *liber homo* and the meaning of the phrase "per judicium parium vel per legem terrae," including the force of the particle *vel*. Of these two the first seems to me of much less importance than the second.

Whatever the barons who framed the Charter may have intended by the words *liber homo,* there can be no doubt but that very shortly they were taken to include all freemen.[11] The effect also of c. 60 upon this clause, as upon

cise it until after certain expedients of a judicial character had been tried. If the pope were proposing to base his action against the Charter upon his legal rights as suzerain, he could find nothing to justify action in c. 61. Indeed if he were appealed to because of civil war between the barons and the king in which the barons had faithfully observed the clause, he would be obliged, if he acted legally, to interfere in favor of the barons and against the king. Nor would the pope's right to the annual *cens* be in any way affected, nor the responsibility of England to pay it. He might no longer have a claim upon John, if the matter were pressed to an extreme against the king, but he would have a claim on the barons for the same payment under the regular operation of the principle. If the lord lost his rights over his vassal by an act of injustice, he lost his obligations to his own lord for that fief as well. The vassal became responsible for his share of his lord's obligations to the next higher suzerain, and more also by becoming responsible to him for what he owed his former suzerain. This is the form which confiscation of the lord's rights took, the correlative to confiscation of the vassal's holding. See Viollet, *Etablissements de Saint Louis,* II, 80 (Bk. I. c. 56 (52)) and notes; *ibid.,* III, 334; and cf. *ibid.,* I, 161, and Digby, *Real Property,* p. 73. It is very likely that the blunt requirements of c. 61 may have excited the anger of John and of the pope, but there was nothing in the clause of which either could complain on the ground of legality. It should be added also that the plain purpose of the clause was to prevent extreme action against the king, and that it would do so if John would keep his promises.

[11] In June, 1217, a writ directing the charter to be read in the county courts says of the liberties granted: "quas baronibus et omnibus aliis de regno nostro per commune consilium regni nostri concessimus . . ." *Rot. Litt. Claus.,* I, 336. In June, 1225, it is said: "Cum omnibus de regno nostro sicut bene scitis concesserimus libertates quasdam scriptas in magna carta nostra de libertatibus, priori et monachis Dunholm de juri deesse non pos-

the whole Charter, should not be overlooked. If it implies that in the body of the Charter neither barons nor king were thinking directly of the rear vassal who was not at the same time a king's vassal, it also says that the mesne lord must allow him the same rights that he claims for himself, and by inference the king must do so also in the rare cases in which in 1215 the king would come directly in contact with the rear vassal, who was not also his own vassal, in matters covered by the Charter. The effect of c. 60 would be to extend the benefits of c. 39 to all holders of land by military or serjeanty tenure. If we remember how very few the freemen were, outside these feudal tenants, who would come into direct judicial contact with the king upon the matters specified in c. 39, we shall conclude that c. 60 makes the range of c. 39 practically universal.

That those who originally framed c. 39 meant only the king's feudal tenants, seems to me still the more probable opinion. The recent arguments to the contrary leave the question in my mind where it was. I understand Professor Powicke to suppose (*Essays,* p. 108) that one who does not hold that the barons intended to include the common freeman must hold that they intended to exclude him. That in my opinion is not the alternative.[12] The barons were simply not thinking about the common freeman at all. They had in mind only their own class and their sufferings from the illegal or extra-legal action of the king.[13] The common freemen had not suffered in the

sumus . . ." *Ibid.,* II, 73. The meaning of "magna carta" in this quotation is probably indicated on the same page below where we read "in majori carta nostra de libertatibus," and again "in minori carta nostra de libertatibus foreste." It should be noticed also that it would be impossible to apply these words to the technical baronial "liberties."

[12] It is necessary to remember that the ordinary feudal vocabulary of the time made it almost impossible in the use of the words *liber homo* to exclude the common freeman. He would have to be excluded by some round about, qualifying expression which would argue, if found, very deliberate intention.

same way from these things. The king had not the same interest to interfere with their rights that he had in the barons' case.[14] In framing the clause the barons were thinking only about their own case, but they had no conscious intention of excluding anybody. They merely used the ordinary feudal language of the time with no particular thought of its range of meaning. That the words had a wider connotation even then than they had in mind was fortunate. It was still more fortunate that during the next hundred years, from causes that were then just beginning to work strongly in England, the class they overlooked increased in importance in the state with great rapidity, while their own class, as they then regarded it, declined as rapidly in relative importance and lost interest in the things which in 1215 they considered especially important.

I cannot admit that the meaning of *liber homo* is to be determined in this clause by the usage of the Charter. I should say rather that the usage of the time is so various

[13] Some of the changes in the language of the original Charter made in the reissues of 1216 and 1217 show that the barons in drawing up the Charter did not have in mind all the implications of the words they used. See the changes in c. 20. *Origin*, p. 257.

[14] After describing briefly the position of the free tenant "in the economy of the manor," which was the position of practically all the common freemen in 1215, Mr. Powicke refers to c. 39 as "protecting them and their tenements against illegal interference from the king and his officials." *Essays*, p. 110. The evidence that the common freeman was consciously included in c. 39 would be materially strengthened if it were shown specifically that the king had been doing this in the particulars named in the clause, and how he did it in manors not his own and for what reasons. In this connection it must be remembered that c. 20 affords protection in a different case from any mentioned in c. 39. It relates only to the operation of the courts of new procedure. That is conclusively shown by c. 21. See below, note 18. The problem of showing how c. 39 applied practically in 1215 to the case of the common freeman as a class, determined in his relations as he was by his position in the economy of the manor, is one that deserves investigation in the further study of this clause of the Charter.

that the meaning of the phrase in every document and every clause is to be determined by its own context. Nor can I accept Professor Powicke's interpretation of the words in some of the other clauses. He believes that *Liber homo* in the Charter included the common freeman in all cases, and only admits a doubt as to c. 34. But in c. 15 the non-feudal freeman is by the very terms excluded. The case supposed could arise only in case of a feudal tenant.[15] That the common freeman was consciously included in c. 27 is highly improbable. The clause was intended to protect tenants-in-chief against the king in a matter in which protection was very hard to secure. It is identical in meaning with c. 7 of Henry I's coronation charter.[16] Clause 34 can refer, I think, only to the possessor of a baronial court in the technical sense, not in 1215 to the possessor of a domanial court.[17] There are only two

[15] Cf. Madox, *Exchequer,* I, 599-600. C. 15 also shows that c. 12 applied to no one but king's vassals. The rear vassal, who would always be a freeman, had to be protected by special mention.

[16] See Glanvill, VII, 16, 2.

[17] Sir Paul Vinogradoff says (*Essays,* p. 82) that c. 34 means only "that when free men had courts they were not to be deprived of their privileges; free men who had no courts were not concerned in c. 34 at all," as if this were opposed to my view. I do not see that it is. I should say that the statement is of course true, but that it is the same as saying that the common freeman is not included. That is, the essential point is that the barons used the words *liber homo* when they knew, if they thought about it at all, as they probably did not, that the common freeman could not have any interests in the provision. All that is asserted of c. 39 is that they used the same words in the same way, not thinking of the application of them to any but their own class. At any rate the new form of statement does not materially advance the discussion, because the meaning of *liber homo* must be independently determined in each separate case, and the question as to c. 39 is who were consciously included in the term. Professor Powicke (*Essays,* p. 108, note 1) asks the question concerning c. 34 whether any manorial court could not suffer from the writ and therefore be protected by the prohibition. Taking the question to refer to the technical manorial (domanial) court as defined above in Chapter VI, it is to be said that it is barely possible that it might in 1215, though very unlikely. The vast majority of cases which led to the use of the writ *praecipe* concerned feudal holdings and, though con-

clauses in the Charter, 20 and 30, in which the common freeman was consciously included beyond a doubt.[18]

I have attempted no exhaustive study of this point. Such a study would require more space here than its relative importance would justify, especially as the conclusion must always remain largely a matter of opinion. To me the balance inclines decidedly in one way, but the evidence is of such a sort that every re-examination leaves the question enough in doubt to warn against dogmatism.

The interpretation of the *judicium parium* portion of the clause seems to me much more important because it not merely bears more directly upon the intention of the barons in the Charter as a whole but also because questions of procedure are involved in its understanding which have a bearing on the future development of law and which it is important for that reason to keep free from confusion. I must be allowed to say in this connection that I read with a good deal of surprise the state-

ceivably one might concern a common freehold and might be begun in a domanial court, such cases, important enough to lead to the use of the writ, would certainly be very rare in those courts down to that date. After the rise of the court baron they might fall into a court which was to all intents manorial. In a few cases the franchisal court might be affected, but if the hundred court tried no pleas of land (above, Chapter VI, note A), the cases would be few and unimportant. But in any case the question is not what class of courts were protected, but whether a non-feudal freeman would possess at that date a court of any kind from which cases would be evoked by the writ.

18 It should be noticed that c. 20 belongs to that portion of the Charter which relates to the results of Henry II's judicial reforms, in which the common freeman had a well defined place by inheritance from the old county court, and therefore it was impossible not to have him in mind in such an enumeration as that of cc. 20-22. The reference to him here cannot legitimately be used to show that he was consciously in mind elsewhere in the Charter. In c. 30 the tenant-in-chief certainly had a greater interest than any common freeman, but I think the latter must have been consciously included for it would be through him in some part at least that the tenant-in-chief would suffer.

ment that I had pushed the baronial interpretation of c. 39 to its logical conclusion,[19] for I never have believed and never have said with reference to this clause that "the barons desired to place themselves beyond the scope of the judicial system elaborated in the reign of Henry II and Richard I."[20] The evidence of such a desire must be found outside this clause, and I supposed I had expressed this opinion so that it would be understood in my note on this clause above referred to, particularly on p. 272 of *The Origin,* where I intended to say that the view I had just stated and illustrated was one with which I did not on the whole agree. I seem to have failed, however, and must try to make my position clearer. The con-

19 *Magna Carta Essays,* p. 96.

20 I cannot avoid the feeling that the criticism of my views is due in part to some little lack of clearness regarding judicial procedure and its bearing on the meaning of the clause. I am confirmed in this feeling by the sentence which follows the one cited above (*Essays,* p. 96). In this sentence the opinion is attributed to me that the barons "meant no particular form of procedure, certainly not the processes of indictment and presentment." This is a correct statement of my opinion, but it should be obvious that to hold it is to maintain that the barons were not thinking of the judicial system elaborated by Henry II and intended no attack upon it. If they had been attacking that system, they would have had procedure, including indictment and presentment, most of all in mind. Professor Pollard also goes astray in the matter of procedure in commenting on this clause. In *History,* II, 173, he says: "The 'or' is here disjunctive: the custom of the country is the ordeal or combat, and the 'doom' of his equals is the novel system of 'recognition,' " and in *History,* V, 34-36, he argues at length in support of that view, citing though without exact reference Bracton's use of the word *judicium* of the conclusion reached by jurors. The passages in Bracton are ff. 185b, 289, and 290b. Vernon Harcourt, *The Steward,* p. 288, calls this a "gross blunder" on Bracton's part, quoting Maitland's words in P. and M., I, 152, note 2, but the term is too severe. The correct explanation is undoubtedly that given by Maitland in P. and M., II, 622, that Bracton is using the word "in a loose, untechnical sense," as, for example, we often use it for opinion. Professor Pollard's only reference is to Vinogradoff in *Magna Carta Essays,* p. 91, where the distinction is clearly set forth and reference made to Pike, *House of Lords,* pp. 169-170, where it is also explained.

clusion which Professor Powicke states on p. 103 of his essay is one with which I entirely agree. He says: "The conclusion is forced upon my mind at least that the thirty-ninth clause was intended to lay stress not so much on any particular form of trial as on the necessity for protection against the arbitrary acts of imprisonment, disseisin, and outlawry in which King John had indulged."[21] That is to say, the barons were not thinking in this clause of the judicial system elaborated by Henry II. If they had been, they would necessarily have been thinking chiefly of the new criminal procedure established by the Assizes of Clarendon and Northampton. But why should they be thinking of this? They had not as yet been troubled by it. They never were seriously troubled by it.[22] They were demanding the traditional curia regis trial by judgment of their peers which was still habitual in their case, not as against some other form of trial, but against no trial at all, against condemnation without trial of any kind.

While I agree with the conclusion which Professor

21 After pointing out what the clause would probably mean if the barons were thinking of procedure (see p. 268), I said: "As I have already said, it seems to me more likely that this [procedure] was not what they were chiefly thinking of, that they were here less concerned with the contrast in procedure between the old *curia regis* and the new royal justice than with John's tyrannical treatment of his vassals without any process of law of either kind." *Origin*, p. 272.

22 There was undoubtedly some danger that the barons might lose their ancient right of trial by their peers through the development of the royal justice. The advance in France in this special particular was more rapid than in England, probably because of the institution of the Twelve Peers of France. This fact was no doubt responsible for Peter des Roches's taunt in 1233 that there were no peers in England and that the king decided all cases by his justices. Roger of Wendover in Matthew Paris, ed. Suard, III, 252. The barons were evidently troubled by the taunt but they did not understand its meaning and did not know what to say. That is, the tendencies of the new procedure were clearer to Peter des Roches than they were to the barons.

Powicke reaches, I cannot agree with the line of argument by which it is reached nor with the important subordinate conclusions of the paper. In order to maintain the disjunctive use of the particle *vel* in the clause[23] and the translation "by the judgment of peers or by the law of the land," Professor Powicke feels obliged, quite correctly I think, to show that a *judicium parium* is not the only way by which a case might be decided in the curia regis.[24] In both the necessity of proving this point and

[23] There is a possible application of the phrase "vel per legem terrae," allowing of a disjunctive meaning for the particle, which may be worth considering. In the enumeration in the first part of the clause of the things the king might do, there are some which required no *judicium parium.* "Capiatur vel imprisonetur" certainly did not in every case and going upon one or sending upon him might not. Possibly it was with the intention of making the pledge all-inclusive and complete with regard to the acts specified that the phrase was used. The chief objection to this suggestion is that it supposes a refinement of legal care in this particular clause which does not characterize the Charter as a whole nor the group of related documents. Or if we are to suppose such care, there would be no objection to Sir James Stephen's interpretation (*Criminal Law,* I, 162-163; *Origin,* p. 264) that the king promises judgment by their peers to those who are his vassals and as the law provides to those who are not. This interpretation could also be applied to the letter of May 10 and thus avoid the blunder of putting vassals and non-vassals on the same footing in the king's court. Those who insist on a disjunctive meaning for *vel* in this part of the clause seem always to overlook its probable meaning in the first part. See *Origin,* p. 262. I understand Professor Tait to hold (*E.H.R., l.c.,* pp. 261-262, 263) that if *vel* is translated conjunctively the clause must be interpreted as an attack on the judicial reforms of Henry II. The opinion must be due, I think, to the belief that the *judicium parium* was not normally a part of the law of the land.

[24] It seems a little unexpected, considering the place which judgment by peers had held in the whole western world for centuries before Magna Carta to have it relegated to such an unusual position in England as is given it in Professor Tait's rendering of Professor Powicke's conclusion: "As an ultimate resort in exceptional cases, a special protection against the arbitrary power of the Crown, something superimposed on the ordinary law of the land rather than a rigid alternative to it." (*E.H.R., l.c.,* p. 262.) Of course if *vel* is used conjunctively judgment by peers is not made an alternative to the law of the land but a part of it, as historically it undoubtedly was. I cannot avoid the impression from the language used by both writers that

the way of proving it, Professor Tait agrees with him. To support this contention several cases are cited which are quite as important with reference to the understanding of procedure in general and the contemporary development of law as with reference to this particular question.

The first case cited is a quarrel in 1205 between King John and the Earl Marshal as to the right of the earl to hold lands of the king of France after the loss of Normandy.[25] The marshal offers the judicial duel; the king insists on "the judgment of my barons." Professor Powicke supposes that the duel was offered as an alternative to a *judicium parium* and that therefore there may be trials in the king's court in which there is no judgment by peers, or, as Professor Tait says, that it was "by no means the only form of trial even for barons."[26] This

they may regard judgment by peers as the thing conceded by the king, as a right granted by him which he might have withheld. That can hardly be the case, however, since it was a right which had everywhere been possessed by feudal vassals from the earliest days of feudalism. What the king granted was that he would not take the right away, that he would respect it.

25 The incident is related in the *Histoire de Guillaume le Maréchal*, ll. 13149-13244. This is the account of a poet not of a lawyer, but it seems correct technically where it can be tested. Professor Powicke cites in a note a case of disagreement between the barons of Poitou and the king related in Roger of Hoveden, IV, p. 176. The barons ask for a judgment of peers; the king insists upon a trial by combat. The principle is exactly the same, and the explanation is plainly suggested in the context. King John has brought together a court from his various lands, as was the frequent practice of the Angevin kings in France, and the barons, seeing a foregone conclusion, are objecting, as they were technically quite right in doing, that this is not a court of their peers and demanding one that is.

26 If we say, as I think we must from any evidence at present available, that still in 1215 every *judicium curiae* was a *judicium parium*, then it follows that there was no "legale judicium," nor any "judicium per legem terrae," known at that date which was not a *judicium parium*. With reference to the *judicium parium* and the jury's verdict, as in note 20 above and at note 50 below, it is interesting to notice a case referred to by Professor Powicke in his review of *Curia Regis Rolls*, Vol. I, in *E.H.R.*, XXXIX, 272, a case "where a man, against whom his lord, Thomas de Burgh, had re-

opinion appears to rest upon a misapprehension of the procedure in the curia regis. The duel was a form of proof, not a *judicium* nor a substitute for a *judicium.* It stood in the same relation to the judicium as did the witness proof, compurgation, or the ordeal. What form of proof should be offered and by which party, was always determined by a *judicium parium* and, in theory at least, the proof was always followed by another *judicium* making the final judgment of the court. In practice I suspect that after some forms of proof, especially the duel and the ordeal, the final judgment was more theoretical than actual, very informal at any rate and perhaps taken as logically involved in the medial judgment. In no sense, however, can the duel be said to be an alternative to a *judicium parium.* The particular issue in this case was clearly not between the king and the marshal, but between the king and the barons of his court. Apparently

covered seisin in his court, came before the justices at Westminster, and with his lord's consent 'posuit se super visnetum et super pares suos ut recognoscatur in curia Thome si frater ipsius Willelmi fuit seisitus die qua obiit de predicta terra.' Here the 'peers' cannot be the suitors in the lord's court, for the man had already been before the court. The parties come into the king's court and agree to a new trial by jury in Thomas's court. They put themselves upon the neighborhood ('visnetum'). This, needless to say, is not a 'judicium parium,' but it shows that the verdict of a jury could be described as a verdict of one's peers.'' The case is unique but is so perhaps because the record is incomplete. As it is, it furnishes William no standing in the king's court nor any ground on which the case could be reopened. Perhaps it was allowed on petition of William and consent of Thomas. In any case it seems to me clear that the jury was a jury of Thomas's court, and that therefore the ''peers'' must be suitors of that court. They could not well belong to any other court. But the chief point to be emphasized, as Professor Powicke has pointed out, is that the verdict of a jury is a verdict of one's peers. But the statement should be generalized to declare that every man who has a jury, except a baron, has a jury of his peers. Perhaps it should be added that ''peer'' had no reference to social or class standing. It meant one in the same legal relation to a lord, or in simplest terms a member of the same court. In the domanial court the free and the unfree were peers of one another for the business of the court.

they wished to choose a form of proof which would avoid a decision of the question on its merits, while the king was determined they should not do so but should put themselves on record in regard to holding lands of the king of France while vassals of himself, as they would be obliged to do in a *judicium parium.*

From the time following Magna Carta, two cases are cited. One is a civil case of 1234 which is printed in *Bracton's Note Book,* pl. 1106, a case in which the king admits disseisin "sine summonitione et sine judicio." According to the heading of the record, the case is a *coram rege* case before a single justice, and according to the record itself the king was actually present. As I understand Professor Powicke, he thinks that the judgment was rendered in this case by the justice and that no one else had any share in making it, that is, that there was no *judicium parium.*[27] I sincerely wish that this could be shown beyond question. The year 1234 falls of course near the beginning of the transitional period when the method of making judgment

[27] The judgment rendered by the court in this case allowed the plaintiff to proceed to recover by the assize of *mort d'ancestor* "vel per breve de recto secundum legem terrae." *Vel* in this case Professor Powicke translates conjunctively: "by assize of *mort d'ancestor* and writ of right," and on the next page he says the decision points "to the legal process by assize and writ, to a possessory and proprietary action." (*Essays,* pp. 104, 105.) I think in this case *vel* must be translated disjunctively. The judgment allows the plaintiff to proceed either by a possessory or by a proprietary action as he pleases, but if he chooses a writ of right the possessory action would be useless. See *Bracton's Note Book,* pl. 37. Professor Powicke rightly emphasizes the "secundum legem terrae" of the record. That this phrase is applied to the assize and the writ of right in 1234 is interesting and noteworthy, as showing that the new procedure is now reckoned a part of the "lex terrae," but by that date it was so firmly fixed in use that probably it would be looked upon by hardly anyone as unusual. In 1217 (*Bracton's Note Book,* pl. 1306) when the defendant tried to transfer a bench case *coram rege* the council decided "quod assisa procedat secundum legem et consuetudinem regni." In 1200 it is noted in a record that an inquisition ordered by the king is not "secundum consuetudinem regni." Palgrave, *R.C.R.,* II, 189; Thayer, *Evidence,* p. 65.

was changing from the medieval method of the *judicium parium* (*judicium curiae*) to the modern method of the justice-made judgment,[28] and just how this change was made has never as yet been shown.[29] It may be said, however, that all the *coram rege* cases of that date which can be studied in details of procedure are cases before the council, and council cases were then, and have always continued to be, decided by a *judicium curiae*. The naming of the justice in the title of the roll and the title itself at that date say nothing about the particular cases on the roll, either as to whether they are really *coram rege* cases in the later sense, as many of them are not, or as to the method of judgment making, and there is nothing in the record of this case to indicate that the justice made the judgment. The technical phrases used are all quite regular of an ordinary council case using the old, that is, the *judicium parium*, procedure: "per judicium curie sue"; "in curia sua fiat judicium"; "consideratum est."

The second case cited from the later period is the famous case of the outlawry of Hubert de Burgh or rather the two cases, his and that of Gilbert Basset and others,

28 Incidentally I cannot help expressing my surprise at the readiness, it would seem almost without critical examination, with which the theories of M. Fréville in his article in the *Nouvelle Revue Historique de Droit Français et Etranger*, 1912, pp. 714 ff., have sometimes been accepted. (*Essays*, p. 102, note 2.) M. Fréville's theory of the transformation of judicial procedure in Normandy between 1150 and 1250, as being from the justice-made judgment to the *judicium curiae*, implies a process of change the exact opposite of that which had been going on throughout almost the whole of Frankish history, and exactly opposed to the tendencies of Henry II's reforms. Such a thesis requires not merely unusually strong supporting evidence, but evidence gathered and interpreted by the strictest scientific method. Careful examination will show that a large proportion of M. Fréville's evidence cannot be accepted in the use which he makes of it.

29 Sir Paul Vinogradoff in his essay in the Commemoration volume (pp. 87-93) makes an important and interesting contribution to this phase of the subject, upon one part of which the reviewer remarks (*E.H.R., l.c.*, p. 262) that it "hardly seems called for."

and their reversal in the great council on May 23, 1234. The two cases are for the present purpose virtually one and may be so treated. As such it forms a very interesting but a very difficult case. I have said elsewhere that it is not clear what should be said about it,[30] and I am still in doubt. My doubt, however, does not involve the question of a *judicium parium.* In that respect the case is quite regular. The difficulty in the case arises from the fact that the original proceedings in outlawry, as given in the earlier records, do not seem to justify the allegations upon which the outlawry was reversed in the great council.[31] Professor Powicke has considered only the record of the reversal and therefore did not notice this feature of the case.[32] Outlawry was of course not a punishment for the offence specified in the indictment or appeal, but for contumacy in refusing to appear and answer, though there must be, or must be assumed to be, a presumption of guilt, and it was therefore not a part of the trial originally begun. In the original cases which led to these sentences of outlawry, the king apparently elected to proceed against Hubert de Burgh by inquest before justices specially appointed, as in 1233 he had a right to do,[33] and against Gilbert Basset by the older method of appeal and suit. If this is true, it would follow that their claim in these earlier cases to be tried by their peers, though in real justice it met the issue raised by the king, did not do so technically. It was not a demand for a dif-

30 *The Origin,* p. 289, note 14.

31 *Bracton's Note Book,* pl. 857.

32 There is a considerable body of material bearing on this case, but reference need be made here only to *Close Rolls, 1231-1234,* pp. 161, 545. The latter is in Shirley, *Royal Letters,* I, 429.

33 In 1189 two methods of outlawry are in recognized use: ''per commune rectum comitatus vel hundredi,'' and ''per appellationem per justitias.'' See the proclamation of Queen Eleanor, *Gesta Regis Henrici,* II, 74-75; and see the reversal of an outlawry ''in toto parliamento nostro'' on grounds of defective procedure in *Close Rolls, 1247-1251,* pp. 106-107.

ferent form of procedure in the cases begun, but for a different kind of case and a different tribunal. They were right in phrasing their demand as for a trial by their peers, because indirectly this raised the question of a *judicium parium* to be made in the great council, because that was the procedure of the great council, but this was not the main issue raised by the demand. That was the kind of court. I do not think that either the barons in their demand in 1233 or the great council in its act of reversal in 1234 were thinking directly of c. 39 or of procedure in itself. If they had been, the point would have been made clear in the judgment. The demand in 1233 for a trial by their peers was a form of demanding a great council trial and, the case being in 1234 before the great council for reconsideration, the demand had been conceded. I am inclined at present to think that, whatever might have been true at any date prior to Henry II, the original proceedings in outlawry in these cases in 1233 were quite regular,[34] and that the reasons for reversal were put in the elaborate shape in which they appear in the record of 1234, because the reversal was a foregone conclusion and must be made to appear well founded on some ground or other, or the ground of reversal must be confused.

Whether this is true or not, it is certainly true that this case can be made to show no alternative to trial by peers, and no violation of that principle except as that may be involved in the original trial of Hubert de Burgh by inquest before justices, that is, by the new procedure. If that point be insisted upon here in his case, it would seem to prove too much. For it would show that in 1233 and 1234 the barons in making their demand thought c. 39

[34] The writs referred to in note 32 above as found in *Close Rolls, 1231-1234,* show that some care was taken to conform to the customary procedure in outlawry.

to be a declaration against the new procedure and an attack upon the judicial system elaborated by Henry II. As I have said above I do not think this was the case, and I do not think c. 39 was in mind at either of the later dates. There can be no question, however, but that before very long the progress of the new procedure in criminal cases raised this issue consciously and that then c. 39 was regarded as a protection for the baronage against the newer forms of trial. It was a hundred years after 1234 before the issue was so raised as to be settled, and when it began to be consciously formulated as an issue, is doubtful.

Professor Powicke has much to say about administrative or prerogative arrest and punishment which is of interest and value. The passage could profitably be extended into a special study of the subject, for it has never been thoroughly investigated. In the meantime there is nothing in the evidence cited, nor in any evidence so far as I know, to indicate that administrative arrest or administrative punishment were ever recognized as a legal alternative to a *judicium parium,* or to any form of trial. In his interpretation in this matter of the "Edictum regium" of 1195, which may be taken as typical of the evidence cited, Professor Powicke sees in it a more decided departure from the system of criminal justice established at Clarendon than I can. It seems to me plainly to relate to extraordinary cases, and I can find nothing in it to show any contemplated change in the ordinary trial procedure of the courts.[35] There are new

[35] Roger of Hoveden, III, 299-300. Those named in the edict to carry its provisions out are "milites ad hoc assignati." In his account of what followed Hoveden says: "Ad haec igitur exsequenda missi sunt per singulos comitatus Angliae viri electi et fideles qui per sacramentum fidelium hominum de visnetis multos ceperunt et carceribus regis incluserunt." If Hoveden intended to describe a regular iter of the justices he would not need to change a word in this sentence. In saying that those arrested "non delib-

regulations as to arrest, emphasis is somewhat different, and there is no direct reference to action before itinerant justices nor in form to the jury of presentment, but it should be remembered that every itinerant justice was a special commissioner, and the action provided for is to take place before special commissioners according to the edict, and that the "per sacramentum fidelium hominum de visnetis" of Hoveden is the action of the jury of presentment. So far from making any change, the document seems to me to indicate that the Clarendon procedure was working on the whole very well when the criminal could be got hold of. That is the difficulty to which the edict is directed—the difficulty of arresting the suspected man. To the same purpose is a writ of 8 November, 9 John, not cited in the *Essays*,[36] and also the passage cited on p. 116 of the *Essays* from the *Close Rolls, 1237-1242*, p. 356. This was one of the great practical problems of the time, to get the accused man arrested and before the court, and this fact explains largely the toleration of administrative arrest and imprisonment in this sphere.

I understand, however, that Professor Powicke considers also that the operation of administrative arrest under such measures as the edict of 1195 created a situation affecting the common freeman, depriving him of a *judicium parium*, and that c. 39 was consciously intended to restore his right in this particular. If the fact can be

erandos nisi per regem aut ejus capitalem justitiam," the edict is using the ordinary formula for the suspension of bail. See the regular practice in the cases of treason and homicide, Glanvill, XIV, 1, 4, and 3, 1; Bracton, ff. 119, 121b; Somerset Record Soc., XI, case no. 969.

[36] A mandate directing the suspension of bail. "Rex etc. Justiciariis et omnibus fidelibus suis salutem. Prohibemus districte ne quis appellatus de morte hominis replegietur vel in custodia tradatur vel ostagietur nisi per speciale praeceptum nostrum, sed in gaola firmiter teneatur donec coram justiciariis judicium suum habuerit. T. Domino J. Norwicensi apud Wudestok, viii die Novembris." *Pat. 9 J. m. 4.* From Madox, *Exchequer,* I, 494, note *u.*

established with a good degree of probability, it will be an important contribution to the subject, for it will furnish what does not now exist, an adequate reason for including the common freeman among those to be protected by the clause. There can be no doubt of the prerogative punishment of barons which deprived them of their right to a *judicium parium;* complaints of John's action in this regard are well enough known, and to my mind without a doubt this abuse is the chief explanation of c. 39. But I understand the prerogative action contemplated in the edict of 1195 to be something quite different in purpose and form, intended to enforce the law in a point which experience had shown to be very difficult to enforce, not to violate it, and likely to meet with the approval of all but criminals. It will be necessary to show that this was not the case, but that the law-abiding common freeman was directly affected in his right to the ordinary trial, or subjected to oppressive action by the king in this respect.[37]

[37] There seems to me to be a tendency in the arguments I am considering to overestimate the public importance of the common freeman in 1215. I have no doubt there were at this date, and had been very likely from the Conquest, individual cases of such men who held a considerable local place. I think it likely that already members of the class had begun to improve their position economically and in local standing. But certainly the evidence of such a process is greater for the fourteenth century than for the thirteenth. Cases must have been rare at the date of the Charter, of non-feudal freemen not living in manorial or borough relations. And yet these would be the only men whom the king could touch in the ways specified in c. 39, except in his own manors, without a violation of property or other rights similar to those protected by c. 34. I do not know of evidence to show that the king had done anything of this kind. Even in the local juries of the new judicial system, where was used the machinery of the county court in which the common freeman had his peculiar field of public action, knights seem always to have been preferred to freemen if there were knights enough. Certainly no evidence has yet been produced to show that in the opening years of the thirteenth century the common freemen occupied such a place in the community, either as a class or as individuals, as to call down upon themselves the oppressive acts of John which he is required to abandon by

In the study of the operation of the judicial system as affecting the interpretation of this clause, there seems to be some difficulty in distinguishing the old procedure from the new, that is, from the procedure introduced by royal innovation after 1066: royal commissioner, jury, indictment or presentment, writs, assizes, etc. It is important to be able to distinguish the one from the other if we are to consider c. 39 as involving a question of judicial procedure. Indeed otherwise comment may go decidedly astray. In its simplest form the distinction is easy to make, but it is complicated in the study of cases with another problem which is not at all easy—the problem of determining just what the relation was between the new and the old in the actual operation of the courts in the period from the Assize of Clarendon to the virtual disappearance of the old, say roughly to the end of the thirteenth century. The subject has never to my knowledge been investigated. Primarily, of course, the new procedure belonged to the new courts and should not appear in the old courts at all, but it gets an entry into county and hundred courts through the sheriff's relation to pleas of the crown and when he is acting as a royal commissioner, and before long not merely these courts but baronial and even domanial are using all the new forms so far as their needs require. On the other hand the old procedure, appeal, foreoath, *judicium curiae,* witness proof, compurgation, ordeal, etc., had always belonged just as normally in the king's special local courts as in the central curia regis or in the old county court, and had been used in them from 1066 on, so that here again new and old appear side by side as normal procedure.[38] Accordingly we

c. 39, or to lead the barons naturally and consciously to reason that they ought to be included with themselves in the protection demanded.

[38] Compurgation continues for some time in rather frequent use in connection with the new procedure for allegations, chiefly negative, of which other forms of proof are not easy to use, as for example when the defendant denies that he has been summoned. See P. and M., II, 632.

have in the same series of records pleas wholly of the new procedure (*Select Pleas of the Crown,* nos. 5, 6, 12); partly new and partly old in the same case (nos. 8, 13, 16, 39, 40); and wholly old (nos. 4, 11). It is not the place here to enter further into this subject, particularly as I do not think that the barons had directly in mind any contrast between new and old procedure in c. 39.[39]

In leaving this phase of c. 39 I must allow myself to say that its interpretation appears to me one of those historical problems from which it is almost impossible to exclude the subjective element. The weight of the later interpretation still rests unconsciously on our minds. We cannot bring ourselves to believe—it is, I am tempted to think, more largely a matter of belief than of proof—that is, we refuse to believe that the people were not then in existence in something like the later sense, or that the barons did not feel an obligation to include them in the details of the "constitutional" guarantees which they secured. *Liber homo* must have included intentionally every free man because we cannot believe otherwise, and our minds revolt emotionally from a cold and hard interpretation of the charter as a legal document rigorously out of the legal ideas and facts of the time. I am afraid I think that it must be so interpreted, if our purpose is to find out what it meant in 1215.

To one portion of c. 39 less study has been given than it deserves. It has ordinarily been assumed without question raised that the disseisin of c. 39 refers to the same kind of cases as those in which the writ of *novel disseisin* was commonly used and that therefore they would fall under the provisions of c. 18. Consequently some little inconsistency is found in the attitude of the barons in

[39] See above, Chapter VIII, at note 17.

these two clauses. While c. 39 demanded a *judicium parium*, c. 18 must mean, I think, that the barons accepted the verdict of an assize jury, as the rolls show that they did.[40] The explanation, if not one of procedure merely, is probably to be found not in any inconsistency of the barons but in the fact that they did not have in mind in c. 18 the kind of disseisins referred to in c. 39.

We may distinguish for convenience in this matter two kinds of disseisins which came before the courts in the twelfth and thirteenth centuries, with one of them falling into two subordinate classes. One class is made up of those cases in which the king is the disseisor; the other of those in which the disseisor is a private individual, most often either the lord of the disseised or a rival claimant for the ownership of the land. This second class may be neglected for the purposes of c. 39. The cases in which the king is the disseisor may be further divided for the present purpose into two classes: first, those in which the disseisin takes place on some ground of civil right, as for example by the judgment of a court for distress, or as land escheated for alleged lack of heirs, or mistakenly involved in an honor or other estate falling

[40] Vernon Harcourt, *The Steward*, p. 223. *Bracton's Note Book*, pl. 1213, has been cited as an instance of a claim by a baron of a judgment by peers in a civil case. P. and M., I, 393, note 1; Baldwin, *King's Council*, p. 56. This is due, I think, to an incomplete study of the case. The record is one of pleadings merely. There is no judgment in the record of the case. The defendant, the earl of Chester, is fighting for a tactical advantage and he takes three exceptions, one after the other. He asserts on three different grounds that he ought not to answer to the suit: first, because the summons was not regular; second, because the countess of Lincoln was not present; and third, because the case is a common plea and ought not, contrary to Magna Carta, to follow the king. It was in introducing his first exception that the earl referred to the judgment of his peers, but plainly he does not appeal from the court to his peers but to the court and to the judgment of his peers. The court before which he was pleading was the court *coram rege* and therefore beyond all question a court of his peers, and it is to this that he appeals. It is their decision which sustains or overrules the exception.

into the king's hands for any reason, or an unintended disseisin because of uncertain boundaries. The second class is made up of disseisins by the king as a punishment, as for instance in forfeiture for default of service or for treason, or as an act of oppression.[41]

If now we examine c. 39 to determine whether both these kinds of disseisins by the king are included or only one, it seems clear to me at least that only the second is meant.[42] All the other acts of the king described in the clause are acts of punishment or oppression. If that kind of disseisin is intended, it falls exactly into place in the list, but if disseisin of the first kind is referred to, an exception is made which is difficult to explain. Further it seems equally clear that the reference is not to disseisins as a punishment inflicted as the result of a judicial process, but arbitrary disseisin at the will of the king, prerogative disseisin. It is of such action that the barons complain throughout the clause; what they demand is that the disseisin shall take place only as the result of a judicial process. Arbitrary disseisins, we know, did occur in well known cases like that of William de Braose along with other of the acts enumerated in the clause.[43] It occurred, or what looks very like it, in less known cases, sometimes almost as if by royal caprice. Henry II disseised a man of his lands because he refused a king's huntsman his dinner.[44] Richard because "malevolentiam habuit versus eundem Willelmum" dispossessed him of

[41] It is not pretended that this is a classification based on the nature of the cases. Bracton, f. 168b, makes two classes of royal disseisins: one where there clearly is a disseisin, and one about which the fact is not so clear, as in a dispute about the boundaries of fields.

[42] *The Origin of the English Constitution*, p. 272.

[43] *Ann. Waverley*, pp. 261-262; Roger of Wendover, in M. Paris, ed. Suard, II, 523-524.

[44] *Bracton's Note Book*, pl. 769. It is to be noticed that the courts did not recognize Henry's act of disseisin as legal nor did they Richard's. *C.R.R.*, I, 285.

his inheritance. John disseised a royal falconer of his lands because he failed to keep an appointment to look after the king's hawks.[45] Of Geoffrey de Lucy it is said that because King John "iratus fuit cum eodem Gaufrido disseisivit eum de tota terra illa et de aliis terris suis."[46] It is commonly said that Magna Carta did not bring disseisins by the king of the kind referred to in c. 39 to an end, and it is certainly true that there are cases after the accession of Henry III in which he acknowledges disseisin "injuste et sine judicio." This phrase is, however, formal language of the writ of *novel disseisin* and is applied to civil as well as criminal disseisins.[47] I have not been able to find a case in which there is an arbitrary or prerogative disseisin as punishment or an act of oppression among those attributed to Henry III in the cases which came before the courts. That such acts continued, however, I have no doubt.

It has been suggested to me in correspondence that a person who was disseised by the sheriff under the judgment of a court in consequence of a writ of *novel disseisin* brought against him might appeal to c. 39 and demand a judgment of his peers. This, I think, could not happen. It implies three things: First, that the barons

45 *Rotuli de Oblatis et Finibus,* p. 43.

46 *Bracton's Note Book,* pl. 1593.

47 The barons may very likely have had in mind in some instances the disseisins which occur in advance of the trial of serious accusations like treason, as that in the case of Bishop William of Saint-Calais, above, Chapter II, note 9, but the king certainly had precedent for his action in these cases. As to Henry III, see what is said of his treatment of William de Ros, M. Paris, IV, 228, and of Robert de Ros, *ibid.,* V, 506, 569. These are chronicle accounts and do not indicate how far the disseisins actually went nor what may have been the result of a subsequent trial, if one took place. See also Bracton's "utlagatus per breve domini regis et per solam voluntatem domini regis, ordine juris non observato," f. 421. Hubert de Burgh's allegations that he had been disseised "per voluntatem regis" (*Bracton's Note Book,* pll. 1136, 1141) may mean no more than that his outlawry had been reversed.

objected to the assizes and to the use of a jury in civil cases, of which I do not think there is any evidence. Second, that they could object to an assize jury as not peers, which I also think was not the case. Villeins were frequently objected to as members of a jury and sheriffs were amerced for placing them there, but the demand and concession of knights upon civil juries is an Edwardian matter, not of the earlier thirteenth century.[48] It implies, third, that c. 39 was intended to cover civil cases, which I believe to be an error.[49]

One point seems usually overlooked in the discussion of this question. The change made by the introduction of the assizes concerned procedure only, not substantive law. As a change in procedure, they affected proof only, not the judgment. The jury did not make a judgment; they merely formed a verdict on certain questions of fact. After their verdict followed the judgment, as it always had after the proof, and nothing about the assizes changed the manner of making the judgment or affected the question of who should make it. A baron could no more object to the absence of his peers from the jury than he could from his opponent's suit or list of compurgators.[50]

48 The ordinary reference for this is *Year Books, 30 and 31 Edward* I, (R.S.), p. 531.

49 The writ ''de nova constitutione'' (*Close Rolls, 1234-1237,* p. 337) shows that the defendant sometimes refused to abide by the assize verdict but it also shows that he had no legal remedy against it. The ''nova constitutio'' is cap. 3 of the statute of Merton and is given on the same membrane of the close roll cited above (p. 338), but it adds nothing to the writ except to show that the assize was not the only way of recovering seisin. A case of the use of this writ is recorded in the Gloucester cartulary, II, 263-264. In the peace between John and the chancellor in 1191, the assizes seem to be reckoned among the legal and legitimate methods of disseising. Hoveden, III, 136. On the general subject of disseisin see Bracton, f. 294b, and cases in *Close Rolls, 1247-1251,* pp. 49, 210.

50 See above, note 20.

NOTE A

MAGNA CARTA AND THE PREROGATIVE

One of the general results derived from the Charter and affecting the constitutional history of the future has, I think, been very little noticed. For it would seem that the Charter checked that natural development of the royal prerogative in the constitution at large which would have been the expected accompaniment of the decline of feudalism and practically confined it to the field of law and the courts, where its applications were limited and where also it was likely to come more or less completely under the rule of precedent. This rule of precedent is what actually happened in those fields where, after the thirteenth century, prerogative had the freest opportunity, in the equity courts and to a less extent in the council and in those prerogative courts which were derived more directly from the council or maintained more completely their identity with it, like the star chamber. At least this is what the first half of the seventeenth century tried to maintain in regard to this department of prerogative action. It is a noticeable feature of English constitutional history as compared with French that there was evolved no prerogative taxation and nothing that can really be called prerogative legislation. That it was the direct influence of Magna Carta which checked any tendency to prerogative taxation is, I think, without doubt. The familiar fact that from 1215 to almost the close of the century no attempt at unauthorized taxation was made and that afterwards any experiments in that direction were almost immediately brought to an end, we are justified in attributing to the direct outgrowth of the principle laid down in the Charter as restored in broader form to the legal tradition in the Confirmation of the Charters of 1297. In regard to legislation, I think it can be shown that it was upon the basis of these same principles, as established in regard to taxation, that the new or parliamentary form of legislation was founded, and that from them it derived its power to drive into the background the older forms of feudal legislation, from which prerogative legislation would naturally develop, and finally to subject completely to itself such of these forms as survived the fourteenth century, as in the case of proclamations. As a result there was no broad development of prerogative in England history.

NOTE B

MAGNA CARTA AND THE LIMITED MONARCHY

The great age of prerogative is before the Charter, in the period of Henry II and his two sons, and, when something like an absolute monarchy again appears in the sixteenth century, it makes little use of the prerogative except in the courts, including the judicial action of the council. The royal initiative, acting in what was really an opposed direction constitutionally, made use of parliament or secured from parliament in advance permission to act. In the early seventeenth century, when somewhat wider prerogative action was attempted, the experiment was checked and its success finally prevented by an opposition which based itself directly on Magna Carta and its later developments by means of an interpretation which was historically, but not logically, mistaken.

In one way this is only saying that the limited monarchy, the complete triumph of the principle that the king must keep the law, was an outgrowth of the fundamental principle of Magna Carta, and the fact should not be overlooked that, as compared with this general effect of the Charter, all specific results that came from it are insignificant.

CHAPTER X[1]

THE THIRTEENTH CENTURY

With the minority of Henry III the council stands out for us clearly for the first time in a double aspect. It has a definite place, or perhaps we ought to say, it is assuming a definite place in the judicial system, and it is assuming an equally definite place in relation to the central executive of the state, a place of responsibility and au-

[1] I must confess frankly at the beginning of this chapter that a considerable part of it is hardly yet ready for publication. It will very likely be judged that it would have been better to follow the more usual course and withhold it all until it could be put into final form, and such a judgment I should not attempt to dispute. But there is much still to do before a definitive discussion is possible of all the topics of the chapter. I think it will be evident from what follows in the text as it stands that a full discussion of the evolution of council and curia during the thirteenth century may easily extend to a volume by itself. Still that is the course which I should have preferred to adopt if it had not been, in the first place, for the warning of age. I cannot be at all sure that any other opportunity will be afforded me to state the conclusions that I believe are warranted in the way in which I should like to put them. And in the second place, these conclusions seem, at least to my mind, necessary both to complete the development we have been following and to indicate how the results of the past have their share in the transformations of the end of the century. The thirteenth century is no more the beginning of a new epoch of growth than it is the logical conclusion of a past epoch; nor do the influences in the century which are new have more to do with the transformations which take place in it than those which are old. I wish here, however, to make it clear beyond mistake that in many parts of this chapter I am not stating conclusions which I have proved to be true but rather what, as a matter of opinion, based on the study of the earlier stages of the same development, I think will be proved by future investigation. In saying this I do not wish to imply that I have any doubt about the strength of the argument which is derived from following out the developments of the past to the results which seem to be plainly their logical conclusions in the thirteenth century.

thority with reference to governmental policy. These are the two outstanding features of the council in all its future history, and it is in the minority of Henry III that they begin to be distinguishable as two separate lines of activity or, it would be more accurate to say, two lines of activity that are separating from one another. As functions of the council they run back, as I have tried to show, as far as our earliest knowledge, though until now with no apparent tendency to differentiate into the germinating principles of two independent institutions. Indeed we should really notice here that, as we look forward into the distant future, we can see that the promise of the early thirteenth century of differentiation into two conspicuous and coordinate institutions, each to assume one of these functions and to hold a high place in the constitution, is not fulfilled. After the thirteenth century the political, governmental function of the council appears distinctly to lead in determining its field of action as council. No institution corresponding to the political council is to be found in any such prominent position in the judicial system; indeed there seems for many generations to be, compared with the earlier times, scarcely any recognition practically of its judicial powers, though they remained potential.[2]

This eclipse of one side of the council is, however, more apparent than real and is due to the manner in which the evolution had taken place. The council in the course of its development had left behind it the most conspicuous and determining of the country's judicial institutions in exchequer, king's bench and chancery courts and the latent possibilities in its own surviving judicial powers at the end of the thirteenth century had equally conspicuous institutions still to produce. Had all these been

2 See Baldwin, *Select Cases before the King's Council* (Selden Soc.), pp. xv-xx.

united into a single institution corresponding to the political council, it would have taken fully as prominent a place in the constitution and the process of differentiation would have seemed to us much more plain. As things really were, however, if the facts of the minority of Henry III seemed to promise the differentiation of the council into two coordinate and controlling institutions, the one political and the other judicial, what really took place was something near but not quite that, was the evolution from one side of the second of the council's offshoots, the court of king's bench, and from the other of the political and governmental council. The latter retained still its original judicial possibilities from which were to be derived later the court of chancery and much later still the prerogative courts of the sixteenth century. There is then a double development as affecting the council which begins, or at least becomes apparent to us, in the minority and which follows its course throughout the thirteenth century.

If now, standing at the beginning of the reign of Henry III, we look forward to the position which the council occupies in the general government and especially in the judicial system under Edward I, though the judicial differentiation is still incomplete, we cannot fail to be astonished at the transformation which has taken place in the interval. In the chancery records and in the court rolls of the earlier time, say of the reign of John, notwithstanding the evidence they give of increased activity, we get only occasional glimpses of the council as the central supervising body and do not find its authority forced upon our attention. We can reach the conclusion that it is the supreme governmental organ for the everyday carrying on of all national business only by a not altogether easy process of study and inference, and even then the result is not obvious to all. The contrast at the end of the century is most striking. If we include in the meaning of the word *consilium*, or *concilium*,[3] as I think we must, all references to *parliamentum*, the commanding position of the council in all departments of government is undeniable.[4] In administrative supervision, in the direction of government policy, in legislation and above all in judicial activities,[5] the council is the one central and controlling power. To bring it forward so clearly into this position is the work of the thirteenth century after the reign of John.

So far as it is possible to separate the two, it is in the judicial development that we are first interested. By way of introduction, to review briefly the history which prepared the more rapid advance of this period: down to the reign of Henry II there were only two sets of courts which were open to litigants, local courts, including the

[3] The distinction between these two words, *concilium* for the great council and *consilium* for the small, which can be said to be maintained not with absolute uniformity but with a considerable degree of strictness to near the end of the thirteenth century, seems to be no longer so carefully observed under Edward I. See otherwise Professor J. F. Baldwin, *A.H.R.*, XX, 330-333.

[4] The prominence referred to in the text belongs especially to the small council. There is little to show with any certainty that under Edward I the great council takes a more prominent part in government than before. The two lines of activity, in which it seems at first sight to be gaining a greater share in the business of government, taxation and the making of statutes, are occasional only, and it is not yet altogether clear how active in them the great council, as great council, was. Consent to taxation seems still largely a matter of separate classes, and statutes to be as often made by some other body as by a great council. There is great need of more detailed study of these problems.

[5] For a not very long period at the close of the thirteenth and the beginning of the fourteenth centuries, a very interesting and rapid development in the use of petitions of grace and favor, not yet reduced to curbing formalities and the control of chancery, as they were soon to be, gave to the council, as will be noticed later, a prominence in the records of judicial action which it had never had before and was not long to continue to have.

baronial as really local, exercising the jurisdiction indicated above, and royal courts, the curia regis.[6] Down to that date there was no curia regis for any litigant except the council in its two forms, great and small, and occasional, sporadic delegations from it granted for the trial of special cases;[7] now and then these delegations were itinerating and in that case they probably heard king's pleas[8] as well as the suits of private men. In jurisdiction the curia regis of this date was peculiarly a court for the tenants-in-chief but it was apparently omnicompetent. It is to be said, however, that the impression which we get from this first Anglo-Norman century[9] is that there was little litigation in any of the existing courts, and this impression does not seem to be due entirely to the small number of the courts or to the scantiness of the records but in part at least is the general impression made by the time. Possibly there was an increase of litigation towards the close of the period which may have made a demand for improved facilities.

The reforms of Henry II introduced into this situation four things which were new, new as parts of the established constitution. First, a new procedure, the prerogative procedure, a vast improvement over the older; second, regularly recurring delegations from the curia regis, the itinerant justice courts, making them accessible to all; third, a central court of like delegation practically always in session; and fourth, the authorized, or we may

6 Above, Chapters V and VI.

7 As described in Chapter III above.

8 This is in fact the particular purpose which is stated in the account of the first iter of which we know anything. (But see above, Chapter III at note 42.) In 1096 William II sent four "optimates" into Devonshire, Cornwall and Exeter "ad investiganda regalia placita." Bigelow, *Placita*, pp. 69-70, from the *Monasticon* (1846), II, 497. In translation in Adams and Stephens, *Select Documents of English Constitutional History*, p. 4.

9 That is, from the Conquest to about 1166.

say required, reference of difficult questions from the new courts to the council for settlement. These changes immediately show results which were reflected in the business of the courts. Litigation was made much easier and simpler. The new procedure indeed attracted litigation and may be said to have tended to increase the amount of it. The council was given a new position in the judicial system. It was relieved of much of the litigation which under the older arrangement would necessarily have fallen to it but which was now shunted off upon the newer courts.[10] The enactment that difficult questions should be referred to the council gave to it a recognized superiority in the matter of decisions and the interpretation of the law which not only gave the council a defined position in the judicial system, but also formed the starting point of a new development which was under way long before it was consciously perceived. It is important, however, to keep in mind the fact that its jurisdiction was not changed. It was still competent to hear as a court of first instance any case that would have been brought before it in earlier days.

The increased amount of litigation shows itself at once in the records. More than twenty curia regis rolls of the reign of Richard and the first and second years of John are in print,[11] and the Public Record Office *Lists and Indexes*[12] catalogue, from the term beginning 10 John to the end of the reign, 139 membranes, omitting the undated rolls and those made up entirely of essoins. This business continued to increase throughout the reign of Henry III and, even in the minority, shows itself in the

10 It is remarkable that in *Curia Regis Rolls,* Volume I, a collection of common pleas rolls, there is no evidence of judicial action by the council and very few references indirectly to counsel taken of the barons. See above, note A at the end of Chapter VIII.

11 See the list in *Curia Regis Rolls,* p. viii.

12 No. IV, 1910, p. viii.

patent and close rolls, the only records yet in print from which one can gain an impression of the continuous judicial development. The pressure of this increasing business is of course the impelling force behind the legal and judicial development of the period. This period, which follows from the accession of Henry III to the death of Edward I, is one of unparalleled legal advance, certainly as far as any earlier period is concerned, and also as compared with any later age which did not invoke the aid of legislation.

So far as regards the evolution of the courts, while it is not very difficult to say *a priori* what ought to appear in the evidence about them after 1215, a little reading of the cases reveals the fact that, so far at least as the evidence at present in print enables us to go, the courts do not seem to have developed as we should *a priori* expect them to, in some particulars at least. Indeed the puzzling features of the rolls are so numerous that all that we can yet do is to describe the probable course of development and guess at what seems actually to be taking place without insisting upon any definite conclusions.

It is, I think, clearly enough established that in the early part of the reign of John the central court of common pleas sat in two divisions, to use Maitland's expression,[13] one at Westminster and the other, called *coram rege,* accompanying the king wherever he might go. It seems equally clear, as shown in Chapter VIII above, that the court accompanying the king was not the ancestor of the later *coram rege* court. It was in all respects, jurisdiction, competence, relation to other institutions, exactly the same as the central court which sat at Westminster. We may conjecture that its name, *coram rege,* was not yet

[13] *Select Pleas of the Crown,* p. xvii. See above, note A at the end of Chapter VIII.

used in the technical sense and meant no more than that it did accompany the king wherever he was in England. Some difference of name was necessary to indicate in which particular division a case was to be, or had been, tried. The reason for this peculiar arrangement, the reason why a division of the court of common pleas travelled with the king, was probably because this court was at that date the highest, and in fact the only, permanently organized court of the new procedure. It was still, as it was to Glanvill, *capitalis curia regis*.

The judicial development of the council, which was soon to give rise to the real *coram rege* court, was not yet far enough advanced to give it, to the contemporary observer, the aspect of a court among the other courts. It had no fixed place of meeting and no rolls; it kept no terms and its decisions are recorded irregularly on the rolls of one or another court, or perhaps not at all. That development had undoubtedly begun in the reference of difficult questions from the new common law courts to the council, called often in the records reference to the king, but it is the rapid increase of business for the courts that makes this practice an important feature in the judicial system that is forming. That increase also brings new business to the council through its original jurisdiction, through the growth of its function in errors, and through its relation to the prerogative in the matter of petitions, which apparently from early in the reign of Henry III begin to increase in number and in judicial importance. The ten years of Henry III's minority is the period which brings the council as a court of law out into view, plain to us though perhaps not so plain to contemporaries, and establishes its relation to the other courts in such a way as to begin a growth into the later common law jurisdiction of the court of king's bench. This process is differentiation as well as growth—a differentiation marked by the growing technicality of the phrase *coram rege.*

Into the preliminary stages of this evolution, as they had been unfolding in the reign of John, entered Magna Carta c. 17 as a sign of change.[14] On the surface the clause would seem to mean that men had begun to feel the inconvenience of having two central courts of common pleas and to recognize that such a division was not necessary. The two courts are identical in jurisdiction; one can do the work of both. To abolish one of them is an easy thing to do and would be economical. Hereafter, if c. 17 is followed, the jurisdiction in ordinary common pleas of any court called *coram rege* is at an end[15] until the phrase *coram rege* appears exclusively in its technical sense, as meaning really *coram consilio.* In this new sense the *coram rege* court, as the king's bench court in its earliest stage, first inherits from the past of the council, besides its incipient jurisdiction in errors, original jurisdiction over the common pleas cases of barons which they may care to bring before it, and second rapidly develops a similar jurisdiction over common

[14] "Communia placita non sequantur curiam nostram sed teneantur in aliquo loco certo." Stubbs, *S.C.,* p. 295. However difficult it may be from the existing records to say with certainty just what change was actually made by c. 17, there can be no doubt that those who drew it up intended to make a definite change which they understood. We have the same difficulty in proving from the records just what was the change undoubtedly intended by the legislation of 1178. See above, Chapter VIII, note 11.

[15] The statement in the text should be qualified by noting that, even if Magna Carta c. 17 be regarded as binding legislation, there is nothing about it which forbids common pleas cases being brought originally *coram rege,* if both parties agree and the council will entertain the case, or if one of the parties fines with the king to have the case transferred *coram rege.* The most that c. 17 could accomplish is to do away with the bench of justices travelling with the king, coordinate with the other bench sitting at Westminster.

pleas in which the king has a direct interest,[16] as an annexation from the territory originally belonging to the central court of common pleas, the two courts for some time sharing these cases between them.

There should be found, speaking still *a priori,* after the date of the Great Charter no rolls which are headed *coram rege* and which are at the same time both terminal rolls and made up of common pleas from various counties, like the *de banco* rolls of the Westminster court and like the *coram rege* rolls of John's time. The common pleas rolls of the time should contain references of difficult questions to the council in varying forms of expression and occasional notices of this or that done *coram rege,*[17] but the rolls of justices travelling with the king and having it as their business to hear common pleas should no longer appear.[18] In other words the term *coram rege* and the opportunity and place for a court which is actually with the king, now abandoned by the court of common pleas, should be left open to be appropriated by any court which can step into the vacancy and do business really *coram rege.* As the council had now for nearly

16 It is clear that by this time men are beginning to feel that a court which is devoted to the trial of ordinary causes between common men is not properly suited to try cases in which the king is a party, or in which the honor or dignity of the crown is concerned. See Maitland, *Bracton's Note Book,* I, 58, and note 2. An early instance in the rolls of noting the king's interest is Palgrave, *R.C.R.,* II, 95 (1199). This is one particular of what is in this period clear upon all sides in all sorts of things, the increasing perception of differences, the growing strictness with which distinctions are being made and the drawing of dividing lines where formerly no divisions were seen, all evidence that differentiation is going on.

17 For example, in the *Staffordshire Historical Collections,* IV, 13, 4 Henry III, is notified the making of an attorney.

18 Professor Powicke thinks it likely that rolls of this kind continued to be made up until Henry III began to hold pleas after his minority. *E.H.R.,* XXXIX, 266. Professor Vinogradoff prints a case from a *coram rege* roll of 10 Henry III. *Villainage* (1892), p. 421. The case however is a common pleas case and the roll was probably cited by an old title.

four decades been doing an increasing judicial business, strictly *coram rege,* that is, in close attendance on the king, with the king always in theory present and often in reality, and as there had been during the later part of this time a growing tendency to consider the term *coram rege* to mean technically in the king's presence and not to take it in the wide sense in which Glanvill had used it, nothing could be more natural than that this council court should step into the vacancy and that *coram rege* after 1215 should mean the council only.[19] Rolls to which, as part of the original record, contemporaries gave the title *coram rege,* if there are any in the period, should be rolls of council action only, and on them should be found no common pleas business except for the two reasons mentioned above, the original business of barons or pleas in the king's interest, or unless they are cases referred to the council because of some difficult question involved or because the common pleas judges did not wish to assume the responsibility of solving the difficulty. It seems far more likely, however, that for some years to come there will be no *coram rege* rolls because it is unlikely that the business will yet have grown to such dimensions as to call for a separate roll. *Coram rege* business should be found entered on the rolls of the other courts and in the chancery records. Theoretically it seems probable that real *coram rege* rolls, when they be-

19 Of this court after 1235 Professor Baldwin says (*King's Council,* p. 54): "The substantial identity of the court known as *coram rege* and the council is abundantly shown in the plea rolls themselves. Conciliar cases alternate with *coram rege* cases without any material distinction. A *coram rege* case becomes a case before the council without change of venue or break in its continuity." Evidence of this statement is drawn from rolls of later date, but that of 1234-1235 contains a council record (*Bracton's Note Book,* pl. 1117) and some cases are plainly before the council though that is not named. Cf. pll. 1108 and 1127. It may be added that in *ibid.,* pl. 741, there is an entry of council action on a common pleas roll of 1233 in the old fashion.

gin, will be made up of business done at different dates and in different places with no evidence of continuous sessions or of terminal appointments.

When we come to trace out what actually took place after 1215, so far as the evidence in print allows us to do it, the facts seem to correspond fairly well with what we should expect *a priori*. The bench of common pleas justices travelling with the king did disappear and no further rolls of such a court are to be found. The reference of cases *coram rege* from one common pleas court to another, as a means of getting at the king, also ceases. References *coram rege* during the minority are all clearly references *coram consilio*,[20] and these references do not appear in set or technical forms of expression. If there is a difference between *coram consilio* in the minority and references made directly to the king under John, it would seem to be in this, that there are fewer indications in the later period that the council is acting as a trial court. Such indications are, however, not lacking, and the difference is exactly what we should expect from the high degree of development which the court of common pleas had now reached.[21] The council also in its relation to the

20 A verbal change becomes necessary because, when the king is in France or a minor, the fiction, it usually is a fiction, of the king's physical presence cannot be maintained. The verbal change, however, indicates no change in courts or trials. *Coram consilio* is exactly the same court as the technical *coram rege* and does exactly the same things. Such modern accounts of the change as imply that some method of deciding judicial questions which had been earlier in use ceased for the time being, while the king was abroad, and was later resumed are much too strongly stated. See especially Holdsworth, I, 195: during the minority there could be no *coram rege* court and "one court tried all the cases"; Baldwin, *King's Council*, p. 52; P. and M., I, 177. The court of common pleas travelling with the king did cease, but the minority of the king had nothing to do with the fact and it did not affect the trial of any plea.

21 Or it may merely seem so to us because the common pleas and eyre rolls of the minority are not in print, so that the records of council action which they undoubtedly bear are not accessible.

judicial system has undergone development and appears definitely as a court of superior jurisdiction, both as a court of errors and as a source of authority. No rolls of pleas before the council appear, which also is as we should expect, since there were no terminal sessions nor any judicial business which belonged regularly to the council. It is natural that its action should appear as occasional only, as business is referred to it from some outside source or, as of old, some baronial plea is brought to it as a court of first instance, and that the record of its action should be found on the common pleas rolls, in writs of execution, or in incidental references in other documents. To say that there were no council rolls in the minority, is not to say that there was then no judicial action by the council, but that as yet that business had not grown to a point where it was recognized as the work of a distinct court. It is not until 1234-1235 that we get our first evidence of the existence of a roll of the new *coram rege* court. The earliest *coram rege* roll from which extracts are made in *Bracton's Note Book* is that of 18-19 Henry III, and this is the earliest which Bracton cites in the *De Legibus.*[22] It is also the earliest *coram rege* roll which is given for Henry III in the Public Record Office *Lists and Indexes,*[23] and the Abbreviator of the sixteenth century used no earlier one. Maitland says he believes that this is the first of that series which is now extant. If this is accepted as the date of the first roll, it provides just about the length of time that would seem to be necessary for the new court to become well established in its place and duties, as a clearly recognized court, after the withdrawal of the old common pleas *coram rege* by c. 17

[22] *Bracton's Note Book,* I, 57-58. Professor Woodbine confirms Maitland's judgment that the "anno regis xvi" of the printed text of Bracton in f. 241b should be "anno regis xviii."

[23] No. IV (1910), p. 3.

of Magna Carta. Such a recognition is certainly implied by its possession of its own roll.

Two rather serious difficulties appear at this point which cannot at present be accounted for and must be left unexplained. One is the recording upon the *coram rege* roll of so much common pleas business which does not seem normally to belong there, as has been noticed above.[24] This apparent anomaly continued for some time but came to an end before the close of the century. In Phillimore's *Placita Coram Rege* for the Trinity term of 25 Edward I, 1297,[25] there cannot be shown to be any case which does not rightfully belong in the court of king's bench. It is possible that when the place of the older common pleas justices acting *coram rege* was taken by the council and, somewhat later but very possibly a little time before the rolls begin, by justices acting for the council, there was continued for a time something of the miscellaneous jurisdiction which the older *coram rege* court had exercised, and that only by degrees was a clear dividing line drawn between the field of their court and that of the justices at Westminster. This hardly seems a satisfactory explanation, but there does not seem to be anything else to suggest at present.

The second difficulty is not serious but arises from exceptional facts which, as in the first instance, cannot at present be fully explained. In 1224 the sheriffs were di-

[24] See the figures given above in note 41 of Chapter VIII. Maitland notices the miscellaneous jurisdiction of the bench during the minority. *Bracton's Note Book,* I, 58. Naturally as still *capitalis curia regis* it must hear many cases which later belong to the king's bench until the development of the council *coram rege* court begins to mark off a jurisdiction for that court. How long it would take such a court after 1234 to develop itself out of the judicial function of the council as exercised at the accession of Henry III to a point where it could absorb the king's bench cases from the Westminster court, cannot be said, but certainly in the thirteenth century the point was not likely to be reached in one year.

[25] Published by the British Record Society, 1898.

rected to send the assizes of *novel disseisin* from four counties to the shire towns to be heard *coram rege*.[26] In 1226 a similar mandate directed that the assizes of *mort d'ancestor* and *novel disseisin* from five counties should be summoned *coram rege*.[27] Why this was done is not indicated nor in what court the assizes were to be tried when they came before the king. These facts, however, can have no bearing on the development of the real *coram rege* court, because the business concerned is that of itinerant justices or assize justices, and not that of the coun-

26 *Rot. Litt. Claus.*, I, 631. Maitland, *Pleas of the Crown*, p. xviii. These mandates were probably responsible for Professor Baldwin's statement (*King's Council*, p. 52): "After Henry came of age, in 1224, the pleas *coram rege* reappear, and henceforth there are to be found two sets of rolls, which at first were maintained with imperfect regularity, namely the *coram rege* and the *de banco rolls*."

27 *Rot. Litt. Claus.*, II, 154. Maitland, *Bracton's Note Book*, I, 58, note 4. The *Plac. Abbr.* (p. 101b) gives, under date of 10 Henry III, extracts from a roll entitled "Assise Mortis Antecessoris et Assise Nove Disseisine apud Salop, coram Dn'o Rege." The records are all of itinerant justice business. With these cases are to be classed undoubtedly those cited by Madox, *Exchequer*, I, 150-153, of the king's judging "in itinere," from pipe rolls of John and Henry III. The titles are among others "Amerciamenta de Itinere Regis," "Amerciamenta per Regem," "De Amerciamentis et Finibus . . . coram Rege itinerando." He quotes from rolls of 5, 22, and 30 Henry III. Cf. *Close Rolls, 1247-1251*, p. 446 (1251). There seems to be no room to doubt that in these cases the *coram rege* is untechnical, referring to the physical presence of the king in the place where the court is held, and that it does not mean a court which is *coram rege* whether the king is present or not. Nor is there any doubt that the business mentioned is itinerant justice business. The chief interest seems to be in the assize of *novel disseisin*. I have said in the text that the facts which cause this difficulty cannot be explained, but I question whether the explanation is not sufficient. The fact at any rate seems to be fairly well established that often, when the king was "itinerating," there was someone in his train taking assizes and occasionally hearing other itinerant justice business. Such a court *coram rege* would not compel litigants to follow the king about the country, as did the common pleas *coram rege* of John's time, but would hear cases in the county and have all the convenience of an extra iter. It would not fall under the condemnation which led to c. 17 of the Charter.

cil in any sense. The king whenever travelling was probably equipped to do the business of an iter if he thought it necessary or cared to do it.

The words *coram rege* make reference of course to a physical fact, and the reference is made in so general a form, with so little of specific characterization, that it may be used popularly or untechnically for any and all forms of the curia regis in which the presence of the king is presumed. If the king is "itinerating" and taking advantage of the fact to do assize business which may have fallen into arrears, or which it seems desirable to hear for any reason, the assizes will naturally be summoned *coram rege* at some place where he is to be.[28] It probably would have been difficult to find another phrase at once so simple and expressive. If in an earlier time the king is travelling with justices in his train who are holding a central common pleas court with the same terminal sessions as the other central court at Westminster, it will naturally be distinguished from that court as being *coram rege*. And finally the council, whose business will practically always be presumed to be done in the king's presence, will just as naturally be described as *coram rege*. All this variety of usage is quite possible and instinctive so long as no technical assignment of the phrase has been made.

It is, however, no mere physical fact which is the distinguishing characteristic of the technical *coram rege* court which is the ancestor of the king's bench. That is rather its authority. It is the fact that it speaks with and for the king, that it expresses the king's decision and his rightful prerogative, that because of this it is the highest

28 The summons is *coram rege* instead of the usual "coram justitiariis itinerantibus." See Stubbs, *S.C.*, p. 354. I think, however, that these cases were heard as the assize justices heard theirs, with no assembling of the county court which met the regular justices of the eyre.

court of the land,[29] from which there is no appeal to anything higher until the evolution of parliament begins to draw to itself the jurisdiction of the old great council, surviving in the house of lords, as if it were something different from the council and of greater authority. So long as the courts are not sharply differentiated and especially so long as the development of the council's judicial business has not reached a point which necessarily calls attention to its activity in this direction and to its authority, it is not likely that *coram rege* will begin to be used in a technical sense of any court. It seems most probable that it is the authority of the council in its judicial decisions that finally attaches the technical meaning to *coram rege* as the designation of a particular court, the council court, the court where the king's decisions are made and where cases affecting the king are tried. It is only slowly, however, that this court becomes *coram rege* in a technical sense. We can hardly date such use before the time when Bracton wrote, and it is not long after that until it begins to be called king's bench, though it never quite loses the earlier name.

It is a little difficult within a reasonable space to indicate the extent of the council's activity either upon the judicial or the political side in this the first period of its history in which it attracts particular attention to itself. Professor Baldwin in the first part of the second chapter of *The King's Council* has given some evidence of what the council was doing during the minority, but it did not fall within his plan to go into this early history very fully, and the references which follow here are listed

29 See the interesting discussion of the position of the eyre and of the king's bench in relation to one another and to the other courts in the introduction to Bolland's *Select Bills in Eyre,* pp. xv-xix. The argument is, however, incomplete because Mr. Bolland confuses the common bench with the king's bench.

without regard to whether they have been cited in that work or not. It must be emphasized also that the evidence here gathered does not pretend to be complete or to give a complete picture of the council's activity. The general purpose of this chapter, as has been intimated, is to do no more than record a present stage of investigation, with the hope that opportunity may in time be afforded to carry it to completion, but with the special desire that present results and impressions may be preserved in any case. The references which follow immediately have been chosen to indicate something of the council's judicial activity. They are by no means the full list which could be given and they do not go beyond the year 1223, but it is believed that they show that the council continues through these years all its earlier forms of judicial activity, and that the foundation is then well laid for the judicial position of the council at the end of the century, as well as for the development of the *coram rege* court of 1234 and, upon the basis of that court, of the king's bench. In the list of references from the close rolls I have included a few which are not primarily to judicial action because I am not to make any further use of that collection.

In some of the following cases the council is not explicitly named but must be intended. "Coram W. Marescallo rectore nostro et regni nostri" is the same as *coram rege* or as "coram archiepiscopo" during the absence of Richard I, or as "coram consilio" during that of Henry III in 1253,[30] *Rot. Litt. Claus.*, I, 301, 347; judgment is rendered "coram magnatibus (fidelibus)" of the council,

[30] For Richard I see Maitland, *Three Rolls of the King's Court,* Pipe Roll Society, XIV, 14, and Palgrave, *R.C.R.*, I, 9, and for John, *ibid.*, II, 156. For Henry III see the memorandum entered on the close roll, 37 Henry III, m. 3, that after the sailing of the king "factae fuerunt heae Litterae subsequentes coram consilio ipsius Regis in Anglia, et continuatae usque ad annum ipsius Regis xxxviii." Madox, *Exchequer,* I, 68, *a.* The

ibid., pp. 310, 404; an acknowledgement before them is the basis of a judgment, *ibid.,* p. 320; ''coram nobis'' occurs occasionally, *ibid.,* 361; a mandate of the council to the justices itinerating in Kent covers more than one point: the justices are to amerce all those falling ''in misericordia'' before them except earls and barons, who are to be amerced by the council; they are to adjourn to a specified day before the council all claims of franchises made before them; and they are to refer all difficult questions to the council, *ibid.,* p. 383b, text also in Madox, *Exchequer,* I, 529, *o*; on page 469b one such question is stated; attorneys are made before the council, *ibid.,* p. 405; another entry on the same page (405b) shows the exchequer used for the same purpose, and another (405b) records the day given for a suit ''coram consilio,'' while on the next page (406) one party is ordered before the exchequer to explain why he sold a marriage which the king claims, and in the next entry but one another party is ordered before the council to explain why he committed waste in the king's woods—a case exactly the same in principle as the preceding one; in two cases land seized ''in manum'' by the justices of the bench for default is ordered restored, and itinerant justices are instructed to defer certain pleas of the crown until it is provided by the council where and before whom they are to be held, *ibid.,* p. 406 (cf. p. 210); on the same page Philip Marc is summoned to be ''coram consilio'' to answer concerning all the revenues of certain manors, and complaint is made to the council that a certain market is to the injury of one of the king's; a petition comes to the council personally presented by a messenger, *ibid.,* p. 415b; the rolls of the exchequer are examined by the

record quoted, *ibid.,* II, 10, note *x,* shows how the phrase ''Loquendum cum domino Rege'' was interpreted in practice, in most cases at least. It was a reference of the question to the council.

council and directions issued in accordance with what is found; and the function of a court of errors is exercised, *ibid.*, p. 549b. It will be noticed that sometimes council and exchequer seem identical (*ibid.*, pp. 361, 438b, 477a and b, and cf. Madox, *Exchequer*, II, 27 *b*), and sometimes the council seems to be regarded as superior to the exchequer. There is further evidence to the same effect, and such a situation is naturally to be expected in what is the last stage of the exchequer's differentiation. Other instances of judicial action by the council within the period are: *Bracton's Note Book*, pll. 12, 67, 81, 167, 1306, 1593; *Patent Rolls, 1216-1225*, pp. 113, 134, 135 (181), 145, 173, 225-226; *Excerpt. Rot. Finium*, I, 19, 44, 45, 95. A comparison of Maitland, *Select Pleas of the Crown*, no. 192, with Bracton, f. 151b (ed. Woodbine, II, 427), shows that the judgment recorded was rendered by the bench upon instructions by the council. The justices of the Jews suspend a case before them that a conference may be had with the council, Cole, *Documents*, p. 311.

It is still more difficult to present here the full evidence of the general activities of the council. Instead of attempting to do that I have chosen to try to show what part the work of the council plays in a single important source, hoping in that way to convey some idea of the impression which a study of all the sources together produces. I am giving a list of references to the work of the council as gathered from the patent rolls to the end of 1223 (*Patent Rolls, 1216-1225*), including a few which may possibly be references to the great council and omitting some earlier cited and some which are merely duplicates and also omitting all those instances to which reference is made in the index of the volume as published by the Master of the Rolls. These are then: pp. 21, 31, 48, 54, 69, 71, 77, 81, 85, 93, 108, 109, 122, 125, 146, 152,

153, 154, 157, 173, 174, 177, 180, 193, 197, 208, 212 (219), 221, 223, 224, 230, 231, 233, 234, 235, 236, 238, 241, 244, 255, 256, 258, 262-263, 263, 265, 271, 279, 280, 281, 287, 298, 303, 307, 320, 322, 324, 326, 327, 330, 331, 333, 334-335, 341, 346, 349, 350, 352, 354, 358, 361, 364-365, 366, 368, 374, 375, 376 *bis,* 377, 379, 380, 382, 384, 385, 388 *bis,* 389, 396, 399, 406. In addition the index of the volume gives twenty-two references for the same period.[31]

An examination of these references will show that the council, as the final deciding, authorizing and legislating body was recorded as occupied during these years about the following matters, there being usually more than one reference to each kind of activity, which shows that the action of the council in the given case was not an isolated one: negotiations with barons who have been in arms against King John concerning their return to allegiance; recovery of castles into the king's hands both from the insurgent barons and from the supporters of John, with the destruction of some castles and the return of others to their former holders; arrangements made necessary

[31] It would be exceedingly ungrateful to make any complaint of the indexes in the Calendar series of the Master of the Rolls considering the difficulties under which they are made and the improvements which have been brought about in them as the work of publication has gone on. Every scholar owes a debt of gratitude to the unselfish labors which have made them possible. It may perhaps be allowable merely to suggest that what the student of institutions desires especially is to have indexed every reference to a particular subject which is made in the text. It is more important to him to be sure that he has at his command every passage in which the subject is referred to than to know that he has some references to every subject of which the text treats. The omission of a single passage from those which the student considers may result in a wrong conclusion. This is especially true of the earliest records when the art of making records is still primitive, and one passage may mention an essential particular which is not found in others. Perhaps this is after all a council of perfection, for the same difficulty stands in the way of a perfect index that stands in the way of a perfect calendar, that the maker must know all the things for which any future student will ask.

by the presence of Louis of France, and negotiations with him, with Scotland and with the Welsh; regulations in great variety for the government of Ireland, Poitou and Gascony, the Welsh borders and the Channel Islands, and concerning the interests of individuals in these lands; the making of truces, the raising of loans, and arrangements for the debts of King John; the bestowal of the custody of counties, bishoprics, abbeys, honors, of castles, wardships and parks, and of the exchequer of the Jews; regulations about Jews in general and special protection for the Jews of Hereford; the gift of churches to convents, of income to the bishop of London, to the monks of Beaulieu and to a faithful clerk; the election of bishops; the perambulation of forests, deforestation, and inquests concerning essarts; the appointment of procurators at the court of Rome and the securing of loans for their expenses; consent to marriages belonging to the king; pardon for outlawry and flight; the removal of serjeants "ad pacem custodiendum"; presentation to prebends; the prohibition of tournaments; grants to cover losses in war, of the mint of England and of the chamberlainship of London; the appointment of itinerant justices, of justices of assize and of jail delivery; assizes are put in respite, and the holding of them without the king's special warrant is prohibited; regulations concerning the dower of Berengaria, the lands of a crusader, the establishment of a fair, the capture of robbers, the taking over of the castle of one who has died, the sale of fallen wood, and against the wrongful possession of a church by a convent. The council legislates; agreements are made before it; and many are summoned before it to hear instructions.

The showing here made from this one set of rolls indicates clearly enough how minutely the details of government were supervised by the council, but it is by no means all that it has to say of the council's activity. The reading of only a half dozen pages of these rolls, or of the close rolls as well, will convince one that only a small portion of the business actually done by the council is explicitly attributed to it in the records. Item after item in which no mention is made of the council is exactly the same in kind as others in which the council is said to be the acting authority. It seems wholly accidental whether the council is mentioned or not, and in most instances it is not, but the less important interest ascribed to its care implies the more important. Directions for the sale of fallen wood are ascribed to the council but not for the making of a regard of the forests five days later, pp. 399, 402.

But the most important transformation which affects the position of the council in this period does not appear in this list of particulars and seems wholly to have escaped the formal records, except as they give us the materials of inference. This is the new and very decided emphasis upon one of its older functions, the conciliar function proper, the function of advice and counsel or, in its wider aspect, the determination of the general policy of the government, which was forced upon the council by the fact of the minority. Here is the beginning of a change as great in its results as any one of the successive differentiations by which exchequer, king's bench, and chancery as a court of law, were established. But it was not a differentiation. No new institution to exercise this special function was thrown off. Nor does the change show itself so much in the transformation of the council into something new, for it still remained actively and effectively all that it had been, as in giving to it a different aspect and atmosphere, which in no long time comes to be its predominant aspect, the one in which through all its later history we naturally regard the council. In other words from now on the function of the council as political adviser of the sovereign attracts more and more attention to itself and crowds the other functions, which it still possesses, out of sight. To us it means that the council begins in this reign the change which gives it by degrees its modern position and function in the state. Or we may say that it begins now to stand out more clearly as the direct ancestor of the privy council and the cabinet. It was undoubtedly this manifestly greater prominence of the council in the general conduct of government which led the older writers to date the beginning of the council as a new institution from the minority.[32]

Gradually, almost imperceptibly, in the thirteenth century, the council's judicial function, which in earlier times had been the function which made the deepest impression on the records as we have them, fell into the background, gradually absorbed by the king's bench, growing more and more independent, and shunted upon a new track by the sudden outburst of petitions towards the end of the century, until these were in turn absorbed by the development of chancery. The judicial function, however, was not destined entirely to disappear. There was indeed a conspicuous revival of it at the end of the middle ages, and as a limited appellate jurisdiction it has remained in existence to our own time. Thus it happened, because the differentiation of the judicial function was easier and simpler, that the council as council was the surviver in the main line of descent and that, as no new institution appeared to exercise the function of advice and counsel, this function came to be regarded as the especially characteristic council business.

It must, however, be strongly emphasized, in order to

[32] Stubbs, II (1875), p. 40; Bémont, *Simon de Montfort,* p. 111; Anson, *Law and Custom of the Constitution,* II, Pt. I, 64; Maitland, *Constitutional History,* p. 200; *Select Pleas of the Crown,* p. xviii.

keep before the mind the connection with the past, that the institution which continues, because it was the continuing stock, was the old small curia regis, unchanged in make up, or changing its composition very slowly,[33] and retaining in theory at least all its original functions. It was still made up to the end of the century of the officers of the royal household, and barons who might be in attendance on the king, and the justices were still members of it because they always had been. It was still the organ of the king's prerogative, still the highest source of equity, still the seat of supervisory administration, and the ordinary legislative body of the state. Even on those few occasions when it was absorbed for this last purpose into the great council, it was still in all probability the small council which was the initiating and directing influence in legislation, as we know it was as late as the sixteenth century. It was still the old small curia regis, forced forward into a new position in the state by the long minority of Henry III in troublous times.

At the beginning of that minority there was committed to the earl marshal with the legate and the bishop of Winchester the care of the king and the kingdom, but the appointment was the act of the small council—"ex communi consilio"—composed of those barons and officers who were at Gloucester at the coronation of the young king. From this appointment their authority was wholly derived with the sanction of the great council, or rather of the small council expanded as nearly into a

[33] Attention has already been called (Chapter VIII, note 36) to an interesting record of council action among the fragments of uncertain date from John's reign which the Abbreviator printed (*Plac. Abbr.* p. 95) apparently from a common pleas roll, and very probably from a *coram rege* common pleas roll. It indicates very neatly the casual composition of the council. The king consults "super hoc illos qui tunc cum illo erant." The same thing appears in *Bracton's Note Book,* pl. 857. The king gets together "omnes magnates in curia sua tunc existentes."

great council as the king's party could manage, held shortly at Bristol. No special council of regency was created. This fact is clearly to be seen from the council's varied functions as enumerated in the list of its activities above. It is equally evident that it cannot be considered, as it was until recently, that it is in the minority that the existence of the council begins, for its activities all grow naturally out of its earlier history. That it was generally so considered is emphatic testimony to the sudden prominence into which the council was brought by the needs of the new government as the supreme controlling institution in a more conspicuous way and concerning more conspicuous affairs than ever before. The council became for the time being the king, and from being the organ through which the king's decisions were carried out and his commands enforced, it became the organ which made the king's decisions and commands. This exact position it of course did not retain, but the sharp emphasis of the minority upon the conciliar function proper was never lost. It is in the chroniclers, decidedly reenforced after about 1230 by the records, that the evidence of this emphasis is given.

As a natural result a transformation began in the council itself. It began to assume features of the modern council and continued to grow throughout the century more and more like it. By the end of the reign of Henry men were appointed to it as to an office; an oath of faithful service in the office was prescribed for them which especially tended to give the council an official and definite character; summonses began to be issued to attend its meetings, as if one were not expected to attend unless summoned, or at least as if some who had attended earlier meetings were not expected to attend all.[34] In

[34] For the present purpose the evidence for the transformation into an official council has been fully enough presented by Professor Baldwin in

other words it began to have the appearance no longer of a generic institution merely, occupying a somewhat indefinite position in the constitution, in possession of vague but extensive powers which it was continually exercising, which had been its character in the twelfth century. It becomes increasingly evident from 1216 on that the council was growing into a specific institution, with a well marked out place in the constitution and a definite function to perform which no other institution shared. It was becoming the official political adviser of the government. The facts in which this transformation appears would be simple and easily understood if it were not for the fact that the council in this new character retains all its earlier general powers and exercises them occasionally, or often, as in the matter of petitions. Considered as they should be, not as evidences of confusion, but as guides to mark out for us the course of evolution through the past, these survivals are conclusive proofs of the continuous development of the small council from William I to Edward I, and then on into privy council, star chamber and cabinet.

Clearly all the influences which affected the council in the course of the thirteenth century were preparing it for the commanding position which it occupies in the reign of Edward I. But in that reign another transformation appeared, an even more conspicuous one, in the field of history, affecting a closely related institution and one which has always attracted to itself the paramount in-

Chapter II of his *King's Council.* The drift towards an official council in the thirteenth century undoubtedly accelerated the differentiation of the exchequer, king's bench and chancery as courts of law. The short time required for the differentiation of chancery as compared with the exchequer is especially noteworthy. The stages through which this differentiation of chancery as a court passes are clearly parallel to those of the differentiation of the exchequer, but in a single century chancery has reached a point of independence which the exchequer reaches only after two.

terest of students of the English constitution. Almost unavoidably their attention has been diverted from the small council. It was indeed a momentous institutional change which affected the great council and gave rise to the later parliament.[35] But the constitutional history of the reign is not to be understood by studying that transformation alone, leaving unstudied, or studied but superficially, various puzzling problems relating to the position of the small council and its share in the public business, for these, bearing the past in mind, are really more likely to hold the key to what takes place than the change in the great council.

At any rate this change in the structure of the great council is here to be left to one side, as not belonging directly in our field.[36] In general what I believe will finally be found to be the fact in regard to the relation of the great and small councils to one another under Edward I is that in such matters as meetings, bodies and action, nothing was done that was new. Absorption of the small council in the great during its session, the continuation of the session by the small council with all the powers and authority of the great after that has been allowed to disperse,[37] the presence in either council of non-feudal elements at the summons of the king including

[35] In saying this, however, we are drawing upon our knowledge of the great rôle which parliament was to play in the later history of the constitution. This of course could not be foreseen and it does not seem likely that the men of the time would have considered that all other institutional interests were overshadowed by the change made when new elements were introduced into the great council. It could not have seemed a violent or striking change when regarded in the light of the past.

[36] See note A at the end of the Chapter.

[37] With regard to a meeting of the small council in preparation for a meeting of the great council, or in continuation of its session after it had dispersed, see *Origin*, pp. 199-201; *Trans. Royal Hist. Soc.*, Series IV, Vol. V, 67-68; *Ann. Burton*, pp. 251-253. See several instances noted in note A at the end of Chapter IV.

the justices, meetings of a part only of the great council by itself as if assembled for a particular kind of business or a particular piece of business, none of these is new.[38] Nothing was done which was not in accordance with precedents running far back in the history of the past. We are naturally affected by the evidence we have from the time of Edward very much as we have sometimes been in regard to the beginning of the political council as a new institution by the evidence from the minority of Henry III. There is so much more evidence in the contemporary records and there is such a marked increase of business that it is possible for us to see some things that have escaped us before and various things seem to be new which can nevertheless be traced back into the age of less business and more scanty records.

The impression of a new beginning is confirmed by the coming into use of new names and phrases like "parliamentum" and "consilium in parliamento."[39] We should,

[38] It was of course new to summon to the meeting of the great council men who stood for, and might speak for, local communities. In regard to them two things are to be said. In the first place the principle that the king might summon whom he would had always been admitted and apparently always acted upon. It was new to act upon it on such a scale and in favor of whole classes. Secondly, there is no clear thirteenth century evidence that the new elements were admitted to what we should call membership in the great council. Such evidence as we have of their sharing in its powers, leaving one side the uncertain case of the trial of David of Wales (Stubbs, *S.C.*, p. 460, no. VI *a*), show them acting rather as distinct classes, as in the adoption of the statute of merchants or the share of the knights in the statute Quia emptores. I do not know of any evidence that the knights of the shire were considered in any special way to represent the minor tenants-in-chief in this transformation of the great council. They represented the community of the county as the burgesses represented the community of the borough. Pollard, *Evolution of Parliament*, p. 51.

[39] On early uses of the word "parliamentum," see Professor A. B. White in the *Modern Language Review*, 1914, IX, 92-93. See also, and on other uses, Pollard, *Evolution of Parliament*, p. 32, note 1, and pp. 45-47. The word comes into use probably first in Italy about the middle of the twelfth century and becomes quite general in all the Latin countries in the

however, not allow the use of these new expressions to induce us to believe that some new thing, some new institution, or some newly made over institution, or some new way of doing business, had just come into existence of which they were the peculiar sign. A difference of name in successive stages of an institution's history may accompany a change in its identity or some modification of its structure or organic character, but not necessarily. They quite as frequently signify nothing in the way of change, except perhaps in language. This is particularly true of the variety of names applied to the Teutonic, Frankish, and Anglo-Norman central assembly in the course of its long history.[40]

The use of the word "parliamentum" goes back into a time when certainly there was as yet no sign of change in the national assembly, and when it was used not of the national assembly alone but of the small council as well. And if it is to be regarded as referring to an institution, it is at most only a translation of "colloquium" which was in similar use some centuries before the Norman

next century. On its use in France, see Borrelli de Serres, *Recherches sur Divers Services Publics,* pp. 288 ff. It is quite common in England by the middle years of the thirteenth century and is applied to all sorts of conferences and colloquies as well as to the more formal meetings of courts and summoned assemblies. For its use of private courts, see the *Cartulary of St. John of Colchester* (Roxburghe Club, 1897), II, 355; and *Archaeologia Cambrensis,* Series IV, Vol. II, 241. Uses in which the word seems equivalent to the term "session" are cited: in Vinogradoff, *Studies,* VI, Pt. 2, 218 (1255), "Et datus ei dies in parliamento"; and in *Trans. Royal Hist. Soc.,* Series IV, Vol. V, 61, "Ideo datus est dies ad parleamentum." Both these are documentary sources. On "consilium in parliamento" see above, Chapter VII, note 49. If the explanation there given is adopted, the words mean no more at most than ". . . per archiepiscopos, episcopos, comites et barones nostros, et consilium nostrum" (Rymer, *Foedera,* I, 1, 156, of 1219), and similar phrases which are not infrequently found and imply either a strongly reenforced small, or a great council.

40 Called in the Frankish period, for example, *curia, placitum, conventus, colloquium, synodus, concilium.* See above, Introduction.

Conquest.[41] The use of "parliamentum" in the thirteenth century seems, however, most simply explained, and for the great majority of cases, if we consider that the primitive meaning is retained in the use of the word, and that the emphasis is upon the method of doing business and not upon the institution which does it. The American Indians had a somewhat similar usage when they called a council held with the representatives of the national government a "great talk." If we can consider that this is in most cases the meaning of the word under Edward I, its best translation for such instances would be "session."[42] A parliament is a session of the council, and "consilium in parliamento" is the council in session, probably in one of its regular terminal sessions. But whether it is the small council, or the great council with the small council for the time being absorbed in it, should

41 The *Annals of Tewkesbury* (pp. 147-148) under date of 1252 say "Dominus Rex tenuit magnum parliamentum Londoniae cum magnatibus Angliae" in one paragraph and in the next "Rex habuit magnum colloquium Londoniae cum magnatibus Angliae," which may possibly indicate a slight difference of meaning in the writer's mind.

42 But not "parliamentary session" (P. and M., I, 178; Vinogradoff, *Studies*, VI, v), which would be a meaningless expression to Fleta, who would not be able to see a difference between sessions which seem to us to be different in kind because we know the later history. I mean by this no more than that, if we use such a phrase as "parliamentary session" to help ourselves in making distinctions, we should not understand it to mean that the same distinctions could be perceived by the men of that time. As an example of the use of the word where it undoubtedly means no more than a meeting of the great council, or a general meeting of the magnates of the kingdom, but where it might easily be taken for the name of a definite institution, showing how easily this transition could be made, is the following quotation from a letter from Henry III to the justiciar, Hugh Bigod, dated 16 January, 1260: ". . . vobis mandamus quod, omni parliamento postposito et penitus remoto, habito super his tractatu cum magnatibus de consilio nostro qui praesentes fuerint . . . nullum parliamentum citra adventum nostrum in Angliam statuentes aut fieri permittentes, quia cum ibidem venerimus . . . de parliamento habendo providebimus . . ." Shirley, *Royal Letters*, II, 150. Cf. Bémont, *Simon de Montfort*, pp. 350-351.

mean no greater difference to us in functions, competence and methods than it did to contemporaries, and they plainly saw no difference in any of these particulars between the parliament of 1305 as at first assembled and the small council which continued its session after the merely great council portion of it had dispersed. This use of the word is in harmony with the attractive and instructive, but not quite convincing,[43] analysis of the parliamentary meetings of Edward's reign which Professor Pollard has given in the third chapter of his *Evolution of Parliament,* and it fits as well into the various facts of the period. The frequent use of the word under Edward is another evidence of the great prominence of the council as the directing organ of government.[44]

43 At least Professor Pollard does not seem to me to have taken into account quite fully enough the writ for the parliament of 1275 nor the meeting for the trial of David of Wales in 1283. Stubbs, *S.C.,* pp. 441 and 460. Nor does it seem to be quite in accordance with the way things naturally develop that such sharp distinctions should be made so early between meetings and names. *The Evolution of Parliament,* pp. 46-54.

44 The relation of the council to the body which finally obtains an exclusive right to the name parliament—but which is still to the end of Edward's reign best characterized as the great council plus the new representative elements—and the position which it occupies in a meeting of that body, have been most carefully studied for the parliament of 1305 by Professor Maitland in his *Memoranda de Parliamento* (R.S.) and by others following his lead. He discusses this relationship in his introduction under these topics: 1. The continuation of the session after the great council has gone home by the small council as a "full parliament." 2. The composition and position of the council. 3. The discussion of affairs of state, especially foreign affairs. 4. Legislation. 5. Taxation. 6. Judicial business. It is an interesting fact which Professor Pollard notes, *Evolution of Parliament,* pp. 90, 28-30, that the word *magnum,* used earlier of the national assembly, drops out of use during the time of Edward I and the assembly is no longer called "magnum concilium" or great council. But this fact again should not lead us to suppose that the institution itself disappeared, as it certainly did not, or that any change occurred in it which is indicated by the falling out of use of the name. It returns to use under Edward II. Professor Pollard supposes that the difference is brought about by the strong government of Edward I, which is very probably true.

Whatever may be the final conclusion of history in regard to these particulars, we drop here from further discussion, as explained above, the transformation of the great council at the end of the thirteenth century and the relation to it of the small council. There remains to be considered a wide movement which is distinctly characteristic of the thirteenth century and belongs within our field because it is closely related to the development of courts and council, but whose general scope only can be indicated here. What I have put together under this head will, I think, when first looked at in detail, give the impression of a somewhat artificial combination of unrelated particulars. But the point I wish especially to emphasize is that behind all these special facts there is a common impelling force, that the connection between them is one of living growth, and that they are all bound together as successive or contemporary phases of a single movement, expressing itself as naturally in one as in another. The movement is in character and partially in effect institutional, but its largest direct contribution is to the body of the law, and it is not directly but through its enlargement of the content and field of the law that its most permanent institutional results were brought about. The immediate practical results in which it reveals itself are in the development of writs, in the increased number of statutes and their more evident influence, in the greatly enlarged use of petitions and in the development of the court of chancery.

It should be evident at once that what lies back of all these apparently distinct features of the time is the demand for new law and for new conveniences of litigation. The development of new writs, recourse to a statute, the employment of petitions, are all attempts in different ways to meet this demand, and the development of the chancery court is a direct result of one consequent enlargement of the field of law. But the demand for new law is nothing ultimate. It must always be itself a result of something which lies farther back. If we are seeking for the ultimate force from which the demand for these changes arose, we must ask how there came to be just at this time an insistent demand for new law, and we are brought by that question into contact with the deeper forces of history. The thirteenth century is one of the world's great ages of rapid advance, not merely in England but throughout the whole western hemisphere.

It is not possible here to go into any detailed discussion of the underlying causes of this world movement nor of the innumerable ways in which it affected the life of mankind. It is sufficient here to say that they were chiefly economic and social—social largely because they were economic—and that this was as true of England as of any other part of Europe. It is well enough known that the thirteenth century in England was an age of great social as well as political, institutional and intellectual changes. These changes force themselves upon our attention. We cannot avoid recognizing them. But they have never yet been studied as a common whole nor the attempt made to carry them back as a single movement to show how they were derived from the more primary economic changes which lie in the background. In the field of law and institutions some few detached things have been done. For example, as a fact of minor importance, we know that economic changes by the middle of the century had destroyed the interest of the barons in protecting their baronial courts by means of the provision in c. 34 of Magna Carta. We are familiar with the more important fact that social changes impelled the transformation of the feudal great council into the modern parliament. How the price revolution of the early century affected the government of King John and became one of the primary influences which led to the granting of the Great Charter, has long ago been pointed out. I am here merely calling attention to the fact that the economic and social change gave the initial and common impulse to lines of growth which seem at first remote from such a cause and unites into an organic whole particulars which seem unconnected.

In creating a demand for new law the economic change often works at first hand and not through an intermediate social result. A new economic interest created is a strong impelling force. The man who sees that economic gains for him lie in a certain direction is anxious to reach them and, if he finds in his way some insurmountable obstacle in the law as it stands, he begins to demand a change in the law. If there are men enough who demand the change, or if they are men of enough influence, it is likely to be made. To take an example to which we shall return later: almost from the moment when the growing economic value of land began to be perceived by the landlord class, a movement began which runs through centuries of English history—the movement for the approvement of commons or, as it was later called, of enclosures—the attempt of the landlord to turn to his own use and profit a portion, or all, of the common land of the manor.[45] But at the beginning of the thirteenth century there stood in the way of the lord's attempt the old customary common law doctrine of common of pasture—the right of the tenant to pasture his beasts on the common.[46] This right had stood for generations and the courts were bound to recognize and enforce it. No change in procedure, within the competence of the court acting by itself, could give the landlord the opportunity which

[45] See below at note 53.

[46] See statements of the common law rights of pasture in *Bracton's Note Book,* pll. 1624, 1881.

he sought. The difficulty could be got about only by some change in the substantive law. Here are indicated two of the ways by which changes were brought about during the century. To these we may add a third and anticipate so much of what is to follow by saying that there were three ways: 1, changes effected by changes in procedure; 2, changes which could be made only by legislation; 3, changes resulting from opening a new field of law, the development of equity as distinct from the common law. It may be premised also that, while here as in other ages men were occasionally conscious of the economic interest by which they were moved, they were often entirely blind to it and thought themselves acting upon other reasons.

The phase of this combined movement which comes both logically and historically first, is the use which was made of the writ or changes effected by changes in procedure. Already in the twelfth century the writ had been the instrument of a revolution by which English law and judicial institutions and to some extent the constitution of the state had been transformed. We have seen above to what an extent that revolution had progressed in the construction of a new judicial system, national in character, in the attack on the baronial jurisdiction of the lords, and in the definite beginning of the common law. There was no demand which the thirteenth century was likely to make for the expansion of procedural law which the writ, in the place which it occupied at the end of the twelfth, was not fully prepared to meet. Indeed the whole machinery, spirit and method of a self-developing law was in existence as the thirteenth century opened. The judiciary was already confident of its powers. The judges were not afraid to deal with the new or to modify the old. If any question of unusual difficulty arose which delegated judges hesitated to settle, it could be referred to the council and determined without passing outside the limits of the judicial system by legislation established.

The expansion of the law and the making of litigation more convenient by the invention of new writs and the division and subdivision of old ones, the multiplication and clear definition of the forms of action, were already well under way before the accession of John. The development of the writ of entry, which is one of the characteristic features of this movement in the thirteenth century, began certainly as early as the reign of Richard. The whole history of English law would have been different, if the promise which the judicial system gave at the beginning of the century of a broad expansion, of elasticity, and of ability to provide for the new demand, had been fulfilled at its close. The reasons for that failure we are not to consider here. It is with the actual advance which was made that we are concerned.

Professor Maitland has studied in his articles on the Registers of Writs[47] the numerical, as well as the legal, results of this expansion and how they show themselves in the formal lists drawn up for the convenience of the lawyers. An increase in the number of writs available, in what is only a little more than a century, from about fifty to several hundreds,[48] though the distinction between many of them may be but slight, indicates very keen activity and a remarkably rapid growth. But no numerical statement can indicate the real character of this expansion. A merely cursory examination of the titles in the Registers of Writs will show that comparatively few are wholly new writs. It will be seen that nearly all of them are formed under the older writs by the introduction of

[47] *Collected Papers,* II, 110-173. First published in the *Harvard Law Review,* 1889, III, 97-115, 167-179, 212-225. Also reprinted in *Select Essays in Anglo-American Legal History,* II, 549-596.

[48] Maitland mentions a Register of Writs of Edward I's time at the British Museum which contains 471 writs. *Collected Papers,* p. 155.

more specific particulars. It is a process akin to division and subdivision by which the scope of the original action is limited and made from the beginning more clear. The writ of entry is formed under the writ of right by the introduction into it of specific allegations, which apparently begin to occur in the pleadings before they do in the writ, and which compel the defendant to answer along a definite line or to fall back upon the ultimate defence of ownership.[49] This is fairly typical of what took place in all directions. The result must have been to economize the time of the court and to simplify the process of litigation. As one follows the unfolding of this development, as it is now scantily revealed to us in the court rolls, it is difficult to avoid the belief that those who presided over it were intent, consciously and deliberately, upon economy of time and simplicity of litigation. That any part of the administration of English law later became a ''horrible tangle'' was no fault of theirs and in spite of their efforts.[50] Whoever first introduced the word *quare* into a writ, or very likely first into pleadings, in an early stage of this expansion, deserves the fame of a great discoverer.[51] But the records give us only here and there a faint glimpse of personalities. There are no famous names.

Maitland's edition of *Bracton's Note Book* is easily accessible. It gives the record of cases, falling between 1217

49 See note B at the end of the Chapter.

50 ''Glanvill I, 5 allows the king to issue this writ *praecipe* whenever he pleases. Had this prerogative been maintained, the horrible tangle of our 'real actions,' our 'writs of entry,' and so forth, would never have perplexed us.'' P. and M., I, 151, note 5.

51 For example, in the index of the *Select Civil Pleas* (Selden Soc.), representing an earlier stage of this history, under the word ''actions'' the list of *quare* writs shows the extreme flexibility of the early writ and how many forms of action had a promising beginning for which there was no future.

and 1240, which were especially studied by *Bracton* in the preparation of the *De Legibus,* and it is possible in it to follow, not the earliest stages of this expansion, which begins indeed in the twelfth century and even before Henry II, but stages of it in which new actions were still in the course of formation, at least somewhere midway in the process of division and subdivision which was still going on in the same way as from the beginning. By selecting any action in which change is taking place and arranging chronologically the cases in which it is employed by the use of the index of actions in the first volume, the change may be studied. Trespass may serve as an example[52] or, to take a somewhat difficult one in another sphere, the change which is going on with regard to the king's interest in criminal cases. Or, in something more simple, the relation of the *quare impedit* (*quare non permisit, quare non admisit*) to the assize of *darrein presentment* may be seen, though the beginning is not shown in Bracton's cases. But any collection of cases, preferably of the early thirteenth century, which has an index of actions, may be used to get a glimpse of this process as it actually went on.

It should be added before leaving this phase of the subject that neither the increase in the number of actions which a litigant might employ, nor the simplification which resulted from their clearer definition, measures the full significance of this movement. In the history of the common law, it is of greater permanent importance that, as one of its direct results, there were opened up great new fields of fruitful interest and of growth. What followed by degrees, for instance in the development of the action of trespass, is like the gradual occupation of a new continent. An entry, damages, and the new writs formed

52 See Woodbine, "The Origins of the Action of Trespass," *Yale Law Journal,* June 1924, XXXIII, 799-816, to be followed by a second article.

about the assizes, open within their possibilities similar regions to be occupied. These lines of expansion have all of them sometime still further to be studied from this point of view, with attention to the careful thinking which someone, or many, must have given to the matter of relationships and other aspects of the movement as it went on. It is especially true that further study must be given to the changing relation of the king to the administration of the law in the courts, or as a participant in its administration, as one like other men affected by its processes and subject to them in certain formal ways, a changing relation which shows itself for example in the development of the criminal jurisdiction of the king's bench, in the *quo warranto,* and in the more frequent appearance in the records of those who "speak for the king."

In turning to the subject of legislation, I of course cannot undertake to maintain, as it may have been thought was implied above, that every change in the law was a direct result of economic changes or was made necessary by an otherwise insuperable obstacle to progress in the preexisting common law. But I do maintain that a good deal of legislation was occasioned in this century by changes of some kind in the society of the time and that a good deal of it did modify, and was recognized as modifying, existing law. Both these facts will be evident, I think, in the list of legislative acts given below.

I have used above the matter of enclosures, or approvement of commons,[53] to illustrate both the direct influence of economic changes on the development of law and also the fact that the desired change in the law could sometimes be secured only by legislation. I am bound to say that the proof that I am justified in this interpretation of the facts is not so full as I could wish, but it seems

[53] See above in text at note 45.

to me that no other is admissible. Since Professor Vinogradoff's discussion of the subject thirty years ago[54] no new material bearing upon it has appeared in print. At least I have found none. All that can be done is to reexamine his evidence and to restate his conclusion with no essential modification. The two cases cited by Vinogradoff from the court rolls[55] do not seem to be quite in agreement with one another, though both are marked by the annotator "contra constitutionem de Mertona." The earlier one, pl. 1975, seems however to state the principle of the statute in a somewhat peculiar application, but it is evident that whatever the courts may have done, the lords of manors did not feel their position in approvement quite secure without the sanction of legislation, and the most that can be claimed for the courts is that they had shown the road for the council to follow. The legislation is very frank about the economic motive[56] and is clearly intended to protect the landlord in the circumstances enumerated from any claim arising from common law rights. It enacts a clear modification of the law in all "ubique" cases.[57]

Taken all together there is a large body of legislation in the reign of Henry III,[58] as we should expect after the

[54] Vinogradoff, *Villainage in England* (1892), pp. 271-275.

[55] From *Bracton's Note Book,* pll. 1881 and 1975.

[56] "Quia multi magnates de regno nostro Angliae, qui feofaverunt milites et libere tenentes suos de parvis tenementis in magnis maneriis, questi fuerunt, quod commodum suum facere non potuerunt de residuo maneriorum suorum, sicut de vastis, boscis, et pasturis, desicut ipsi feofati sufficientem possent habere pasturam quatenus pertineret ad tenementa sua, ita provisum est . . ." *Ann. Burton,* p. 250. See also the writ formed on the statute, Bracton f. 227b.

[57] See above, at note 46.

[58] I am omitting from the present discussion all consideration of the great statutes of the end of the century because it seems to me that their peculiar importance is rather as foundation of the future than as culmination of the past. At least for the purpose of this study, they appear to me to add only confirmation, not new conclusions.

beginning made in the exercise of that function in the preceding century[59] and in a reign of nearly sixty years full of change. A part of it is administrative regulation, a part is declaratory merely, but a good part of it creates new law or modifies old. The point in which I am at present most interested is that an act of legislation duly adopted and put into force was binding upon the courts whatever the old law might be.[60] A new administrative regulation must be obeyed by itinerant justices, sheriffs, and the exchequer in its annual accountings. The meaning fixed by a declaratory act must be accepted. An addition to the substance of the law by the council, or a change in its substance, becomes as valid law as anything that existed before.

Many problems which arise naturally in the history of this movement I am not pretending to solve, or even to consider, at this time. I am attempting no discussion of how or by whom the process of legislation was carried on in this age; nor to decide what documents were statutes in our sense of the word and what others were not, nor whether the term statute was then used in anything like our meaning; nor to mark out the difference between statutes and ordinances; nor to settle the question to what extent the courts may have thought themselves justified in putting their own interpretation upon the language of statutes.[61] Whatever view we may take of

59 See for example above, Chapter V, note 33.

60 Even the famous "nolumus leges Anglie mutare" of the barons in the matter of bastardy (*Bracton's Note Book*, I, 104 ff.) shows that they were fully conscious that they had the right and power to change the common law if they willed to do so.

61 This is the subject of Mr. T. F. T. Plucknett's interesting book: *Statutes and their Interpretation in the First Half of the Fourteenth Century*, in "Cambridge Studies in English Legal History," 1922. Even in the cases which he cites, pp. 57-60, from the reign of Edward I, in which the courts certainly take large liberties with the statutes, their conclusion is

these problems, the fact remains in my opinion unquestionable that there was during the thirteenth century a considerable body of enactment of one kind or another by which the common law was changed and enlarged, by which the courts were bound, and to some of which I am assuming a present right to apply the name statute somewhat in the sense we give the word today. This body of legislation and its effect seems to me the matter just now most in need of discussion.

No complete list has ever been attempted of the legislative acts of Henry III's reign that have come down to us in any kind of mention and one really complete is never likely to be possible. But, because a list as full as a careful examination of our present material permits, will give a more adequate idea of the activities of the reign in this direction than anything else can, I am attempting that. Logically and chronologically the list should begin with the Great Charter. Though this was not in legislative form and was probably not formally adopted by the council, it was issued with the sanction of what passed as a great council about a fortnight after the consecration of the king, and it was treated as a statute by the courts, that is, a definite declaration by the Charter of the law upon any point settled that point for the courts. The further question whether it was also regarded as fundamental law in this period need not be here discussed. To be considered fundamental law, it must have been held not merely to overrule the common law, any statute did that, but to overrule and render void statutes themselves. Such a view of the Charter could, I think, result only from considerable experience with statutes and a good deal of thinking about the different kinds of

ultimately a matter of interpretation and is not based on any doctrine that the common law is superior to the statute. They rather imply that the statute would govern if it applied exactly to the case.

law and their relation to one another. Professor Maitland regards certain clauses in the excommunication issued against violators of the Charter in 1253 as an "effort to convert every one of its clauses into a fundamental, irrepealable law.[62] By the middle of the century there had certainly been a good deal of experience of the kind needed, and it is not impossible that Professor Maitland's interpretation may be correct. If it is, however, I am inclined to think that it gives us the ideas of one man, or a few, rather than any general feeling. That the courts regarded the Charter as having the same force that a modern statute has, is shown plainly enough in *Bracton's Note Book*. See pleas 743, 1213, 1220, 1227, 1248, 1328, 1478. Plea 1730 also indicates clearly that the provisions of the Charter were considered binding law though the subject of dispute and contention. Bracton cites the Charter as law not infrequently: ff. 87, 87b, 105b, 116b, 168b, 281, 414b.

The following legislative acts should be studied.[63]

[62] P. and M., I, 158. Text in *Statutes of the Realm*, I, 6 and Rymer, *Foedera*, I, 1, 289. The excommunication is against the makers of statutes which violate the Charter and strictly interpreted the language does not imply that the statutes will be void. It implies possibly the contrary. Nor is it quite certain in what meaning the word statute is used.

[63] Will the reader kindly notice that what I am here concerned with is the character and effect of defining and directing acts adopted by any body having what we would now distinguish as legislative powers. This would include at least the great council, the formal small council meeting by itself, exchequer as council, and *coram rege* as council. I am not pointing out in every case the overruling authority of the enactment because it seems to me in many places abundantly clear. Plucknett in his *Statutes and their Interpretation*, p. 21, says of bodies adopting legislation under Edward I: "Legislation was by no means the monopoly of parliament [great council]." "One statute is made by the Council, Judges of both Benches, and the Barons of the Exchequer sitting in the Exchequer, another by the Council with the advice of the Judges and the consent of the king at ("ad") a parliament, while Hengham tells us that he and his companions made the statute of Westminster II." I quite agree, but I may point out that it is highly probable that in the eyes of contemporaries in all these

Probably during the minority it was provided that no subject of the king of England need answer to a subject of the king of France until the French courts were open to English subjects.[64] In 1219 the justices were instructed how to treat those accused of crimes before them now that the ordeal had been prohibited,[65] and the holding of assizes in private courts without permission was strictly forbidden. In 1221 the council regulated the operation of the itinerant justice system in Ireland.[66] In 1223 it provided that there should be exchanges of precious metal in England only at London and Canterbury.[67] In 1225 an earlier "constitutio" concerning cloth was modified for the benefit of the Londoners.[68] In 1230 an administrative regulation of exchequer business was made by an unusually large council. In 1232 the method of the grand assize was modified for tenants in gavelkind in Kent.[69] In 1233 the council made regulations concerning watch

instances it was the same body which was acting, and that body was technically the small council, even where the action is said to be at a parliament. In each case some special feature of the council's membership is emphasized, as in some the share of the king is referred to and in some not. For what reason the difference is made we cannot now say, but adding together the various persons specified does not take us outside the known council membership. Neither is it a new thing that part of the council should act as the whole, and a different part in another case, nor is it new that the small council, as distinguished from the great, should exercise the legislative function.

64 *Bracton's Note Book*, pll. 110, 1396. Baldwin, *King's Council*, p. 59, says "made in 1220," but there is no evidence for a date in the records cited.

65 *Patent Rolls, 1216-1225*, p. 186; Rymer, *Foedera*, I, 1, 154; Thayer, *Evidence*, pp. 37-38; Holdsworth, II, 221 and note 5. *Pat. Rolls, 1216-1225*, p. 202.

66 *Rot. Litt. Claus.*, I, 451.

67 *Pat. Rolls, 1216-1225*, p. 366.

68 *Ibid.*, p. 523; Madox, *Exchequer*, II, 27, *g*.

69 *Statutes of the Realm*, I, 225; *Close Rolls, 1231-1234*, pp. 32, 83; Rymer, *Foedera*, I, 1, 202; Maitland, *Collected Papers*, II, 142.

and the keeping of the peace.[70] In 1234 it enacted that suits might be made to royal and private courts and pleas prosecuted and defended by attorney without special writs,[71] and a declaratory act was adopted regarding holding hundred courts and the sheriff's turn. Later in the same year the statute concerning special bastardy was adopted,[72] and apparently in the same meeting of the council the application of the assizes of darrein presentment and utrum to certain clerical cases was modified.[73] Probably in the next year an act of the council enlarged the list of things from which tithes were to be paid from the royal domains.[74] In 1236 an assize of wine was made and London merchants were forbidden to go to meet foreign merchants to make early purchases;[75] the Gascons were forbidden to reduce the size of their casks[76] and the Cistercians to buy wool or hides to sell again or anyone to sell to them for this purpose.[77] The statute of Merton also belongs to the year 1236, a considerable body of legislation on at least five different subjects.[78] In 1237

[70] *Close Rolls, 1231-1234*, pp. 309-310; Rymer, *Foedera*, I, 1, 209-210.

[71] *Close Rolls, 1231-1234*, p. 551. Given in the *Statutes of the Realm* as c. 10 of the statute of Merton. Cf. *Bracton's Note Book*, I, 104 ff.; Holdsworth, II, 221; *Close Rolls, 1231-1234*, p. 588; *Ann. Dunstable*, p. 139.

[72] *Bracton's Note Book*, I, 104 ff., and pl. 1117; H. G. Richardson in *Transactions Royal Hist. Soc.*, Series IV (1922), V, 67-68. Given in *Statutes of the Realm* as c. 9 of the statute of Merton. Cf. *Close Rolls, 1234-1237*, pp. 201-202. Holdsworth's reference, II, 221, to this and the next above should be transposed.

[73] *Bracton's Note Book*, pl. 1117; *Trans. Royal Hist. Soc.* Series IV (1922), V, 68.

[74] *Close Rolls, 1234-1237*, p. 140.

[75] *Ibid.*, p. 512. The latter part of this regulation is called in the document itself *assisa* and in the next document on the close roll *statutum.*

[76] *Close Rolls, 1234-1237*, pp. 512-513.

[77] *Ibid.*, p. 532.

[78] *Statutes of the Realm*, I, 1; M. Paris, III, 341; *Ann. Burton*, pp. 249-251; *Bracton's Note Book*, I, 104 ff. C. 11 of the statute is interesting as indicating a debate in the council which resulted in no legislation at that time.

a "constitutio" had lately been made concerning hearing the accounts of those who were directing royal works;[79] and it was provided that keepers of the king's manors should have the custody of all parks and domain woods belonging to their manors on certain conditions.[80] In 1237 also it seems probable the enactment was made changing the limitation of time on various writs which is given as c. 8 of the statute of Merton,[81] and the new writ of cosinage was adopted by the council.[82] In 1238 it was provided that nothing should be taken from merchants, foreign or other, except by the king's writ and the view of legal men,[83] and regulations were made touching the keeping of the king's forests[84] in continuation of those made the year before.[85] In 1242 the council ordained that in the future no chapters should be held by the Jews in England[86] and provided a form in which the merchants of Flanders should prove the ownership of their goods during the war with France.[87] In 1242 also was adopted, I think, the assize of arms usually assigned to 1252. If so it was enacted not long before the king's departure for Gascony on May 9. There is no ground for a *teste* by the archbishop of York in May, 1252.[88] The writ of 28 Henry III printed by Madox must have been based upon legisla-

79 *Close Rolls, 1234-1237*, p. 482.

80 *Cal. Pat. Rolls, 1232-1247*, pp. 186-187.

81 *Bracton's Note Book*, I, 106, and pl. 1217.

82 *Ibid.*, pl. 1215.

83 *Close Rolls, 1237-1242*, p. 56.

84 *Cal. Pat. Rolls, 1232-1247*, p. 216.

85 *Ann. Burton*, pp. 251-252.

86 *Close Rolls, 1237-1242*, p. 464.

87 *Cal. Pat. Rolls, 1232-1247*, p. 303.

88 Printed as of 1252 in Rymer, *Foedera*, I, 1, 281, and Stubbs, *S.C.*, ed. 9, p. 362, and cf. Vinogradoff, *Oxford Studies*, VI, 1, 25, note 2. It is given its proper place on the close roll. See *Close Rolls, 1237-1242*, pp. 482-484. See also Vincent, *Lancashire Lay Subsidies* (Lanc. and Cheshire Record Soc. XXVII), pp. 67-70.

tion, as it states, but no date is indicated though it is probably of this reign.[89] In 1246 by an act of the council the laws and customs of England were extended over Ireland.[90] In 1248, or shortly before, it was provided that extents of wardships and escheats coming "in manum" should be made by the king's escheators and not by the sheriffs.[91] In the same year regulations were made directing how the king's money was to be made,[92] fixing the amount of interest to be charged for small sums by the Jews of Oxford,[93] and forbidding mutilation privately inflicted "nisi pro conjuge."[94] In 1251 advantage was taken of the dedication of the abbey of Hailes to adopt legislation limiting for the future the right of the defendant to vouch the king to warranty.[95] In 1256 an enactment was made against the alienation of land by tenants-in-chief without the king's consent.[96] In the same year was made an assize of bread[97] and regulations for the amercement for delay at the exchequer of sheriffs and of towns answering by their bailiffs,[98] and on the method of reckoning the extra day in leap year.[99] The Provisions of Oxford adopted in 1258 show how far the council thought itself justified in going in modification of the constitution of the state,[100] as do also the abortive provisions

89 Madox, *Exchequer*, II, 249, note *ff*.

90 *Cal. Pat. Rolls, 1232-1247*, p. 488; Rymer, *Foedera*, I, 1, 266. Cf. *Cal. Pat. Rolls, 1232-1247*, p. 177.

91 *Close Rolls, 1247-1251*, p. 105.

92 *Ibid.*, p. 45.

93 *Ibid.*, p. 114, and cf. p. 216.

94 M. Paris, V, 35; P. and M., II, 483, note 2.

95 Bracton, f. 382b; M. Paris, V, 262; P. and M., I, 159, note 4; Vinogradoff, *Oxford Studies*, VI, 2, 25, 51. Cf. *Bracton's Note Book*, pl. 1306.

96 G. J. Turner in *Law Quarterly Review* (1896), XII, 299-301; P. and M., ed. 2, I, 335 (not in ed. 1); Holdsworth, II, 221, note 12.

97 *Ann. Burton*, p. 375.

98 M. Paris, V, 588.

99 *Statutes of the Realm*, I, 7; *Bracton's Note Book*, I, 42, 82.

100 *Ann. Burton*, pp. 446-453; Stubbs, *S.C.*, pp. 378-387.

of 1244.[101] The Provisions of Westminster of 1259 are interesting, both as probably in themselves intended to be legislation and as the basis of later legislation in the statute of Marlborough of 1267.[102] Their history and contents are instructive on the sources of reform demands and their growth into legislation.[103] The reforms commanded this year by the king with his council at the exchequer, chiefly of abuses by the sheriffs, include some that are of a legislative character.[104] Apparently in 1260 an ordinance (*condictum*) was made "by the whole council" that every magnate should have the power of correcting the excesses of his bailiffs and sergeants when complaint was made of their trespasses.[105] In 51 Henry III a regulation was made by the king in the exchequer about the payment of the arrears of sheriffs and the treatment of the king's writ concerning them.[106]

In addition to the acts included in this list, there are three undated enactments which should be noticed: a provision concerning minor heirs for the protection of the feudal right of marriage;[107] another that no man captured for felony should be disseised until he had been convicted;[108] and a third that the king should have the wardship of all born fools.[109] In the list thus completed there are many broad gaps, in some of which it is more than likely that legislation was adopted, the traces of which have disappeared or have not yet been discovered.

101 M. Paris, IV, 366-368.

102 Stubbs, *S.C.*, pp. 389-394, from *Statutes of the Realm*, I, 8-11.

103 See the article by E. F. Jacob: "What were the Provisions of Oxford?" in *History* (1924), IX, 188-200.

104 Madox, *Exchequer*, II, 102-103. Text in Prynne, *Brief Animadversions on the Fourth Part of the Institutes*, p. 53.

105 *Cal. Pat. Rolls, 1258-1266*, p. 97.

106 Madox, *Exchequer*, II, 11, note *c*.

107 Bracton, f. 91b.

108 *Ibid.*, f. 136b.

109 Maitland, *Collected Papers*, II, 185-187.

We have now come to the more formal statute of Marlborough of 1267. Though that relates mainly to issues raised during the previous fifteen years and by no means brings to an end legislation of the type which prevails in the above list, it seems to me in relation to this particular topic, the legislation of the reign of Henry III, to belong rather to the future and to introduce the great statutes of the reign of Edward I. In regard to these I wish merely to call attention to the extensive changes which they made in the common law, in the development of the writ, for example, and in the land law.[110] In making a list of the legislative enactments of Henry's time, I have not called attention to the effect of any of them upon existing law, but in numerous instances it is obvious,[111] and we may confidently assert that in this particular a complete preparation had been made for the legislation of the English Justinian.

Concerning the method of legislation, it may be added that various references to it, direct and indirect, put it beyond question that the consent of the magnates was necessary to changes in the law and to new legislation. Bracton opens with a statement practically to that effect[112] and may be said almost to close with another, of

[110] Professor Woodbine in his *Four Thirteenth Century Law Tracts*, p. 40, notes that while Bracton and Hengham, in his *Magna Summa*, refer to decided cases for their authority, the later writers of the century refer to the statutes instead. The same thing is true, he tells me, of the annotations on the margins of the Bracton manuscripts by their users. For these later writers the authority of the statutes outweighs the authority of the courts.

[111] It may be added that the effect of statutes was the same in France. *Tres Anc. Cout.*, pp. lxv-lxvi.

[112] F. 1b, ed. Woodbine, II, 21. "Quae quidem, cum fuerint approbatae consensu utentium et sacramento regum confirmatae, mutari non poterunt nec destrui sine communi consensu eorum omnium quorum consilio et consensu fuerint promulgatae." This passage states with exactness the division of function in the practice of the feudal state. Cf. f. 107b.

less extensive application, that certain writs granted and approved by the common counsel of the whole kingdom cannot be changed without their consent.[113] Bishop Grosseteste expresses the same idea with emphasis,[114] and it is implied in c. 11 of the statute of Merton which records a failure to legislate because king and magnates could not agree.[115] The same rule was officially recognized to exist in Ireland,[116] and to limit the action of the king in England.[117] In 1248 the king prohibited the collection of first fruits from churches in lay gift because the magnates "in ultimo parliamento nostro" were unwilling that they should be paid until there could be another conference with them, "sine quibus super hoc nichil volumus attemptare."[118]

The improvement of courts and processes in the judicial system of England since the accession of Henry II, while not infrequently of help when quite small pieces of land were in question, had been mainly of advantage to the larger holders of land and men of wealth. There has, however, recently been discovered abundant evidence of a practice in the common law courts at the end of the thirteenth century,[119] at least in the courts of the eyre, by which the same advantage was secured by many poor men.[120] This practice consisted in sending in to the eyre

113 *Ibid.*, f. 413b.

114 A well known passage: ". . . nec tam idiota sum quod credam ad alicujus suggestionem te vel alium sine principis et magnatum consilio posse leges condere vel commutare." *Epistolae* (R.S.), p. 96.

115 *Statutes of the Realm*, I, 1. Quoted Holdsworth, II, 220, note 3.

116 *Close Rolls, 1234-1237*, p. 501.

117 *Cal. Pat. Rolls*, 1232-1247: "the king being beyond seas without his council cannot at present make any ordinance."

118 *Close Rolls, 1247-1251*, p. 109.

119 Bolland, *Eyre of Kent*, pp. xxi-xxx, and *Bills in Eyre*, pp. xv-xix. See above, Chapter VII at note 3, and note C at the end of this Chapter where a case in the bench is cited.

120 *Eyre of Kent*, pp. xxv and xxviii.

courts petitions of grace and favor, appealing to the king's prerogative powers, or to the implied powers in these courts which stood in a peculiar sense in the place of the king,[121] for a remedy which seemed to the petitioner impossible in the common law. The procedure has already been briefly described above in Chapter VII, and a full account of it is given in the books of Mr. Bolland there referred to, especially in the *Eyre of Kent*, Vol. II. If with the abundance of this evidence in mind we look back over the thirteenth century, we shall be tempted to say that there was a sudden outburst of activity in petitioning the eyre courts which had no earlier introduction. There is no evidence of such a practice in any available itinerant justice roll, and Mr. Bolland says that the earliest of the bills in eyre which he has found is of 14 Edward I.[122] If this absence of evidence really indicated that there was no earlier introduction, then we should find here a most unusual chapter of institutional history.

The new activity in the use of petitions in the eyre courts at the end of the century was, however, no isolated phenomenon and should not be so studied. It was accompanied with what seems like another similar, sudden outburst of petitioning, not the common law courts but the council, the king or the king in council, by men of higher economic standing. This other kind of petitioning has also been described at length and may be studied in the petitions printed in Professor Maitland's *Memoranda de Parliamento* (R.S.) of the parliament of 1305. It can there easily be seen that the petitions to the council concern more important persons and larger interests than those to be read in Mr. Bolland's *Select Bills in Eyre*, but that they do not differ from them in nature nor in the

121 *Eyre of Kent*, II, xxix; *Bills in Eyre*, p. 6, no. 11, and p. xv.
122 *Bills in Eyre*, p. xv.

kind of interest described.[123] Indeed it must be evident, I think, in any study of these two sets of petitions together that they are two parallel sides of the same movement. They both rest upon the same institutional principles; in both alike the petitions are addressed to the king's prerogative of grace; both ask extraordinary remedies not otherwise to be had; and what I believe to be more important seems also to be clear, the same impulse lies behind the peculiar activity of the time in both directions.

In regard to the antecedents of this procedure, it is to be remembered that petitions to the king to interfere by his prerogative power, where other remedies could not be had for any reason, had always been available, and that petitions had been the method, or something very similar, by which the ordinary law cases of magnates had been brought before the council as a court of first instance. In the matter of petitions we can cite a few cases, fewer than we could wish, from the preceding part of the thirteenth century[124] and we are tempted to say *a priori* that the practice must have been in occasional use because in such a way only could the precedents be kept alive upon which was based the later system of equity jurisprudence. The fact that the petitions of the poor to the courts of the eyre left no traces behind them in the earlier thirteenth century should also not be regarded as proof that they were not in use. Besides noting, as said above, that such a conclusion would imply a most unusual situation in institutional history, it may be added of the common law courts that, as the common law system itself originated in an identical interference in the preexisting system for an identical purpose,[125] this application of the

123 Exception should perhaps be made of the fact that the petitions to the council sometimes concern matters in which the king has an interest.

124 See above, Chapter VII, notes 2 and 58.

125 See above, Chapter VII.

prerogative would be entirely to be expected and normal in the common law courts at any time in their early history.

The reason why petitions of either kind left so few, or no, traces of their use is probably to be found in the fact that they were not written.[126] Apparently the most important change affecting either of these lines of judicial action at the end of the century was the introduction of the written petition in place of the oral. Indeed, apart from the much greater frequency of use, there is no evidence of any other change. Such a change may well have been made by legislation and have been the subject of a statute or ordinance, but if so it has not survived to us, and we know of no requirement that writing should be used in these petitions. All that we know is that the practice of writing became common soon after the accession of Edward I. Here at any rate we are chiefly concerned with the fact that by this means for a time at least the poor man was enabled to enjoy almost as fully as the rich man ever could the advantages of the new system of justice. The use of bills in eyre slowly dies out in the fourteenth century and scarcely survives into the fifteenth. It had no influence upon the formation of the equity system.

Turning now to the common impulse which we have said above seems to lie behind the peculiar activity of the close of the thirteenth century in both kinds of petitioning, we may be sure that it is not to be found in a requirement that petitions should be written. That is a matter purely mechanical and might be a deterrent in some cases

126 Perhaps also because, like all council cases before the fourth decade of the century, they lay too far outside the regular business of the courts to affect their rolls, unless relating to business already before the court, and the council had no rolls of its own. See note C at the end of the Chapter.

if it facilitated others. The impulse had its beginning without doubt in the natural result which followed the discovery of a new method of litigation which opened the courts to a wide range of cases shut out by the growing strictness of the common law procedure, or supposed by the parties to be shut out. That it was not truly a new method does not affect the point. It was apparently to the mass of men at the time a new discovery, and quite naturally the same result followed in the increased use of the newly discovered method, in increased litigation of the kind that we have seen above to follow, on a somewhat smaller scale so far as our evidence shows, the opening to the public of improved methods of litigation by the reforms of Henry II.[127] In this way the increased use of petitions links itself in with the increase in the number of writs and the more frequent use of the legislative power as common results in the field of law of that wide movement of change which is characteristic of the thirteenth century.

It is not, however, as a characteristic of the age of Edward I, nor even as one expression of the thirteenth century age of change, that this new activity in the use of petitions has its most significant effect. Its permanent significance is rather to be seen in the fact that it transforms the occasional uses of the past into the regular and systematic operation of what is soon to be judicial machinery of a new sort, new at least as occupying a distinct field, the field of equity jurisprudence.

By a first interference of the prerogative in the common law of his time to secure justice more easily and generally than it could be secured by the ordinary and existing processes and to grant remedies not provided by the existing judicial system, Henry II established a new judicial system and a new common law which absorbed

[127] See above in this Chapter at notes 11 and 12.

the old.[128] This was as truly an exercise of the crown's equity powers as can be found at any later time. The new system was really at the start an equity system and for a long time it remained flexible and able to provide new remedies. Indeed the bills in eyre more than a century after Henry's changes show that those courts still retained, for a certain class of men at least, the power to grant justice freely and without restricting formalities. On the other hand the petitions to the council imply that men who could not plead poverty were frequently interested in cases to which now the common law courts were not open, because of the growing hardness of their rules, or were believed not to be open. They appealed to the equity powers of the king, which had not been diminished by Henry II's use of them but had continued in the interval, one may believe, to be exercised occasionally through the council. They appealed not now for the establishment of a new judicial system but for a special interference in a particular case. What these petitioners to the council did obtain, however, was in a sense the establishment of a new judicial system. For it was their action, their petitions and the answers returned to them, which developed these equity powers of the king in council from the sporadic instances of the past into the regular and systematic exercise of the future in equity law and equity and chancery courts. The outburst of activity in petitions to the council under Edward I was the bridge over which the equity powers of the crown, which had been so signally exercised in the creation of the common law system, but which might easily have been swallowed up in the rising flood of formalism, passed securely to their modern exercise.

It is at this moment also that the chancery appears in constant use as an organ of action in these equity cases

128 See above, Chapter VII.

and in direct connection with these petitions to the council. It can easily be seen in Maitland's *Memoranda de Parliamento,* cited above, how frequently the petitioner is referred to the chancery or to the chancellor for the preparation of his remedy.[129] It is this tide of business, its increasing amount and importance, that brings about what is, apart from parliament, the greatest permanent contribution of this age, to the national constitution, the development of chancery into an independent court of law with all which that carried with it. It is not meant of course that the development is complete in this age. It is meant that from this point and in the increased use of petitions is to be seen the beginning of that steady growth which leads, in perhaps another hundred years, to the independent court of chancery and to the chancellor's position as head of the equity system. As a completed study, the evolution at this point remains still to be worked out, but a considerable beginning has been made by Professor James F. Baldwin in his *Select Cases before the King's Council* published by the Selden Society.[130] The evolution is, however, very simple and one who keeps in mind the past relationships of the institutions and institutional processes concerned will have little difficulty in understanding how the evolution went on.

We have considered the age of Edward I primarily as an age in which we could find clearly indicated the results of lines of advance which distinguish the two preceding centuries, especially in law and courts of law. In leaving for the present at least a further discussion of this age,

129 Of definite references of the petitioners to other "courts, places or persons," about two thirds are to the chancery or the chancellor.

130 Baildon, *Select Cases in Chancery* (Selden Society) takes up the subject at a later point.

one cannot refrain from saying that its truest greatness is measured not by what it contains of the results of the past but by the way in which it transforms these results into the beginnings of the future. The beginning of parliament, of equity and the equity courts, of the independence of the king's bench, and more outside our field but not less important, the formulation of the right of consent to taxation and its restoration to the tradition of Magna Carta, make it in truth one of the greatest of all the ages of institutional history.

NOTE A

THE STANDING OF BOROUGHS IN THE GREAT COUNCIL

As I have said in the text, I do not propose to discuss here the change in the structure of the great council which began to be made in the last half of the thirteenth century by which it was transformed into the modern parliament. Standing at the year 1300, the view of this book is towards the past, not towards the future, and what it would emphasize in the council meetings, great or small, and the parliaments of Edward's time, is those features of them which are not new, which do not show that changes are under way. One exception only it is of interest to make because of its bearing on what has gone before. One of the difficulties in accounting for the transformation of the great council into the modern parliament is the difficulty of finding an institutional ground, if there was any, upon which the new elements, knights of the shire and burgesses, could be admitted into the old great council. Upon what legal right in a society feudally organized could they stand? In reference to this difficulty Professor Pollard has suggested that the boroughs were represented on tenurial grounds, "because they are collective tenants-in-chief on the king's demesne." *The Evolution of Parliament,* p. 157.

It is no doubt true that by the end of the thirteenth century a large proportion of the towns of England were held by their citizens or burgesses collectively "ad feodi firmam," on payment of the annual farm, and are therefore properly to be called tenants-in-chief. Indeed some of the records speak of them as holding "in capite." See citations from the pipe rolls in Madox, *Exchequer*, I, 285, *x;* 501, *k;* 503, *n.* It is also true that Magna Carta c. 14, in specifying those who are to be summoned by the sheriff to a meeting of the great council, says in general terms without qualification "omnes illos qui de nobis tenent in capite." Plainly in the language used the boroughs held in fee-farm were included. Yet we know that in practice they were not included until the very end of the second Anglo-Norman century. They did not attend before 1265. The explanation is that we have in the language used in the Great Charter one of the traps which writers of the feudal age, not yet alive to the necessity of strict technical accuracy even in legal documents, are continually setting for the modern student who does not keep in mind the fundamental principles of feudalism. No contemporary of Magna Carta in reading clause 14 would have supposed for a moment, despite the language, that it was intended to include any tenant-in-chief from whom that particular form of service was not due. What determined the service due from any individual holding was either the customary interpretation of the class of holdings to which it belonged or a definite specification in the grant of the service to be rendered. If a desired service was not included among those customarily understood to be due from a given holding, it could be attached to that holding only by the insertion in the deed of gift of a clause to that effect. As a duty created by tenure, attendance at the great council when summoned was technically court service. As a customary service due from the tenant, although not specified in the grant, it was a feature of military tenure. It was not due and could not be called for by the king as merely a customary service from any other form of tenure, leaving one side the question which might be raised regarding some forms of serjeanty tenure. Magna Carta c. 37 distinguishes clearly between the fee-farm and military tenures and indicates with equal clearness that military service might be attached to a fee-farm holding. In that case court service would be due but it would be a feature of the military, not of the fee-farm tenure. In the thirteenth century no one would have thought of questioning this principle or of departing from it in practice. The fee-farm tenure is in one respect the most perfect illustration of the principle which the time affords. Custom attached to the tenure only one service, the payment of a farm, the amount of which needed always to be specified. But from the very fact that custom in its interpretation of this tenure placed so little limitation on the bargaining possibilities of lord and tenant, it was the easiest of all tenures to which to attach all sorts of miscellaneous services, and it was so used. We find attached to it all kinds of obligations from nothing at all except the farm to full military service. See for examples and references, *Magna Carta Commemoration Essays*, p. 39, note; below, App., note 25. It would have been entirely regular to attach court service to the king to any fee-farm grant to a borough, that is, the duty of attending the great council when summoned, but as a matter of fact there is no instance of it in all the borough charters of the twelfth and thirteenth centuries. Nor is there even any condition of actual service in the field in time of war except under strict limitations. And the same is true of the payment of aids, another customary feature of the military tenure. These things can all easily be determined by an examination of Ballard, *British Borough Charters, 1042-1216,* especially pp. 89-94, and Vol. II, *1216-1307,* especially pp. 114-121. It is indeed uncommon in the case of boroughs to add anything to the farm, except reserved remainders of their original services before they obtained their charters. The specification of the farm is not infrequently followed by the words "pro omni servitio," which is the phrase commonly used definitely to exclude any service not specifically named. It is therefore impossible to find in the fee-farm tenure a legal basis for the attendance of the boroughs in parliament. The phrase tenant-in-chief was rather loosely used but where used without qualification it very rarely refers to any class except military tenants. By a like process of narrowing a general phrase to a specific meaning, "servitium debitum" commonly, always I think in official documents, refers only to military service.

An interesting parallel to the language of c. 14, afterwards more definitely defined, is to be found in Edward Grim's "Life of St. Thomas," Robertson, *Materials,* II, 390. Henry II, determining to hold a great council to try the archbishop ("solemne statuens celebrare concilium") caused to be summoned "omnes qui de rege tenerent in capite," and later he calls those who passed sentence on the archbishop "principes," necessarily the same persons. William Fitz Stephen in his account of the same events, after saying that the king "generale edicit concilium," *Materials,* III, 49, indicates later, p. 52, its composition as "the bishops, earls and barons of England." He adds, p. 67, that when in the course of the trial a difficulty arose about getting a judgment "evocantur quidam vicecomites et secundae dignitatis barones, antiqui dierum, ut addantur eis et assint judicio," implying that they had not been called until this point was reached. The Anonymous Author, *Materials,* IV, 41, mixes together in one statement the earlier and the later summoned, as if all had been present from the beginning: "rex edicto publico convocavit episcopos et abbates, comites etiam et proceres, et omnes officiales suos, omnesque omnino qui alicujus essent auctoritatis vel nominis." William Fitz Stephen undoubtedly states the facts as they actually occurred and the passages illustrate not merely the ordinary composition of the great council but the prerogative right of the king to summon others to attend it even in considerable numbers.

It is really not necessary to find in past precedents an institutional principle in accordance with which the new elements could be admitted to the great council. The step was really within the competence of the king, though it was action upon an unprecedented scale, the summoning of a class instead of individuals. It should be added that, if the explanation first suggested in *The Origin of the English Constitution,* pp. 317-323, of the purpose and manner in which the delegates from the counties were brought into the council in 1254 is correct, then it is very doubtful if either county or borough representatives during the reign of Edward I were admitted to meetings of the council as members of it or had any voice in its general decisions. Their function was probably limited to giving information and to decisions which concerned themselves alone.

It may be allowable to add here that another trap for the unwary similar to that set in c. 14 is set in Magna Carta c. 12. In speaking of the aid for the marriage of the eldest daughter of the lord, the clause is stated as if *eldest* were the rule, and not merely what was in practice the usual fact. The rule was any one daughter for whom it might first be taken. See Du Cange, *Gloss. Med. Latin., s. v.* "auxilium," and *Origin,* p. 254.

NOTE B

THE WRIT OF ENTRY

Palgrave, *R.C.R.,* I, 22-23 and 91, both of the year 1194, show the writ of entry in process of formation, the first untechnical and still in the pleadings, the second probably in the writ but with uncertain and mixed forms. The use of formulae of the writ of *mort d'ancestor* in the second case is interesting. As we should expect, the formula of a limited entry lingers in pleadings after it has become established in the writ. See *Select Civil Pleas,* nos. 156 and 157 (1203). Maitland (*Forms of Action,* p. 333) supposes the writ of entry to have developed from Glanvill's writ of right for debt, particularly from that for the recovery of land pledged for the debt for a term which has passed. (Glanvill, X, 9.) This suggestion was first made by Bigelow (*Procedure,* p. 165) in very strong language, asserting that only the change of one word and the dropping of one clause was necessary to give us the writ of entry, though this change would leave the writ still lacking the characteristic formula ("in quod idem A non habet ingressum nisi"), a formula certainly later essential to all forms of the writ except this single form and one which seems clearly to indicate the reason and road of its development. Glanvill's writ X, 9 does limit the scope of the action in somewhat the same way, but not through such a form as to lead to the introduction of the formula into the writ, though it might possibly suggest its appearance in the pleadings. If we look at the matter with the presumption created by the way in which such forms usually develop, it would seem to be more likely that Glanvill's writ came to be classed as a writ of entry (Bracton, f. 318, ed. Twiss, V, 7) after the writ of entry had been somewhat developed and the similarity of the limitation of the action in the two cases could be recognized, than that Glanvill's writ gave rise to the writ of entry. It is not evident in the scanty records that we have that in early cases which employ the forms of the later writ of entry the "a terminum qui praeteriit" form is earlier or more frequent than others, in fact in the early cases entry by custody appears to be the most frequent specification and the earliest cited above are entry by dower and entry by custody.

I cannot presume to assert that what I have to say here of the writ of entry is correct in any point in which it differs from the accepted doctrine. (P. and M., II, 63-75; Holdsworth, III, 11-14.) The writ is, however, unusually interesting from any point of view and it seems to me peculiarly so as giving us a glimpse into the legal mind of the thirteenth century. Even if the suggestions here made cannot be established, it may be of some value to note how the history of the writ strikes one who regards it as primarily an institutional development. By that I mean one who considers that its peculiarities are to be explained historically, when that explanation is possible, rather than as the expression of juristic ideas.

As intimated above (at note 49), the writ appears to me clearly to have been developed directly from the ordinary writ of right by the introduction of a formula specifying the defect in the tenant's title which narrowed the scope of the action and shut the tenant up to the answer of one specific question, though the number of possible sets of facts from which an answer might be drawn in one case or another still remained very large. So long as the change has gone no farther than this, no step has been taken outside the field of the ordinary writ of right. The change is really one of economy and simplification. But it seems very early to have occurred to someone that this new formula might be used with good effect where, let us say as the best example, the assize of *novel disseisin* could not be used because the disseisor had died. The disseisor's heir has entered into the disputed land, not now as a disseisor but as an heir, as of right. The land is to him and, until some question is successfully raised about it, in law his right and inheritance. His possession cannot be directly attacked; it must be attacked in an action which raises the question of title. Therefore the complainant, who would have brought a writ of *novel disseisin* if the ancestor had not died, brings a writ of right but specifies the disseisin as the defect in the tenant's title. These facts would be the same in essence in any of the kinds of entry specified. This is the step which carries the writ into an entirely new field and leads to all the subsequent enlargement of its use. It creates a situation which is characteristic of all the later history and explains its peculiarities. A writ of right action is used to get a judgment on a question of disseisin, or in other words to accomplish the purpose of a possessory action. It is not strange that it comes to be considered practically a possessory action. As a plaintiff declared in one instance: "cum habuerit seisinam suam qualem tunc habuit respondebit omnibus de jure." (*Bracton's Note Book,* pl. 1133.) The action seemed to him an ordinary possessory action. So it seems in the main to Bracton, though in discussing the writs of entry he says he is treating "de causa proprietatis" (f. 317, ed. Twiss, V, 2), and so it was treated practically in the courts. But however this may be, the question which the plaintiff does raise is the question of title. The defendant is ordered to surrender *juste* to the plaintiff certain land which the latter claims to be "jus et hereditatem suam," and then the writ goes on to specify the way in which the defendant comes to appear falsely to have a title. So that if the court decides in favor of the plaintiff, it has decided that the defendant has no title because he did enter into possession in the way asserted and that can give him none.

It seems clear that Bracton (ff. 318-327b) is treating the writ from its practical effects rather than either from its historical descent or from its real meaning. He represents it as extending the field of the assizes of *novel disseisin* and *mort d'ancestor*. That is what it really does do in practice, but the action is not thereby made in anything except practical effect a possessory action. The forms of the writ remain the forms of a writ of right and the tenant answers in the same way. The facts indeed, from the form of the tenant's answer, are sometimes too obvious to be overlooked, and Bracton is forced to what seems a very awkward explanation that the writ of entry is turned by the pleadings into a writ of right. It would seem to be much simpler to explain the facts historically and to cover all cases by saying that the writ of entry is always in essence a writ of right used to accomplish the purpose of a possessory action.

The double character of the writ had, however, on another side important historical consequences because the writ of entry was the expedient chiefly used to avoid the limitation set upon the royal jurisdiction by Magna Carta c. 34. (P. and M., I, 151, note 5; Maitland, *Forms of Action,* p. 338; McKechnie, *Magna Carta,* p. 354.) It could be allowed to do this because it was reckoned in practice a writ introducing a possessory action merely and not a trial of the question of title. For some reason, which we cannot now state, the barons did not regard the royal possessory action as infringing their rights of jurisdiction. It can easily be understood that their interest in the possessory action would be a financial one only, but the economic interest was coming to be a leading one in the early years of the century, and the loss of fees and fines in such an action might be considerable. This point is made towards the end of the century by the author of the *Mirror of Justices,* who says: "the prohibition of the *breve quod vocatur Praecipe* is disregarded, for every day so many writs which are possessory in form are issued, and this too by statute, that the lords lose the cognizance of matters concerning their fees and the profits of their courts." (Quoted from Holdsworth, II, 332, note 3.) But the barons had not objected, so far as we know, to the possessory assizes when they were first introduced, nor was any objection expressed in Magna Carta, rather the contrary (cc. 18, 19). If Bracton's argument that the writ of cosinage was not a violation of c. 34 of the Charter because it was possessory only and left the question of title still to be determined was what convinced the council which approved the writ, as it seems to have been (*Bracton's Note Book,* pl. 1215: "nec tollat alicui curiam suam ubi locum habere possit breve de recto"; cf. Bracton, f. 281), it is likely that similar reasoning would sanction the writs of entry. Bracton's argument was undoubtedly honest, and the baron could easily see that by retaining the right to try the question of *jus* he was retaining the right really for him most fundamental—the right to determine who should be his tenant. What he did not see was that, whatever may have been true of the writ of cosinage, the argument as used for the writ of entry was fallacious because the trial under that writ really settled not merely the question of possession but the question of *jus.*

Professor Maitland (*Forms of Action,* p. 316) suggests that the assizes may have been accepted by the barons without objection because the king was "able to represent the great step that he took as no interference with the proprietary rights but a mere protection of possession." As I have said in effect elsewhere (*Origin,* p. 103), it hardly seems possible that the king could have maintained, or even have advanced, such a claim while the world was still ruled by feudal law. It was everywhere recognized as one of the lord's most immediate duties to protect his vassal in his possessions. It is possible that before the last half of the twelfth century this had been done rather by the battle axe than by court process. Or it is possible that in the practical jurisprudence of the time before Henry II the suit was always for title, even if according to later distinctions the issue was really one of possession. Or in other words that the distinction between the action for *jus* and the action for possession is one which developed in the royal courts or chancery rather than in the courts of the lords. The establishment of the assizes, however, before 1180 shows that before that date there must have been considerable thinking on the subject by someone and the distinction must have been in the mind of those who carried through that legislation. See also the last references in note 25, Chapter V above, cases which are in date near to the time when the possessory assizes were introduced.

NOTE C

QUERELAE AND BILLS IN EYRE

In regard to the origin of bills in eyre, or written petitions in the common law courts, Miss Helen M. Cam has shown (Vinogradoff, *Oxford Studies,* VI, Part I, especially pages 133-138) that they "probably originate in the instructions to hear *querelae* given to the commissioners who held the inquest of 1274." (Holdsworth, II, 336, who accepts Miss Cam's conclusions.) These instructions are not in the commission of 1274 as we now have it (*Hundred Rolls,* I, 13; Rymer, *Foedera,* I, 1, 517), but are inferred from "the fact that *querelae* of the very nature that the directions invite are found upon the returns of 1274-5." (Miss Cam, *l.c.,* p. 136.) This fact may be weakened somewhat as evidence by what is said below of the early occurrence of *querelae,* but it is not an unfair inference in general that items frequently recurring in the returns to an inquest imply corresponding instructions to the commissioners. I do not, however, feel entirely sure how far justices of the early part of the century may not have felt themselves justified under their instructions in entertaining *querelae* of a similar kind against royal officials; nor how far such new instructions may have been due to a growing feeling on the part of the justices in eyre that they were bound to a strictly literal interpretation of the articles of their commission. To be exact about the date of these instructions, as Miss Cam says (*l.c.,* p. 32), "as the records stand, we know not whether to assign [them] to 1274, 1276, or 1278." As we have them they occur at the end of the 41 *nova capitula* of the eyre, and these down at least to c. 34 are drawn from the commission of 1274. (*Statutes of the Realm,* I, 235-236.)

As these instructions stand therefore, the most natural explanation of them is that they were inserted at the end of the *capitula* to authorize the justices of the eyre to entertain complaints concerning the abuses into which the commissioners of 1274 were to inquire, that is, virtually to carry on that inquest. These were largely abuses committed by royal officers who made use of their position for extortion. Apart however from the fact that the justices might perhaps now act in a new range of cases, nothing new was required of them by these instructions. If they were given to the commissioners as well, as some of the records in the *Hundred Rolls* imply (see the case of Petronilla de Assildeham below, *Hundred Rolls,* I, 137), they probably were intended to authorize them to exercise in this range of cases a function which the justices had always exercised, and they would do no more than this. *Querelae* of exactly the same sort had been acted upon by the justices from the beginning of the common law courts. An instance almost at the beginning of the second oldest roll that we have is especially instructive, in comparison with the case cited by Miss Cam, *l.c.,* p. 134: "Willielmus de Einsford' junior queritur quod Hugo de Bello Campo et mater ejus Alienora detinent ei totam hereditatem suam occasione dotis ipsius matris sue. Et ipsa venit et dicit quod ipsa non vult respondere inde sine viro suo. Willielmus habeat breve ad summonitionem predictionem Hugonem quod sit apud Westmonisterium a die Mercurii proximo post festum Sancti Edwardi in xv dies inde responsurus. Idem dies datus est eidem Alienore in banco." Palgrave, *R.C.R.,* I, 3-4. It seems clear that the complaint is an oral one made directly to the court without a writ (*Bracton's Note Book,* pl. 269). The writ of summons to Hugo is a judicial writ, issued by the court as a process necessary to the continuation of the case before it. Unquestionably if Hugo should fail to appear at the day specified, another judicial writ would be issued by the court directing that Hugo be attached by pledges to appear at another day specified. Many *querelae* appear upon the rolls in this stage. The usual beginning in the twelfth and thirteenth centuries which appears in the record is: "A queritur quod B . . . ," which is the form followed in Miss Cam's typical *querela* (*l.c.,* pp. 134, 185): "Petronilla de Assildeham queritur de Ricardo le Brun . . . quod." The *querelae* on the rolls of the common law courts concern a variety of matters, many of them not equity; a large proportion of them are cases which would later be classified as torts. They are often tried throughout by the old procedure. Some of the early cases show the features which led Professor Powicke to remark of the bills in eyre that "they prove the necessity of methods of accusation open to individuals," though hardly at so early a date "the break down of the criminal appeal." Powicke in *E.H.R.*, XXX, 333, cited by Holdsworth, II, 341, note 3. If these instructions add nothing to the earlier practice except perhaps a new range of cases, there is nothing new to be accounted for at the time unless it be that here we have the requirement made that such complaints should be brought before the court by a written petition or bill. Such a requirement as that is of a kind which might very well have a definite beginning, as by ordinance or other legislation. There appears to have been no such requirement during most of the reign of Henry III. Erlich in Vinogradoff's *Oxford Studies,* VI, 2, 22, 26 f. If it begins to be made about the time of the inquest of 1274, no evidence of the fact has been offered. It was probably rather practice than requirement, though the judges may have made it a rule. The apparent permission in the statute of Rageman (Miss Cam, *l.c.*, pp. 136-137) to the justices to determine *querelae* without a writ is probably not new legislation but a passing remark about what had always been done. If it had been a new enactment it would almost certainly have been given more emphasis. Instances of *querelae* in the common law courts are cited here of different dates but no exhaustive list from any roll has been attempted. Maitland, *Three Rolls of the King's Court,* pp. 7, 41, 43, 48; Palgrave, *R.C.R.*, I, 34, 54, 373, 376; II, 6 (10), 36, 51, 82, 91, 120, 126, 230, 255, 260; Maitland, *Select Civil Pleas,* nos. 7, 13, 27, 32, 54, 71, 86; *Select Pleas of the Crown,* nos. 61, 105, 159, 174, 177, 178; *Bracton's Note Book,* pll. 16, 78, 137, 489, 918. It will be noticed in reading the rolls that not all cases where *queritur* is used are instances of this procedure, and it is very likely that there are errors in this list. Certainly *querela* and *queritur* are words to which no technical meaning can be attached.

There is perhaps a question which can be raised at this point in regard to these early *querelae* which seems at first sight a serious one. How was it possible that a case between private men could get into the royal courts without a writ authorizing the use of the king's machinery and specifying for what purpose, that is, defining the action? Would not in this way the king fail to get the revenue which was one chief object of the new system? The answer is to be found without doubt in the fact that this survival of the old procedure could not be prevented. The new system of justice was absorbing the old, but the old was not yet entirely absorbed and, as we have seen above, the old still survived in not infrequent cases of more than one kind. Chapter X at note 39. The appeal was probably always introduced orally and almost always tried by the old procedure. If we go back to the earliest beginnings of the new system, to the local king's courts of William I, there was no new procedure. The writ does hardly more than to establish the court and authorize its use. There was as yet no clear characterization of the action to be tried, limiting the operation of the court, and the whole procedure in the court itself was oral and scarcely modified at all from that used in the Saxon courts. The court remained permanently what it had been. It should not surprise us that in the later king's courts, besides appeals, other kinds of cases still go their course by the old procedure or do so in part. It must also be remembered that by no means yet had writs been developed for all the various forms of action they were one day to describe. The process of writ formation was in rapid operation but it might not infrequently happen that the complainant could find no writ existing to suit his case and was obliged to bring it to the attention of the court by word of mouth in order that the justices might provide a new writ or allow the case to go on without one. The records appear to give us not a few such cases and show the justices issuing judicial writs to continue the proceedings, and old Saxon judgments are rendered. It seems highly probable also that in Book I, c. 5—the introduction to the *praecipe* writ—Glanvill is describing a similar process and one which would prevail almost necessarily at the beginning of the new system. The plaintiff goes in person to the king—to the king's chancery probably—

or directly to the justices and makes his complaint in order to get the writ: "Cum clamat quis domino Rege aut ejus justiciis de feodo aut de libero tenemento suo, si fuerit querela talis quod debeat, vel dominus rex velit, in curia sua deduci, tunc is qui queritur tale breve de summonitione habebit." Something like this certainly continued possible for a long time, at least for writs not yet "de cursu." In 1310-1311 John Soke, a litigant appearing in person, says, "For God's sake can I have a writ to attaint this fraud?" to which Stanton, J., replies, "Make your bill and you shall have what the court can allow." Cited by Holdsworth, II, 342, note 1, from *Year Book, 4 Edward II* (Selden Soc.), p. 21. This occurred in the common bench court.

Financially the king was not left without returns. Amercements remained the same; a judicial writ might have its price; a grand assize or a jury if appealed to was not a free gift. The selling of writs by no means exhausted the sources of revenue from the new judicial system.

APPENDIX

INNOCENT III AND THE GREAT CHARTER.[1]

THAT John expected the pope to release him from his obligation to the Charter upon some ground or other is, I think, reasonably certain. That the pope honestly believed that he was acting with competent authority in doing so, is even more clear from the evidence. But no attempt has ever been made, so far as I am aware, to show by an analysis of the evidence upon what basis of legal right the pope supposed he was resting his bull of 24 August, 1215, or to subject his right to annul the Charter to a legal criticism. I can hope here to do no more than to make a beginning in that direction.

To determine the legal basis of the pope's action, one turns first of all to the bull itself, but the answer which it gives is too indefinite to be satisfactory.[2] One naturally expects to find the pope's action based upon the vassal relation of England to the papacy. This relationship is indeed clearly mentioned in the bull, but it is not emphasized. It is put forward as one fact among others explaining the pope's interest in the case; but his interest in the

1 The following essay was contributed to Magna Carta Commemoration Essays, 1917, published by the Royal Historical Society in celebration of the seven hundredth anniversary of the granting of the Charter. While not precisely in line with the main development followed in the present volume, it is included here as illustrating the general legal environment in which that development took place. My thanks are due to the officers of the Royal Historical Society for permission to republish the essay. There are some slight additions and changes in the footnotes.

2 Rymer, *Foedera,* I, 1, 135; Bémont, *Chartes des Libertés Anglaises,* pp. 41-44.

fact that John was a crusader is more strongly insisted on.[3] Nowhere is the feudal relationship asserted as the ground of right on which the pope was acting, nor is there any attempt made to show that the Charter reduced the value of the fief or its ability to perform the service by which it was held, nor are these facts even asserted. In the formal phrases of annulling at the close of the bull, it is the apostolic authority which is put forward, and there is no mention of the feudal relationship.[4] So far as the language of the bull is concerned, there is nothing in it to prevent our saying that, if the relationship had not existed, the pope would have taken the same action.

If now we turn from the bull to the other contemporary evidence, documentary and chronicle, which has come down to us, the information we gain is no more definite, but certain things bearing on the question stand out rather clearly.

I. The feudal dependency of England upon the papacy was recognized by all parties during the whole period, with the single exception of Philip II of France and his son in their debate with the pope. They, however, do not deny the fact of the relationship, but the right of John to enter into it and its legality.[5] John of course makes the matter entirely clear in his two charters, recording his

[3] "Cum igitur debeamus et libenter velimus . . . dicti Regis qui vasallus noster existit conservare justitias et injurias propulsare, maxime cum idem propter caracterem crusis assumptum specialiter sub nostra protectione consistat. . . ."—Letter of Innocent III of 18 June, 1215. See also the bull "Miramur plurimum." The reference to the vassal relationship in any portion of the bull of 24 August, except the historical, is only indirect.

[4] ". . . ex parte Dei omnipotentis patris et filii et Spiritus sancti, auctoritate quoque beatorum Petri et Pauli apostolorum ejus ac nostra, de communi fratrum nostrorum consilio, compositionem hujusmodi reprobamus penitus. . . ."—Bull of 24 August.

[5] Roger of Wendover (ed. Coxe), III, 364, 365-366.

oath of fealty, of 15 May, and 3 October, 1213.[6] He there calls England for the first time "patrimonium beati Petri" a phrase recurring again in connection with the Charter. In his letters in 1215 John also refers frequently and clearly to the relationship, as does also the pope, and the phrase "patrimonium Petri" occurs several times. Too much emphasis has, I think, been placed upon the barons' recognition of the vassal relation in their letter to the pope in February, 1215, for rhetorical purposes merely, but they certainly do recognize it, according to the statement of John's envoy.[7]

II. In certain cases John had acted, or seems at first sight to have acted, as the pope's vassal:—

1. He sought a confirmation from the pope of his grant of freedom of election to the churches of 15 January, 1215.[8] That this is the act of a feudal vassal seeking a

[6] Rymer, I, 111, 115, containing John's oath of fealty in written form, which was not usual. For another instance see the fealty of Henry II to Louis VII, Bouquet, XVI, 16. That an ecclesiastic had some influence upon the wording of this document seems to be indicated not merely by the phrase "patrimonium beati Petri" but also by the other phrase by which fealty was sworn not merely to Innocent III, but also "ejusque successoribus catholice intrantibus," a specification which would hardly have occurred to an English layman, but which would have seemed very necessary to a Roman having in mind the recent and foreseeing the possible history of the papacy.

[7] See Norgate, *John Lackland*, p. 246.

[8] This depends upon the statement twice made by M. Paris in what appear to be his separate additions to Roger of Wendover (M. Paris, II, 606 and 607). John's request has not been preserved, and the papal confirmation, which is addressed to the English prelates only, does not allude to it. The confirmation is Potthast, No. 4963, and is printed "from the original" in Rymer, I, 1, 127. Apparently no confirmation was asked of the earlier issue of this grant on 21 November, 1214. Having carefully considered suggestions made to the contrary, I still hold to the opinion expressed in *The Origin of the English Constitution*, p. 258, that it is very doubtful if any heir of John would have considered himself bound by a grant like this. Henry III certainly did not consider himself bound by what it means, fairly interpreted.

confirmation from his lord of a grant which would be invalid without it, is exceedingly doubtful. It probably would have been sought in any case; the prelates would naturally desire this sanction added to the king's grant. The confirmation is "auctoritate Apostolica confirmamus," and there is no reference in it to the feudal relationship nor to feudal rights. The language of all the clauses of confirmation and sanction follows closely the model which had long been in use in the papal chancery for similar confirmations issued in large numbers to monasteries and churches with reference to lands and rights by whomsoever given.[9] It is not possible to cite this case as evidence of action upon feudal principles.

2. Confirmation was also sought from the pope of the arrangement made with Berengaria in 1215 in regard to her dower rights. In this case the papal confirmation is lacking, though one was sent to Berengaria in answer to her request,[10] and one was no doubt sent to John. We have, however, John's requests, two separate requests of even date, in regard to two distinct agreements.[11] In these no reference is made directly or indirectly to the feudal position of the pope. In the one which concerns the main agreement, there is no request for confirmation, but, in the language of the agreement, the pope is asked "ut praesenti compositioni addat securitates quas viderit expedire et nos ratum habebimus quicquid inde statuerit." In the second the word "confirmat" is used but clearly not in a technical sense, and the meaning of the

[9] Examples may be found in almost any cartulary. See *Ramsey Cartulary*, II, 146, a confirmation by Innocent III, 1199, of gifts present and future ("auctoritate Apostolica confirmamus"), in which the language with insignificant variations is identical, and the following document (p. 147) a similar confirmation by Alexander III. Some of these phrases occur again in the bull of 24 August, annulling the Charter.

[10] Potthast, No. 5141; Bouquet, XIX, 607; Migne, *Opp. Inn.*, III, 992.

[11] Rymer, I, 1, 137; *Rot. Litt. Pat.* I, 181-182.

request is the same as in the first, not that the pope will make legal something which is otherwise beyond the capacity of the contracting party, but that he will add further, unknown, sanctions to the agreement. This is quite in accordance with what would at any time be normal, considering the question between the parties and the pope's earlier interest in the case. In a letter on the subject addressed to John in 1207,[12] he had clearly stated the grounds of his right to act in the case, his special duty towards widows, and commanded ("mandamus") him to represent "in praesentia nostra" what he was going to do. This case is also clearly non-feudal.

3. In his letter of 29 May, 1215, John said that he had declared to the barons that his land was the patrimony of St. Peter, held of him and of the Roman church and of the pope, that he emphasized to them his obligations, and claimed his privileges as a crusader, and then appealed through the earls of Pembroke and Warenne against the disturbers of the peace of the land.[13] Roger of Wendover states that John's messengers to the pope, presumably those whom he says the king sent soon after granting the Charter, in the account of events which they gave the pope, mentioned an appeal by the king before the entry of the barons into London.[14] In his bull of 24 August, the

[12] Potthast, No. 3171; Rymer, I, 1, 97.

[13] Rymer, I, 1, 129. The appeal was "contra perturbatores pacis terræ nostræ," no doubt the source from which the pope obtained this phrase used afterwards in the bull "Miramur plurimum" ordering the excommunication of the barons. The repetition of phrases from one of these documents to another, and the borrowing—by England of papal phrases, and by the pope of English phrases—is interesting. That John in this letter puts more emphasis on his crusading than on his vassal relationship, may be due to the fact that he is replying to a request from the pope for a report on his preparation for the crusade. It gives him an opportunity to make clear the effect which the baronial opposition was having upon Innocent's cherished plans which he did not neglect.

[14] Roger of Wendover, III, 322.

pope says that John had twice appealed to him. There is no further evidence for these statements, but there is no reason to doubt them. It should be noted that they give us no clear evidence of the ground on which the appeal was made.

4. Roger of Wendover in the account just referred to makes the king's envoys say that at some indefinite time before the granting of the Charter John publicly protested before the barons that, because the kingdom of England belonged to the Roman church "ratione dominii," he could not and ought not to decree anything new without the consent of the pope nor to change anything in the kingdom to his prejudice. This same statement is also made by the pope in the bull of 24 August.[15] Here is clearly an appeal to feudal law. The pope's attention was called to a principle upon which he might act against the Charter, and that principle was clearly in his mind when the bull was drawn up. Nevertheless it was not made the

15 The language on this matter is so nearly alike in Roger of Wendover, III, 322, and the papal bull, as to raise the question of their dependence upon one another. Wendover could easily be following the bull in these particular phrases, but he adds other particulars which could not be so derived, and it is quite possible that he was following a letter presented to the pope by the envoys, not now surviving, which the pope also follows, as was his constant practice throughout the struggle—in regard to his information from England. Some confirmation of this may possibly be found in the reference to the occupation of London, of which Wendover says, "quae caput regni sui est proditione sibi traditam," and the pope, "que sedes est regni proditorie sibi traditam." Roger of Wendover (III, 319) says that John sent Pandulf to the pope against the Charter soon after it was granted, and Walter of Coventry (II, 222) says that he sent the Chancellor, Richard Marsh (cf. McKechnie, p. 44, who seems from his reference to be following Petit-Dutaillis, *Vie de Louis VIII,* p. 59, where it was, I suppose, a misprint). Neither of these statements is correct, and the letter of John to the pope in regard to a mission of Pandulf's, which is printed in Rymer, I, 1, 135, as if it belonged to this date, must probably be dated *c.* 13 September (cf. *Dict. Nat. Biography,* XV, 176). It was entered in the patent roll of 17 John (m. 15 d.) in close connection with other letters of that date (*Rotuli Patentes,* p. 182).

basis of the pope's action. In regard to the point of law, we may so far anticipate the later discussion as to say that in the first part of his statement John was quite wrong, and in his second more nearly right.

5. In the bull of 24 August, the pope says that after offering to the barons "secundum formam mandati nostri justitie plenitudinem exhibere," which they refused, the king "ad audientiam nostram appellans obtulit eis exhibere justitiam coram nobis, ad quos hujus cause juditium ratione dominii pertinebat."[16] This is the first appeal mentioned by the pope, and if the appeals have been correctly indicated in 3 above, it is the one made through the earls of Pembroke and Warenne. In his letter 29 May, John, in mentioning this appeal, does not add these legal particulars, and the source of the pope's information is not evident. Judging by his general practice, however, he was probably following English information from some source. It is also quite possible that John, in order to confuse the situation, may have made an appeal in some such terms. It is out of the question, however, that any practical result should follow from such an appeal, or that it should be legally defensible. It is theoretically possible that the pope could create a lay court of peers for the trial of an appeal by John, but not actually possible. The king of Sicily was in the midst of his campaign for the throne of Germany. The king of Aragon was a minor. The pope's royal vassals in Hungary and

[16] The offer which most nearly corresponds to this in form is that which John in his letter of 29 May (Rymer, I, 1, 129) says he made to the barons in the presence of brother William, that is, on the day the letter was written. He says: "optulimus praedictis baronibus quod de omnibus petitionibus suis, quas a nobis exigunt, in vos benignissime compromitteremus, ut vos qui plenitudine gaudetis potestatis, quod justum foret statueretis." This offer, however, as stated, does not mean legally what the pope asserts, and the date seems hardly to agree with the pope's implied chronology. Clearly he puts the offer before, and John after, the offer of arbitration by a chosen body of eight.

the Balkans could hardly be expected to appear in Rome for such a purpose. A lay court of the pope's vassals in Rome and its neighborhood could easily have been called together, but it would hardly have been a court of the peers of John. In relation to him they would be in the position of those who held in England "ut de honore" instead of "ut de corona." The legal difficulties are equally formidable. The language used by the pope plainly implies a judicial proceeding. If the pope states the facts correctly, and the evidence goes to show that he did, on the arrival in England of his letter of 29 March, John offered to the barons—"quod . . . in curia sua per pares eorum secundum legem et consuetudines regni suborta dissensio sopiretur." This, however, would not be a suit at law. With reference to the barons' complaints, the king would be in the position of a defendant, but as king he could not be sued. He states the situation with technical correctness in his letter of 29 May, which is probably the source of the pope's information.[17] He says: "et praeterea eis optulimus quod de omnibus petitionibus suis, per considerationem parium suorum justitiae plenitudinem eis exhiberemus." That is, the barons' case could come before the curia regis only by way of petition, and the answer would be a matter of equity, that is, an act of the curia as council, not as court, if we may make a distinction perfectly valid in 1215, but which perhaps the men of that day could not have drawn. In such a case John could have no appeal to his suzerain on technical grounds. Every action of the council was technically his action, and no decision of the whole baronage against him

[17] The technical expression is also correct in the two papal letters of 29 March. For the situation created in the curia when all the barons were against the lord, see Beaumanoir, *Coutumes de Beauvoisis,* c. 44 (ed. Salmon), I, 33 (ed. Beugnot). The appeal there referred to is the appeal for default of right.

would have any legal validity if he withheld the "Rechtsgebot." The only technical appeal possible would be by the barons. They, however, refused the king's offer and then John appealed, on what grounds we do not know. It could not have been on grounds of legal technicality, but the general appeal to his lord for protection was always open to him, though it could have been made in this case only by a quibble. Equally difficult is the pope's statement that John offered to do the barons justice before him to whom "hujus cause juditium ratione dominii pertinebat." In the relation of England to the papacy, no right of judgment pertained to the pope "ratione dominii" except in cases brought before him by way of appeal. It is necessary to say that the pope is here using language which is apparently technical, but which cannot be justified upon such grounds, but only if it is regarded as used in the most general and non-technical sense.[18] John's curia was as fully competent to judge finally every case between the king and the barons after as before he became the vassal of the pope and without any reference to his overlord. His position was not that of an English vassal of the king, but that of one of the sovereign great barons of France, and, under the terms by which the fief was held, he could not even be called upon for court service as a matter of right.

III. Although John calls attention several times to his feudal relation to the pope, and seems disposed to make what he can of it, he clearly does not trust to it as sufficient. On 4 March, 1215, he took the cross, thereby gaining the ecclesiastical protection and extensive privileges

[18] Of course some lords had a right of judgment in cases arising in their vassals' holdings "ratione dominii" because of the limited right of jurisdiction of the vassal. But that right could not exist here. All lords had such a right by way of the regular appeals, but that right also could not be in force in this case.

granted to the crusader, but also securing the interest of the pope in regard to the plans which Innocent had most deeply at heart. In this new relationship John undoubtedly secured all that he needed, and the skilful use which he could make of it is shown in his letter of 29 May in which he puts the situation in such a light as to make clear to the pope his inability to take any steps towards the crusade because of the trouble the barons were making.[19] On this ground alone the pope would undoubtedly have felt himself justified by existing law and practice in acting as he did. Not merely did the privileges granted crusaders relieve them from contracts which interfered with the carrying out of their vows,[20] but the popes assumed the right to protect a crusade, and crusaders, from any interference with the undertaking. In his excommunication of the crusaders of the fourth crusade, for their attack on Zara, Innocent based his action wholly on ecclesiastical grounds, and did not allude to the fact that the king of Hungary, whose territory was thus violated, was his vassal whom he would be bound to protect in the possession of his fief.[21]

IV. According to Roger of Wendover's account of the embassy to the pope soon after the granting of the Charter, Innocent was informed that the barons had demanded "quasdam leges et libertates iniquas quas dignitatem regiam nulli decuit confirmare." The same chronicler informs us that John, angry at the demands

19 Innocent was dependent for his information as to the facts and merits of the struggle in England mainly upon information given him by John. As stated by the king his case must have seemed very strong to the pope, who seems to have understood fairly well a good many of the details.

20 See for example the regulations for the third crusade, in Rigord (ed. Delaborde), I, 85-88. These indicate not merely the privileges granted crusaders in the matter of debts, but also by their limitations on those privileges they show what larger things were popularly expected.

21 Potthast, Nos. 1848, 1849; Migne, *Opp. Inn.*, I, 1178, 1179; Bouquet, XIX, 420, 422.

of the barons presented in their preliminary schedule, cried out "Et quare cum istis iniquis exactionibus barones non postulant regnum," and attributes a similar exclamation to Innocent when certain clauses of the Charter were shown him in writing.[22] If these statements refer to specific demands, it would be exceedingly interesting to know which ones they were. If regarded as intended to furnish a legal basis in feudal law for the pope's action against the Charter, they are certainly much too strong for anything which it contains. The only clauses which demand extreme concessions from the king I have discussed elsewhere sufficiently, I think, to show that taken all together they would not justify such statements.[23]

If finally we turn to feudal law, as understood either in England or on the continent, to inquire if, by its principles alone, the pope would have been justified in annulling the Charter, the answer must be, I think, in the negative. The details of the law which would apply to this case differed in different countries, but the underlying principle was the same everywhere: without the lord's consent the vassal might do nothing with or in his fief which reduced its value to himself to such an extent as to endanger his ability to perform the service by which he held it.[24] In some cases this principle was extended to mean that no reduction, however small, like the emanci-

22 Roger of Wendover, III, 322, 298, 323 respectively. The pope in the bull of 24 August calls the Charter "compositionem . . . non solum vilem et turpem, verum etiam illicitam et iniquam, in nimiam diminutionem et derogationem sui juris pariter et honoris."

23 In *Origin*, Chapter V.

24 The legislation upon this question, as far as tenants-in-chief are concerned, is about the oldest in feudal law, and goes back to a point before feudalism in the later sense had been fully established. See *Mon. Ger. Hist., Capitularia Regum Francorum*, II, 14, c. 1, and the references in note 1 to earlier legislation, and p. 15, c. 5 (A.D. 829). In the intermediate period a great deal of laxness prevailed both in Italy and England in regard to the

pation of a serf, could be made in the capital, or permanent, value of the fief, undoubtedly with reference to the possibility of escheat, as is stated in the English statute of mortmain. In applying this principle to the case of Innocent III and John, it must first of all be remembered that John did not hold England by indefinite feudal, or

application of the fundamental principles. In Italy imperial legislation at the middle of the twelfth century endeavored to check these tendencies and may be supposed to have been within the memory of the papal curia. See the law of Lothar III of 1136, *M.G.H.*, Leg., Sec. IV, tome I, 175, and those of Frederick I of 1154 and 1158, *ibid.*, pp. 207 and 248, c. 3. This legislation was taken up into the *Libri Feudorum.* Conrad II's legislation of 1037 has no provisions on the subject. In England the legislation of the thirteenth century, both in regard to mortmain and the principles of the statute of *Quia emptores,* shows that the fundamental feudal principles had been consciously recognized, however lax the practice may have been. In the kingdom of Jerusalem peculiar freedom was allowed in the matter of subinfeudation for military reasons. See *Livre de Jean d'Ibelin,* c. 182, ed. Beugnot, I, 284, and note b. The fundamental principle is, however, the same. It is the assize, or the local usage, which makes the difference. None of the feudal law codes of the thirteenth century gives any great space to the topic, or particularly emphasizes any part of it, unless it be grants in mortmain. Particularly good discussions of various phases of the subject may be found in Viollet's notes to the *Établissements de S. Louis,* I, 30, 163; III, 104-107, 124-126; IV, 298-303. It is in French feudal law that the principles were finally worked out in the most elaborate way. This may be best obtained from Loysel's *Institutes Coutumières,* ed. Dupin et Laboulaye (1846), nowhere in one place, but see the various terms in the Index. The result may be indicated as follows: The general principle covers: (1) Abridgement of the fief; (2) dismemberment of the fief, or the division of it into a number of fiefs, all holding of the immediate overlord, as results from the statute *Quia emptores,* and (3) "Jeu de fief," or subinfeudation. It is under abridgement of the fief that Magna Carta would come, if anywhere. That is again subdivided into: (1) grants in mortmain; (2) emancipation of serfs; and (3) abridgement proper in which certain definite income from the fief, including the relief, is fixed by agreement between lord and man at a sum considerably below the normal value. It is this last arrangement which creates what is known technically in French law as the "fief abridgé," and it is under this only that Magna Carta could be brought, but it is absurd to suppose that any financial provision of the Charter would render uncertain John's ability to pay his annual *cens* of 1000 marks. There are no regulations in any feudal code or law, early or late, concerning customs, services, or relationships, which have not an

by military tenure, but by a clearly defined money payment only. That is, England was a "feudum censuale," which is the term applied by Innocent to the exactly similar relation of Aragon to the papacy.[25] In both John's charters of 1213 making the concession to the pope, and in the pope's acceptance of 2 November, 1213, the money payment is distinctly said to be "pro omni servicio et consuetudine, quod pro ipsis facere deberemus," saving St. Peter's pence. This definition of the service is per-

economic value, or which would justify the statement attributed by Roger of Wendover, III, 322, to John that he could not "de novo aliquid statuere" without the knowledge of the pope. The *Tratado de la Regalia de Amortización* of Rodriguez Campomanes, Madrid, 1765, reviews the legislation of all the countries of Western Europe on that subject, but traces only partially the earliest forms and does not discuss allied matters. The same is true, with even less on early legislation, of C. I. Montagnini, "Dell' Antica Legislagione Italiana sulle Manimorte," in *Miscellanea de Storia Italiana,* tome XIX, Turin, 1880. It deals with the subject in detail only from the fifteenth century. Reference should be added to the legislation on this subject in the reissue of the Great Charter of 1217, c. 39, and also in that of 1225. Cf. *Bracton's Note Book,* pl. 1248, and *Cal. Pat. Rolls, 1232-1247,* p. 234.

25 . . . "illud ei [Sedi Apostolicæ] constituens in perpetuum censuale." . . . Letter to Peter II, not dated. Potthast, No. 2322. Text in Jean Dumont, *Corps Universel Diplomatique,* I, 132. There was nothing in the fact that John's service was merely a rent payment to make his typically feudal oath of fealty, or the use of the word "vassal" for him, seem out of place. The idea "held of another" was fundamental in feudalism, and from it passed with feudal incidents to relationships not originally feudal and in reality never becoming such. Here it is important to notice that with this idea as a starting-point anything in the way of service could be added or omitted according to individual conditions, and a fee-farm tenure be made clearly feudal, or clearly a common freehold, and the immense variety of services attached to serjeanty tenures be created at will. That a fee-farm tenure might owe military service is directly stated by Magna Carta, c. 37. Interesting examples of the varieties of this tenure may be found in almost any cartulary. See for reservation of forensic, or royal, service, which might often be military, *Gloucester Cartulary,* I, 209, 272 (many others); for service at a free court, *ibid.,* I, 333, 385 (many others); wardship, *ibid.,* I, 303; "servitium esquierii," *ibid.,* I, 336; the ordinary judicial duty of the "advocatus," *Ramsey Cartulary,* II, 260, 265; with "liege fealty," *ibid.,* II, 261; with castle guard, *Testa de Nevill,* p. 52b (*Book of Fees,* Pt. I, 593).

fectly clear and normal, and it limits not merely John's obligations but also the pope's rights. Under it the pope would be in duty bound to protect the king in the possession of his fief against any outside attack or any internal revolution which would deprive him of it, but he could find no ground in feudal law on which he could object to any arrangement entered into by his vassal for its internal management which did not seriously affect his ability to pay the specified annual sum. If all the financial clauses of the Charter be put together and interpreted as they must have been understood in 1215, the absurdity of supposing that they would justify the annulling of the Charter by the overlord will be apparent. But the pope and the king apparently understood the weakness of such a case, notwithstanding John's extreme statements and the pope's seeming endorsement of them; neither of them trusted the feudal relationship as a sufficient ground of action against the Charter, and the fact accounts for John's assumption of the cross, and for the way in which the pope passed over his feudal rights in the bull of 24 August. It is upon his ecclesiastical rights that Innocent founded his action and upon them alone.[26]

[26] It must be noticed that this inquiry is directed only to ascertain if the pope had a legal basis for his action against the Charter, on which he believed himself justified in annulling it. While the result of the investigation is negative only, that is, that there is to be found no basis for the action in strict law, as the law then was, it seems worth while to establish the fact, and to add that the question is left open on what other ground, very likely of his ecclesiastical pretensions or his claims to world supremacy, the pope may have believed himself justified in acting as he did. If it is suggested that a legal basis might be found in the general feudal duty of protection, including protection against rebellion, which the suzerain owed to his vassal, it is to be said that in strict law no such duty existed when the rebellion was due to the lord's violation of his obligations towards his own vassals. This was the ground on which the rebellion against John rested its right according to the barons, and we are bound to say justly so far as law goes. If the pope had a right to interfere in the quarrel, bare law alone considered, it would be against John, not in his favor. He does not, however, make any reference to a right of this kind.

NOTE A

The pope's letter of 18 June, 1215, to which reference is made above, is in the Public Record Office, Papal Bulls, Box 52, No. 2. The upper left-hand corner has been destroyed at some time in the past, so that the entire address and portions of diminishing length of the first ten lines have been lost, and a single word and portions of words, as indicated in the text, have been lost elsewhere in the letter. The lines contain an average of 202 letter and word spaces. The address was probably general to the people of England. The letter seems to have a special reference to John's letter to the pope of 29 May, and in the first portion it follows rather closely the pope's letters of 19 March. The text was printed by Prynne in his *History of King John* (1670), p. 27, who supplied the address "Innocentius Episcopus nobilibus viris universitati Baronum Angliæ hanc paginam inspecturis, salutem et Apostolicam benedictionem" (which can hardly be correct), and portions of the missing words, distinguishing his additions in two cases only. Modern historians have mostly not noticed its existence. Ramsay, *Angevin Empire,* p. 486, note 1, refers to Prynne's text (reference a misprint) and says the letter "does not read quite like one of Innocent's utterances." Gasquet, *Henry Third and the Church,* pp. 13-15, gives a reference to the original, says it was "addressed to Langton and the other English bishops," which it certainly was not, and gives an otherwise inaccurate abstract of its contents. There is no reference to it in Potthast. As the letter is highly characteristic of the method in which the papal letters were composed during this conflict, and may be called in some respects a first draft of the bull of 24 August, it seems worth while to print it in a new and more accessible edition. A comparison of the text with that of the other letters, papal and royal, of the crisis, beginning with that to Eustace de Vesci of 5 November, 1214 (Rymer, I, 1, 126), will show the characteristic borrowing of phrases of which I have spoken. I have referred in the notes by date to some of the more important or interesting cases. The punctuation is that of the original.

It will be noticed that in this letter the pope says that he has given directions to the archbishop and his suffragans to excommunicate the barons unless within eight days they come to an agreement with the king according to the form which he had earlier recommended to their messengers. The only papal letter which we have corresponding to this statement is the bull "Miramur plurimum" preserved without date by Roger of Wendover (III, 336). The dating of this bull is admittedly difficult. Its place among the events of Roger of Wendover's narrative can give us no clue. In Walter of Coventry (II, 223), a bull of similar purport is said to have been shown to the bishops at a meeting at Oxford on 16 August. It is dated by Potthast (No. 4992) end of August, and most modern historians have accepted Walter of Coventry's date as that at which it was presented. Sir James Ramsay (*Angevin Empire,* p. 478) concludes against August in favor of 16 July. The most serious objection to considering the bull "Miramur plurimum" to be the one referred to in the letter of 18 June is the definite statement that the barons were to be allowed an interval of eight days in which to come to an agreement with the king. That statement is not in the bull "Miramur plurimum." It may have been contained in a supplementary letter, or have been committed to the messengers to be made known orally, as not quite consonant with the dignity of a formal papal command. It should be noticed that the bull shows no knowledge of the Charter. I am inclined to believe that it should be dated 18 June, and the meeting at which it was shown the bishops 16 July, though I am not prepared to assert this definitely.

TEXT OF THE POPE'S LETTER OF 18 JUNE

. . . partibus Anglie nuper auribus nostris
. . . odo Regni Anglie; sed etiam aliorum . . .
. . . quasdam inter eos et Carissimum . . .
. . . opus esset cum humilitate ac devotione repetere[1]
. . . super hoc iidem Barones suos ad nos nuntios destinassent;[2] et nos Ue . . .

[1] March 19. The single reference in these notes must not be understood to mean that it is to the only instance of the use of the phrase.

[2] Cf. Rymer, I, 1, 120. The letters referred to by the Pope are those of 19 March.

. . . dedissemus litteris in preceptis. ut conspirationes et coniurationes[3] presumptas. a tempore suborte discordie inter Regnum et sacerdotium, apostolica denu . . . es; ne talia decetero temptarentur, iniungerent baronibus antedictis; ut per devotionis et humilitatis ind[i]cia tam animum Regis placare.[4] quam recon . . . es, quod ab eo ducerent postulandum; conseruando sibi regalem honorem et[5] exhibendo seruitia debita.[6] quibus ipse rex non debebat absque iudicio spoliari;[7] ac insuper . . . prefatam in remissione sibi peccaminum iniungendo. quatinus benigne pertractans nobiles antedictos, iustas petitiones eorum clementer admitteret[8] plena eis in uniendo. morando. et recedendo secu . . . essa pariter atque data. Ita quod si forte non posset inter eos concordia prouenire; in curia sua per pares eorum[9] secundum Regni consuetudines atque leges mota deberet dissensio terminari; Barones ipsi nostro non expec[10] tato responso, postquam idem Rex signum crucis assumpsit in subsidium terre sancte; contempta iustitia quam ipse Rex superhabundanter offerebat eisdem;[11] contra dominum suum arma mouere temeritate nefaria presumpserunt. non timentes taliter crusis negotium impedire; ac regni periculum procurare. cum pecuniam quam pro liberatione terre sancte deberet expendere;[12] in destructionem etiam terre sue profundere compellatur. Quodque nefandum est et absurdum. cum ipse Rex quasi peruersus deum et ecclesiam offendebat; illi assistebant eidem. Cum autem conuersus deo et ecclesie satisfecit; ipsum impugnare presumunt.[13] sicque uidetur quod conspirationem inhierint detestan-

3 5 November, 1214; 19 March.

4 19 March.

5 19 March. ''em honorem et'' written over an erasure.

6 19 March, 1 April, 29 May. The reference without doubt is to scutage.

7 1 April.

8 19 March. This letter is even more closely followed than these notes indicate.

9 10 May, 29 May.

10 End of line 10.

11 Cf. 29 May.

12 Cf. 20 May.

13 Cf. John's letter to the Pope, 13 September, *Rotuli Patentes*, I, 182.

dam; ut eum taliter de Regno possint eicere.[14] hominio et fidelitate sibi prestitis penitus uiolatis. quod quam crudele sit actu. et horrendum auditu; cum perniciosi exempli materia sit et causa nostris temporibus inaudita; manifeste cognoscit. quicumque iudicio utitur rationis. unde ualde dolendum existit. cum hoc in iniuriam summi dei. ecclesie Romane ac nostrum contemptum. Regis et Regni obprobrium et periculum. et terre sancte ad cuius subsidium se deuouerat Rex prefatus, nimium detrimentum redundat. Cum igitur debeamus et libenter uelimus pacem Regni Anglie procurare. ipsius turbationes[15] propellere, ac dicti Regis qui uasallus noster existit conseruare iustitias et iniurias propulsare. maxime[16] cum idem propter caracterem crusis assumptum. specialiter subnostra protectione consistat; prefatis Archiepiscopo et Suffraganis eius in obedientie uirtute districte[16] dedimus in preceptis. quatinus nisi prefati Barones infra octo dies[17] post susceptionem litterarum nostrarum, ab eis uel aliquo ipsorum diligenter ammoniti. receperint et seruauerint formam descriptam superius a [nobis] nuntiis eorum presentibus cum multa deliberatione prouisam; iidem omni cauillatione postposita;[12] eos et fautores ipsorum sublato cuiuslibet contradictionis et appellationis obstaculo; excommunicationis mucrone percellant et terras illorum [ecclesi]astico subiciant interdicto, facientes utramque sententiam per totam angliam singulis diebus dominicis et festiuis sollempniter publicari. Ne igitur propter quosdam peruersos uniuersitatis sinceritas in Anglia corrumpatur. que hactenus ab infidelitatis contagio fuit prorsus immunis. Uniuersitati uestri per apostolica scripta precipiendo mandamus. et in remissionem iniungimus peccatorum. quatinus prefato Regi aduersus peruersores huiusmodi oportunum impendatis auxilium et fauorem. ita quod in confusionem ipsius et aliorum Regnorum, non possit tanta nequitia preualere, sed tempestate sedata;

14 Cf. Roger of Wendover, III, 323, and the ''Miramur plurimum.''

15 Cf. the ''Miramur plurimum'' with 29 May. It was impossible for anyone to interpret the phrase honestly as meaning anyone but the barons.

16 ''Miramur plurimum.''

17 Roughly the period between the exhibition of the letter at the supposed meeting of 16 August and the proclamation of the excommunication at Staines (Walter of Coventry, II, 223-224).

Regnum ipsum optata tranquillitate letetur. Scientes procerto. quod si Rex ipse remissus esset aut tepidus in hac parte, nos Regnum Anglie non pateremur ad tantam ignominiam et uilitatem deduci, cum sciamus per dei gratiam et possumus talium insolentiam castigare. Dat. Terentin'. xiiii Kal Iulii. Pontificatus nostri Anno Octauodicimo.

An endorsement in a later, but thirteenth-century, hand, possibly not much later than the original, reads: "Innoc' de turbacione orta inter Regem I. et barones Anglie verbum ultimum competens est. Examinatur."

INDEX

www.ingramcontent.com/pod-product-compliance
Lightning Source LLC
La Vergne TN
LVHW101455200926
848483LV00001B/131